Muslim Political Discourse
in Postcolonial India

Hilal Ahmed's book is a pioneering exploration of the politics of historical monuments, an interdisciplinary work linking the analysis of law, history and politics. It offers a remarkable analysis of the ways in which reinterpreted images of the past work as resources for mobilization and action in the political present. The book also offers a fascinating analysis of the politics around the Jama Masjid in Delhi – showing how religious monuments transform into sites of the political public sphere. Ahmed provides an insightful examination of the construction of historical memory and a sophisticated exploration of the complex effects of democratic mobilization on the political identity of Indian Muslims.

Sudipta Kaviraj
Professor of Indian Politics and Intellectual History, Middle Eastern, South Asian and African Studies, Columbia University, New York

What could be more concrete, more singular in meaning than a building? In fact, many different actors have made signage, use, disputation, and rituals have made India's built past centrally important in defining nationalism and belonging. Citizens absorb the assumptions of national identities as wholly natural, and the historical meanings attached to sites and buildings are part of those identities. Hilal Ahmed's book provides a fresh and original analysis to understanding cultural and political life in India's culturally plural society today.

Barbara Metcalf
Professor of History Emerita, University of California, Davis

Hilal Ahmed analyses the way in which political groups, both Hindu and Muslim, have used the great monuments of the Indo-Islamic tradition for political mobilisation. His book is one of the most important and innovative pieces of research of recent times. No scholar in the field should ignore it.

Francis Robinson
Professor of the History of South Asia, Royal Holloway, University of London

Muslim Political Discourse in Postcolonial India

Monuments, Memory, Contestation

HILAL AHMED

Routledge
Taylor & Francis Group
LONDON NEW YORK NEW DELHI

First published 2014 in India
by Routledge
912 Tolstoy House, 15–17 Tolstoy Marg, Connaught Place,
New Delhi 110 001

Simultaneously published in the UK
by Routledge
2 Park Square, Milton Park, Abingdon, Oxon OX14 4RN

Routledge is an imprint of the Taylor & Francis Group, an informa business

© 2014 Hilal Ahmed

Typeset by
Solution Graphics
A–14, Indira Puri, Loni Road
Ghaziabad, Uttar Pradesh 201 102

All rights reserved. No part of this book may be reproduced or utilised in any
form or by any electronic, mechanical or other means, now known or hereafter
invented, including photocopying and recording, or in any information storage
and retrieval system without permission in writing from the publishers.

British Library Cataloguing-in-Publication Data
A catalogue record of this book is available from the British Library

ISBN 978-1-138-02016-0

For

Nazima, Sarmad, Maaz and Raheel

Contents

Tables and Figures	ix
Preface	xi
Acknowledgements	xiii

1.	Introduction	1
2.	Monumentalisation in Colonial India: Discovery of 'Indian Muslim Architectural Heritage'	50
3.	Monumentalisation in Postcolonial India: Conservation, Law and Muslim Politics	97
4.	Jama Masjid and the Political Memory of a Royal Muslim Past	140
5.	Babri Masjid and the Muslim Politics of Right to Heritage	192
6.	Conclusion	275

Appendices	284
Select Bibliography	290
About the Author	316
Index	317

Tables and Figures

TABLES

4.1	Imam's Politics Compared: Memory, Law and History	184

5.1	Narratives of the Babri Masjid–Ram Temple Dispute	205
5.2	Legal Issues and Political Implications of Babri Masjid Case: 1949–94	225
5.3	Internal Dynamics of Muslim Politics on Babri Masjid in 1986	236
5.4	Positions of BMMCC and AIBMAC on Babri Masjid	255
5.5	Negotiation on Babri Masjid Dispute	271

FIGURES

2.1:	Legal Classification of Indian Buildings (1810–63)	68
2.2:	The Process of Monumentalisation and the 1904 Act	82
2.3:	Classification of Ancient Monuments by *The Conservation Manual* (1923)	86
2.4:	Conservation of Religious Places of Worship (1904–47)	87
3.1:	Powers of the Central Government	105
3.2:	ASI's Version of Qutub Mosque	109
3.3:	Right to Heritage: A Legal Interpretation	118
3.4:	Secularism(s) Compared and a Few Unsolved Issues	125
4.1:	Erstwhile Office of the Archaeological Survey of India (ASI) at Jama Masjid	141
4.2:	Sunni Majlis-e-Auqaf Board	142
4.3:	Jama Masjid 'Speaks'	144
4.4:	Clearance of Shops Near the Wall of Jama Masjid by the DDA (1975)	152
4.5:	Bullet Marks at Jama Masjid	155
4.6:	Black Banner at the Jama Masjid	168
4.7:	Jama Masjid in June 1987	168
4.8:	Reopening of the Jama Masjid	170

Tables and Figures

4.9:	Jama Masjid	173
4.10:	The Wazukhana of Jama Masjid	176
4.11:	Pamphlet Distributed in Different Mosques by the YWS Activists against L. K. Advani's Visit	179
4.12:	PAS of the Jama Masjid	185
4.13:	Imam Abdullah Bukhari in Tahmad and Kurta	189
4.14:	Ahmad Bukhari and Abdullah Bukhari Wearing Robes	190
5.1:	Kar Sewa Puram Ayodhya	197
5.2:	Babri Masjid Site in 1858	210
5.3:	Site Plan Submitted by the Mahant in 1885	212
5.4:	Babri Masjid in 1949	215
5.5:	Babri Masjid (1986)	220
5.6:	Babri Masjid (1990)	223
5.7:	Babri Masjid Agitation: February to November 1986	238
5.8:	The Ideological Composition of the Coalition	241
5.9:	The Imam Formula	265

Preface

This book has emerged from my doctoral thesis, *Politics of Monuments and Memory*, which was submitted to the School of Oriental and African Studies, University of London in 2006–07. Unlike other conventional studies on the history of 'monuments'/ archaeology or Muslim politics, communalism/secularism, the book makes a modest attempt to establish a link between two very different sets of issues: the questions related to the process by which historic buildings become monuments — primarily in historical and legal terms or what I call the *process of monumentalisation*; and the manner in which these historic/legal entities are transformed into political objects. From this vantage point, I try to understand the postcolonial Muslim political discourse. Concentrating on multiple ways by which Indo-Islamic historic buildings are interpreted as 'political sites', I explore the political construction of a *collective memory* of a royal Muslim past.

The book simply offers an 'introduction' — a slight reframing of issues in relation to a particular kind of contextual Muslim politics of 1970–90. For that reason, it follows a very different style of writing. Each chapter asks a few conceptually conscious and empirically rooted questions; the subsequent discussion offers a possible interpretation to these questions based on a re-reading of various sources; and finally an analysis is offered. I adopt this style simply to arrange and produce the vast empirical information that I managed to collect during the course of this research. It does not mean that the empirical details are given priority over the conceptual treatment of the subject. I do take up the complex issues of theoretical kind such as the discursive nature of Muslim political discourse. However, I admit that the arguments offered in this book, from my point of view, can be treated as 'first-level generalizations' — which can further be developed into a more sophisticated intellectual position on Muslim political engagement in south Asia.

In any case, the significance of these 'first level generalizations' on postcolonial Muslim politics need to be emphasised for two obvious reasons. First, the specificity of Muslim politics in India xii *Preface*

has not been adequately studied. As an inseparable constituent of a larger conceptual package called 'Muslim issues', Muslim politics is always understood either in relation to Muslim backwardness or communalism. It is, I believe, important to look at the ways in which a Muslim issue is articulated politically. The book tries to offer a historical explanation to modern Muslim politics in this sense, especially its north India-dominated version, simply by moving away from the prevalent notions such as *Muslim separatism, Muslim communalism* and for that matter *Muslim secularism*. In my view, such frames of analysis, distract serious empirical and theoretical studies and might lead us to an unnecessary discussion on 'political' correctness.

Second, the linkage between 'official history', law and political action, which I try to make in this book, has its own explanatory importance. The book offers an 'analytical angle' to approach these vast areas by concentrating on a few identified questions that revolve around a discursively constituted historical practice called 'Muslim politics'. One may criticise this 'selective treatment' on the basis of the vastness of the subjects like archaeology, law and above all, history. However, I do not find such rather *predictable* refutations useful. If we are ready to accept the 'interdisciplinary research' in the true sense of the term, we have to recognise the selective preferences of a researcher in dealing with his/her research questions. This is precisely what this book underlines. To put it rather polemically, I would say that this intellectual attempt is simply a reply to those political scientists and historians, who still do not deviate from set disciplinary questions!

To deal with this rather unconventional take on Muslim politics, I draw on a variety of sources: archival material, interviews, speeches of political leaders, legal documents and visual sources such as pictures of mosques, etc. These sources are put together to construct a narrative, which is simply an interpretative exercise. I do not suggest that this is the only and/or fixed explanation of these sources. Of course, there could be various possibilities to explore them. But, I urge the readers not only to look at the narrative critically but also pay equal attention to the sequence of various sources, which gives a structure and flow to the arguments I offer.

2 May 2013

Hilal Ahmed
Wellington

Acknowledgements

Writing an 'acknowledgement' could possibly be one of the most difficult tasks for any researcher. No one can draw a clear dividing line between what exactly has been borrowed from sources — individuals, institutions or society — and what precisely has been his/her own original contribution. Thus, in my opinion, the best feasible way to acknowledge the social nature of academic research is to pay tribute to a few processes by which ideas are generated, systematised and shaped in different forms.

The present research, in this sense, is also a product of a few specific, though highly peculiar social processes — it could be my mother's favourite bedtime stories in which many *jinns* came out from *Viran Masjid* and *Khandathar* and hid in the dark corners of our *gali* (street); it could be my Hindi teacher's lecture at the Arya Samaj-run DAV school on *Musalmano Dwara Hindu Mandiron Ka Vidhwans* (desecration of temples by Muslims in medieval India); it could be those post-*Isha salat* discussions in our mosque (particularly during the time of curfew) in which elders used to talk about *Masjid ki siyasat* (Politics of mosques), *Asar-e Kadima* (old buildings), and *Muslamone ki wakf milikiyaten* (wakf properties of Muslims); it could be the reminiscences of those 'encounters' when the *chowkidar*s (guards) of the protected monuments did not allow us to offer *Namaz* inside the historic mosque; or even it could be those sweetest memories when I went for my first date with an intention to propose to my girlfriend for a lifelong association and our hunch for a romantic place brought us to the Safdarjung's Tomb — again a protected monument of national importance! All these 'critical' events shaped my interests in historical buildings and finally I found myself working on a book on 'politics of monuments'!

The transition of these varied processes into an academic research project is also very interesting. In fact, the entire credit goes to my teachers, colleagues, friends, and students, who actually shaped my personality and helped me in contextualizing my own interests, anxieties, apprehensions, issues, and problems into a rather sophisticated discourse of academic research. I am thankful to late I. P. Sharma, Nafis-ul-Hasan, Maninder Nath

xiv *Acknowledgements*

Thakur, Deepak Verma, Manoranjan Mohanty, Riaz Ahmad, John Sidel, Louiza Odysseos, Francis Robinson, Ian Talbot, Barbara Metcalf, Imtiaz Ahmad, Mathew Nelson, Mukulika Banerjee, Emma Tarlo, Markus Daechsel, David Washbrook, Peter Robb, Daud Ali, Nivedita Menon, S. K. Chaube, Ashish Ghosh, M. P. Jain, Manish Jain, Ruma Dutt, Jinee Lokaneeta, Munaf Zeena, Azimudin Sayed, Nilanjana Kaviraj, Syed Zahid Ali, Bilal Ahmed, Javed Ahmed, Mohammad Usman, Arif Anjum, Mohammad Ahmad, Mohammad Arshad, Mushir Ahmed, Bushra Sultana, Azra, Sultana, Mohammad Ashiqueen, Mohammad Naseem, Mazhar Ahmed, Mohammad Irfan, Mohammad Rashid, Mahjabeen Rashid, late Qamar Jahan, late Faiz Ahmed, Zumrud Jahan,Sartaj, Tani Bhargava, Abhay Prasad Singh, Mohammad Nadim, Shafiquddin, Ujjawal Kumar Singh, and Anupama Roy for their help, comments and criticisms.

A special thanks to Sudipta Kaviraj, my thesis supervisor and one of the best minds of our time, for encouraging me to think critically and innovatively, and of course independently. I do not have adequate words to express my gratitude for his contribution as a teacher.

The practical help given by a number of people in India, particularly during the time of fieldwork is priceless. I am grateful to my respondents at Delhi, Ayodhya, Kanpur, Lucknow and other parts of north India for their readiness to discuss political issues with me. Hashim Ansari, Zahid Raza Rizvi, Yunus Siddiquie, Zafaryab Jilani, Nawabuddin Nakshabandi, Shankrachraya Mahant Adhyoshnadji, and N. K. Sharma deserve special thanks. This study is highly indebted to Syed Shahabuddin and his journal, *Muslim India*, which he published for two decades.

Over the years, I have realized the intellectual significance of the Centre for the Study of Developing Societies (CSDS) — the 'Centre' in my academic and personal life. My brilliant colleagues at the Centre — Abhay Kumar Dubey, Awadhendra Sharan, Peter R. deSouza, Prathama Banerjee, Priyadarshini Vijaisri, Rakesh Pandey, Ravi Sundaram, Ravi Vasudevan, Ravi Kant, Hemachandran Karah, Sanjay Kumar, Sarada Balagopalan, Sanjeer Alam, Madhu Purnima Kishwar, Ananya Vajpeyi, Avinash Jha, and Praveen Rai have helped me in reshaping my arguments. A special thanks to Ashis Nandy, D. L. Sheth, Shail Mayaram, Rajeev Bhargava and Aditya Nigam — who read various drafts of my work very

Acknowledgements   xv

critically and suggested ways to improve it. I am also grateful to the CSDS library and staff — late 'Dada'— Sujit Deb, K. A. Q. A. Hilal, Himanshu, Ghanshyam, Manoj, T. K. Singh, and others for their love and support.

I am grateful to the Ford Foundation International Fellowship Program (IFP) for giving me the IFP fellowship for my doctoral research. Especially I am thankful to Joan Dassin and Mary Zurbuchen for their personal interest in my work. I must express gratitude to IFP India office, particularly to Vivek Mansukhani, Neera Handa, and Akta Sawhney. I am also thankful to the School of Oriental and African Studies (SOAS) Registry and the Faculty of Law and Social Sciences, SOAS for providing financial support. The institutional support extended by the Faith in the Future Limited (London) and the North London Muslim Community Centre was extremely useful.

I am also thankful to the library and staff of the Oriental and India Office Collections (Asia Pacific and Africa Collection) at the British Library, SOAS Library, the Senate House Library, Hackney Central Library, Stamford Hill Library, North London Muslim Centre Library, *Impact International* Document Collection (London), Nehru Memorial Museum and Library (Delhi), National Institution of Urban Affairs Library, Delhi Urban Art Commission, INTACH Library (particularly Ms Nasreen Begum and Mr. O. P. Jain for their help), Ratan Tata Library, Central Reference Library (Delhi University), Supreme Court of India Library, Delhi High Court Library, Delhi Public Library, National Archives (India), All India Muslim Majlis-e-Mushawarat Library, Jamiat Ulema-e-Hind Library (special thanks to Salem Saheb and Mazhar Bhai), and Raza Library, Rampur.

I am also thankful to the editorial team of Routledge, New Delhi, for their careful reading of the manuscript and professional attitude.

The final version of the manuscript was completed during my stay in Wellington. I am thankful to the New Zealand India Research Institute of the Victoria University of Wellington, especially its Director, Sekhar Bandyopadhyay, for inviting me as Visiting Fellow for the academic year 2013–14.

My ideas have been shaped and influenced by four individuals in the past few years in a significant way. Yogendra Yadav, one of the most energetic and creative contemporary social scientists, is

xvi *Acknowledgements*

one of them. As a superb teacher, he taught me how to collect and analyse micro-level data/information; and as a colleague, showed me the political value of intellectual labour. Madhulika Banerjee has always been a source of inspiration for me. She has taught me how to establish a balance between intellectual labour and family commitment. M. Ghazali Khan gave a new direction to my thinking during my stay in London. He encouraged me to look at the idea of politics from different vantage points. Finally, Maulana Athar Hussein Dehlavi — a friend and philosopher — who has been guiding me in almost every aspect of my life. I must say that he made the fieldwork, particularly the interviews with politicians and bureaucrats, so smooth and easy.

My children — Sarmad, Maaz and Raheel — have always been central to my personal and professional life. Actually, Sarmad worked very hard to read many drafts of this manuscript and helped me in typing at various levels. In fact, he asked some very interesting questions about my research. Maaz and Raheel took some time to understand that 'Papa was doing some work'. But after this realization they also started contributing in this research in their own sweet ways.

My wife Nazima Parveen has been travelling with me since the very day when we visited the Safdarjung's Tomb and agreed for an enduring bond. As an intellectual she provided valuable comments, as a friend shared every problem of life, as a responsible companion worked very hard to provide time so that I could finish my work, and as the administrator of the family set out some rules to systemize the life of a highly unorganized person like me. I must confess that my life is still lyrical, just because of her! In recognition of our shared dreams, anxieties, and differences, this study is dedicated to my family: Nazima, Sarmad, Maaz, and Raheel.

1

Introduction

The academic literature on Indian Muslim communities discusses the term 'Muslim politics' in a number of ways. Popular demands such as the protection of Urdu or Muslim Personal Law, the programmes, policies and activities of Muslim organisations or pressure groups, sermons, speeches and statements of influential Muslim personalities and the Muslim voting pattern in elections are often studied as the constituents of Muslim politics in postcolonial India. A few illuminating studies have already made attempts to conceptualise the political power structure among Muslims by employing a Marxist and/or elitist framework of analysis. However, despite such a variety of academic writings, our knowledge of different forms and trajectories of post-1947 Indian Muslim politics is rather limited. A strong conviction that there is only one form of Muslim politics in India, which eventually characterises an indispensable dichotomy between Western modernity and Islam, seems to dominate academic discourses. It is believed that Muslim politics as a manifestation of minority communalism could either be juxtaposed with secular politics or completely ignored as a kind of reaction to assertive Hindu nationalism also known as *Hindutva*.[1] There is an underlying assumption that an upper-class, upper-caste, male Muslim elite divert common Muslims from secular/national issues for the sake of their vested interests. This assumption is often accepted uncritically. As a result, the internal complexities of Muslim politics and the ways in which Muslim political actors

---

[1] The term 'Hindutva' refers to the politics of Hindu rightists that has emerged in the mid-1980s. Interestingly, the Supreme Court of India has taken it too literally and conceptualises the 'Hindutva' as a way of life (AIR 1996 SC, 1113). However, it should be noted that the rightist Hindu groups, which are often called the constituents of 'Hindutva family' popularly known as the *Sangh Parivar*, do not follow any single political ideology. In fact, the Ram Temple issue gave them an opportunity to form an informal political coalition.

2 *Muslim Political Discourse in Postcolonial India*

function become less important and intellectual energies are devoted to reproducing the existing intellectual and political divide between secularism and communalism.

The present study is a modest endeavour to go beyond this dominant and all-inclusive view of Muslim politics. Instead of examining wide-ranging issues such as the *acceptable* role of Muslims in a secular environment or the strategies for their political empowerment, this study narrows down its focus. It identifies the political reception of Indo-Islamic historic architecture as a vantage point to enter into the contemporary Muslim political discourse in north India.[2] Concentrating on the multiple ways in which Indo-Islamic historic buildings are interpreted as 'political sites', this study explores the political construction of a *collective memory* of a *royal Muslim past*.

This work deals with three different kinds of *contestations*. The first contestation is characterised by the clash between the modern concept of a secular monument, which looks at historic sites as dead entities, and various Islamic traditions, which commemorate these buildings as living sites. This study examines how these two very different approaches to the past overlap each other and shape the idea of an Indian Muslim architectural heritage in colonial and postcolonial India. The placing of Indo-Islamic buildings in the official discourse on national heritage is the second kind of contestation. I try to examine a few popular images of such buildings such as dead historical monuments, symbols of Islamic conquests, emblem of Indian's shared heritage and so on to find out why an additional explanation is always attached to describe these sites. The appropriation of Indo-Islamic buildings by Muslim leaders as political symbols, illustrates the third kind of contestation. The study looks at the ways by which historic sites are used as political symbols for fashioning appropriate mobilisation

---

[2] In general, the term 'historic' signifies a momentous, well-known and important date in history, while 'historical' refers to a kind of belonging to, or dealing with the past. In this sense, important events and dates are historic and information and data from the past are historical. However, I use historic and historical interchangeably for describing Indo-Islamic buildings in this study because: (*a*) these buildings signify important events or phases in a historic sense, and (*b*) these buildings are treated as historical source/information to deal with the past.

Introduction 3

strategies. Reconsidering the secularism versus communalism debate and the Muslim homogeneity versus Muslim plurality debate, this study tries to understand how the contested images of Indo-Islamic buildings are re-invented by the Muslim political groups in postcolonial India. In this sense, instead of arguing for or against the notion of a single Muslim community in India, the purpose of this endeavour is to look at how the collective political existence of India's Muslims is conceptualised as a 'political community' in variety of ways. In other words, I intend to study the structure of postcolonial *Muslim political discourse* — an intellectual process by which specific notions of Muslim identity are produced and meanings of political acts are determined.[3]

The study of Indo-Islamic historic buildings as political sites is also very relevant to understand the shifting nature of Muslim politics in postcolonial India. In fact, if we look at the Muslim *political* demands in the post-1947 period, the proper management of the *wakf* properties including the non-functional historic mosques had always been recognised as an important issue.[4] Although, the demands such as freedom to offer *Namaz* inside the declared

---

[3] Sudipta Kaviraj reminds us: '[t]he first step in developing the critique of any ideological discourse ... must be to disbelieve its autobiography, the history, it gives to itself' (2010: 88). Following this suggestion, I also try to avoid the 'secular-communal' binary. In my view, these ideological labels are intrinsically associated with the dominant narrative of modern Muslim politics.

[4] The term 'functional site' referred to those buildings, which were being used for a variety of purposes including, religious worship. On the other hand, the term 'non-functional site' was employed for those buildings, which had been almost abandoned by local communities such as non-functional religious places, ruins and/or dilapidated structures. However, the distinction between functional and non-functional sites should not be confused with a similar kind of difference between 'living sites' and 'dead sites'. In fact, this clarification is very crucial to understanding the local reception of officially declared historical monuments in postcolonial India. It is true that the non-functional sites are 'dead sites' in the actual physical sense. Nevertheless, we cannot ignore the local religious meanings of these sites, which are very different from objective secular meanings. In this sense, these non-functional buildings are supposed to possess certain historical values, but in more subtle metaphysical terms.

4   *Muslim Political Discourse in Postcolonial India*

and protected historical monuments and the right to manage and control all functional and non-functional Islamic religious places of worship were not portrayed as crucial political issues before 1970s, their significant presence in the dominant Muslim political discourse cannot be ignored.

However, in the 1970s and 1980s, the right to worship and control over the Indo-Islamic historic sites emerged as one of the main Muslim political issues. For instance, the Delhi riots of February 1975 transformed the Jama Masjid of Delhi and its *Shahi* Imam into a symbolic Muslim political authority. In the same manner, in 1979, an organisation, the *Masjid Basao Committee* (Rehabilitate the Mosques Committee), was formed in old Delhi to restore the religious status of abandoned historic non-functional mosques. These efforts were given an organised form in 1984, when the All India Muslim Majlis-e-Mushawarat (AIMMM) submitted a memorandum to the government and demanded that all protected historical mosques, which had been under the control of the Archaeological Survey of India (ASI) as protected monuments, should be opened for regular prayers. Even, after the emergence of the Babri Masjid issue in 1986, a private bill was introduced in the Parliament to amend the Ancient Monuments and Archaeological Sites and Remains Act (1958) for expanding the scope of right to worship inside the protected historical monuments. All these developments clearly demonstrate the fact that the 'right to heritage' had been recognised as a point of reference to redefine Muslim claims in this period.

This interesting shift in Muslim demands has not been studied so far. In fact, in the last 20 years, especially before and after the demolition of the Babri mosque in 1992, *Hindutva* has acquired a central place in the academic research on religious revivalism, fundamentalism and communalism. However, the response of the Muslim political groups, their political strategies and the emerging configurations of power relations among the Muslims of north India are not adequately analysed. The present research is an attempt to understand these issues.

I

WHAT IS MUSLIM POLITICS?

What is postcolonial Muslim politics? This question is directly related to different approaches to Muslim politics and the manner,

Introduction 5

attitude and perceptions by which this term has been conceptualised. In fact, this kind of exploration is useful in two senses. First, it would help us in situating the research agenda of the present study in the existing literature on this subject. Second, such a review will also help in highlighting the strengths, problems and weaknesses of these 'positions' in detail.

I identify two dominant perspectives on Muslim politics — the *Muslim homogeneity perspective* and the *secular heterogeneity perspective*. The vast literature that conceptualises Muslim community as a single political unit and concentrates on the Indian legal-constitutional discourse of minority rights could be called the Muslim homogeneity perspective. The writings of Iqbal Ansari and Syed Shahabuddin are examples of this trend. In contrast, the secular heterogeneity perspective rejects the idea of oneness of Muslim community and asserts that Muslim politics represents a kind of *communal* politics. I discuss four versions of this thesis: (*a*) social assimilation and Muslim politics, (*b*) class analysis of Muslim politics, (*c*) the instrumentalist approach to Muslim politics, and (*d*) the modern-liberal explanation of Muslim politic.[5]

Muslim Homogeneity and the Legal-Constitutionalist Explanation of Muslim Politics

Let us begin with the legal-constitutionalist position which conceptualises Muslim politics as politics of minority rights. This position is based on two general premises. First, there is only one homogeneous Muslim community in India, which has some particular collective interests. Second, these interests are legitimate because the Constitution of India recognises the Muslim community as a legally identifiable religious minority and Muslim demands are nothing more than a claim for the proper implementation of given

---

[5] The literature on Indian Muslims does not deal with the question of Muslim politics directly. These studies raise diverse issues and propose a number of distinct, and even, contradictory arguments. However, despite several conceptual and methodological differences, almost all major studies make very explicit observations and comments on Muslim politics. In fact, the clear adherence of these scholars to define *ideological* positions gives us an opportunity to classify various interpretations of Muslim politics.

6   *Muslim Political Discourse in Postcolonial India*

minority rights. These two premises are linked to make a general argument that the Muslims in India are socially and economically backward and in order to tackle this multidimensional backwardness, there is a need for a Muslim politics of rights. I discuss the writings of Syed Shahabuddin to elaborate this position.

According to Syed Shahabuddin, the religion and caste determine the basic logic of Indian identities. He writes: '[w]ithin the territorial framework of the Indian state ... our primary identity is still defined by religion; our secondary identity by caste; our tertiary identity by our social function' (1987: 435–36). The basic framework of the Indian state, he says, was established to accommodate these identities and to ensure plurality of Indian social life. In his opinion, the state in India adopted an *India-specific* secularism that on the one hand respects all religious traditions, but at the same time, maintains equidistance from all religious groups. It has created a federal structure and re-organised states on linguistic bases, identified rights of distinct ethnic and social groups and granted religious freedom to minorities, and applied the concept of protective discrimination to provide reservation to backwards classes. In Shahabuddin's view these examples show that the Indian constitution established a system for the specific needs of Indian social life. He argues that the Indian legal constitutional framework is capable of producing and sustaining the social equilibrium of Indian civil society.

Now the question arises: if the system is well-equipped for dealing with any kind of social disruption, what is the significance of mass politics? For Shahabuddin, the centralisation of power is the most important problem of the Indian political system, because of which the established institutions are not performing the required functions. Shahabuddin identifies two aspects of this centralisation. First, there is a lack of adequate representation of different groups in the democratic institutions and therefore power gets centralised. Second, the dominant group is not only using the state apparatus for its own vested interests but also trying to demolish the fundamental structure of Indian state (ibid.: 437).

Within this broad framework, Shahabuddin explores the contentious issue of religion and politics. He argues that: '[r]eligion stands for eternal and universal values ... provides ethical foundation of

Introduction 7

human existence . . . gives a Man a permanent value system . . . a permanent set of principles to determine our conduct and behaviour in changing situations and circumstances'. On the other hand, he notes, 'politics is the management of human society. Management means dealing with problems and situations as they arise and with demands of consumption with available resources and technologies'. For him: '[t]here is no logical basis for comparing or contrasting religion and politics. People and societies go on changing; religion remains changeless. Religion is constant, politics is variable'. In this sense, 'politics without the anchor sheet of religious values can only be tyrannical and oppressive'. Therefore, Shahabuddin seems to assert that there should be a principled separation between the boundaries of the state and religion. He says: '[a] secular state in a multi-religious society must not only guarantee freedom of religion and of conscience but act as an umpire in the case of conflict between one religious group and another and lay down norms for the reconciliation of conflicting claims'. In this framework, the state should not interfere with the internal religious issues of religious communities. These groups should be given freedom to define the essentials of their own religions.[6] At the same time, Shahabuddin suggests, 'we should begin by stopping religious penetrations in the state affairs' (1987: 435–37)

According to Shahabuddin, the 'Muslim community' is a political community in India because all the basic characteristics of a political community apply to Indian Muslims. He notes 'it is a pan-Indian community which sometimes reacts uniformly to a given stimulus but it is by no means a monolithic or homogeneous community, linguistically, ethnically or culturally' (ibid.: 435). He further argues that religion provides a basic logical unity to the Indian Muslim community; however, the external push such as anti-Muslim violence gives it the momentum to speak the language of a political community. He writes that, 'no doubt Muslim Indians see themselves, above all as a religious community, but they have

---

[6] He argues: '[e]very religious community must be free to define the essentials of its faith and the secular state must respect these essentials and protect them from external interference. A secular state should not take the task of religious reforms even in the name of social reforms' (Shahabuddin 1987: 435–36).

8   *Muslim Political Discourse in Postcolonial India*

to realise that they can protect their religious status or religious rights flowing from the constitution only through political action. Once they are conscious of this imperative, they become a political community' (Shahabuddin 1988: 146–47).

Shahabuddin highlights an important sociological aspect of the Indian Muslim community. He draws attention to the fact that the Muslim community in India is highly diversified. In his opinion there are different social and linguistic communities in India that follow Islam as a religion. In fact, the understanding of Islam among these communities is also not at all homogeneous and there are several Muslim sects and sub-sects. However, at the same time, he forcefully argues for the common concerns of this plural Muslim community. In his opinion, it does not mean that these Muslim communities do not recognise Islam as the primary marker of their identity. He notes, however: '[c]ommon concerns and priorities are more often overshadowed by local preoccupations and problems' (ibid.). In his opinion, the question of being a political community and becoming a political community is contingent upon the ways by which Indian Muslim communities react to the 'external pushes' and internal self-perceptions. Thus, for Shahabuddin 'being a religious community and becoming a political community, in larger and in national sense, are indeed, only two faces of the same coin- inseparable from each other' (ibid.).

Thus, Muslim politics could have four possible aspects from this perspective:

- (*a*) There is one collective Muslim politics, which represents the collective interest of Indian Muslims.
- (*b*) The Indian Constitutional framework is capable of protecting the plural character of Indian social life.
- (*c*) Collective Muslim politics functions as the first push to the political systems so that they can work effectively without any failure. The active participation of Muslims in free, fair and regular elections at every level of the political system could be an example of this kind of democratic politics.
- (*d*) Collective Muslim politics also ensures that the broad objectives of India-specific plurality are achieved. This is the kind of mass participation that Shahabuddin calls mass politics for social justice.

Introduction 9

This position on the collective existence of the Muslims in India as a political community can be criticised on two counts. First, it is true that despite several kinds of differences, there can be a few common issues that could affect the entire Muslim community in India. It is also true that the community does/can respond and behave collectively as well as politically at certain points of time. But these momentary and short-lived 'political' reactions cannot be taken as evidence to justify the homogeneity and oneness of Muslim political behaviour.

Second, this position does not accord much importance to the ideological stands of different Muslim organisations and political leaders. It assumes that an Islamic content in the ideologies of Muslim organisations or political leaders always influences their political actions. However, it would be inappropriate to assume that universally-accepted Islamic religious practices and ideals such as performing *Namaz* or paying *Zakat* as prescribed by the Quran could be taken as salient features to assess the Islamicness of any organisation or individual. On the contrary, we find a variety of political interpretations of these ideals at different levels. The Islamic content in the activities of Muslim organisations or the politics of Muslim leaders swings like a pendulum. The ideal-textual-high Islam which evokes the Quranic logic of umma and the conception of a single Muslim community in India is one extreme end of this swing, and the immediate cultural-local political considerations are at the other end.

Social Assimilation and Muslim Politics

In the early 1970s, sociologists like T. N. Madan and Imtiaz Ahmad started questioning the prevailing notions of Muslim identity in India and the ways in which Indo-Muslim communities had been analysed in sociological studies. Indicating the limitations of these writings, Imtiaz Ahmad argued that sociological studies on India did not give importance to the social structures of non-Hindu Indian communities and consequently generalised the sociology of Hindus as the sociology of India. In the absence of such sociological researches on non-Hindu communities, Ahmad wrote emphatically: 'We may have Hindu, Muslim or Christian sociology,

10   *Muslim Political Discourse in Postcolonial India*

but hardly a sociology of India (Ahmad 1972: 177).[7] This search for an 'Indian sociology' became the theoretical foundation of four volumes of essays by various authors on different social aspects of Muslim communities of South Asia, which were edited by Imtiaz Ahmad in the 1970s and 1980s. These essays provide a broad analytical perspective on the social and religious aspects of Muslim communities. These studies substantiated a broad argument that a synthesis has been worked out in South Asia between the high Islamic ideals and custom-centric traditions and therefore, these two components co-exist as complementary and integral parts of a common religious system.[8] Ahmad's various introductions in these volumes very clearly reject the political agenda of Islamists who always define Indian Muslims as a distinct religious and political community. In the third volume Ahmad (1981: 18) writes:

> Muslim fundamentalists may assert and maintain that there is one, only one version of what is orthodox from the Islamic point of view

---

[7] In my view, Ahmad's work highlights three limitations of sociological researchers on Indian Muslim communities — the *limits of historicism*, which questions the tendency to employ historical facts/categories available in historical literature to understand contemporary Muslim societies; the *limits of macro generalisations*, which somehow make a conscious endeavour to identify a fixed 'model' for analysing diverse Muslim social groups in India; and finally *the limits of grand India specific explanation* that does not allow the study of specific social formation(s) (Ahmad 1972). This is an interesting critique. It points towards the rigid boundaries of conventional sociological thinking about Indian Muslims. At the same time, Ahmad seems to suggest that the social and cultural linkages between 'India' and its non-Hindu communities ought to be studied to compile a sociology of India. Thus, Ahmad's prime intellectual objective has been to examine the complex sociological 'merger' between the ever-evolving local cultures (which should not be entirely understood as Hindu culture) and the non-Hindu communities. In this sense, Ahmad's work introduces us to a highly complex process of social assimilation.

[8] It is important to clarify that the authors in these volumes do not take any given ideological position. In fact, Imtiaz Ahmad's introductions are very carefully written. These introductions do not attempt to divert the basic thrust of different essays despite upholding and endorsing a basic theoretical formulation. Consequently, these volumes not only introduced the Islamic assimilation in India and its various shades as a strong intellectual position but also helped in generating a healthy academic debate on Indian Muslims.

Introduction **11**

and whatever does not conform to it is to be dismissed as hetero-dox ... Clearly it seems to me that Islamists' vision has tented to obscure the inherent and underlying pluralism within Indian Islam as a practised religion.

Does this plurality of Indian Islam as a finding help us in understanding different forms of Muslim politics in India? Obviously, a simple reading of the broad argument presented in these four volumes can legitimately be employed to refuse the agenda of those Islamists who purposefully project Indian Muslims as a single and politically identifiable religious community. But, for a profound understanding of the implication of this argument one has to examine the manner by which the sociological plurality of Indian Islam is applied to understand Muslim politics.

We now turn our attention to the writings of Imtiaz Ahmad. In an article published in 1972, he writes: '[o]bjective scholarship would require that Hindus and Muslims [and I should say other religious communities as well] should be seen as constituting a single social field and analysis should concentrate on the social and political processes among them in constant interaction' (Ahmed 1972a: 85). This argument very clearly suggests that Muslim politics is inextricably linked to the wider socio-political processes in India and therefore has to be analysed contextually.

Imtiaz Ahmad identifies a process of Islamisation among Muslims, which, in his opinion, is similar to the process of Sanskritisation among the Hindus and illustrates the basic thrust of collective Muslim politics in postcolonial India. The process of Islamisation, he writes:

'[i]nvolved the spread of the custom, ideology, and practice of the orthodox Muslims belonging to the upper strata of Muslim society ... like Sanskritisation, Islamisation helped in the spread of a relatively uniform Muslim culture throughout the country and it was aided by the presence of certain orthodox movements, such as *tabligh* and *tanzim*' (Ahmad 1969: 1142).[9]

---

[9] The concept of Islamisation, in this case, is seen on historical and social bases. However, Ahmad does not clarify the exact meanings and historical significance of the terms like 'tabligh' or 'tanzim' in medieval India. These words originated in the later colonial period when organisations like Tablighi Jamaat and the Jamaat-e-Islami came into existence. Later in this article, the words like 'communal' and 'Islamisation' are used interchangeably, particularly to describe the Muslim political attitude in postcolonial India.

12　　*Muslim Political Discourse in Postcolonial India*

According to Ahmad, the process of Islamisation in postcolonial India is a result of the growing Sanskritisation of Hindu society. The increasing Hindu communalism in India created a sense of fear among the Muslims and consequently the Islamisation became a form of political and social expression of Muslim grievances. He notes (Ahmad 1969: 1152):

> [i]t is a matter of common knowledge that when a religious minority feels seriously threatened, the machinery of its faith begins to wear out and its traditions begin to falter against those of the majority, it turns worriedly in, upon itself and its members cling even more intensely to the faltering traditions. That something like this has happened in the case of the Indian Muslims seems quite certain.

Imtiaz Ahmad gives another and quite different analysis of Muslim politics in an article published in 1974. He identifies two main political approaches adopted by Muslims in postcolonial India — (*a*) 'Muslims sought to participate in the political system through consolidating themselves as a communal pressure group and using their combined strength in the population as a basis for political horse trading' (Ahmed 1974: 24–27). The formation of the Muslim Majlis-e-Mushawarat could be the example of this approach; (*b*) The participation of Muslims through secular national politics. In this case, Ahmad notes, supporting a particular party was the main tactic. Ahmad rejects these political approaches. He writes that, 'given the segmented character of their community and the presence of a number of distinct strata within it, each with its own specific problems and grievances, a third possibility for the Muslims to participate in the political system would have been for each distinct strata to create a solidarity of social and economic interest with corresponding segments in other religious communities, and to work for their common problem in a collective fashion' (ibid.). In his view this approach would reduce communalism, secularise Muslim demands, and enlarge the support base for Muslims.

But, why did Muslims actually fail to adopt such a well-defined political approach? Ahmad finds a few reasons for this failure, which not only outlines his understanding of Muslim politics but quite significantly contradicts his own theoretical position. First, he talks about the Muslim self-view. According to him, 'the Muslims perceive themselves as an undifferentiated monolithic community sharing common interests and aspirations all over the

Introduction **13**

country' (ibid.). Therefore, he suggests that they could not recognise their own multiple identities and thus, failed to take up a truly 'secular' political strategy. Second, the 'continued involvement of the Muslims with the idea of Pakistan and the attraction for the politics that led to its creation', he writes, had been an important reason for the failure of Muslim politics. He notes that, 'the Muslims or at least a sizeable section amongst them began to see Pakistan as a source of their identity as well as security in a predominately Hindu India' (ibid.). After the 1965 War, Ahmad further notes, a section of young Muslims were attracted towards separatist politics.[10]

So, what is Muslim politics? Is it a kind of separatist politics? Is it reflecting a general trend of Indian politics? Or is it something that emanates from social Islamisation? We do not find answers to these questions. Instead, we could identify a broad perspective on Muslim politics, which is based on the following six propositions:

(*a*) The social hierarchies among Muslims and the Islamic plurality in India are the constant and uniform factors which could legitimately be employed to study Muslim politics in India.

(*b*) There is only one Muslim politics in India, which promotes separatism and communalism in the country and consequently is an anti-thesis of secular politics.

(*c*) This Muslim politics is a direct result of Islamisation.

(*d*) Islamisation is a process which has emerged because of increasing Sanskritisation.

(*e*) There is no independent agenda of Muslim politics. It does not invent potential issues for itself. Instead, it simply responds either to the agenda of the state or the politics of Hindu rightists.

(*f*) There is no problem with the constitutional ideal as well as legal structure related to secularism in India. However, for achieving a truly secular state, a secular society is needed.

---

[10] Interestingly Ahmad justifies this point by pointing out the increasing mass base of the Muslim League in north India. He writes in a footnote that the bulk of the League's workers 'are still not voters or have become voters recently' (Ahmad 1974: 27, n. 2). With this additional observation he rationalises the existence of Muslim separatism!

14   *Muslim Political Discourse in Postcolonial India*

Therefore, there is no need for Muslim politics of any kind.

The writings of Imtiaz Ahmad repeatedly tell us that 'Islam' and 'Muslims' are plural concepts in the Indian context. In this framework, Muslim politics is taken as a 'static entity' which is juxtaposed with the Islamic religious plurality. In this sense we can point out two basic limitations of Imtiaz Ahmad's works on Muslim politics.

First, it seems that Ahmad takes two different positions on Muslim politics. In the first case, he analyses the causes of Islamisation and locates this trend of Muslim politics in a more general context of Indian politics. In his later analysis, Ahmad finds a few separatist tendencies among Muslims and conceptualises Muslim politics as communal politics. However, despite drawing two very different conclusions, Ahmad applies the notions of plurality of Indian Islam and caste division among the Muslims as the fundamental principle in both the cases to understand the Muslim political responses. In this sense, Islamisation is introduced as a kind of political orthodoxy in the first analysis, which is severely criticised and refuted by taking a more rational, progressive and secular political approach in the latter case. Ahmad suggests that 'one will have to launch a mass programme of social reforms to effect the changes required for the acceptance of a broad based secular approach to organised politics' (1974: 27).

Second, we find a strong adherence to secularism in Ahmad's writing that eventually does not allow him to appreciate the fact that political ideologies of Islamic organisations and their polit-ical actions do not always follow similar trajectories. He strongly assumes that the political ideologies are fixed and cannot be changed. A strict dividing line is drawn between the Muslim communalism and secularism without analysing different forms of 'communal' or 'secular' politics.[11]

---

[11] His criticism of Theodore Wright's study of Jamaat-e-Islami can be a good example to further illustrate this point. Wright analyses the role of Jamaat-e-Islami in the process of modernisation of Indian Muslims. He compares the activities of the Jamaat with the *Bilalians*, a movement of the Black Muslim communities in the United States (US) in the 1960s. Introducing the concept of 'inadvertent modernisation', Wright argues that the activities

Introduction **15**

Class Analysis of Muslim Politics: A Contradiction between 'False Consciousness' and 'Liberation Theology'

Let us move on to the class analysis of Muslim politics. As pointed out earlier, one finds a few very comprehensive studies on Muslim politics in the 1970s which discuss the political power structure among Muslims and the nature of the organised Muslim demands.[12] The term 'Muslim elite' is used by these commentators to underline the internal division between Muslim masses and Muslim leaders. I focus on the writings of Moin Shakir and Asghar Ali Engineer to show two different Marxist approaches to the study of Muslim politics.[13]

Moin Shakir's books *Muslims in Free India* (1972) and *Islam in Indian Politics* (1983) are relevant for us. Broadly speaking, Shakir's understanding of Muslim politics is based on two general assumptions. First, that the 'politics of the Muslim community has been the politics of Muslim elite which cannot be equated with the entire community ... elite competition, elite solidarity and elite mobilisation of larger population determines the tones of "Muslim

---

of the Jamaat-e-Islami, a radical Muslim group in Indian subcontinent, could also be seen as a kind of 'inadvertent modernisation' (1983: 83–95). In this sense, Wright's essays very clearly question the ways by which Jamaat or the radical Islamic politics is understood in India. Rejecting his argument about inadvertent modernisation of Jamaat-e-Islami, Ahmad argues that: '[a] nascent democracy still struggling to achieve the goals of secularism and communal harmony when these goals are daily threatened by the propaganda carried out by communal and obscurantist organisations cannot look upon them as secular organisations merely on the hope that their operation might potentially promote inadvertent modernisation' (Ahmad 1983: xlii). This criticism simply does not pay attention to the complex interplay of law, politics and religion in India.

[12] Zafar Imam's essay, 'Some Aspects of Social Structure of the Muslim Community in India' (1975) is also very relevant here. Although the essay is primarily concerned with the social structure of Muslims in India, with particular reference to urban–rural divide and the impact of different laws on Muslim class structure, it offers us a short and systematic class analysis of Muslim politics.

[13] It is important to mention Ali Ashraf's book *The Muslim Elite* (1982). His objective is not to show the power structure among the Muslims of Bihar. Rather, he wants to look at the growth patterns of a few influential individuals. In this sense, this book does not analyse Muslim politics.

16 *Muslim Political Discourse in Postcolonial India*

Politics"' (Shakir 1983: 1–2). He further writes, 'the position of the elite is strengthened by an emphasis on the identity of religion, choice of symbol of disunity, and an urge for the solidarity of community' (ibid.). Second, this sort of Muslim elite politics as well as the situation of common Muslims in India cannot be understood without analysing the working of Indian bourgeoisie democracy (ibid.).

Applying a Marxist perspective, Shakir offers a critical overview of the class character of the politics of the Muslim elite. In his opinion, there are two important characteristics of the Muslim elite: (*a*) they come from the upper Muslim castes, and (*b*) they are economically well-off (ibid.). In his opinion, these elites can further be divided into two broad categories — the religious leaders and the Muslim leaders in other secular parties and organisations.[14] However, Shakir does not find any political hostility between these two types of elites. Instead, he notes that the religious as well as political leaders follow a similar kind of non-democratic reactionary politics (ibid.: 89–90).

Shakir argues forcefully that the majority of Muslims are economically backward and belong to the lower classes of Indian society. To prove this point, he does not give us any data or statistics. On the contrary, he offers us a long descriptive analysis of the Indian capitalist system, its political manifestation as a 'bourgeois democracy' and its relationship with foreign capital / international capitalist system. And finally we are told that the 'rich in the Muslim community are bound to get the benefits' out of this sort of capitalism. In this formulation, the actual emphasis is on the functioning of capitalism in India, which is taken as 'the explanation' to demonstrate the class position of poor Muslims. Shakir does not see any kind of specific impact of postcolonial Indian capitalism on poor Muslims (ibid.: 20).

According to Shakir, common Muslims are secular and do follow secular politics. On the bases of Muslim voting patterns, he declares that the common Muslims have rejected the communal politics of the elites (ibid.: 96). He again does not analyse any specific survey on Muslim voting pattern. Instead, he describes a very general political picture to prove this point.

---

[14] According to Shakir, the Muslim communist leaders or the Muslim leaders in communist parties do not follow this kind of politics (1983: 89).

Introduction **17**

He makes two arguments: (*a*) In order to ensure cultural security to the different minority groups, secularism, in the true sense of the word, should guide the state's policy. There should be a real separation between religion and state, i.e., depriving all the religious communities of any support from public funds' (ibid.: 117); (*b*) For the poor Muslims as well as the other deprived sections of Indian society, the hope lies only in politics, not the politics of an elitist nature; not the politics which serves the aims of establishment; but the politics of emancipation; politics of scrapping the capitalist framework with such a framework which is capable of serving the interests of the entire society (ibid.: 119).

Activist-scholar Asghar Ali Engineer takes a different position. In fact, he offers us a more creative Marxist analysis of Muslim politics. His criticism of the Muslim elite focuses more on the misuse of true Islamic principles. In his opinion, the Muslim elite mobilises Muslim masses by propagating a pro-upper class perspective of Islam. As a result, Islam, which primarily emerged as a political movement for the liberation of poor, women, needy and destitute of Arabian society in the 7th century, has become a tool in the hands of these upper-class Muslim elite. Engineer forcefully argues that a pro-poor Islamic understanding can be used as a political strategy to counter the hegemony of Muslim upper classes. Therefore, he goes on to develop a liberation theology in Islam (Engineer 1990: 1–16).

Liberation theology in Islam, he argues: '[c]oncerns itself primarily with here and now . . . it does not support the status quo which favours those who have as against those who do not (ibid.: 1). He further writes (ibid.: 1–2):

> I am afraid the theology in its received form does not imply human liberation . . . it concerns itself exclusively with liberation in purely metaphysical sense and outside the process of history . . . it is because the received theology has been an ally of establishment and the theologians benefactor of status quo . . . Hence it is necessary to develop a liberation theology if religion has to be meaningful to the oppressed and weak who follow it most.

Engineer's search for a liberal, democratic and radical Islam thus becomes a theoretical tool to examine the historical evolution of Muslim politics in India. In his book, *Lifting the Veil: Communal Violence and Communal Harmony in Contemporary India* (1995), he

18   *Muslim Political Discourse in Postcolonial India*

looks at the question of Muslim politics and the legitimacy of the so-called Muslim issues. Instead of evaluating the specific Muslim issues and their validity, Engineer offers us a grand analysis of Muslim politics.

Discussing the sharpening sense of Islamic identity in post-Independence India, particularly after the 1980s, Engineer points out that, 'the increasing awareness among different sections of Indian society about their social situation' is an important factor. 'This increasing awareness has become possible on account of the broadening and deepening of democratic processes' (Engineer 1995: 51). According to him, after Independence, 'a section of Muslims too, benefited from economic development and began to acquire higher social status. They too became aware of their political bargaining power and used it in exchange for some benefits, though they were more in the nature of emotional gratification. As Dalits and Muslims became more aware of their bargaining strength and began to assert, the upper caste Hindus felt uneasy at the erosion of their monopoly over power and began to retaliate violently' (ibid.: 52). As a result several inter-communal riots against Muslims took place in India in the late 1950s and early 1960s.

The international assertion of Islam in the 1970s gave more strength to the Muslim identity. During this period, the Muslim leaders in India adopted a more radical approach and continued to mobilise the (Muslim) masses in the name of Islam. Engineer notes that the Shah Bano case is the best example to show this kind of politics. The Shah Bano controversy gave a new impetus to the Hindu rightwing forces. In this regards, the Babri Masjid–Ram Janam Bhoomi issue further communalised Indian society. At the same time, the Indian ruling establishment continued to encourage communal polarisation and provided legitimacy to communal organisations such as the Vishwa Hindu Parishad, the Babri Masjid Action Committee and the Bajrang Dal. Thus, for Engineer, there is one communal politics in India and Hindutva and Muslim politics are its two different forms. The politics of secularism based on the notion of rights and liberties can be the best vantage point to counter this communal politics. As an activist, the intellectual agenda of Engineer has changed quite rapidly in later recent years, becoming more concerned with the erosion of secular values and the inter-communal riots.

Introduction **19**

Let us now summarise the Marxist position(s) on Muslim politics. A broad overview of these two positions suggests:

(a) There is a 'communal' Muslim politics in India.
(b) There are several kinds of Muslim elites; practically there is no difference among them. They use the religious ideology of Islam for their own vested interests.
(c) There are options for Muslims: they should join the 'struggle for emancipation' with other deprived sections of society.
(d) Islamic adherence is a personal affair of Muslims therefore it has no role to play in public life (Moin Shakir's position).
(e) Islam emerged as a social movement. It can be reinterpreted from a rational modern point of view for, (i) exposing the false Islamic agenda of Muslim elite, and (ii) mobilising common Muslims effectively for the wider politics of emancipation of the Muslims in India. This 'liberated' form of Islam will eventually follow a secular agenda (Asghar Ali Engineer's position).

The class analysis of Muslim politics suffers from two kinds of conceptual problems. First, it is assumed that the ideological differences between different Muslim leaders or organisations are not at all important. For example, Moin Shakir's analysis very clearly tells us that Muslim politics is a communal politics of the Muslim elite. He even makes an attempt to locate the agenda of Muslim politics within the general Marxist framework. But, in order to take a Marxist position on this kind of politics, Shakir deliberately avoids studying the complexities and varieties of the political discourse of Muslim elites. For example, to empirically prove his generalisations, Shakir analyses three Muslim organisations — the Jamaat-e-Islami, the Muslim Majlis-e-Mushawarat and the Muslim League. Interestingly, Shakir does not tell us about his methodological priorities in focusing only on these three Muslim organisations. The Jamaat-e-Islami is a pressure group, the Muslim Majlis-e-Mushawarat is an umbrella organisation of different Muslim groups and the Muslim League is a registered political party. In any case, these organisations cannot be taken as the representative sample to make a general argument on Muslim politics. On the basis of these generalisations, we cannot find any specific assessment of the activities of the Jamaat-e-Islami in the

20   *Muslim Political Discourse in Postcolonial India*

1960s, the political pact between the Imam Bukhari of Jama Masjid and the Janata Party in 1977 and the political agenda of Muslim Majlis-e-Mushawarat in 1962. Shakir's study does not look at the changing political forms of Muslim politics.

The second problem is related to the application of Marxism. Moin Shakir points out that the difference between the organic intellectuals and the traditional intellectuals, as described by Gramsci, is absent among the Muslims in India. At the same time, Shakir notes, the Muslim leaders have a considerable influence over the Muslim masses. They are the defenders of traditional values and religion. In this situation, therefore, Shakir suggests, we need to see the politics of the Muslim elite in entirety (1983: 6–7).

It is important to note that Gramsci's distinction between organic and traditional intellectuals is based on a concrete historical context. He discusses the ways by which the hegemony of a class/group is crystallised by these two kinds of intellectuals in different historical moments.[15] Thus, for applying this distinction between organic and traditional intellectuals on Muslim politics,

---

[15] The term 'intellectuals' in Gramsci's analysis, refers to those individuals in a social group, who play a particular organisational role. Gramsci identifies two types of intellectuals: the 'traditional' and the 'organic'. The organic intellectuals are those who formulate the ideology and interests of a particular class or social group. Gramsci writes, 'every social group, coming into existence on the original terrain of an essential function in the world of economic production, creates together with itself, organically, one or more strata of intellectuals which give it homogeneity and an awareness of its own function, not only in the economic but also in the social and political fields' (1971: 5). On the other hand, the traditional intellectuals are those intellectuals who have been formulating the ideology of that particular social group for sustaining an older hegemonic project. Gramsci sees an interesting relationship between the traditional and organic intellectuals. He notes, 'one of the most important characteristics of any group that is developing towards dominance is its struggle to assimilate and to conquer "ideologically" the traditional intellectuals, but this assimilation and conquest is made quicker and more efficacious the more the group in question succeeds in simultaneously elaborating its own organic intellectuals' (ibid.: 10). In this sense, the new organic intellectuals assimilate within the given hegemonic project, but at the same time, conquer it by re-formulating a new hegemony for the social group.

Introduction **21**

we need to seriously look at the traditional hegemonic project of Muslim politicians in postcolonial India and at the same time find out the internal dynamics of Muslim politics for understanding the process of assimilation and contradiction at the level of leadership. On the contrary, Shakir gives a static image of Muslims as a social group. He does not go into the complexities of Gramsci's argument. Instead, he proposes that his adherence to a particular understanding of Marxism, or in this case Gramsci, can be used as 'the theory' to explain everything.

These problems can also be found in the writings of Engineer, though in a different form. Despite applying a very creative understanding of Marxism, he also seems to believe that the there is only one Muslim politics in India. We do not find any systematic analysis of the functioning of this politics in his writings. In fact, there is a missing link between his theory of liberation theology and his analysis of Muslim politics. In contrast, Engineer's several fact-finding reports on riots have generated a huge empirical data / information on communal politics in India, which indicates a strong possibility of an alternative kind of analysis of Muslim politics.

The Brass Thesis: Muslim Politics as an Instrument of Muslim Elite

It is important to clarify that Paul Brass has never worked exclusively on Indian Muslims. His earlier work was on the role of religion and language in the process of nation formation. Similarly, his later works on ethnic violence identify a few socially institutionalised communal networks that promote different forms of collective violence in India (Brass 2002). In both the cases, Muslim politics has been taken as a case study to comparatively analyse a few wider theoretical concerns. However, despite this fairly comparative focus of Paul Brass's writings on Muslim politics, his general thesis on symbol manipulation has been frequently employed by several authors for explaining the role of Muslim elites.

Brass offers a historical analysis of Muslim separatism in Uttar Pradesh and links it to the Muslim politics of 1950s and 1960s.[16]

---

[16] Brass's two major works, his book *Language, Religion and Politics in North India* (1974) and his essay, 'Elite Groups, Symbol Manipulation and Ethnic Identity among the Muslims of South Asia' (1977) are noteworthy. These two studies discuss the complexities of Muslim politics in post-Independence India in great detail.

22   *Muslim Political Discourse in Postcolonial India*

He suggests that the Muslim demand for the protection of Urdu could possibly be connected to an unwritten 'informal rule', which marks the attitude of the central government towards the political demands in post-Independence India. In his opinion, the demands, particularly the regional demands based on language and culture are accommodated easily. However, the demands that are explicitly based on religious differences are not accepted by the Indian political system (Brass 1974: 17). Therefore, instead of Islamic uniqueness of Muslim culture in India or the political rights of Indian Muslims, Urdu as a political symbol was adopted by the elites to mobilise Muslim masses for political action (ibid.: 183–85). Therefore, in post-Independence India, Brass suggests, Muslim political demands are consciously linked to cultural issues.

Brass identifies three kinds of Muslim leaders (elites) in post-Independence India: (*a*) the educated elite such as middle-class lawyers, doctors, teachers, and journalists who are further divided into two broad categories — one, the secular and Marxist Muslim elites who tended initially to work with Congress and later join other leftists and secular parties. Second, the educated conservative Muslim elite who remained less concerned with secularism than with the interests of the Muslim community; (*b*) The Ulema from different religious schools, and, finally (*c*) the backward caste/class Muslim elite (ibid.: 235–36).

Brass locates these elites in four kinds of socio-political Muslim organisations: the religious political associations such as the Jamaat-e-Islami, Jamiat Ulama-i-Hind; the non-economic interest organisations such the AnjumanTaraqqi Urdu; the occupational and class association such as the Bihar Momin Conference; and inclusive political organisations such as the Muslim Majlis-e-Mushawarat (ibid.: 235–53). He discusses the attitude of national and regional political parties on the question of Urdu in Bihar and UP and the role played by Muslim elites. He concludes that the political realities of post-Independence India, particularly the legal system based on constitutional democracy and a few 'unwritten' rules, radically affected the nature of Muslim political demands.

Thus, Brass's work on Muslim politics suggests that:

(*a*)   The Muslim politics becomes defensive in nature and thus converted into a kind of politics of minority rights in post-1950 India.

Introduction **23**

(b) 'There was no effective Muslim leadership available to protect and defend the rights of Muslims' in this period (ibid.: 273–74).

(c) The defensive Muslim politics which has been revolving around the cultural issues such as the protection of Urdu virtually failed to effectively mobilise Muslims for political action in postcolonial India.

It is true that Brass's work recognises the political agendas of different kinds of Muslim elites in India, yet, his analysis suffers from other types of problems. I identify three problematic issues. The first problem is related to the application of instrumentalism for exploring the dynamics of Muslim politics. This question has been discussed and analysed more systematically by Francis Robinson in a decade-long debate with Paul Brass. Robinson argues that Brass's overemphasis on instrumentalism does not allow him to look at the significant roles played by political ideas and ideologies in the wider context. He also points out that Brass's analysis is based on the assumption that the elites, or in this case the Muslim elites, always function rationally and select political symbols for mobilising the masses. Robinson argues that the Brass thesis does not examine the ideological framework of Muslim elites. He further notes that in this construction, the Muslim elites seem to stand apart from their societies and their cultural tradition (Robinson 1979: 84).

The second problem is, if we focus on Brass's work on the Urdu movement in postcolonial India, we find that he simply describes the major Muslim political demands and different kinds of Muslim leaders. He concentrates on political responses of political parties, legislative bodies and other institutions to the Urdu movement to substantiate his general argument about the role of language and religion in Indian politics. The strategies of Muslim leaders and their relationship with local Muslim communities is virtually absent in his analysis. As a result, Brass concludes that Muslim politics has become defensive in postcolonial India. This kind of limited analysis prevents Brass from seeing the radical agenda of Muslim leaders that was further reflected in the political demands of the 1970s and 1980s.

The third problem relates to the need to see Brass's treatment of political symbols critically. In Brass's opinion, the existence of a pool

24   *Muslim Political Discourse in Postcolonial India*

of symbols to draw upon is one important requisite to transform an objectively different group of people into a subjectively conscious community (Brass 1974: 44). In this sense, he uses the term 'symbol' as a given and undifferentiated entity. He seems to believe that the symbols are easily available choices for the elites. He does not look at the different ways by which an object/issue is converted into a symbol. In this scheme therefore, Islam as a religion and Urdu as a language are understood as symbols merely because these have been the available options for the Muslim political elites in India.

Secular Modernists and the 'Communal' Muslim Politics

Mushirul Hasan's book *Legacy of a Divided Nation: India's Muslims since Independence* (1997), which claims to offer an analysis of the experience of Indian Muslims in the last five decades, is quite relevant to understand the secular modernist position on Muslim politics. This book or what Hasan calls 'historian's journey' begins with the description of Partition and concludes with the demolition of the Babri Mosque. In his view both the events symbolise the 'heightened religious consciousness, the renewed salience of Hindu–Muslim schism and the weakness and ultimate retreat of the state in dealing with Hindu and Muslim extremism' (ibid.: 22). He clarifies that his main engagement in this book, 'is with their *legacy* and, in a more general sense, with current debate about the possible direction of Indian society, future of secularism, and the fate of religious minorities' (ibid.).

Hasan strongly believes that the Muslim community in India is highly diversified and the idea of a single Muslim community was invented in British India by the colonial authorities and Muslim separatists. Quoting Paul Brass, he says that Muslim elites invented the idea of Muslim nationhood for their own vested interests. He argues, quite radically, that it is 'necessary to deconstruct the language of minorityism and uncover the motives of those practitioners of modern day politics who purported to represent the *millat*, or the "community" as a whole, but were actually exploiting Islam and communitarian solidarity as shield to cover their political design' (ibid.: 51).

Hasan identifies a link between colonial and postcolonial Muslim politics and develops an argument against Muslim communalism. Criticising the *minorityism* of Muslim elites in contemporary India, he argues that the Muslim leaders still follow the path of Muslim

Introduction **25**

League's politics of 1940s. He discusses several Muslim communal organisations such as the Tablighi Jamaat, Jamaat-e-Islami and Jamiat Ulama-i-Hind and the Muslim Majlis-e-Mushawarat to substantiate the point that despite various ideological differences, Muslim politics is still dominated by communa' and anti-democratic tendencies (ibid.: Chs. 4–5).

He uses this secularist argument to compare the Muslim politics of minorityism with a new kind of Muslim liberal modernist secular intelligentsia, who represent a completely different picture of secular Muslim culture. He writes (ibid.: 227):

> [t]he intelligentsia — artist and intellectual — creates mirrors through which we see ourselves and *windows* through which we perceive reality. It is these mirrors and windows that define the boundaries of ideas and institutions. The intelligentsia's role — both as creators of a cultural outlook and the product of the milieu — is central to this writer's view of what happened in India in general and among certain Muslim groups in particular.

Hasan discusses the roles of institutions like Aligarh Muslim University and Jamia Millia Islamia, and the contributions of Muslim individuals and families such as Mohammad Habib, Dr Ansari and Maulana Azad in protecting the secular democratic character of postcolonial India. The way he elaborates the notion of a liberal modernist agenda, particularly in post-Babri Masjid India, makes this aspect very relevant for understanding his approach to postcolonial Muslim politics. He writes: 'the secular modernists represent different groups from mixed social and cultural background . . . I describe them as *secular modernist*, in recognition of their secular framework of analysis and their commitment to secularism' (ibid.: 319).

Hasan further notes some broad characteristics of these secular modernists. He points out that, (*a*) these individuals fight to protect the basic Nehruvian model of Indian democracy; (*b*) They believe that communalism and Hindu–Muslim strife need not imply the failure of secular experiments and finally; (*c*) they belong to nationalist, secularist family backgrounds. This last characteristic is very interesting. He discusses the family background of these secular modernists to highlight an 'Indian secular tradition'. Emphasising the secular contribution of a few progressive Muslim families, he talks about the family of Mohammad Habib (Aligarh historian),

26 *Muslim Political Discourse in Postcolonial India*

and his brother, Mohammad Mujeeb, and Habib's son Irfan Habib, who contributed a lot to the secularisation of India; the family of journalist Seema Mustafa, who is a part of the Kidwai clan, the home of Rafi Ahmad Kidwai (her grandmother was a freedom fighter and social activist); the family of Hasan Suroor, a London-based journalist, whose father, despite being a British civil servant, was a sympathiser of Congress and whose mother gave up her *burqa* (veil) to participate in social activities (Hasan 1997: 320). Hasan concludes that these progressive intellectuals inherited secular values from their families and upheld the cause of secularism in India.

Thus, we can draw the following five inferences from Mushirul Hasan's analysis of Muslim politics:

(*a*) There is only one communal Muslim politics in India, which is anti-secular, because it does not follow the given and prescribed notion of secular politics; it is anti-modern because of its aggressive attitude towards social reforms and finally, it is anti-Indian because it ignores the composite Indian culture.

(*b*) Postcolonial Muslim politics is an extension of colonial Muslim politics. There is no difference among forms, contents and mobilisation patterns of these two well-defined political projects.

(*c*) The Partition and the demolition of Babri Mosque as events are comparable; the retreat of the colonial state in late 1940s and the postcolonial state in 1990s are very similar and therefore, the aggressive Hindutva politics and the politics of Muslim organisations of 1980s and 1990s can be compared with the Muslim separatism of the 1940s.

(*d*) Actual Muslim politics can be contrasted with the contribution of secular Muslim institutions and secular Muslim literature. In this sense, Muslim intellectuals, particularly, the secular modernist intellectuals, can be legitimately compared with communal Muslim politicians.

(*e*) The secular project of liberal modernists is based on moral and non-*political* progressive considerations.

There are however, a few serious problems in this conceptualisation. First, the postcolonial Muslim politics cannot be understood simply as an extension of colonial Muslim politics. It is true that the

Introduction 27

comparisons between these two historical contexts can be useful in understanding long-term trajectories of Muslim politics. But, one kind of historical assessment could not be used to explain a very different sort of political context. In this sense, the similarities as well as the *dissimilarities* between the communal politics of the Muslim League in the 1940s and the Muslim politics of the Babri Masjid Action Committee in the late 1980s become equally important. A sweeping generalisation in this regard may not be able to locate the specific trajectories of Muslim politics in India. Second, despite being committed to the Islamic pluralism in India and the diversity of Muslim community, he virtually fails to pinpoint multiple political responses of this diversified Muslim community in postcolonial India. His entire discussion is centred on the most dominant version of Muslim politics. Third, Hasan does not elucidate his understanding of secularism/or a secular ethos in the Indian context. We are told about the composite Hindu–Muslim culture of UP, the idea of tolerance among different Indian religious traditions, the political commitments of people like Mahatma Gandhi, Jawaharlal Nehru, Maulana Azad and a few liberal Muslim intellectuals and their families as examples of secularism in India. There is virtually nothing on the principles and ideas on which the Indian version of constitutional secularism is based. Fourth, Mushirul Hasan's understanding of the world of politics is quite problematic. He wants us to believe that secular individuals, institutions and literature can be juxtaposed with the actual day-to-day politics. No one can deny the fact that literature reflects the mindset of a society or a community. However, it does not mean that literature and political action can be put side by side in a comparative mode. This kind of comparison ignores the independent and creative roles of literature and political action in particular social settings. Moreover, if we focus on Muslim communities in India, we have to recognise a complex relationship between literature and society. The low level of literacy and educational backwardness of Muslims in India is a well-known fact. The majority have a limited access to literature or written information. Because of this fact, Muslim political elites tend to use some unconventional forms of media such as public address systems of mosques, religious processions and so on. The kind of literature Hasan discusses in his book, in this sense, cannot be treated as mass literature. Finally, in his attempt to show the real face of secularism in India, Hasan goes on to argue that the family

28   *Muslim Political Discourse in Postcolonial India*

links and the secular background of an individual can/should also be seen as significant *facts*!

This brief discussion shows that most of the existing approaches to postcolonial Muslim political experiences offer an essentialist understanding of Muslim politics, which is almost incapable of explaining the relationship between Muslim elites and common Muslims. Thus, there is a need to re-examine the multiplicity of Muslim politics at various levels and its actual functioning. For that reason, this study concentrates on a specific kind of Muslim politics of monuments and memory. I attempt to understand the nature as well as the function of various social, political and cultural power structures in a historical perspective that determines the political actions of Muslim elites in different social contexts. At the same time, I also look at the strategies and symbols by which Muslim elites make politically appropriate configurations to mobilise Muslims and carve out an important space for themselves in the so-called secular political sphere.

However, Indo-Islamic historic architecture as a vantage point introduces us to several different types of issues, including, the most controversial question of politics. In fact, the study of politics of architecture/art is usually not encouraged in India. It is argued that historic sites are neutral, artistic and apolitical entities, which can/should not be seen as 'political sites'. It is strongly believed that art and politics are two very different spheres of social life. The various forms of art are appreciated as impartial, positive, universally-accepted activities while politics is regarded as a corrupt and unfair practice for achieving power. Therefore, it is suggested that the historic buildings should be kept outside the corrupt, irrational domain of politics. Furthermore, conventional disciplinary boundaries are also underlined to justify this strict separation between art/architecture and politics. In this context, an important and straightforward question arises: Is it possible to approach Indo-Islamic sites as political monuments for making sense of Muslim politics?

II

ARCHAEOLOGY/HISTORY/POLITICS: INDIAN HISTORICAL SITES AS 'MONUMENTS'

There is a large literature on architecture and/or colonial and postcolonial conservation policies, religious and charitable

Introduction 29

endowments, desecration of places of worship, Indian secularism and so on. However, these studies focus on specific issues and do not look at the 'politics of monuments' in relation to the legal ambiguities and postcolonial archaeological explorations. As a result, the political reception of historic sites in India is still an unexplored area of academic research.

For example, the literature on heritage, archaeology and conservation deals with the evolution of different styles of architecture and the artistic significance of particular historic building(s). Various publications of the Indian National Trust for Arts and Cultural Heritage (INTACH) and the ASI can be the examples of this kind of literature.[17] Most of the early colonial writings in the 19th century established this genre, which was subsequently followed by Indian authors in colonial and postcolonial India. This type of literature is primarily concerned with the physical characteristics of historic buildings, forms and styles of architectural features, internal composition, material used, specific construction methods/techniques, and most importantly, their objective history. Interestingly, in these works the colonial/western supremacy in the field of archaeology is usually recognised as an indispensable 'external push' that gave traditional-minded and ignorant Indians a sense of 'built heritage'.[18]

---

[17] For example, the INTACH publication *Delhi: The Built Heritage: A Listing* (2000) is a valuable document. This work lists 1,208 historic buildings of Delhi. Interestingly, despite showing commitment for a 'people's centric heritage', this collection does not look at the popular perceptions and the memories associated with these sites.

[18] Let us take two examples to illustrate this point. James Fergusson, in the introduction of his book *The History of Indian and Eastern Architecture* (1910: 4), points out: '[i]t cannot, of course, be for one moment contended that India ever reached the intellectual supremacy of Greece, or moral greatness of Rome; but though on a lower step of the ladder, her arts are more original and more varied and her forms of civilisation present an ever changing variety, such as are no where to be found'. In the similar manner, Sourindranath Roy in his book *The Story of Indian Archaeology 1784–1947* (1996), which was published by the ASI, suggests: 'non-scientific historiography of Hindus and Muslims failed to develop a true spirit for Indian archaeology' (ibid.: 8). Western archaeologists and historians, according to Roy, provided the much-needed stimulation to Indian archaeology.

30   *Muslim Political Discourse in Postcolonial India*

Similarly, existing literature on laws related to monuments and religious endowments suggests that no serious intellectual attempt has been made to study the complex legal side of historical monuments.[19] It is true that the literature on religious endowment does make some useful arguments about the legal status of historic-religious places of worship. But, the complex relationship among three sets of laws: the laws related to protected historical monuments (such as the Ancient Monuments and Preservation Act, 1958), the laws related to Islamic wakfs (such as the Wakf Act, 1995) and the laws related to the protection of religious places of worship (such as the Protection of Religious Places of Worship Act, 1991) have not been examined thoroughly. In fact, the legal issues related to 'secular monuments' are generally accepted without any critical discussion.

Politics of Monuments in India: Different Approaches

In recent years, the traditional art history paradigm has been challenged significantly. Scholars have questioned the methodological basis of art history, its subject matter and the interconnectivity of art with other social activities. A more interdisciplinary and culturally sensitive approach is gradually becoming popular to study some of the untouched areas of the historic architecture in India. The works of Thomas Metcalf, Tapati Guha-Thakurta, G. H. R. Tillotson, Monica Juneja, Richard Davis, Richard M. Eaton, John Lang, Madhvi Desai, Miki Desai, Sunil Kumar, and Nayanjyot Lahiri illuminate different dimensions of Indian historic architecture, which could not be traced by the traditional framework of art history. Most importantly, the study of political questions related to the history of historic architecture and its varied interpretations are some of the common concerns that unite all these recent attempts. It would be misleading to club all these writings in one single category. I try to identify three possible positions on

---

[19] Arjun Appadurai's book *Worship and Control under Colonial Rule* (1981), which is an ethno-historical analysis of conflict in a single south Indian temple over a period of 200 years, is an exception in this regard. Appadurai discusses the religious activities and issues of management and control in the context of colonial laws on religious endowments. In fact, he offers a sociological analysis of the Religious Endowments Act, 1860.

Introduction **31**

the complex relationship between art/architecture/archaeology and the political power in a colonial situation.

Thomas Metcalf, Tapati Guha-Thakurta and Nayanjyot Lahiri contend that the growth of Indian art/archaeology could be seen in relation to the colonial politics of knowledge. Metcalf (1989) studies the use of Indian architectural styles in the public buildings by the colonial state as a kind of political appropriation. Guha-Thakurta examines the growth of archaeology in India as a discipline and traces its relationship with the Indian Museum. The museum, Guha-Thakurta (1992) argues, re-constructed the visual aspects of the past and brought history into the domain of colonial knowledge. Nayanjyot Lahiri explores different dimensions of the monument policy of the British Raj during the time of Lord Curzon (1899–1905). She contends that we need to critically examine the dominant image of Curzon as a saviour of Indian monuments.

G. H. R. Tillotson and O. P. Kejariwal do not accept the view that the works of early Indologists could be reduced to the colonial project of knowledge that had a direct connection with political power.[20] Tillotson (1998) argues that the dominant paradigms of art/science during the Victorian England had influenced the British art historians and authors. The European concepts and categories of aesthetics were deployed to understand and describe the Indian art/architecture. He seems to suggest that the element of politics in the writings of British/European authors should be con-ceptualised in a complex manner. O. P. Kejariwal demonstrates the fact that there was not any direct relationship between the colonial state and the early Indologists. In fact, he argues that many a time the colonial state stopped funding for archaeological explorations (Kejariwal 1988: 226–29).

---

[20] The debate on 'orientalism in Indian context' could also be mentioned here. David Cannadine, John M. Mackenzie and Peter Heehs approach this question from three different angles. Cannadine's argument that the self-perception of the British Empire and its aesthetic represents a kind of cultural assimilation, has a direct bearing on the political question (Cannadine 2001). Mackenzie's study (1995) of orientalism suggests that the Western approaches to the orient, particularly in the field of art and architecture, were interactive. Peter Heehs (2003) traces six styles of orientalist discourse in the writings of colonial and postcolonial authors. Heehs concludes that a more balanced approach to orientalism is needed (ibid.).

32   *Muslim Political Discourse in Postcolonial India*

Partha Mitter represents the third position. His seminal works, including his celebrated book, *Much Maligned Monsters: A History of European Reactions to Indian Art* (1977), deal with the political question at two levels. At a more general level, he questions the 'dominance of Western classical canons by showing it to be the product of a specific historical and cultural situation rather than one with a timeless and universal quality' (ibid.: xiv). He shows that the terms of discourse in a colonial situation are always determined by the nature of power relations. However, at a more complex level, he clearly demonstrates the fact that the European reactions to Indian art were more closely linked to the European religious and philosophical traditions. In this sense, he gives equal importance to the historical evolution of different European aesthetic traditions.

The literature on postcolonial archaeology is expanding. The Ayodhya issue and emergence of the 'people-centric' interpretative archaeology have influenced some of the recent writings on the political images of historic sites. The writings of Tapati Guha-Thakurta (2004), Dilip Chakrabarti (2003), Sheena Panja (2002), Maria Antonella Pelizzari (2003), A. G. Krishna Menon (2003), and more recently, Santhi Kavuri-Bauer (2011) provide a critical point of view and suggest different perspectives to study conservation, archaeology and the idea of monument in postcolonial India. It would be too early to club all these intellectual responses into any one analytical category. Nevertheless, this emerging area of research offers us a critical overview of the official understanding of Indian historic sites and conservation practices.[21]

What is the relevance of these approaches for studying Muslim politics? This brings us to our conceptual and methodological priorities. Metcalf, Guha-Thakurta and Kavuri-Bauer's position is useful for examining the colonial archival sources on Indian archaeology/architecture. Following Mitter, the complex relationship between the colonial power and the academic/artistic initiatives could be analysed. Similarly, Tillotson's argument can

---

[21] Guha-Thakurta's book *Monuments, Objects, Histories: Institutions of Art in Colonial and Postcolonial India* (2004) is relevant here. In this book she tries to bring in the question of 'contemporary' in a significant way. She argues that the issues like Ayodhya offer us an opportunity to re-examine the ways in which Indian past(s) had been conceptualised in colonial India.

Introduction 33

be applied to look at the interactions between Western ideas and the indigenous elite (more specifically in our case, the Muslim elite). However, for clarifying the placing of these varied and often conflicting approaches on historic sites and their political use in postcolonial India, a broad conceptual framework is needed, which I discuss in the next section.

III

HISTORY/MEMORY DICHOTOMY: PROCESS OF *MONUMENTALISATION* AND THE MUSLIM POLITICS OF MONUMENTS AND MEMORY

It is quite common to use terms like 'historic architecture' and 'monument', interchangeably to describe old buildings or historic sites. There is, however, an important conceptual difference between these two terms. Historic architecture is a broad category and it could be used to describe a number of old buildings, ruins and protected monuments. On the other hand, the basic function of a monument is to commemorate an idea, event or person.[22] In this sense, a 'monument' could have two interrelated aspects:

---

[22] The Oxford English Dictionary defines 'monument' as 'an object commemorating a person or event [and/or] a structure of historical importance' (OED 1999: 331). The Cassell's Dictionary of Word Histories, quite similarly, notes that the word *monument* signifies 'anything by which the memory of persons or things is preserved, especially a building or permanent structure' (Room 2002: 392). The Encyclopaedia Britannica defining the term 'monument' notes: 'it is a word whose many meanings are all related to its original roots, which signifies a memorial ... More specifically in architecture, a monument is a structure erected for the primary purpose of commemorating a person or event' (1967: 775). In India, officially the Hindi/Sanskrit word *smarak* is used for monument. This word originates from the Sanskrit word *smriti*, which means memory. The non-functional historical monuments are often called *Veeraan* buildings (Uninhabited) or *Khandhar* (ruins) or *Bhutha* buildings (the buildings where the ghosts live). In literary Urdu, the Persian terms like '*Asar-a-Kadim*' (old buildings) and *Tarikhi-Imarate* (historical buildings) are frequently used for the historical monuments. But these expressions are not common in the day-to-day life practices. In fact, I do not find any particular word or a group of words (at least in popular Hindustani) that can exactly translate the term 'monument'!

34 *Muslim Political Discourse in Postcolonial India*

(*a*) the object/structure that is intentionally erected to symbolise a person or an event and (*b*) the associated idea/story that has to be remembered/commemorated.[23] In India, a monument is also a legal entity. The artistic and historical values of a particular historic building determine its status as an officially declared historical monument that commemorates significant historical events related to the nation's past. Thus, any historical building could be converted into an official national monument or alternately any officially declared national monument could simply cease to be 'a national monument' at any point of time.

This substantial difference between historic architecture and a monument is very crucial in understanding the process by which a particular building or a group of buildings is converted into a protected historical monument or monumental complex in India.[24]

---

[23] Alois Riegl makes a distinction between intentional and unintentional monuments. An intentional monument is 'a human creation, erected for the specific purpose of keeping single human deeds or event (or a combination thereof) alive in the minds of future generations'. For him, this type of monument is concerned with commemoration. They recall a specific moment or complex of moments from the past and make a claim to immortality to an eternal present and an unceasing state of becoming. The idea of commemoration remains the prime objective behind the construction of these types of monuments. Riegl believes that all the antiquities of the middle ages can be called intentional monuments. An unintentional monument for Riegl is: '[a] remain whose meaning is determined not by their makers but by our own modern perceptions of these monuments'. All historical buildings can be clubbed in this category. Riegl (1982) also informs us that an intentional monument can also become unintentional when it survives much longer and finds new meanings in a completely new social set up.

[24] Françoise Choay argues that in the aftermath of scientific revolution in Europe, the images of the past changed quite rapidly. The notion of *monuments* (objects that were built intentionally to remember a person or event) was replaced by the idea of a *historical monument*, so as to recognise the historical cognitive values associated with old buildings (Choay 2001: 10–17). As a result, the scientific conservation became a crucial aspect to re-produce the past through the preservation of the old buildings as historical monuments. The invention of printing provided further help in producing the images of monuments. It became easier to produce the history of monuments through the publication of books, journals and newspapers. The invention of photography further enhanced the capacities to record the past (ibid.: 123–29).

Introduction **35**

This process deals with a number of issues: a particular building is differentiated from other buildings; its physical characteristics are identified as symbols; its architectural properties are measured; certain historical and artistic values of the building are determined; its history is traced and finally it is preserved as a heritage of a nation, community or people. In a broader sense, we may call this the 'process of monumentalisation'.

The dichotomy between history and memory is the most significant aspect of the process of monumentalisation in India.[25] It demonstrates an interesting struggle between these two very distinct ways to commemorate the past. The clash between the official history of Indo-Islamic sites and the collective memory of local Muslim communities is a very clear example of this rift. We find that the official history of Indo-Islamic historic buildings introduced the contested idea of a separate Indian Muslim architectural heritage. On the other hand, various forms of collective memories associated with these sites are crystallised by Muslim political groups and transformed into a memory of a royal Muslim past. This history/memory dichotomy, thus, can be adopted as the conceptual framework to understand the making of Indo-Islamic buildings as historical monuments and their re-making as political sites in contemporary India. This framework is useful in studying

---

[25] Maurice Halbwachs suggests two crucial differences between history and memory: (*a*) History notes only those events of the past which are important and significant for the present community, society or nation. It starts when the social and collective memory stop operating. In contrast, social memory consciously or unconsciously contains every bit of information as a shared feeling. Halbwachs argues that memory 'is a current of continuous thought whose continuity is not at all artificial, for it retains from the past only what still lives or is capable of living in the consciousness of the groups keeping the memory alive' (1980: 80); (*b*) History attempts to make broad observations dividing the past into periods. The memory on the other hand does not go beyond a limited time frame. Halbwachs notes: '[h]istory ... gives the impression that ... everything is transformed from one period to another ... it divides sequences of centuries into period ... each period is apparently considered a whole, independent for the most part of preceding and following, and having some task-good, bad or indifferent-to accomplish'(ibid.: 81). Halbwachs's distinction between history and memory thus suggests that history does not adequately address the dynamics of collective remembrance.

36   *Muslim Political Discourse in Postcolonial India*

the 'sites' of monuments, in this case — Jama Masjid and Babri Masjid. At the same time, this could also explain the wider historical processes by which these sites acquire political significance.[26]

More specifically, I employ this history/memory framework to examine three sets of questions: (a) the monumentalisation of Indo-Islamic sites in colonial India, (b) the continuity and discontinuities of the process of monumentalisation in postcolonial India and (c) the political reception of Indo-Islamic buildings and Muslim politics of monuments and memory. Let us discuss these questions to understand the conceptual structure of this study.

Monumentalisation and the Idea of an Indian Muslim Heritage

In general, the term 'architectural heritage' characterises a kind of relationship between the architectural objects of the past and their successors, who collectively inherit them, preserve them and hand over them to future generations. It may be a community, a society, a nation, or more broadly, the world.[27] However, this simple idea of a shared architectural heritage cannot be applied to Indo-Islamic buildings and their functional as well as symbolic connections with

---

[26] Pierre Nora's concept of *lieux de memoir* is very significant here. Nora argues that the modern acceleration of history — the most dominant mode to commemorate the past in the modern societies — has replaced the pre-modern 'real' and inviolate memory (1996b: 2) As a result, Nora points out, we have *lieux de memoir* or sites of memory where our 'modern memory' is crystallised. For Nora, a lieux de memoir is 'any significant entity, whatever material or non-material in nature, which by dint of human will or the work of time has become a symbolic element of the memorial heritage of any community' (1996a: xvii). Thus, Nora calls for a new history of memory through the study of these sites of memory. His aim is to recover the symbolic meanings of these *lieux*. From our point of view, this line of argument can help us in two ways: (a) it could be significant to trace the popular meanings of Indo-Islamic sites and (b) it could also be used to understand the placing of these symbolic meanings in the political projects of Muslim groups.

[27] The Oxford English Dictionary (OED) defines the term 'heritage' as 'history, tradition and qualities that a country or society has had for many years and that are considered an important part of its character' (OED 1991: 408). The word 'heritage' originated from old French word *heriter*. It also means 'a land or other property that passes by descent or course of law to an heir' (Room 2002: 279).

Introduction **37**

various Indian Muslim communities. In fact, there are two significant aspects of Indo-Islamic buildings, which do not correspond to the modern idea of heritage. First, the Indo-Islamic sites represent at least two types of architectural traditions: (*a*) the regional architecture that evolves from the local architectural practices and responds to the local cultural norms; (*b*) the pan-Islamic norms that actually grew in the centres of Islam but gradually diffused and were transmitted to different regions. These pan-Islamic standards link these buildings to the religious practices of a worldwide Muslim community. Thus, Indo-Islamic sites accommodate region-specific designs of building construction and at the same time follow the basic Islamic architectural spirit. In this sense, the idea of a common Muslim heritage has to recognise both of these powerful architectural elements.

Second, the question of a Muslim heritage should also be seen in relation to the notion of the Islamic wakf. The term 'wakf' in its literal sense means 'detention' or 'stoppage'.[28] It signifies the sacred act by which a portion of movable and immovable property/wealth is dedicated in the name of God for the benefit of the Muslim community. Although, the concept of wakf was not fully developed in the initial stage of Islam, Islamic *fiqh* (jurisprudence) has given considerable importance to this kind of Islamic philanthropy.[29] Different schools of Islamic *shariat* have recognised various religiously valid purposes for which Muslims can dedicate properties as wakf. For example, dedicating some land or building for the benefit of the entire Muslim community is a religiously acknowledged wakf. In the same manner, reserving some property for the

---

[28] The Hanafi School of Islamic law conceptualises the wakf as 'the extinction of the proprietor's ownership in the thing dedicated and its detention in the implied ownership of God in such a manner that the profits may revert to and be applied for the benefit of human beings' (Ahmad 2000: 260).

[29] There are three interrelated aspects of wakf. First, the owner of the property, who intends to dedicate his/her property or a portion of it as wakf; second, his/her dedication of that portion of property in the name of Allah; and finally, the society/community, which would be the beneficiary of that dedicated portion of property. Since God is not a physically tangible entity, the society/community that is considered to be the actual heir of that portion of property would exercise its control through the appointed *Mutawali* (manager).

38   *Muslim Political Discourse in Postcolonial India*

comfort of one's own family or specified Muslim community is also an acceptable act of wakf.[30] All the Muslim cemeteries, tombs, historic functional/non-functional mosques, *dargahs* and *khanqahs* in India, are wakf properties. From the point of view of heritage, the Muslim community does not inherit wakf buildings as dead historical monuments for commemorating the past achievements of Muslim rulers. Instead, these sites are taken over and used as living sites for religious observance.[31] In this sense, the existence of a variety of wakf buildings illustrates the cultural plurality of Islamic communities, their intrinsic religious connections, and above all, a continuity of religious traditions, which cannot be explained by the modern idea of a Muslim heritage.

These two aspects, more broadly, show that Indo-Islamic buildings could be described as symbols of Islamic pluralism because these sites accommodate various regional architectural styles and are managed and controlled by various local Muslim communities. On the other hand, the 'Islamic element' in their construction and the universally accepted notion of Islamic wakf link them to each other. The question is how to analyse this religious-architectural specificity of Indo-Islamic historic buildings in a colonial context when the process of monumentalisation conceptualised these sites as an inseparable part of the Muslim heritage?

Richard Eaton's conceptualisation of a 'double movement' is useful to explain this paradoxical equation. Analysing the formation of Islamic identity in South Asia in historical perspective, he talks of a double movement of Islamic identity. The first movement was adoptive in nature. The slow pace of conversion of different rural agrarian communities in India to Islam adopted local

---

[30] The question of family wakf became very controversial in the early 20th century and after a long debate the Wakf Aal-ul-Aulad Act, 1913 was passed. This aspect shows that the concept of wakf recognises the specificity of local social context and gives rights to the local Muslim community as well.

[31] The complex legal structure related to wakf and historic sites and the legal process by which a wakf is created is discussed in the next chapter. Here it suffices to say that Islamic mosque, Islamic cemetery (including the tombs and Dargahs) are built on a land that is dedicated to God in a form of wakf. According to Hanafi Sharia if a mosque is built on a non-dedicated land, it should immediately be demolished or money should be paid for that land (Kashmiri 2004, Int.).

Introduction   **39**

cultures and traditions. The precepts of Islam were redesigned and rearticulated according to the local religious-cultural practices. The second movement reflects an emotive urge to get connected with the imagined centres of Islam. The Indo-Islamic communities, in this sense, inclined to establish an enduring link between their everyday social practices and norms of idealised Islamic discourse. Eaton argues that the 'Indo-Islamic traditions that grew and flourished between 711 and 1750 CE served both to shape Islam to the regional cultures of south Asia and to connect Muslims of those cultures to a world-wide faith community' (2003: 6).

Elaborating this point further, Eaton argues that this double movement is very much evident in architecture. He points out that the architectural forms of two mosques, one built in Bengal and the other in Malabar during the 16th century, could be different. These mosques might be quite similar to other buildings of these regions; yet their structural similarities such as 'an alignment with Mecca, a niche indicating the direction of prayer and ample interior space for worshippers and so on' would connect them to each other (ibid.: 9–11). This is precisely because of the synchronised existence of a double movement: the localisation of Islamic principles and the Islamisation of the local cultures.

But, how did the colonial archaeological explorations deal with this complex double movement of Indo-Islamic traditions? How was the idea of a Muslim architectural heritage conceptualised and appropriated to justify the existence of a single Muslim community? To place these issues in the history/memory framework, I draw on Sudipta Kaviraj's work on the principles of community construction in a colonial context.[32] I examine the enumeration of

---

[32] Kaviraj argues that in the pre-colonial India the principle of community construction was different. These communities were 'fuzzy' in two senses: first, the complex sum of different identities, such as caste, village or region, was fuzzy. There wasn't any overarching community identity available to them that could claim to represent all the layers of social bonds of an individual. Second, communities were not enumerated. He points out: '[t]hey [members of these fuzzy communities] would not represent themselves as a large universal collective group … for the very fact of being one, being involved in some action' (Kaviraj 1997b: 147–48). He argues that colonial modernity provided a clearer self-perception to Indian communities through the processes of statistical counting and spatial mapping.

40   *Muslim Political Discourse in Postcolonial India*

historical monuments to suggest that after such listings of historic sites, it actually became possible to think of a grand, universal contribution of a single Indian Muslim community.

Monumentalisation in Postcolonial India and Secularism(s) of 'National Heritage'

The continuations and ruptures of the process of monumentalisation in postcolonial India are linked to the institutional and legal framework in which ideas like 'national heritage' and 'secularism' are converted into policies. For that reason, I evoke the recent secularism debate to understand the controversial placing of Indo-Islamic sites as an inseparable part of secular Indian heritage and wakf issues in the legal-constitutional discourse.

Broadly speaking, the present debate on secularism has produced two explanations of Indian secularism.[33] The first reaction to secularism is somewhat pessimistic. It criticises the very concept of Western secularism and finds it inappropriate in the Indian context. The works of T. N. Madan, Ashis Nandy and Partha Chatterjee can be placed in this category.[34] In contrast, the second response

---

Consequently, it became possible to think of a homogeneous community, the exact numbers of its members and its common interests.

[33] One may add a third response to secularism: the response of Hindutva. Interestingly, this response has not been seen very seriously. This critique is based on the idea of 'equality'. For example, the documents produced by the Rashtriya Swayamsevak Sangh (RSS), the Vishva Hindu Parishad (VHP) and the Bharatiya Janata Party (BJP), one finds an unquestionable adherence to constitutional secularism in the first place. The problem, these documents argue, lies in the discriminatory nature of some provisions of the constitution that provide unlimited and unrestricted freedom to minorities (http://www.rss.org/New_RSS/Mission_Vision/RSS_on_Minorties.jsp, accessed on 12 May 2004).

[34] T. N. Madan denounces the Western concept of secularism on three grounds: (a) It is not applicable in India on the contextual ground (secularism is a gift of Christianity and as a concept emerged in the West), (b) South Asian religions are *totalising* in a sense that the religious life cannot be separated from the public life; and (c) secularism is impotent to fight against the growing religious fundamentalism. Madan (1998) analyses different religious traditions of South Asia and proposes that secularism should not be overemphasised to reject the religious worldviews. Madan does not reject the possibility of secularism in India completely; instead his purpose is to illuminate the importance of religious traditions. In

Introduction   **41**

is rather affirmative and reassuring. It defends the Indian version of secularism on moral, political and ethical grounds. Rajeev Bhargava's works on secularism are noticeable in this regard.[35]

---

his earlier writings, Madan calls upon the Indian intellectual to work out a clear concept of secularism in Indian context (ibid.). In his later works, Madan identifies the 'civil society' as an arena to discuss religious issues like religious conversions (Madan 2003). Ashis Nandy also rejects secularism, but on different grounds. Nandy's focus is on the cultural–political aspects of Indian public life. He makes a difference between the religion as a faith and religion as an ideology (Nandy 1998). For Nandy, the latter is a perverted and most politicised form of religion. He argues that the secularism as a Western modern idea has been used by the middle classes in India not only to reject the cultural claims of the people but also to politicise religion. The present Hindutva is a result of secularisation of Hinduism (Nandy 2003: 79). Nandy offers a Gandhian solution. He argues that we should explore the concept of tolerance in day-to-day practises of various South Asian religions. Partha Chatterjee is the third most important opponent of secularism. Chatterjee is concerned with actual religious communities and the political dimensions of secularism. He rejects secularism on cultural and historical grounds. He notes that the postcolonial state in India pursed the social reform agenda in the early years. These attempts were justified for promoting secularism. Chatterjee sees the politics of modern secularism in these reforms. The present Hindutva is a result of over secularisation because it operates within the conceptual framework of secularism and describes its adversaries as pseudo-secularists. Chatterjee suggests a politics of toleration. Unlike Nandy, he attempts to trace this kind of politics within the domain of modern state institutions. He argues that the strategic politics of toleration should operate at two levels: (*a*) the minority cultural groups should seek to resist the homogenisation agenda of the state to maintain their specific cultural identity and (*b*) these groups should continue to pursue the reform agenda within their communities to democratise the inner structures (Chatterjee 1997: 261).

[35] Rajeev Bhargava raises two basic questions: Why religion and politics should be separated and what kind of separation the advocates of secularism are seeking. Analysing different philosophical arguments that justify the separation between religion and politics, Bhargava suggests two versions of secularism: (*a*) the ethical secularism that seeks the separation of religion from politics for the realisation of some ultimate ideals (e.g., equality, rationality, egalitarianism, etc.); (*b*) Political secularism that seeks this separation for making the political arena much more workable. Unlike the ethical secularism, Bhargava argues, the political secularism

It is to be noted that the question of historical sites, particularly the religious status and identity of a non-functional protected monument, has not been directly discussed in relation to the debate on Indian secularism. However, the broad arguments, which have emerged out of this debate, could conceivably be employed to examine the secular process of conservation of historical monuments in postcolonial India. For example, following the Nandy–Madan thesis, it can be argued that monumentalisation is a modern process, which is irreconcilable with Indian religious traditions. Therefore, the Western idea of a monument can easily be contrasted with eastern religious places of worship. This is an important point that makes us aware of the politics of colonial modernity. But, this inference does not help us in understanding the Muslim politics of historic sites in contemporary India, which evokes the question of secularism for 'liberating' Indo-Islamic sites from state control.

Rajeev Bhargava's position is more accommodative. From his point of view, it is possible to examine a few 'principles' behind the secularised process of monumentalisation. His argument is valuable in investigating the relationship between the official history of the Indo-Islamic sites and the operation of various kinds of secularisms in postcolonial India. Thus, following Bhargava, this

---

does not go for any ultimate ideal. It is, in a sense, a more practical form of secularism that tries to maintain a peaceful ordinary life by carving out separate boundaries for religion and politics. Bhargava suggests three versions of political secularism: (a) hyper-substantive secularism that excludes religion from politics and seeks to maintain an absolute kind of polity for the realisation of some ultimate ideal (b) the ultra-procedural secularism that seeks an unconditional separation of religion and politics but remains suspicious of all kinds of ultimate ideals and (c) contextual secularism that maintains a principled distance from religion. Bhargava points out that the Madan–Nandy thesis is important to understand first two versions of secularism. However, the contextual secularism cannot be rejected on cultural grounds because it devises culturally specific principles for maintaining distance from religion. The irreversibility of modernity makes contextual secularism much more relevant. Bhargava appreciates Indian secularism for its unique contextual features. In his opinion, the Indian constitution not only makes attempts to separate religion from politics but also tries to pursue the agenda of socio-religious reforms through the judiciary.

Introduction

43

study attempts to examine two kinds of secularisms: the secularism of historical monuments and secularism of minority rights to trace the legal-constitutional implications of the process of monumentalisation in postcolonial India.

POLITICAL RECEPTION OF INDO-ISLAMIC SITES AND MUSLIM POLITICS OF MEMORY

The meanings of a historic site are not static or fixed. These meanings are constructed in multiple ways and gradually transformed into collective memories. Unlike the formation of official secular history, which records the most notable aspects of a period, memories emerge from the continual interaction between a site and local communities.[36] However, this does not mean that the history and memories of historic sites operate in their own ways and do not influence each other. In fact, one of the most fundamental objectives of this study is to look at the placement of official history/ laws and local memories in the political discourse of contemporary Muslim political groups.[37] To expand this aspect, let us talk about two selected case studies.

Jama Masjid, Delhi

The Jama Masjid at Delhi is the first case study. Examining the monumentalisation of Jama Masjid in colonial and postcolonial India, I attempt to understand how the idea of a 'living' Muslim heritage is evoked by its Shahi Imam in the last three decades.

---

[36] Richard Davis uses the term 'community of response' to understand the collective social meanings of images. In his opinion the meaning emerges through the relation of image with viewer, who brings his or her community's own interpretative strategies to bear with the encounter. In this way, the derived meanings are learned, shared and susceptible to change (Davis 1997: 9).

[37] Rudy Koshar's work (2000) on 'German memory' also locates monuments in a historical perspective. Koshar uses the concept 'memory landscape' to study the historic architectural sites and other forms of built environment. Koshar is concerned about the ways by which an object of the past is understood by different groups including the state. In this sense, Koshar's argument goes in two directions: (*a*) how does the historical evolution of the objects of the past take place and (*b*) how these objects are understood and framed in the public discourse by different social groups.

44 *Muslim Political Discourse in Postcolonial India*

I discuss three significant events to contextualise the politics of the Shahi Imam: the riots of February 1975, when the Shahi Imam transformed a personal tussle between him and the Delhi Wakf Board over the control of the mosque into a national Muslim issue by stirring up the memories of the Muslim past; the closure of Jama Masjid in 1987, when the Jama Masjid was closed down for nearly two weeks to pressurise the government to accept a few immediate political demands. In this case, the Jama Masjid was presented as a symbol of India's heritage and its closure was used to highlight the anti-Muslim policies of the then Congress government; finally, the Wazukhana episode, 1996, when the Imam, quite unexpectedly, started constructing a *Wazukhana* (area for ablutions) adjacent to Jama Masjid. Within a few days, this attempt turned into a question of 'misuse' of a historical monument and the local authorities and citizen groups became active. This time, however, the Imam made it a purely legal issue. These events are discussed to look at the relationship between the culture and economy of old Delhi and the memory of a royal Muslim past, which provided a symbolic political authority to the Imam to speak on behalf of the entire Indian Muslim community.

Babri Masjid, Ayodhya

The Babri Masjid–Ram Temple site in Ayodhya has acquired a central place in the popular discourse of Indian politics in the last two decades. Unlike the dominant perception that Babri Masjid is a political–ideological tussle between secularism and Hindu communalism, I find that this disputed site is a revealing example of Muslim politics of monuments and memory. Concentrating on Muslim responses to the Babri Masjid question from 1934 to 1992, I attempt to investigate a variety of political agendas and strategies of Muslim political leaders at various levels. In this case, three questions are discussed: (*a*) What are the Muslim 'histories' of the Babri Masjid dispute? How do such accounts differ from other versions of this case; (*b*) What has been the role of judiciary in the Babri Masjid case? Why did the Muslim positions on legal proceedings change quite considerably in post-1986 period; (*c*) How and why did the Muslim political groups transform the Babri Masjid into a question of secularism and right to heritage? Why did they demand that the mosque should be declared a protected monument? What encouraged them to constitute a 'Muslim political coalition' on

Babri Masjid? How did this 'fragile' coalition work and why did it collapse within two years? I argue that the Babri Masjid case can help us in exploring the adherence of minority groups to legal-constitutionalism. Moreover, it also shows the shifting character of Muslim politics of monuments and memory after the emergence of a secular camp in the late 1980s.

These two mosques as 'case studies' can be compared in four different ways. First of all, the two mosques could be placed side by side on the basis of their religious status. The Jama Masjid is a functional mosque, in which Muslims enjoy an undisputed right to offer namaz. On the other hand, Babri Masjid was a non-functional mosque. Even the point that Muslims did not use this mosque since 1949 (or 1934!) is still being debated in the current legal proceedings. Second, these mosques possess very different kinds of symbolic relevance. The Jama Masjid is symbolically recognised as the 'notorious centre of Muslim politics'. On the other hand, the Babri Masjid has emerged as a symbol of Muslim subjugation and a crisis of Islamic identity in secular India. Third, the nature of conflict in these two cases is different. In the Jama Masjid case, the Imam has been involved in a continuous battle with the ASI and the wakf board. In contrast, the dispute over the Babri Masjid is multi-dimensional. In this case, Hindutva groups, the government, the judiciary, the secular political leaders and organisations and a variety of Muslim political actors are struggling with each other. Finally, although, these mosques are not 'protected monuments of national importance', the question of their monumentalisation and the control of ASI has been an important political issue. This aspect makes them revealing cases to understand the actual functioning of the process of monumentalisation in postcolonial India.

IV

RESEARCHING THE MEMORIES: ON 'METHOD', STRUCTURE AND ARGUMENTS

The present research is a qualitative ethnographic study, which emerges from a critical encounter with three research sites: the archive, the law and policy discourse, and the 'lived' memories, which I collected during my fieldwork. The archive took me to colonial archaeological/legal sources and various significant postcolonial documents. The policy discourse helped me in understanding

46   *Muslim Political Discourse in Postcolonial India*

the mechanism of the legal-constitutional modes by which legal principles are converted into concrete policies. Finally, the in-depth personal interviews and group discussions, which I carried out with a variety of respondents: the ASI and wakf board officials, Muslim political leaders, heads of various Muslim social-political organisations, ulema of different religious schools, local political activists and local Muslims and Hindus, offered me a lived experience to construct a narrative out of rather fragmented memories, claims, suggestions and assertions. Thus, instead of following any formal methodological route, my research journey was guided by the specific questions that I have discussed in previous sections.

This small clarification on methodological moves brings me to the focus of the study. Despite the fact that I discuss the transformation of historic sites into official monuments in colonial and postcolonial India in detail, my main aim is to make sense of the particular kind of Muslim politics of monuments in a historical perspective. In fact, the contemporary political issues are seen as 'questions' for exploring the historicity of this process of monumentalisation. However, this does not mean that the chapters on colonial history and postcolonial legal-constitutional discourse simply provide background information to two selected case studies. These chapters, on the other hand, capture the political trajectories of laws and official history, which are crucial for any kind of political analysis.

The book, thus, is divided into six chapters (including this chapter). Chapter 2 discusses the historical evolution of the idea of a separate Muslim architectural heritage in colonial India. Analysing the writings of colonial and Indian authors, early Indologists and relevant legal documents, this chapter talks about different phases of the process of monumentalisation and tries to show how Indo-Islamic sites became 'contested monuments', even in colonial India. Chapter 3 examines the continuities and discontinuities of the process of monumentalisation in postcolonial India and the legal complexities associated with Indo-Islamic sites. I also discuss various kinds of secularisms and a few contentious and unresolved legal issues. This chapter thus attempts to demonstrate that the images of Indo-Islamic sites as contested monuments was substantiated in postcolonial India and the idea of national heritage uncritically accepted the colonial classification of India's historic sites. It further establishes a link between the

Introduction **47**

legal-archaeological framework introduced by the postcolonial state and the changing nature of Muslim political demands. Concentrating on a major shift in the nature of collective Muslim politics in north India post-1970, this chapter also shows that the Muslim politics of monuments, does not necessarily operate in relation to Hindutva attack on Muslim religious places of worship. Chapter 4 is on Jama Masjid which looks at the placing of history, law and memory in the political project of the Shahi Imam. Discussing three crucial events, this chapter shows how the memory of a royal Muslim past has been conceptualised by the Imam to underline the collective Muslim political existence. Chapter 5 discusses the Muslim politics of Babri Masjid. I look at various ways by which the history of the Babri Masjid dispute has been conceptualised. This chapter also examines the legal issues of the case and different Muslim responses. It shows that the nature of this case forced three ideologically different groups — the liberal-constitutionalists, radical Muslims, and Ulema — to form the first major Muslim political coalition in 1987. The chapter finally argues that the placing of Muslim political demands in newly emerged 'secular camp' affected the nature of collective Muslim politics in post-1992 period. Finally, in Chapter 6, I summarise my main findings and try to make a few observations and possible arguments.

Let me recapitulate this discussion by introducing three main arguments that emerge out of this book. First, Muslim politics in postcolonial India is simply understood as a monolithic entity and is always seen as an inseparable component of a broader conceptual package called 'Muslim issues'. In most of the cases, as I have discussed in the first section of this chapter, a few crucial and fundamental findings on these Muslim issues are extended to develop a general theory on Indian Muslims so as to explain every single aspect of their public engagements, including their politics.[38]

---

[38] Pointing out the limitations of the scholarly debates on Muslim politics in India, Peter B. Mayer makes a similar point. He identifies three dominant positions on Muslim politics: the *Koranic political culture* position (that attempts to find out some intrinsic and essential qualities 'which distinguish Muslims as social actors or which distinctively characterise their attitude towards social and political life), the *Islamic political theory* position (which sticks to the views and ideas of a few Islamic scholars and intellectuals and tries to understand the political response of common

48   *Muslim Political Discourse in Postcolonial India*

In response to this oversimplified understanding of Muslim politics, I suggest that every Muslim 'issue' has its own specific politics, which cannot be explained by any general theory. In fact, it is imperative to rethink about the ways by which political acts are explained and categorised. Thus, concentrating specifically on the shifting character of postcolonial Muslim political discourse, I argue that Muslim politics of monuments and memory revolves around the contested notion of Muslim architectural heritage and links it to the extended meanings of the constitutional right to worship.

Second, Muslim politics is juxtaposed with 'secularism' by employing certain established theoretical formulations such as 'Marxism' or 'Weberian' liberalism either to find out the correct political answers or demonstrating the explanato43ry capacity of these grand theories. Refuting these claims, this study argues that the legal-constitutional discourse of secularism is accepted by Muslim political groups as a broad framework in which the elements of official history and popular memory are strategically placed and redefined for articulating political demands.

Finally, the dichotomy between the notion of a single Muslim community and the idea of a plural Muslim community in India still dominates the academic discourse. The Muslim homogeneity perspective does not accept the plurality of Muslim responses in order to substantiate their legal-constitutional explanation of Muslim politics. On the other hand, the secularists fail to understand the symbols, manners and attitudes by which the notion of a single Muslim community in India is politically produced and sustained. In fact, the secular critique ignores the significant placing of laws in the political agenda of Muslim elites. This study suggests that the homogeneity versus plurality issue should be posed

---

Muslims on the bases of these ideas and conceptualisations) and the *crisis of the contemporary Muslim community* position (which focuses on the problems of Indian Muslims and concludes that the Muslims are 'experiencing' a moral and political crisis in contemporary India). On the basis of an empirical study and a quantitative survey Mayer refutes these positions and other common assumptions about the political participation of Muslims in India. He argues that we need to understand the grassroots complexities of Muslim politics before taking any extreme position (Mayer 1983: 5–48).

Introduction 49

in a different way. We need to look at the ways in which Muslim groups conceptualise the question of Muslim unity. In our case, the contested notion of Muslim historic sites and the gradual formation of the memory of a royal Muslim past are studied as an entry point to trace the various configurations of Muslim unity. I argue that political construction of the memory of a royal Muslim past transforms the local memories into a collective shared memory of a single Muslim community. In this sense, the memory of a royal Muslim past is used by the political groups to underline the collective political existence of India's Muslims.

■

2

Monumentalisation in Colonial India

Discovery of 'Indian Muslim Architectural Heritage'

The objective of this chapter is to examine the process of monumentalisation in colonial India and its intrinsic relationship with the notion of an 'Indian Muslim architectural heritage'. The chapter looks at the colonial archaeological and legal initiatives that not only identified Indian historic buildings as an important 'source' of objective history but also classified Indian historic sites on religious basis and protected them as secular historical *monuments*.[1] In this process, the stereotypical images of Indian religious communities were produced and the dominant colonial notion of Indian history, which had conceptualised India's past as a battle ground of religious conflicts, was substantiated. The monuments became a point of reference to uphold the view that Muslims — the foreign invaders — conquered and destroyed the indigenous Hindu civilisation in medieval India. In order to demoralise the Hindu population, Muslim invaders are alleged to have targeted the Hindu religious places of worship. They demolished these sites and/or converted them into mosques. The desecration of Hindu temples by Muslims, therefore, became a focal point for historical discourse in colonial India. Focusing upon the colonial discovery of the 'Muslim invasion', this chapter re-evaluates a few 'neutral' and 'objective' archaeological/historical 'findings' and attempts to trace the historical evolution of the 'contested' idea of an 'Indian Muslim architectural heritage'.

---

[1] I do not use the term 'colonial archaeology' in an instrumental way. Nor do I evoke the colonial/national binary to justify the famous 'divide and rule' theory. My purpose here is to explore various modes in which Indian historic buildings were understood and categorised and how a discourse of 'Muslim heritage' evolved.

Analysing the writings of colonial and Indian authors, early Indologists, relevant legal documents, the official state policy on historical monument and popular tourist guidebooks in colonial India, I try to suggest that the listing and categorisation of historic buildings on religious basis established a fixed religious identity of these sites. As a result, the collective memories associated with Indian historic buildings were replaced by an objective secular–rational history and every single historical object became a part of a larger 'communal' grouping. In this context, the Indo-Islamic buildings were reinvented either as an architectural contribution of a 'single Indian Muslim community' to Indian nation and/or as a symbol of 'Islamic conquest'.

I would like to make three crucial clarifications here to elucidate the significance of historical material for political research of this kind. First, I evoke the 'past' of the process of monumentalisation simply to ask a few 'second order political questions' (Kaviraj 2010: 39). The legal-archaeological framework and the modes of writings about the Indian historic architecture are explored to trace the complex formation of a few known political debates such as the desecration of Hindu temples by Muslim rulers and/or the historical contributions of Muslims to the nation. Although these debates continued to affect the political imagination of Muslim elites in colonial India, such discussions found a new afterlife in the 1970s and 1980s, particularly after the Babri Masjid episode. My questions obviously stem from this crucial point of departure; however, I do not ignore the contextual specificities of certain historical writings and functioning of institutional mechanisms related to historic architecture. This is the reason why the chapter also pays attention to different attitudes of Muslim intelligentsia and political leaders towards the official history of Indo-Islamic buildings in colonial India. This brief discussion, I suggest, could give us an opportunity to ask an appropriate yet speculative question: Why was there no 'Muslim politics of monuments' during colonial times?[2]

---

[2] The conventional disciplinary boundaries that set out the contours of history and political science might not be able to help us in dealing with the questions I raise. Obviously, I do not want to produce any alternative conception of the past of Indian archaeology/monuments; nor do I offer a 'prehistory of communal or secular politics'. I am trying to historicise the question of monumentalisation simply to understand the ways in

52   *Muslim Political Discourse in Postcolonial India*

Second, despite the fact that I try to unpack an intrinsic dichotomy in the conceptual construction of the terms like Indo-Islamic and/or Indian Muslim heritage in a historical sense, I continue to use these categories in my discussion. This apparently contradictory practice, I suggest, is useful in underlining the distinctiveness of modern historical categories, which we use to describe Islamic buildings in India today. In other words, I do not claim to offer any 'alternative', 'hospitable' or in a more fashionable sense, a 'secular' terminology to get rid of the overtly 'colonial and certainly modern vocabulary' given to us. On the contrary, a modest attempt is made to problematise the dominant intellectual discourse of archaeology/conservation.

Finally, I divide the process of monumentalisation in colonial India into four clearly identifiable phases. The classification of this 'history' into phases is not based on any chronological consideration; nor do I suggest that these timelines could offer any fixed and legitimate sequencing to relevant events and processes that transformed historic buildings into monuments. Instead, the purpose is to offer an interpretative framework to quite well-known historical arguments.

I begin my story rather unconventionally. I describe the first phase of monumentalisation as *period of interaction*, which began in the 15th century. During this period, the early European travellers made initial attempts to grasp the meanings of Indian architecture. By employing European standards and artistic sensibilities, these travellers produced a number of images of Indian buildings. The publication of various travelogues in Europe subsequently introduced these images of Indian sites to contemporary European intellectual and artistic traditions. The second period was the *period of exploration* when Indian culture, art and architecture became the objects of serious research and the early individual initiatives were institutionalised, particularly after the formation of the Asiatic Society of Bengal. The third period was the *period of categorisation*. At this stage, the religious and communal identities of Indian historic

---

which a political discourse emerges around it in a specific context. I evoke Kaviraj's argument here. He says: '[a] study of more abstract questions . . . cannot be produced by the unreconstructed discipline of history. Nor can it be produced by an unreconstructed state theory out of its own internal, purely conceptual, resources' (Kaviraj 2010: 39).

Monumentalisation in Colonial India   **53**

sites were elaborated as analytical categories for conceptualising Indian heritage as a collection of various communal heritage(s). The fourth period can be called *the period of conservation*. In this period, religious categorisation was employed for preserving the artistic and historical values of Indian buildings as 'protected monuments'. A principle of 'strict neutrality' was also laid down for providing legal protection to these sites. In addition, a 'neutral' and objective history of Indian monuments was brought into the domain of education for further reproduction of this knowledge.

I

INTERACTION: INDIAN ARCHITECTURE AND EUROPEAN SENSIBILITIES

In most of the 'histories' of Indian archaeology, the writings of early European travellers, who visited India between 15th and 17th century, are not adequately examined.[3] It is argued that only after the formation of the Asiatic Society of Bengal in 1784, systematic and institutionalised efforts began in the fields of archaeological exploration and conservation of historic sites. It is true that the establishment of the Society was a crucial development, which had a considerable impact on Indian historical researches. However, it does not mean that the period before the formation of the Asiatic Society was insignificant. In fact, the early European reactions to Indian art and architecture could be useful to trace the ways by which Indian buildings were initially perceived. In this sense, the travellers' accounts illustrate various intellectual responses to Indian architecture in two significant ways.

First, the early European travellers actually *invented* different images of Indian historic sites.[4] They applied European artistic

---

[3] All Europeans visitors, in general, could be described as 'travellers'. However, I focus on the writings of those travellers who wrote extensively on Indian buildings and/or religious communities. The vast secondary literature on travel writings, particularly the books published from 1850 to 1930 on this subject, are useful in this regard. The editors of these books very carefully re-compiled the original works of early travellers by dividing the general description into different topics. In this sense, these later travelogues were more classified and reader friendly (Wheeler 1878; McCrindale 1885; Foster 1926).

[4] Mary Louise Pratt points out that the European travellers had a unique opportunity to construct certain images of people and cultures of Asia and

54   *Muslim Political Discourse in Postcolonial India*

canons to understand the architectural styles and cultural/religious complexities associated with these buildings. As a result, they perceived these buildings in their own intellectual context. The accounts of these travellers were the major source of information about the Indian buildings in Europe at that point of time (Mitter 1977: 2). In fact, the export of these images of Indian buildings to Europe facilitated the production of different artistic and intellectual endeavours.

Second, the political context of these writings was very different. Except for the Portuguese occupation of Goa, most of the western and northern parts of India were politically controlled by Indian rulers. The direct political rule of any European trading company or political power was not yet established. In fact, the political interests of European companies were gradually being articulated in this period. Thus, the notions of superiority/inferiority in these travellers' accounts were considerably different from the later colonial writings.

It is also important to look at the intellectual context of 15th century Europe for understanding the responses of early European travellers. This was a period of transition in Europe. The emerging humanism, as an intellectual movement, was challenging the old medieval political and social values by insisting on the rediscovery and reevaluation of the classical civilisations of ancient Greece

---

Africa. Pratt uses the term 'European planetary consciousness', to argue that this new conception of the world offered a new self-image to Europe and led to the 'construction of global scale meaning through the descriptive apparatus of natural history' (Pratt 1992: 15–16). Moreover, as Donald E. Pease argues, these early travellers writing also affected the established literary traditions. The discoveries of new worlds increased the social and intellectual status of European travellers. They wrote with a considerable amount of authority. In this sense their works were significantly different from the traditional medieval literature. The European medieval literary conception of 'auctor', which denoted a writer whose words commanded respect and belief, was challenged by these travellers' accounts. These writings introduced a new kind of 'author', who was supposed to be a faithful companion of the reader (Pease 1995: 105–06). Pease suggests that these 'authors' 'exploited the discontinuity between the things in the New World and the words in the ancient books to claim for their words an unprecedented cultural power' (ibid.: 107).

Monumentalisation in Colonial India **55**

and Rome. The periodisation of history in different phases and the discovery of the 'present' phase as the period of renaissance had made it possible for these humanists to appreciate the artefacts of the past as the symbols of history. As a result, ruins, old buildings and sculptures were acquiring unprecedented intellectual significance.[5] Thus, the impact of these intellectual traditions and on-going debates on the specific status of the 'New World' on early European travellers cannot be ignored.

Functional and/or Non-Functional: Early European Interpretation(s) of Indo-Islamic Buildings

The early travel writings do not make any clear difference between a *historic site* and a *non-historic site*. Instead, the criteria of *functional* and *non-functional* sites were employed quite frequently to classify Indian buildings. For instance, the functional sites are always described with a greater emphasis on cultural and religious activities. In fact, a living relationship between local people and Indian buildings is highlighted to demonstrate the actual placing of these sites into the cultural discourse of Indian communities.[6]

On the contrary, we encounter a variety of European responses to non-functional sites. Although most of the early observations on

---

[5] It should be clarified that the historic buildings were not treated as primary resources for knowing the past. In fact, as François Choay argues: '[f]or the humanists of the 15th century and first half of 16th century ... monuments and their remains confirmed or illustrated the accounts of Greek or Roman authors. However, in the hierarchy of truthfulness, their status was inferior to that of texts, which retained the unconditional authority of verbal testimony' (Choay 2001: 41). Thus, in the humanists' framework, monuments and old buildings were considered as the secondary *sources*, which could also be used to establish the authority of classical texts.

[6] Describing the Indian temples, Linschoten, who visited Goa in the 15th century writes: '[t]hey have on every hill, cliffe, hole or denne their pagodes and Idols in most devilish and deformed shapes, cut (and hewed) out of the stone and rocks with their furnises hard by them, and a cesterne not farre (from them, which is alwaise full of water) and every one that passeth by, washeth their feete therein, and so fall down before their Idoll, some setting before him for an offering fruits, Rice, Egges, Hennes, etc., as their devotion serve, and then commeth the Bramenes their Priest and taketh it away and eateth it, making the common people beleeve that the pagode hath eaten it' (quoted in Wheeler 1878: 186).

56   *Muslim Political Discourse in Postcolonial India*

non-functional sites were limited to the cave temples of Kanheri, Elephanta and Ellora, the descriptions clearly reveal different and almost contradictory European attitudes, reactions and approaches to these type of buildings.[7] The Italian traveller Andrea Corsali's account of a temple, which was destroyed by Portuguese, could be a good example to illustrate these varied reactions. Corsali wrote a letter to Duke Giuliano de Medici in 1515. He writes:

> [i]n this land of Goa and the whole of India there are numerous ancient edifices of the pagans. In small Island nearby called Divari, the Portuguese in order to build the land of Goa have destroyed an ancient temple called pagoda, which was built with a marvellous artifice, with ancient figures with certain black stone worked with greatest perfection, of which some still remain standing in ruins and damaged because the Portuguese do not hold them in any esteem. If I could obtain one of these sculptures thus ruined, I would have sent it to your lordship, so that you may judge in what great esteem sculpture was held in antiquity (Mitter 1977: 34).

Exposing the vandalism of Portuguese, this letter also introduces us to a more substantive approach to non-functional sites. Corsali's account seems to suggest that a section of early Europeans had a keen interest in the protection of a few non-functional buildings. The influence of humanism in this case cannot be ruled out. Perhaps for that reason, the casting and measurement of non-functional sites emerged as the most significant intellectual practice in this period.[8]

---

[7] The writings of those Europeans who spent a considerable time in north and central India are very different from those who stayed in western and coastal India. In fact, the latter wrote mainly on ancient Hindu temple particularly situated in the region of Goa. These travellers did not find many Islamic buildings in this part of India and as a result, there is virtually no discussion on Indo-Islamic historic buildings in these travelogues. M. Anguetil du Perron, a European traveller, who visited the tomb of Aurangzeb's wife in April 1760, is an exception in this regard. He not only described the architectural style of this tomb, but also talked about the functional aspects of this building. Perron writes: '[h]ere is an endowment [Wakf] for four, who are to perform this office day and night according to the intention of the Baegum' (1785: 77–78).

[8] The description of Elephanta by Jo`ao do Castro, who was the viceroy of Goa, is a revealing example. Describing the architectural style of

Monumentalisation in Colonial India **57**

The relationship between architectural forms and the religious practices of local Indian communities is another interesting aspect of these early European accounts.[9] For example, the Hindu temples, which were called *pagode*s, were more or less seen as the resting places of eastern monsters. While at the same time, certain formal aspects of these temples were highly appreciated on purely artistic/intellectual grounds[10] (Mitter 1992: 2). Similarly, the travellers such

---

Elephanta as Roman style, he carried out the measurement of this rock-cut temple and collected other technical details. Partha Mitter argues that this was the first attempt on record to measure an Indian monument (1977: 34).

[9] Partha Mitter identifies two powerful traditions, which actually influenced the attitude of the European people towards the non-European religious practices, arts and architecture in the later medieval period. The popular tales like the *Romance of Alexander,* which were the major sources of information at that time, represents the first tradition. These stories were based on popular memories of a few famous encounters between the European heroes like Alexander and the eastern people. The second influential tradition stemmed from medieval European religious practices. It dealt with 'medieval conception of hell, the field of demonology and the imagery connected with Antichrist in the apocalyptic literature' (ibid.: 9). From the earlier date the Christian Church connected the idea of devil with the pagan religions. It was established that the pagan religions were invented by the devils and Satan. The Indian Hindu and Buddhist icons and religious images were very close to that imagination. Mitter argues that these two traditions, the classical one of the monstrous races and the Christian one of the demons, gradually converged during the late Middle Ages. These traditions had a direct impact on the minds of European travellers who visited India during the late 15th century. They could not relate the eastern Hindu religious philosophies with the complexities of sculpture art in this period.

[10] In these writings, the most frequent expression for Hindu temples is *pagode*s. The Portuguese word *Pagode* originated from the Persian word *butkada,* which means (*but*) Idol (*Kada*) habitation or a temple where an Idol is based. In English, *Pagode* became *pagoda* in the later writing (Room 2000: 434). A similar elaboration of the term *pagode* is found in the writings of Rev. J. Ovington, who visited Kanheri in 1689. According to him a Pagode 'is the heathen temple or place dedicated to the worship of their false gods, and it borrows its name from the Persian word *poul* which signifies idol: hence *poul Ghuda,* a temple of the false gods, and from thence *Pagode*' (Chakrabarti 1987: 8).

58   *Muslim Political Discourse in Postcolonial India*

as Sir Thomas Roe, Francois Bernier and Jean Baptiste Tavernier admired Indo-Islamic buildings for their grandness, internal composition and simplicity. However, as it appears from their descriptions, they could not understand the complex social life of Islam in India.

Let us elaborate this point by focusing on the images of Indo-Islamic buildings in these writings. It is important to note that the European travellers were well aware of Islam and the Muslim societies of Arabia and central Asia. In fact, the crusades and Europe's trade links with Arabia were crucial factors, which actually shaped their attitudes towards Indo-Islamic communities.[11] More precisely, they had a very negative image of Islam: the image of sword and blood. On the other hand, these travellers encountered a completely different religious composition in India. For instance, Bernier writes:

> [w]ho then can wonder that the great Mogul, though a *Mahometen*, as such an enemy of the *Gentiles*, always keeps in his service a large retinue of Rajas, treating them with same consideration as his other *Omrah*, and appointing them to important command in his army? (1891: 40)

Bernier also found it astonishing that Muslims were divided on caste lines and shared cultural life with local non-Muslim communities (ibid.: 259). For a European mind of that time it was an unfamiliar, strange and peculiar social order.[12] In such a context, a negative image of Islam, social composition of Indian communities and European intellectual developments all contributed in the making of certain images of Indo-Islamic buildings.

The famous buildings of Agra and Delhi, like the Taj Mahal, the Agra Fort and the Jama Masjid were almost 'new' and functional

---

[11] Edward Said's conceptualisation of orientalist construction of Islam tells us how the religious wars between Islam and Christianity were seen in the early European writings. Said also points out that the idea of orient was first applied on Islam and then transmitted to other non-European regions (1978: 73–76).

[12] It is important here to note that the term 'Hindu' is not used in these writings. Nor do we find any reference to the numerical strength of any religious community. Instead, the presumed hostility between Muslims and non-Muslims is taken as an explanatory justification.

Monumentalisation in Colonial India **59**

during the 17th century when Bernier visited India. He admired the construction of the Jama Masjid and described the procession of the Mughal emperor, who used to come from the Red Fort to Jama Masjid on every Friday for weekly congregational prayer. Bernier also informs us about the beauty and magnificence of the Taj Mahal. His description of the Taj Mahal is full of comparisons. He says:

> [l]ast time I visited the Tage Mehale's mausoleum I was in the company of a French Merchant, who, as well as myself, thought that this extra ordinary fabric could not be sufficiently admired. I did not venture to express my opinion, fearing that my taste might have been corrupted by my long residence in the Indies; and my companion was come recently from France, it was quite relief to my mind to hear him say he had seen nothing in Europe so bold and majestic (1891: 295).

We also find that the Taj Mahal was a functional tomb at that time.[13] Bernier points out that some *Mullah*s were appointed for reciting the Quran at the tomb and the attached mosque was used for daily prayers.

There is very little information available on non-functional Indo-Islamic buildings in the writings of these travellers. For instance, in Bernier's description, we find a very brief comment on an old city of Delhi, which according to him was situated in the south of the city of Shahjahanabad. He writes:

> [t]wo leagues from the city, on the Agra road, in a place which the *Mahometans* call *Koia Kotubeddin*, is a very old edifice, formerly a *Deura*, or Temple of idols, containing inscriptions of characters different from those any language spoken in the Indies, and so ancient that no one understand them (ibid.: 283)

This description underlines an important aspect of early European attitude. The Qutub monument complex, which became a highly controversial site in colonial and postcolonial India, was not seen

---

[13] The observation of the annual *urs* (death anniversary) of Mumtaz Mahal has been reported by many observers. For instance, the second *urs* of Mumtaz Mahal was held on 26 May 1633, reported in detail by an English traveller, Peter Mundy, in his description of Mughal India (quoted in Begley 1979).

60   *Muslim Political Discourse in Postcolonial India*

as a contested site. Even the bricks and stones of the old temple, with images of Hindu deities on them, used in this structure were not seen as symbols of Islamic conquests.

So, what was the role of these early travellers' accounts in conceptualising the idea an Indian Muslim heritage? The answer may be summarised as follows:

(*a*)   The collection of architectural details actually established a link between Indian architecture and emerging European intellectual/artistic approaches. In this sense, Indian architecture was enumerated as well as categorised on the basis of European principles for the very first time.

(*b*)   The early writings drew a clear distinction between the architectural styles/composition of Indian buildings and the Indian philosophical traditions and religious practices. As a result, Indian architecture became an 'independent' object of study in this period.

(*c*)   Although the religious character of Indian buildings was often seen as an important marker of their identity, the early travel writings did not envisage these sites as 'heritage' of any kind. The Indo-Islamic buildings, in this sense, were regarded as Indian buildings rather than as a 'contribution' of Indian Muslim community.

II

EXPLORATION: HISTORIC BUILDINGS AS A SOURCE OF HISTORY

The commercial links between Europe and India in the late 17th and early 18th centuries had also been facilitating a fresh flow of information related to Indian religion, culture and historic buildings. That was the period of Antiquarianism in Europe. The intellectual tradition established by the humanists was taken over by these Antiquarians in the later 17th century. In their bid to trace the most authentic past of the classical ages, these Antiquarians did not trust the written works of Geek and Latin 'historians'. On the contrary, for them 'the past reveals itself more reliably through its involuntary witness — such as public inscriptions and above all, the entire range of production of material culture' (Choay 2001: 41). Thus, the monuments/historic buildings of the past became the most authentic sources for learning about history. In the mid-18th century this Antiquarian movement took a new intellectual turn. The study of comparative religion became very popular, particularly in England and Germany. The antiquarians began searching the common origin of all religions. They used ethnographic information related to different religions and tried to work out a comparative methodology. The discovery of Sanskrit and other Asian languages encouraged European scholars to work on new areas for further researches.

These developments led to a systematic exploration in the fields of Indian art, architecture and religious/sacred literature (mostly Hindu religious literature). For example, the British antiquarian movement which endeavoured to 'search the local and national past of England' primarily under the patronage of the *Society of Antiquaries* in post-1770s, had a profound interest in Indian art and culture. The publication of a number of articles on Indian buildings, which appeared in *Archaeologia*, the journal published by the Society between 1785 and 1790 demonstrates the fact that India antiquity was being seen as an important area of research.

It is important here to look at the political context of contemporary India. The decline of the Mughal Empire after the death of Aurangzeb in 1707 led to a series of important political changes in the first half of the 18th century. The growth of regional political powers and the increasing influence of European trading companies in India quite significantly changed the political scenario. In fact, following the Battles of Plassey (1757) and Buxar (1764), the English East India Company established itself as a dominant political player in north India. The changed political context had a direct impact on the nature of European researches in India. It is true that in the early phase, the colonial administration did not offer any kind of official or financial support to amateur explorers and learned societies. Yet, the establishment of the Company's rule re-shaped the notion of European superiority in the Indian context and the nature of colonial historical research.

Authentic India and the 'Muslim Invasion'

In the last phase of the 18th century when the systematic explorations began in the fields of Indian languages, science and art, the issues of 'authenticity', 'verification' and 'objectification' became very significant. Most of the writings of this period focus on the

62   *Muslim Political Discourse in Postcolonial India*

notion of the 'authentic/original' past and give priority to reliable 'objective' sources. However, these original 'sources' were very limited at that point of time and it was important to prioritise one set of sources over the others. In this context, Indian literature was identified as the most reliable source. In fact, the idea that the translation of Indian literature would help in learning about India's past was practically viable and politically desirable. It was felt that the translation of written sources would provide a concrete and reliable chronology of Indian history and facilitate research in other related fields. For instance, the early Indologists like William Jones, who recognised the importance of Indian historic architecture, gave priority to literature and epigraphy as reliable sources over historic buildings.[14]

Furthermore, the translation of literature had a direct relation with a few administrative problems. The officers of the Company did not know about the traditional land ownership and revenue systems. Therefore, it was important to trace the most concrete source of information for such practical needs.[15] Moreover, after the establishment of various colonial institutions including the Supreme Court in Calcutta, the translation of Indian religious literature became very crucial for the effective working of these administrative bodies.

---

[14] William Jones identifies: '[f]our general media: languages and letters, philosophy and religion, written memorial of science and arts, and the remains of the old sculpture and architecture' to . . . satisfy the curiosity . . . and to clear the 'clouds of fables' over the history of Hindus' (1788: 421).

[15] Ranajit Guha points out that the early histories of India from the British point of view were written in a period of 30 years (between the Diwani and Permanent Settlement). Guha traces three types of narratives in this period: (a) The comprehensive surveys of Indian past covering a long period of time exploring the relationship between power and property for answering the question 'who owned the land?'; (b) The comprehensive surveys covering the whole sub-continent and again exploring the relationship between political power and landed classes but in a different manner. The question for such a narrative is: how much wealth did the land produce and how it was shared?; (c) The local histories written by the local officials for identifying the relationship between power and property at the local level. These early histories were simply responding to the political needs of the early colonial rule. These histories relied extensively on Indian literature, particularly the religious sources (Guha 1997: 160–62).

Monumentalisation in Colonial India   **63**

In contrast, the works of R. Gough, Thomas Maurice and William Hunter demonstrate a very different approach to historic buildings/Indian antiquities. In comparison to other Orientalists, these researchers gave much importance to the study of Indian architecture. Gough, who was personally very active with the *Society of Antiquaries*, edited an interesting book on Indian historic sites, *A Comparative View of the Ancient Monuments of India, Particularly those in the Island of Salset near Bombay: As Described by Different Writers* (1785). In its introduction, Gough pointed out that his aim was to offer a 'comparative perspective' for further research on Indian sites. He also expressed hope that the East India Company would encourage people to do some serious research on India's classical past (Gough 1785: 2–4).[16] Quite similarly, William Hunter wrote an article on Indian cave temples that appeared in the seventh volume of *Archaeologia* (1785). Comparing the Indian and Egyptian antiquities, Hunter argued that despite being ruled by the Muslims, Indian [Hindu] religious texts were still used by the local Hindus in their day-to-day life. He recommended that a good and able draftsman and an impartial man of letters be sent to India for establishing links between the written sources and the historic buildings (Hunter 1785: 302).

Unlike Gough and Hunter, Thomas Maurice's *Indian Antiquities* (1794) provides an interesting link between the studies conducted by the Asiatic Society of Bengal under William Jones and the English antiquarians based in London. As an extensive and ambitious intellectual project, *Indian Antiquities* was a study of Indian geography, theology, original forms of government and literature. In the third volume of his work, Maurice discussed Hindu theology and traced the history of the five holiest Hindu temples in India. Using the early travellers' accounts and the translations of some of the religious texts as authentic sources, Maurice described India's classical past as a 'non-polluted and authentically Hindu culture' that flourished before the 'Muslims invasion'.[17]

---

[16] Gough writes: '[m]ay we at least rejoice that now peace is restored in all our acquisition, our enquires, may be pursued in a milder manner under the auspices of a Governor General who has established a *printing press*, and a judge who has founded a literary society in Calcutta' (emphasis original, Gough 1785: 4).

[17] Writing about the South Indian temples, Maurice says: '[t]he Peninsula was the region of India last conquered by the Mohammedans; we may

64   *Muslim Political Discourse in Postcolonial India*

Maurice describes the desecration of the Somnath Temple by Mahmud of Ghazni as an important 'critical event', which according to him not only led to the establishment of Muslim rule in India but also polluted the 'original and pure' Hindu religious traditions. This 'event' was seen as a reference point for discussing the subsequent historical developments. For instance, to determine the exact date of construction of the Jagannath Temple at Puri, he traced the actual time of the destruction of Somnath Temple so as to explain the historical connection between these two events. Maurice describes, in great detail, how Aurangzeb destroyed the Hindu temples at Banaras and Ahmedabad in order to ruin the Hindu traditions. In this regard, Maurice's work not only establishes a crucial connection between classical literature and Indian historic sites but also offers a systematic conceptualisation of a 'theory of Muslim invasion'. Perhaps for this reason, his study became a major source of inspiration for those later historians who employed the theory of 'Muslim invasion' as 'the' decisive factor to understanding medieval Indian history.

The Historic Buildings as Objective Sources and the 'Missing Link' of Indian History

In the next two decades (1790–1820), broadly speaking, three important developments — British political control over Delhi (1803), Lat Bhairava riot of Banaras (1809) and establishment of the Calcutta Museum (1814) — changed the direction of historical researches in India by transforming Indian historic buildings into an objective reliable source of history.

In 1803, Delhi, the capital city of Mughal India was acquired by the Company from the Marathas by the Treaty of Surji Arjungaon. As a 'historical city', the ruins of Delhi could be an important source to find out the history of several Muslim ruling dynasties. In this sense, Delhi offered a comparative perspective to colonial researches simply because it was the only city in India that had different types of non-functional Muslim buildings. The 'missing link' between the classical Hindu past and the medieval 'Muslim

---

therefore expect to find in that region as well as the genuine remains of the Indian religion as the unmixed feature of Indian architecture' (Maurice 1794: 23).

rule' could be traced through the historical buildings of Delhi.[18] Moreover, the historical knowledge acquired through the translation of medieval Indian chronicles could also be applied to these sites. In the later part of the 19th century, Delhi became a reference point for 'Indian monuments'.[19] In fact, the historic buildings of Delhi were used to sustain the communal categorisation of Indian historical sites in the later period.

The Lat Bhairava riot (1809) of Banaras was the second important development. Banaras was an important city for the Oriental scholars. The sacred and historical character of this city attracted the Orientalists who were very keen to trace the 'origin' of Indian/ Hindu civilisation. In such a context, the Lat Bhairava riot took place in October 1809.[20] Interestingly, this riot was not only 'used' by the colonial administration to substantiate the fact that Hindu–Muslim communal relationships were one of the major problems of Indian society but was also appropriated by the Orientalists to demonstrate the intrinsic historical opposition between polite and non-violent Hindu tradition and Islamic iconoclasm. The famous Orientalist,

---

[18] In the fourth volume of *The Asiatic Researches,* Ensign James T. Blunt wrote an essay on Qutub Minar. This essay primarily focuses upon the exact measurement of this minaret. Blunt, however, could not distinguish between Qutubuddin Baqtiyar Kaki, a Sufi who was buried in his dargah near the Qutub complex, and Iltutmish, the Sultan who ruled India during the early 13th century. Interestingly, we do not find any mention of Islamic iconoclasm in this article (Blunt 1799: 323–29).

[19] Narayani Gupta points out four important scholarly 'happenings' in the mid-18th century. Thomas Metcalf compiled an album entitled *Reminiscences of Imperial Delhi* (1844); Syed Ahmad Khan's book *Asar us Sanadid* was published in 1847; the Archaeological Society of Delhi was established (1850), and a detailed map of Shahjahanabad was painted (Gupta 2000: 54). These developments changed the colonial perceptions of Delhi. In the later years Delhi was described as the 'architectural representative of Muslim rule' in India. The Qutub complex, like Somnath Temple (Gujarat) and Gyanvaphi mosque (Banaras) emerged as the representative historical site to prove the theory of 'Muhammadan Invasion'.

[20] Gyanendra Pandey offers an extensive analysis of this riot. He shows how different official documents produced various conflicting histories of this event and as a result this local level conflict between Hindus and Muslims became a 'civilisation clash' in the first half of the 20th century (Pandey 1990: 30–31, Table 2.2).

66   *Muslim Political Discourse in Postcolonial India*

James Prinsep's account of this event is a good example to illustrate this point. He published a three volume artistic guide, *Benares Illustrated* (1831) and visited Banaras in the 1820s, almost 11 years after the occurrence of this riot. Quite astonishingly, as Gyanendra Pandey points out, Prinsep not only offered an elaborate description of this riot but also cited a few 'facts' about the actual events, which were even not mentioned in the official colonial reports![21] Employing this authentic 'information', Prinsep makes a broad generalisation about the historic sites of Banaras. For him every Muslim ruler (particularly Aurangzeb) ordered the demolition of a number of temples and construction of mosques 'with the same materials and upon the same foundations . . . leaving portions of the ancient walls exposed here and there as evidences of the indignity to which the Hindoo religion had been subjected' (Pandey 1990: 37). Prinsep's description of the city of Banaras once again reiterated the theory of Muslim invasion and the desecration of Hindu temple. Moreover, Prinsep's description also established a very clear link between a highly localised Muslim–Hindu conflict and the practice of Islamic iconoclasm.

The establishment of an India Museum in 1814 by the Asiatic Society of Bengal was the third important event. The museum was initially established to collect the scientific and historical objects of India. Tapati Guha-Thakurta points out that in the first few years the objective of the Museum was to 'collect' historical and scientific objects rather than 'displaying' the discoveries of the Asiatic Society (1997: 25). However, in later years, the Museum was conceived as a 'knowledge producing apparatus' that had to display a condensed form of India under one roof (ibid.: 22). There was a direct relationship between the historic sites and the growing collection of art objects in the Museum. The historic sites, which were now being recognised as 'objects of knowledge' and/or 'source of history', also had to be conserved and displayed. Since it was practically not possible to bring historic sites to the Museum, it was decided that these buildings ought to be conserved at their original locations. Guha-Thakurta argues that in the later years when the *in situ* principle of conservation of

---

[21] For instance, Prinsep was the first person who 'invented' the fact that the *Muharram* procession by the Muslims was the main reason behind the 1809 riot (quoted in Pandey 1990: 33–36).

Monumentalisation in Colonial India **67**

historic sites was adopted, entire India was envisaged as an 'open air museum'.

The early legal initiatives in the field of conservation also demonstrate the fact that the historical buildings were gradually being recognised as an important legal issue in this period. The Bengal Code (1810) and the Madras Code (1817) were the main laws, which were enacted during this period. It is to be noted that the legal demarcation between a historical building and a non-historical building was not clarified. Instead, the functional status of a particular building was identified as the main criterion. Thus, the functional religious sites such as temples, *Maths*, mosques, Sufi shrines, religious schools and public buildings such as *Sarais*, *Kattras* and bridges were distinguished from those non-functional buildings that had been completely abandoned by the local communities. The functional sites, particularly the religious places of worship, were conceptualised as 'religious endowments' and the managing boards or boards of trustees were established for the 'due appropriation of the rents and produce of lands granted for ... the support of these endowments' (Religious Endowment Act, 1863).[22] On the other hand, these Acts empowered the government to protect 'public buildings' of historical importance; while a few management boards were also established for the conservation and supervision of a few non-functional sites. Interestingly, the artistic/historical values of functional sites were also recognised but no specific legal provisions were made to protect these sites as monuments of any kind (Archaeological Survey of India: 2005). However, these legal initiatives paved the way for the growth of two kinds of laws in later years: (*a*) the laws related to religious and charitable endowments and (*b*) the laws related to historical monuments (Figure 2.1).

This discussion shows that the treatment of Indian buildings as a reliable historical source in the first half of the 19th century that

---

[22] It is important to remember here that these laws were applicable only in those parts of India, where the East India Company had established its rule by that time. However, the impact of these laws was much higher. In fact, these regulations actually became legal 'sources' not only for redesigning of wakf laws in the British India but also in the princely states. For a detailed discussion on the nature and administration of Muslim endowments in British India (see Kozlowski 1985: 41–59).

Figure 2.1: Legal Classification of Indian Buildings (1810–63)

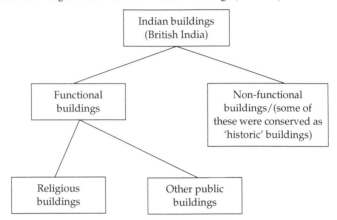

Source: Author.

helped the colonial authors to make three arguments that were subsequently employed to justify the colonial understanding of Indian religious-cultural life:

1. The authenticity argument: It was established that the Hindu civilisation was the most authentic ancient Indian civilisation. The relationship between Hinduism, Buddhism and Jainism was also recognised. However, the Islamic civilisation was described as an alien culture on two grounds: (*a*) Islam as a religion did not originate in India and (*b*) as a religious doctrine Islam did not have any commonality with Vedic Hinduism.
2. The 'historic rupture' argument: Emphasising the fact that many Indo-Islamic sites were built mainly by destroying ancient Hindu temples, it was argued that the Muslim invasion marked a historic rupture in Indian history because it actually polluted the authentic Hindu civilisation.
3. The 'progress-decline' argument: It was demonstrated that the 'great Indian Hindu civilisation, which had been one of the leading civilisations in the past and which had successfully coped with various kinds of cultural and political assaults, including the Islamic invasion, was in a state of decay'.

Monumentalisation in Colonial India **69**

Therefore, for the restoration and revival of classical Hindu civilisation and/or the progress of India, the 'rational-scientific' colonial rule was necessary (Metcalf 1989: 26–30).

These arguments produced a general framework of Indian history in which the Indo-Islamic buildings were placed as the most 'contested historical sites'. But, how was this kind of 'contested image' used to outline the idea of a single Muslim community and its historical existence in India? After all, it was not possible for the colonial authors to pay no attention to the artistic values of Indo-Islamic sites, particularly when an elite Muslim class was emerging, which actually wanted to trace the 'golden' history of Islam and its imprint on India.

III

CATEGORISATION: THE COMMUNITY OF MONUMENTS AND THE MONUMENTS OF A COMMUNITY

The classification of Indian buildings by British and Indian authors, the establishment of the Archaeological Survey of India (ASI) in 1861, the emergence of the notion of centralised conservation of 'monuments', and the introduction of a few legal provisions for the protection of historic sites were some of the most significant developments that shaped the process of monumentalisation and consolidated the idea of a separate 'Indian Muslim architectural heritage' in the period between 1840 and 1902.[23] The works of James Fergusson, Alexander Cunningham and Syed Ahmad Khan published in this period and the formal definition of the term 'monument' was introduced.

---

[23] It is important to underline the wider impact of the events of 1857 on the attitude of colonial administration towards Islamic sites in this period. During the war of 1857, many Islamic religious places of worship were either demolished or occupied by the British. The conversion of Delhi's historic mosques into military stations — the Jama Masjid, the Fatehpuri Masjid and the Zeenatul Masjid — underlines this hostile British attitude. In fact, there was a proposal to sell the Jama Masjid and then to use it as a barrack for the European troops (Spear 1951: 220). The Jama Masjid, however, was given back to Muslims in 1862 (Gupta 1981: 27).

70   *Muslim Political Discourse in Postcolonial India*

The Chronological Categorisation

Let us begin our discussion with Syed Ahmad Khan' book *Asar as-Sanadid* (Vestiges of the Past). It is important to clarify this valuable text should not always be linked to the later Muslim politics that is often called 'Muslim separatism'.[24] It is true that Syed Ahmad Khan's works underline Muslim exclusiveness in a significant way, *Asar as-Sanadid* offers us a very different conceptualisation of Indian buildings, which needs to be situated in its own intellectual contexts.[25]

Written in Urdu, *Asar as-Sanadid* (1847/1854) was a remarkable work in two significant ways.[26] First, this book was based on an extensive survey of Delhi's buildings. Khan discussed all the available historical contributions, documents related to Mughal era, religious books and popular traditions of contemporary Delhi to trace the history of these sites. In this respect, it could be called a pioneering work on Delhi's historic buildings. Second, and perhaps most importantly, this book offered an analytical framework for the classification of Indian historical buildings. Khan does not exaggerate the given Hindu-ness or Muslim-ness

---

[24] C. M. Naim offers a comparative reading of two different versions of this text (1847/1854) to make a similar argument. Describing the successful intellectual reception of this book, Naim (2011) notes: '[h]e had practically abandoned both Delhi and History, and instead set himself well on the trajectory that led him to create a history of his own at Aligarh and elsewhere'.

[25] I would also like to point out the significance of this text for my arguments. This text has been discussed quite extensively by colonial authors as well as by those researchers who have worked on Indian architecture and/or Muslim elite culture of 19th century. However, my focus here is slightly different. I try to look at the ways in which chronological classification of Delhi's buildings continued to affect the historical imagination and contributed to the process of monumentalisation in the mid-19th century. Precisely because of this reason, I discuss this valuable text briefly. I have used three sources here for this text — the 1854 Urdu text, the 1978 English translation of the same text and an elaborated discussion on various versions of this text by C. M. Naim.

[26] It is to clarify that *Asar as-Sanadid* was not the first study of this kind. Sangin Beg's *Sair-ul-Manzil* (1819) and Ram Raz's *An Essay on the Architecture of Hindus* (1834) had been published well before the actual publication of Syed Ahmad Khan's book (Gupta 2002: 55).

Monumentalisation in Colonial India 71

of historic buildings of Delhi; instead, he tries to offer a standard classificatory schema. In fact, one cannot find any attempt in this book to show that Muslims had experienced a 'separate' historic past in Delhi. However, the classification of buildings on the basis of ruler's community paved the way for a very different kind of knowledge formation.

The 1854 edition of *Asar as-Sanadid* consisted of interesting contents and classification. The book was divided into four parts. The first part had three separate tables which gave chronological information depicting the (*a*) Hindu dynasties; (*b*) the Sultans of Delhi, and Mughal emperors, and (*c*) the fortresses and cities of Delhi. The second part further discussed the fortresses and cities of Delhi including the Red Fort and the city of Shahjahanabad. The third part was again a chronological table that dealt with different tombs, mosques and palaces of Delhi. Finally, in the fourth part Khan discussed the development of the Urdu language.[27] We find that the author initially began to write a history of architecture. Subsequently, however, the focus shifted from 'history of architecture' to 'history through architecture'. The original plan of the book seems to operate between the past and the then present of Delhi's historical sites. It offers a 'homogenised past for Delhi' in which a sequence of architectural growth of the city can easily be traced. In fact, the book reflects a historical continuity from earlier Hindu buildings to later Mughal or Pathan buildings (Gupta 2002: 58). An interesting classification of functional and non-functional buildings is also underlined to explain the present status of a particular building.

The book does not establish any direct link between the Indian religious communities and historical sites. Even the Muslim buildings are discussed as Mughal or Pathan buildings. The entire enterprise revolves around four questions: (*a*) who is the original or the 'true' builder of a particular historic building?; (*b*) the location, measurement and architectural characteristics of a

---

[27] Monica Juneja argues that the idea of supplying a certain amount of information in a tabular form was a popular style of writing at that time. The British authors followed this method to provide a sequence to collected information (Juneja 2001a: 12). However, it is to be noted that this style of writing is not quite uncommon in Islamic literature. The Islamic medieval literature, particularly on Sufism also employs tabular form to provide information in a particular sequence.

72　　*Muslim Political Discourse in Postcolonial India*

building and its aesthetic or historical relationship with other buildings; (*c*) the popular meaning of a building and associated local rituals and customs, and (*d*) the history of Delhi's rulers. To find out answers to these four questions, Syed Ahmad Khan employed religious categories. However, these categories were not used as the ultimate marker of the identity of Delhi's buildings. Instead, the shared local meanings of these sites, and the local culture practices were given an adequate importance.[28] In this sense, *Asar as-Sanadid* successfully recorded and compiled the history and memory of Delhi's historical buildings.

Asar as-Sanadid also conceptualised an intrinsic relationship between historical buildings and the 'living' religious communities. The description of these religious communities is based on a broad assumption that each community has its own 'exclusive' status and it does not necessarily come into conflict with other religious communities.[29] Khan seems to argue that these living communities inherit the 'vestiges of the past' in a collective manner as 'shared heritage' without relinquishing their exclusive religious identity.[30]

Asar as-Sanadid was an intellectually sophisticated endeavour to offer a completely new historical perspective to Muslim upper classes of north India that had been suffering from a self-imposed isolation at that time.[31] Interestingly, this new 'history' did not rely

---

[28] In this sequence, Syed Ahmad Khan also places the British as rulers of India and provides descriptions of those buildings which were built by them (quoted in Naim 2011).

[29] Syed Ahmad Khan's descriptions of Nigham Bodh Ghat and Jain Lal Mandir could be taken as revealing examples of his treatment of functional Hindu and Jain sites (Khan 1978: 65–75).

[30] C. M. Naim finds an interesting description of the Kalika Temple in the 1847 version of this text, which also underlines this point. Describing his experience at the temple, Syed Ahmad Khan writes: 'When I arrived to get a sketch done of the temple, the *pandas* gave me the *Prasad* consisting of *batasa*, raisins, and almonds. I took it helplessly, fearing that otherwise they might not let me go inside to make a drawing. I also made an effort to please them. [As the Persian verse goes,] 'I imitated him and became a *kafir* for a few days. I read the Zend texts and became a Brahmin.' (quoted in Naim 2011: 36)

[31] Discussing the Urdu poetry of late 1850s and the identity formation of Indian Muslim community, Ayesha Jalal argues that the Urdu literary

Monumentalisation in Colonial India **73**

on the memories of a glorious 'Muslim' past to make a few remarks on the decline of Muslims. Instead, Khan's book tries to establish a link between the alienation of Muslims and the overall decline of Indian society in the mid-19th century. The deterioration of the historic buildings and the weakening of Delhi's cultural heritage, in this sense, are seen as a part of a general 'collective decay'.[32] Thus, in Syed Ahmad Khan's conceptualisation the Islamic buildings are not presented as 'evidence' for 'Muslim separatism'. Instead, he makes an attempt to narrate the past and present of the city of Delhi by evoking religious categories (Hindus, Muslims, Sikhs, etc.) as cultural idioms. Perhaps for that very reason, the 'Islamic iconoclasm' is taken merely as a historical 'fact', which in Khan's schema, cannot be shown as any kind of 'Muslim achievement'.[33]

We now move on to the colonial perspective on classification of Indian architecture. James Fergusson's *The History of Indian and Eastern Architecture* (1876/1910), is known as the very first and systematic study on Indian buildings that not only explored different styles of architecture but also classified them into analytical categories from a colonial perspective. Fergusson's classification of Indian architecture should be seen in terms of his two broad objectives.

First, Fergusson's prime objective, as he himself pointed out, had been to find out a general history of different architectural styles rather conducting any archaeological exploration (Fergusson

---

traditions of mid-19th century revolved around a deep sense of defeat and depression (Jalal 1998). In this context, the *Asar as-Sanadid* could well be regarded as an effort to look at the past for self-respect and future struggles. However, for Syed Ahmad Khan, the struggle did not mean the struggle against the British; rather it was a struggle to adopt new culture and rule of the British for the well-being of India's Muslims.

[32] The description of *Faid Bazaar* is important here. Syed Ahmad Khan tells us that the drainage system of this bazaar was severely damaged and the British actually repaired it (1978: 21).

[33] The description of Qutub Minar in this book can be a good example to illustrate this point. Syed Ahmad Khan argues that the Quwaatul Islam mosque was erected by destroying 27 Hindu and Jain temples. He also suggests that the first floor of the minaret was built by Hindus (ibid.: 4–5). Interestingly, Khan does not get into the desecration of Hindu and Jain temples. Instead, he focuses on the architectural characteristics and the actual history of this site.

74   *Muslim Political Discourse in Postcolonial India*

1910: x). For realising this objective, Fergusson focused on architectural designs of Indian buildings and classified them into two broad categories: Ancient and Medieval. Buddhist and Hindu sites were placed in the Ancient category, while Medieval architecture was further divided into two sub-categories: regional and the Saracenic. In this sense, Fergusson's classification simply underlined Mill's famous categorisation of Indian history into three periods: Ancient (Hindu), Medieval (Muslim) and Modern (British). The use of religious categories enabled him to argue that architecture of India could be understood as a great *stone book*.[34]

Second, and perhaps more importantly, Fergusson's work on India was a part of his grand research that aimed to find out a general history of architecture of different countries. In fact, his work on India, despite being an independent and detailed version, came in a sequel to his earlier published work *A History of Architecture in All Countries from the Earliest Times to the Present Day* (1867). This second broader objective of Fergusson provided him an authority to establish linkages and making comparison between Indian styles of architecture and the architecture of other countries. The treatment of Indo-Islamic buildings in this schema was very important. He employed the term *Saracenic* architecture for the Indo-Islamic buildings. It is important to mention here that the term *Saracenic* first applied on the antiquities of the nomadic people of the Syrian Deserts and later on all the Islamic art forms (Metcalf 1989: 35). The use of this term as an analytical category from a colonial perspective simply established an intrinsic unity among different Islamic buildings. Now, the Indo-Islamic historic sites became a part of a *Saracenic heritage*.[35]

The works of Ameer Ali seem to follow Fergusson's argument. Ameer Ali wrote primarily on Islamic history and Muslim law.

---

[34] Fergusson writes: '[a]rchitecture of this country may be considered as a great stone book, in which each tribe and race has written its annals and that in a manner is so clear that those who run may read' (1910: x).

[35] In *The Cambridge History of India* (1928) John Marshall refutes the term Saracenic. He argues: '[it] means nothing more than the Arabic tribesmen who dwelt along with border of the Syrian deserts' (Marshall 1928: 568). Marshall proposes the term 'Muslim architecture' and suggests that this term could explain the fusion of different architectural forms more clearly (ibid.: 569).

Monumentalisation in Colonial India **75**

In fact, we do not find any discussion on Indo-Islamic historic architecture in his writings. Yet, Ameer Ali's treatment of Islamic history and his conceptualisation of a single 'Saracenic' nation make him relevant. His first major historical work, *The Life of Mohammed or the Spirit of Islam* was published in 1891. He studied the life of Mohammed and his philosophy for analysing the decline of Muslim culture. Ali argued that Muslims should follow Islamic teachings as well as modern education to come out from the social crisis they were facing. Clarifying his prime objective in his famous *A Short History of the Saracens* (1899), Ali wrote:

> [i]t is a matter of regret that in the West a knowledge of their [Muslims] history should be more or less confined to specialists; whilst in India, a country which was at one time peculiarly subject to the influence of their civilisation, it should be unknown (1899: iv).

The history of Saracen simply reminds us of an intrinsic connection between Indian Muslims and the Islamic world; a link that had a historical and philosophical basis. It might be a strong reason behind his sketchy remarks on India.[36] From our point of view Ameer Ali's work provided a much greater sophistication to the argument proposed by Fergusson on Indo-Islamic historic architecture. He offered an intellectual foundation to the argument that the Indian Muslim community was an inseparable part of a 'Saracenic nation'.

Thus, these three works characterise an interesting sequence. Syed Ahmad Khan's book highlights the exclusiveness of architecture forms by offering a community-based categorisation in 1854; Fergusson's work links that exclusiveness to the wider Islamic heritage by conceptualising the notion of Saracenic architecture in 1877; and finally, Ameer Ali compiles the history of the Saracenic nation by outlining the common historical origin of Muslim communities and the universally applicable philosophical foundations of Islam in 1891. In a much broader sense, this sequence

---

[36] Writing about Mehmud of Ghazni and his 'glorious' expeditions, Ameer Ali does not talk of the desecration of Somnath temple (1899: 307). Instead, a few references to early Sultanate period are mentioned. It is important to point out that Ameer Ali does not study the Indo-Indian Islamic historical contributions for conceptualising the idea of a Saracenic nation.

76   *Muslim Political Discourse in Postcolonial India*

shows how the idea of Muslim heritage was gradually shaped in this period.

The Archaeological Categorisation

Let us discuss the colonial institutional efforts in the field of Indian archaeology and conservation in this period. In 1862, the Archaeological Department was established under the headship of Alexander Cunningham, who had already been recognised as a professional archaeologist. It is to be noted that initially the Archaeological Department was not set up as a permanent institution of any kind; instead, it was created on temporary basis to conduct a comprehensive survey of Indian historical sites.[37] However, this arrangement changed quite significantly in 1871, when 'the appointment of Cunningham was declared to be that of Director General of the ASI and whose duty was to superintend a complete search over the whole country and a systematic record and description of all architectural and other remains' (Marshall 1939: 1). As a result, the first state sponsored search for Indian's past through historic sites began. Cunningham's extensive tours and comprehensive reports produced remarkable factual information about Indian historic sites including those anonymous buildings, which had been almost forgotten. Moreover, Cunningham also introduced the idea of systematic archaeological excavation for tracing the unknown past of India. These extensive efforts of the Archaeological Department under Cunningham were further institutionalised in 1880, when Major H. H. Cole was appointed as the Curator of Ancient Monuments. The Curator was appointed to study the conditions of various historic sites so that the proper conservation plans for these buildings could be made. Major Cole produced three valuable reports on the status of 'monuments' in early 1880s. Interestingly, Cole's reports also classified historic sites or 'ancient monuments' on religious basis (Cole 1882: 1–20).

---

[37] The colonial government did not provide any long-term financial support to archaeological works in the initial period. In fact, Cunningham himself worked very hard to secure funding for his archaeological explorations. This point underscores the argument that there was a complex relationship between archaeological explorations and the colonial state. For a detailed analysis of this aspect, particularly in relation to the origin of ASI and the works of Cunningham see Abu Imam (1966).

Monumentalisation in Colonial India **77**

These archaeological efforts demonstrate four very significant aspects of the process of monumentalisation in this period. First, the term 'monument' was used to describe the old non-functional historic buildings in almost all the official documents of the Archaeological Department. Although it was not the first time that the term monument was used for non-functional historic buildings, the Archaeological Department provided an administrative rationalisation of this term. In a broader sense, all Indian historic buildings were conceived as monuments by which the Indian past could be commemorated. Second, these comprehensive explorations brought Indian historic sites under the purview of a centralised authority and these 'monuments' became an administrative entity. The Archaeological Department established a new kind of secular authority which became instrumental in rewriting the *official history* of Indian monuments. Thus, for the first time in colonial India, the local meanings of historic sites were replaced by an official history and the relationship between Indian buildings and local communities was broken. Third, the use of communal categories for the classification of historical monuments eventually linked them to the other colonial ethnographic researchers. In fact, the Archaeological Department actually 'enumerated' the Indian heritage on a communal basis. Finally, the idea of archaeological excavation gave a new turn to the ongoing debate on Indian's authentic past. The excavation as a legitimate archaeological activity made it possible to search the real authentic and unpolluted Hindu India beneath the Islamic 'structures'. In the later years, particularly after the advent of 'tradition based archaeology' in postcolonial India, Indo-Islamic building became highly controversial. The Ayodhya excavation is the best example in this regard.

The Legal Categorisation

We now move on to the legal initiatives, which further specified the legal status of historic buildings and separated them from other functional religious endowments. It is to be noted that the criterion of functional and non-functional buildings continued to be used for defining the scope of various legal provisions in this period. The functional sites, particularly the religious places of worship, were strictly seen in terms of customs and practices associated with religion. For example, the Indian Penal Code (IPC 1860) devoted an entire chapter on the 'Offences Related to Religion'. Sections 295

78   *Muslim Political Discourse in Postcolonial India*

to 298, which very clearly laid down legal norms for protecting religious places of worship. The Religious Endowments Act 1863, however, was the most comprehensive law in this regard. This Act provided for the control and management of religious endowments by managers or managing committees with a provision for intervention by the civil court.[38] Section 23 of the Act empowered the government to take legal steps to protect those non-functional 'historic buildings', which had been protected by the local authorities since 1810. However, the protection of the historic character of functional buildings was not legally clarified.

In the period between 1867 and 1894, three important legal initiatives changed the nature of state control over the non-functional historic sites quite significantly. In 1867, for example, the instructions were issued by the central government for recognising 'the duty of the government to conserve all historical monuments that had been located ... [and] to encourage explorations of others yet to be discovered historical sites' (Batra 1996: 9–13). The Indian Treasure Trove Act (1878) was the second legal initiative, which empowered the government for the compulsory acquisition of antiquities. Although, this Act was not directly related to non-functional historic buildings, but by implication of this Act in 1885 the directives were issued by the central government, which barred the excavation of any public land without the prior permission of the Archaeological Department (Archaeological Survey of India 2005). The Land Acquisitions Act (1894) was the most important legal initiative. It provided ultimate powers to the government to acquire any land or property including the places of worship. This law also introduced the legal concept of eminent domain of the state to acquire any property in the name of public purpose.

These legal initiatives very clearly show how colonial archaeological efforts were legally rationalised. These laws justified the separation between the local communities and non-functional buildings. It was recognised that the non-functional sites as 'dead

---

[38] Clarifying the powers of religious endowments, this Act separated religious activities from secular activities. Section 21 of the 1863 Act empowered the Board of Revenue to determine what portion of the land or property would remain under the superintendence of the Board for the secular activities and what portion would be transferred to the concerned endowment (The Religious Endowment Act 1863).

monuments' could not form any functional relationship with living communities. Therefore, these sites ought to be treated as 'ownerless' in legal terms. In this sense, the dead non-functional sites became state property. This created a number of confusions and problems. In fact, the legal position of non-functional Indo-Islamic sites, which had a well-defined wakf status, turned out to be highly vague and uncertain. In later years, particularly in postcolonial India, as we shall see, this issue became one of the defining factors of Muslim politics.

So, how did these different kinds of categorisations, primarily on religious basis, transform the images of Indo-Islamic buildings and converted them into an Indian Muslim architectural heritage? To understand this question we have to acknowledge the fact that 'religion' was an important and dominant identity in colonial India and the architectural designs and patterning of Indian buildings also reflected an orientation toward particular religious philosophies. It was very obvious for the early historians and archeologists to accept religion as a broad analytical perspective. However, the manner in which this categorisation was introduced actually reinforced the colonial notion of Indian history in two significant ways:

(a) The listing and categorisation of buildings as a source of history on a religious basis established a fixed communal identity of Indian historic sites. Consequently, the questions like 'who built what' and 'who destroyed what' were resolved and the archaeological efforts were directed to protect and conserve 'what is remaining' and 'what has been destroyed'. In this sense, this categorisation legitimised the colonial discovery of 'Muslim invasion' and 'Hindu resistance'.

(b) The colonial ethnographic researchers also provided a new kind of self-perception to living religious communities by informing them about their collective existence through the processes of statistical counting and spatial mapping (Kaviraj 2010: 187–89). Thus, it became possible to think of a homogeneous community, the exact numbers of its members and its common interests. The listing of 'monuments' on a religious basis through archaeological surveys similarly established a link between the newly enumerated Indian

80 *Muslim Political Discourse in Postcolonial India*

communities and their past contribution/heritage. In this context, the idea of a single Muslim community came into existence simultaneously with the notion of an Indo-Islamic heritage.

IV

CONSERVATION: SECULARISM OF 'STRICT NEUTRALITY' AND THE INDIAN MUSLIM ARCHITECTURAL HERITAGE

It is generally believed that the viceroyalty of Lord Curzon was the 'golden age' of Indian archaeology. Lord Curzon, who was very much interested in the preservation of Indian monuments, played an important role in the process of legalisation of Indian historic sites. The appointment of John Marshall as the Director General of the ASI in 1902, creation of a state scholarship for the training of Indian students in archaeology in 1903, the inclusion of archaeology as a subject in Indian universities, and finally the enactment of the Ancient Monuments Preservation Act, 1904 were some of the important changes introduced by Lord Curzon. All these developments not only converted Indian archaeology into an important area of colonial policy but also laid down the concrete principles for the actual conservation of Indian sites. I now focus on these legal administrative efforts in order to understand their wider implications.

The Legal Monumentalisation

The Ancient Monuments Preservation Act, 1904 was a comprehensive law, which not only defined the term 'monument' in a legal-administrative sense, but also legalised the process by which a variety of Indian buildings could be taken over by the state for proper maintenance and conservation. Moreover, the artistic value and historical relevance of functional historic sites, particularly the functional religious places of worship were also identified. For that reason, the religious activities and secular conservation were legally separated by providing an overarching definition of the term 'Ancient Monument'. According to Section 2 of the 1904 Act, an 'Ancient Monument' refers to:

> [a]ny structure, erection or monument or any tumulus or place of interest or any cave, rock shelter, inscription or monolith which is

Monumentalisation in Colonial India

of historical, archaeological, or artistic interest, or any remain there of and includes:

(*a*) The site of an ancient monument,

(*b*) Such portion of land adjoining the site of an ancient monument as may be required for fencing or covering in or other-wise preserving such monument, and

(*c*) The means of access to and convenient inspection of historical monument (The Ancient Monuments Preservation Act, 1904).

This definition focused on the 'historic' character of Indian buildings without dividing them into functional or non-functional sites. In fact, after the enactment of this Act, it became possible to define all the historic buildings, including the historic places of worship, as ancient monuments. However, to specify this wide-ranging definition of ancient monument, the 1904 Act introduced the concept of 'protected monuments'. Section 3 of the Act points out: 'the [central government] may by notification in the [official gazette] declare an ancient monument to be protected monument within the meaning of this Act'. By this provision, the Act divided Indian buildings into two categories: ancient monuments and protected monuments and elucidated the process by which an ancient monument could be converted into a protected monument (Sections 3 and 4). Furthermore, the responsibility of taking care of the protected historical monuments was given to the state. In this connection, the separate spheres of religion and state were also defined. Section 13(1) of the Act, which gave protection to places of worship from misuse, pollution or desecration, says: 'a place of worship or shrine maintained by the Government under this Act shall not be used for any purpose inconsistence with its character'. Section 13(2b) further explained the nature of the state's protection and empowers the Collector to take necessary action to protect the religious character of such monuments.

The Act of 1904 more broadly suggested four legal ways by which 'ancient monuments' could be declared as protected monuments. First, the Act empowered the state to legally acquire those historically significant buildings, which had been non-functional and which were not owned by any individual or group. In fact, these buildings were considered as 'properties without owner' (Section 4[6]). In this case, the Act recognised the state as the owner of these historic buildings and established legal provision for their

82   *Muslim Political Discourse in Postcolonial India*

conservation as 'protected monuments' (Section 4 [4]). Second, the Act authorised the state to accept a 'gift or bequest of any protected monument' (Section 4 [2]). In this case again, the state was recognised as the guardian/owner of these protected sites. Third, the state was also permitted to propose the owner(s) of historically/ archaeologically relevant buildings to enter into an agreement with the ASI or any other concerned body for the preservation of these sites. It was held that such type of agreement would not affect the ownership rights of individuals or groups. However, after entering into an agreement with the concerned conservation body, the owner(s) would not be able to enjoy his/her right to destroy, remove or alter or deface the monument' (Section 5 [2c]). Finally, Section 10 of the Act stated that if the government 'apprehends that a protected monument is in danger of being destroyed, injured or allowed to fall into decay', it could acquire such buildings under the provision of the Land Acquisition Act, 1894. In this case, the protection of such buildings was considered to be a 'public purpose' of some kind. Figure 2.2 illustrates these legal aspects.

Figure 2.2: The Process of Monumentalisation and the 1904 Act

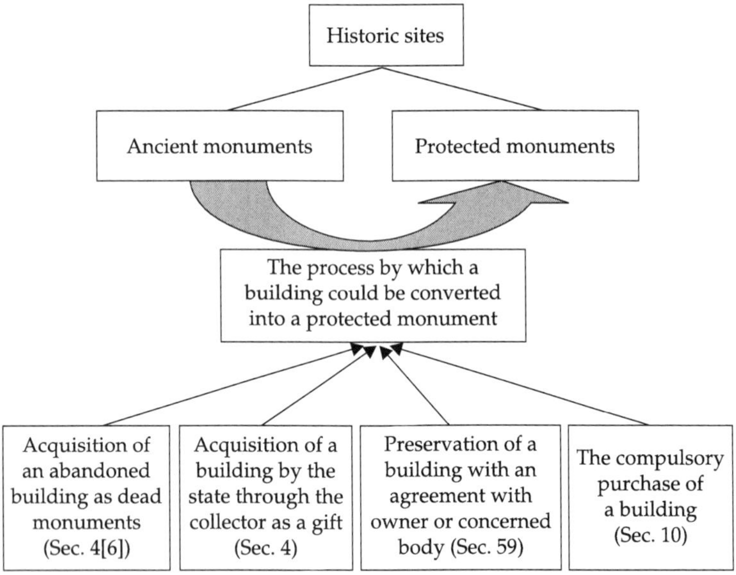

Source: Author.

Monumentalisation in Colonial India 83

Policy of 'Strict Neutrality' and the Nature of State Control

The 1904 Act thus, defined the process of monumentalisation in legal terms. The provisions of this Act and the subsequent official policy on historical monuments, which underlined a strong desire to protect India's heritage, in effect provided four different forms of effective control to the colonial authority over Indian historic architecture. First, the colonial state was legally empowered to identify, select and protect any historic building including, the religious places of worship as a 'protected monument'. In this sense, the state became the one and only authority, which could determine the historic relevance of any particular Indian building. As a result, it now became possible for the colonial state to conserve and popularise its own interpretation of India's past through the conservation of selected historical monuments. Moreover, the 1904 Act legalised the religious classification of protected historical sites in such a manner that every protected site acquired a permanent and fixed religious identity. Thus, the religious places like dargahas and Buddhist monasteries/temples, which had been used by the members of various religious communities, lost their 'specific' religious character. In the later years, this so-called 'neutral conservation' of India's heritage played an important role in converting the Indo-Islamic sites into the symbol of Islamic dominance.

Second, the state's possession of non-functional historic places of worship violated the religious and traditional rights enjoyed by the local religious communities over these sites. Since all the non-functional abandoned sites were treated as dead monuments or 'buildings without owners' (Section 4 [6]; Figure 2.2), the complex religious status of these places of worship were completely overlooked. For example, many non-functional mosques and tombs, which were considered as 'dead sites' under this Act, were actually dedicated as wakf properties in the past by their known and unknown builders.[39] However, after becoming monuments, their wakf status was almost disregarded and the secular state became the ultimate owner/protector of these sites.

---

[39] The legal status of these wakf was not defined at that point of time. However, later laws paid greater attention to define the position of those wakf buildings which were actually abandoned. For an interesting trajectory of this process in British India (see Kozlowski 1985, Chapters 3–4).

84   *Muslim Political Discourse in Postcolonial India*

Third, the religious activities, which were considered to be consistent with the religious character of a particular protected monument, also became a legal-administrative issue. It is true that the state allowed the local religious communities to use these monuments as places of worship; yet these communities were not permitted to make any change in the actual architectural design and/or structure of these buildings. In this sense, the intrinsic relationship between the religious site and the believer was replaced by a right to worship, which might be subject to certain legal conditions. The Indian Archaeological Policy (1915), which set out broad principles of conservation in colonial India, could be taken as an example to further elaborate this point. Clauses 19 and 20 of the policy emphasised that the purpose of the government was to conserve 'what has been left' without interfering in the religious activities associated with a monument.[40] These clauses make it clear that the colonial authorities did not want to get involved in the religious issues. Yet, at the same time, it was established that the archaeological exploration/conservation of 'what has been left' should always be the duty of the state, which was certainly outside the scope of concerned religious endowments.

Fourth, the activities of the Archaeological department were not limited to those buildings which were declared as protected monuments. In fact, on the other hand, *The Conservation Manual* (1923) empowered the department to support a few functional

---

[40] Clause 19 of the 1915 Policy says: '[i]n this country it is impractical to lay down one law which will be applicable to every case. Thus a distinction is drawn between the older Buddhist, Hindu and Jain edifies on the one hand, and the more modern erections of the Muhammadans on the other; and in the case of the latter the view is taken a policy of limited restoration not only desirable but justified on the ground that the art of the original builder is still a living art. It is held also that in the case of monuments which still serving the purpose for which they were built, whether they be Hindu temples or Muhammadan mosque or tomb or palaces where ceremonial function are still performed, there are frequently valid reasons for restoring to more extensive measures of repair than would be desirable, if the buildings in question were maintained merely as antiquarian relic ... the object which Government set before themselves is not reproduce what has been defaced or destroyed, but to save what is left from further injury or decay, and to preserve it as a national heir-loom of prosperity' (The Indian Archaeological Policy 1915: 18–19).

Monumentalisation in Colonial India 85

religious places of worship, which were not protected by the state.[41]
Section 27 of the *Manual*, which lays great stress on the principle
of neutrality in relation to religious affairs, noted:

> [i]t is the policy of the Government to abstain as far as possible
> from any interference with the management or repair of religious
> buildings. But if such buildings were of exceptional archaeological
> interest, and if the endowment attached to them were insufficient
> for their upkeep, the offer of expert advice and guidance or even
> of financial assistance might be made by the Government to the
> owner or trustee, on condition that the repairs were carried out on
> lines approved by the Archaeological Department (*The Conservation
> Manual* 1923: 10–11).

This arrangement authorised the ASI to get involved in the conservation of those buildings, which were entirely owned and
managed by the concerned religious endowments. In fact, the
state 'interference', that was highly unclear in legal terms, affected
the rights of religious endowments/communities in a very significant way. The endowments, which had not actually entered
into an agreement with the state, had to comply with the official
guidelines related to conservation. In later years, as we shall see in
Chapter 5, this unclear indirect state 'support' played an important
role in aggravating the contentious political issues in postcolonial
India.

Let us summarise this discussion by highlighting the legal-
archaeological classification of Indian buildings as ancient
monuments and the status of religious places of worship. For
that reason, the classification proposed by the *Manual* was very

---

[41] John Marshall's *The Conservation Manual* (1923) discusses the
practicality of conservation and provides guidelines to archaeological
officers. The *Manual* is divided into two parts. The first part talks about
the government's orders regarding the maintenance and the conduct
of conservation. The second part provides detailed instructions and
specifications on all questions likely to arise with conservation of historical
monuments. The *Manual* underlines the preservation of the authentic
character of historic buildings as one of the main objective of conservation
in India. Section 25 clearly states that purpose of the conservation was
not to renovate the building but to preserve its authenticity. It says: '[i]t
should never be forgotten that their historical value is gone when their
authenticity is destroyed' (*The Conservation Manual* 1923: 10).

useful, which classified ancient monuments into three categories (Figure 2.3):

(a) Those monuments which from their present condition or historical or archaeological values ought to be maintained in permanent good repair. (Section 3 of the Manual subdivided these monuments into three categories: [a] Monuments owned and maintained by the government, [b] Monuments owned and maintained by the private persons and [c] Monuments owned by the private person but maintained by the owner and government jointly or the government exclusively.)

(b) Those monuments which are now only possible or desirable to save from further decay by such measure as the eradication of vegetation, the exclusion of water from walls and the like.

(c) Those monuments which, from their advanced stage of decay or comparative unimportance are impossible or unnecessary to preserve (*The Conservation Manual* 1923: 2).

Figure 2.3: Classification of Ancient Monuments by *The Conservation Manual* (1923)

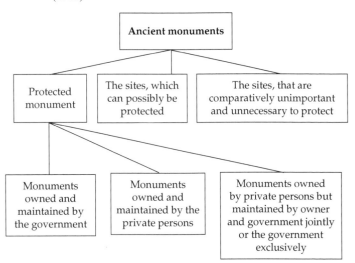

Source: Author.

Monumentalisation in Colonial India   87

This broad classification of Indian buildings not only illustrates the actual process of conservation in colonial India but also clearly demonstrates the nature of state control over the historic religious places of worship. Thus, on the basis of this classification we can identify three types of historic religious places of worships: (*a*) the non-functional historic places of worship acquired by the state as dead monuments; (*b*) The functional places of worship owned by the concerned religious endowment and managed by the state and (*c*) the state support for the conservation of those historically relevant buildings, which were owned and managed by the religious endowments. Figure 2.4 shows this classification.

Figure 2.4:   Conservation of Religious Places of Worship (1904–47)

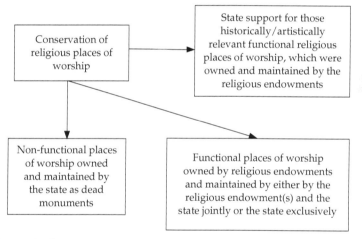

Source: Author.

Conservation and the 'Contested Nature' of Muslim Heritage

The inclusion of archaeology as a subject in Indian universities and growing production of history books, including numerous tourist guides, transformed the images of Indian historic architecture in this period. In fact, the historic buildings, particularly the Indo-Islamic sites, turned out to be the most accessible sources of India's history by acquiring a new contested 'public' character in two significant ways. First, the Indo-Islamic sites became the 'public edifice' of the Muslim conquest. In this sense, the Hindu–Muslim

88   *Muslim Political Discourse in Postcolonial India*

conflict of the early 20th century, which had no connection with these buildings, found a concrete 'historical' foundation. Second, the conservation of these monuments by applying a principle of neutrality also justified the position of the colonial rule as the protector of Indian civilisation. To elaborate these two points let us take G. R. Hearn's tourist guidebook, *The Seven Cities of Delhi* (1907) as an example. Being one of the most well-accepted tourist guides, this book introduces us to the popular colonial perceptions.[42] Describing the Hindu–Muslim relations in contemporary Delhi, Hearn notes: 'Brahmins give water to Hindus … while Mohammedans water-carriers clink brass dishes to summon their thirsty co-religionist (1997: 19).

This simple, and of course, *impartial* observation, cannot be treated as a reflection of famous 'divide and rule' theory. On the contrary, this is an honest attempt to introduce the reader to the social-cultural environment of the early 20th century Delhi. However, the problem arises when these impartial observations are mixed with 'historical facts'. For instance, analysing the influence of Hindu architecture on early Muslim mosques, Hearn writes:

> [t]he old Muhammadan Kings while they could not approve of the carving of images, prohibited by their Koran, were quite willing to use the materials of Hindu temples to build their mosques (ibid.: 94).

No one can deny the fact that temples were destroyed by the Muslim kings in medieval India. But, quite interestingly the desecration of Hindu temples is portrayed here as the most important aspect of the Indo-Islamic buildings. It is true that Hearn did not argue that the desecration of these Hindu temples was the most determining factor for the Hindu–Muslim conflicts of the early 20th century. But, in this case he literally pushed the reader to draw a clear connection between the past and the present of Delhi's contested communal identities.

But, what about the future of this contested past? To answer this straightforward question, Hearn talks about the efforts of the

---

[42] This guidebook classified the historic sites of Delhi into Hindu, Muslim, Jain and British monuments and offered a brief history of the seven cities of Delhi (1192–1906). Thus, a connection between the old Hindu and Muslim regimes and the colonial rule is clearly established.

Monumentalisation in Colonial India **89**

colonial government in protecting the past glory of this city. For example, describing the Red Fort and other buildings of Delhi, Hearn says:

> [n]ow ... the Mughal courtiers rest in their nameless graves, the ashes of Hindu princes have long been consigned to the Ganges ... the Peacock throne was taken by Nadir Shah ... and the last king of Delhi died as a prisoner ... These buildings also would have crumble into dust, were it not for the care of Government (ibid.: 9).

Similarly in the conclusion of the book, Hearn notes:

> [o]n the 1st January ... (1871) the first British Empress of India was proclaimed according to the ancient custom at Delhi; the present emperor also was proclaimed there on January 1, 1903. The many camps around Delhi, the long procession of elephants, the presence of Muhammadan and Hindu feudatories from all India — all combined to recall the splendour which Delhi has known in the past (ibid.: 312).

This discussion, more broadly, shows that the notion of 'neutral' conservation introduced by the colonial state in the early 20th century, cannot be separated from a very long historical process which, as we have seen in previous sections, explored, conceptualised and categorised Indian historic sites on a religious basis. In this sense, the dominant colonial explanations of Indian history, particularly the discovery of 'Muslim invasion' as one of the defining moments of India's past and the stagnation and decline of Indian civilisation in the 19th century, were not affected by this active conservation policy. On the contrary, by adopting the principle of strict neutrality, the colonial conservation policy 'normalised' the dominant colonial classification of Indian historic sites.[43] Moreover, it underlined the claim that India's architectural heritage was declining and therefore, the scientific archaeology based on strict neutrality should be introduced to save India's heritage.[44]

---

[43] It is important to remember that although the conservation policies were limited to the British India, the princely states were also encouraged to adopt similar policies. For an excellent discussion on the trajectories of a wider policy discourse in princely states, see Bhukya (2013).

[44] Partha Chatterjee's conceptualisation of the 'rule of colonial difference' would be useful here to understand the nature of this neutrality in relation

90 *Muslim Political Discourse in Postcolonial India*

On the basis of our assessment of the process of monumentalisation, it can be argued that the notion of an Indian Muslim architectural heritage was 'contested' on three grounds:

(*a*) It was contested on a historical basis because the Indo-Islamic buildings were either linked to the desecration of Hindu temples or conceptualised as symbols of Islamic dominance. The strategic placing of the idea of a Muslim architectural heritage in the overall sequence of Indian history, particularly in the dominant framework of colonial history, was used to symbolise the conflicting nature of India's past.

(*b*) It was contested on an archaeological basis because the conservation of Indo-Islamic sites as 'protected monuments' was in principle, opposite to the larger objective of the colonial archaeology namely the search for real authentic Hindu past.

(*c*) It was also legally contested. The Indo-Islamic historic sites which were declared as dead protected monuments were actually the wakf properties. Since the overarching definition of monument did not consider the wakf character of these sites, Muslim architectural heritage became a symbol of an endless legal conflict.

MUSLIM POLITICS IN COLONIAL INDIA AND THE QUESTION OF RELIGIOUS OF PLACES OF WORSHIP

It is very important to note that despite a variety of extensive debates on India's past, the categorisation of Indian historic sites

---

to conservation practices. The 'rule of colonial difference' argues Chatterjee 'was based on the colonial perception of Indian society. In theory, the modern institutions, which were introduced by the colonial state itself, were supposed to possess certain universally accepted characteristics and could be introduced to any social context. But in practice, Chatterjee argues, these laws were seen as external and superior to native sensibilities. Thus, the colony was an exception to the universally accepted principles of these institutions. The impulse to modernisation under colonial conditions was to be managed in such a manner that colonial difference could be maintained and reproduced (Chatterjee 1993: 19–32). Following Chatterjee, it could be argued that the colonial neutrality in the field of archaeology and conservation was a latent manifestation of the 'rule of colonial difference'.

Monumentalisation in Colonial India **91**

as 'monuments' and the state's control over historic places of worship were never understood in political terms. Even Muslim political groups, including the Muslim League, did not question the ways in which the wakf status of non-functional mosques was almost ignored by the colonial conservation policy.[45] This question becomes more complicated when we learn that wakf issues had been one of the most important aspects of Muslim politics since the 1910s.[46] Quite similarly, one cannot overlook the fact that the idea of a Muslim architectural heritage was also evoked by Muslim intelligentsia to claim the exclusive and distinct status of the Indian Muslim community.[47]

---

[45] For an elaborated discussion of Muslim politics of wakf in colonial India see (Kozlowski 1985: 156–60).

[46] The Muslim League's campaign for validating the *Wakf-alal-Aulad* (the wakf dedicated for the benefit of one's own family) in the early 20th century is a good example in this regard. One finds wide-ranging discussions on wakf issues in different proceedings of Muslim League's meetings in this period. In fact, it was more or less asserted that the wakf could not be seen merely as a charitable endowment and *Wakf-alal-Aulad* was specific to Islamic philanthropic discourse. Even in its second session at Amritsar in 1908, the Muslim League passed a resolution 'asking the Government to appoint a commission to enquire into the number, general purpose, and manner of administration of Musalman endowments designed merely for public benefits' (Pirzada 1969: 82). Interestingly, we do not find any discussion on the legal changes related to wakf institution introduced by the 1904 Act.

[47] The works of two important figures: Mohammed Iqbal and A. R. Chughtai could be cited as revealing examples here. As a poet and a philosopher, Iqbal pays special attention to the question of Islamic heritage. His three long poems *Masjid-e-Qartaba* (The Cordova Mosque) *Shikwa* (Complaint to God) and *Jawab-e-Shikwa* (Response to a Complaint) — use Islamic architecture as a metaphor to stir up the reminiscences of a glorious Muslim past. In fact, in *Shikwa*, Iqbal also makes a few remarks, though in a highly poetic manner, on the conversion of churches into mosques in order to illustrate the contribution of the Islamic civilisation. He writes:

Sometimes we were calling Adhan in the cathedrals of Europe,
Sometimes in the scorching Africa Deserts;
We never cared for the grandeur of monarch
We recited Kalimah under the shade of the sword (Iqbal 2006)

However, Iqbal, like many other Muslim intellectuals of his generation, did not show any interest in producing an objective account of Islamic

92   *Muslim Political Discourse in Postcolonial India*

It may be argued that due to poor urbanisation of major north Indian historic cities and the less-developed tourist/heritage industry in colonial India, most of the non-functional state protected monuments could not be 'commercialised' as tourist spots in the modern sense of the term. In many cases, these sites were located in uninhabited areas outside the main cities. Therefore, it was virtually not possible for native Indian communities, including Muslims, to use these non-functional sites for religious observances regularly. In addition, the religious communities were always allowed to use these protected sites on special occasions. As far as the state protection of functional religious places of worship is concerned, one also finds that such types of buildings were under the control of the concerned religious endowments and the state was just providing some kind of technical and/or financial support for the upkeep of the actual architectural design of these buildings. In this sense, it could safely be suggested that since the state was acting as a responsible neutral custodian, it was not possible for the Muslim elite to make political use of these issues.[48] To some

---

history (Shaikh 2005: 377–81). In a much wider sense, this deliberate ignorance of objective history underlines an interesting intellectual tendency. The Muslim intelligentsia of this period chose literature, particularly poetry, to evoke the memories of a glorious Muslim past. However, such memories of the past were not analysed as 'facts' to write any 'Muslim' history of India (Smith 1961: 321–23). Another reflection of this trend can be found in the paintings of A. R. Chughtai, who chose Muslim historical themes, particularly Mughal architecture, for representing the images of Muslim past (Mitter 1994: 336). Although Chughtai drew heavily on Indian cultural symbols including Hindu icons and figures, his paintings very clearly show an artistic inclination towards the idea of an exclusive Muslim heritage.

[48] The famous Jama Masjid case (1858–62) needs to be mentioned here. As pointed out earlier, the Jama Masjid was captured by the British troops in 1857 and was handed over to the Muslims in 1862. The Management Committee of the Jama Masjid, which was established to take care of the religious activities etc. remained loyal to the British throughout the 19th century (Gupta 1981: 27). But, this 'loyalist management' did not entirely stop the use of Jama Masjid for political activities in the later period. Yet, the Jama Masjid never became a hub of politics in colonial India for two obvious reasons. First, the state did not intervene in the management of religious affairs of the mosque, though its indirect influence cannot entirely be ruled out. Second, the Muslim political elite did not

Monumentalisation in Colonial India

extent, as we shall see in postcolonial India, the urbanisation of cities and the commercialisation of heritage industry played an important role in the emergence of Muslim politics of monuments. But, these practical issues cannot convincingly explain the level of indifference of Muslim elite towards these significant issues. Let us take two interesting cases, the Kanpur Mosque case (1913) and the Shahid Ganj Mosque case (1935–37), as examples in which the 'protection of places of warship' was directly seen as a 'political question', to further elaborate this discussion.

In 1913, the Kanpur Municipality demolished the wadu khana (place for ablution) of a functional mosque in the congested Machchali Bazaar area to make room for a new road (Minault 1982: 39). This incident created a stir in local Muslim political circles. The local Muslim leaders argued that the wadu khana was an integral part of the mosque and thus the Municipality should rebuild it and modify its road construction plan. However, the local authorities did not accept this plea and decided to go ahead with their original scheme. In response to this rigid stand, the local Muslim elite decided to organise a public meeting, which later turned into a direct confrontation between the police and the Muslims. In this violent clash, several Muslims were killed and all the main leaders of the agitation were arrested. This incident, particularly the way in which the local authorities behaved, was severely criticised. In fact, this case was shown as 'desecration of a Muslim place of worship'. The colonial state, however, took this matter very sincerely. Lord Hardinge, the Viceroy, overruled the decision of the local government and decided to drop charges against those people who were arrested by the police. He also agreed to rebuild the demolished corner of the mosque (ibid.: 47–49).

The Shahid Ganj Mosque case, Lahore (1935–37) exemplifies another aspect of Muslim politics of religious places of worship in colonial India. In this case, a property was dedicated by a Muslim

---

identify this mosque as a political symbol of any kind. The demand made by the Muslim League in 1918, that the Jama Masjid must be opened for political activities, in this sense, could not be considered as politicisation of the mosque. In fact, the local administration very clearly suggested that since the mosque was managed by the Muslims themselves, the state could not be held accountable for any permission (ibid.: 203.). For an excellent discussion on Jama Masjid case see, Kavuri-Bauer (2011: Chapter 3).

94   *Muslim Political Discourse in Postcolonial India*

landlord in 1722 as wakf to build a mosque and a madrasa in Lahore. In 1762, however, this mosque and some adjacent land were occupied by the Sikhs, who built a Gurudwara and a shrine of a Sikh leader just next to the mosque. The legal proceedings in this case started in 1850, when the Muslim party filed an application in the local court. However, the court upheld the Sikh claim and Sikhs were allowed to use this place as a Gurudwara (Noorani 2003a: 2–3).

The trouble began after the enactment of the Sikh Gurudwara Act (1925), which was passed for the effective management of Sikh shrines and religious places of worship: The Shahid Ganj Mosque was notified as a Sikh shrine by this Act in the 1930s. The Muslims of Punjab led by the *Anjuman Islamia*, opposed this move and filed a case in the Sikh Gurudwara Tribunal, which was actually established to settle the disputes relating to Sikh religious places of worship. The Tribunal rejected the objections raised by the Muslim side and endorsed the previous legal verdicts that the disputed property was a Sikh temple. This verdict provoked the local Muslims to file another application before the Lahore High Court. This appeal was also rejected on the same grounds. These legal battles affected the local Muslim–Sikh communal relations. In fact, the rising inter-communal tensions led to a series of clashes between the Muslims and the Sikhs. The entire structure of the Shahid Ganj Mosque was demolished and more than 12 people were killed in these riots (ibid.: 9).

After the 1937 elections, Sikander Hayat Khan became the Premier of Punjab. Considering the feelings of local Muslims, the case was reopened. However, this time again the court favoured the Sikh claim and recognised the Shahid Ganj property as a Gurudwara. Moreover, the court also defined the status of a non-functional mosque, which could be adversely possessed by non-Muslims. The Privy Council held that:

> [i]t is impossible to read into the modern Limitation Acts any exception for property made wakf for the purpose of mosque whether the purpose be merely to provide money for the upkeep and conduct of a mosque or to provide a site and building for the purpose. While their Lordship have every sympathy with the religious sentiment which would ascribe sanctity and inviolability to a place of worship, they cannot under the limitation Act accept the contentions that such a building cannot be possessed adversely to the wakf, or that it is not

Monumentalisation in Colonial India

so possessed so long as it is referred to as a 'mosque', or unless the building is razed to the ground or loses the appearance which reveals its original purpose (cf. AIR, 1994, SC 605).

As could be expected, the Muslim elected representatives tried to introduce a bill in the Provincial Assembly of Punjab against this verdict. However, Sikander Hayat discouraged such a move. He maintained that his government would abide by the decision of the court and continue to provide protection to all religious places of worship (Noorani 2003a: 9).

What do these cases show? In the Kanpur Mosque case, the colonial authorities were directly involved in a highly sensitive issue, which in any case was against the policy of strict neutrality. In comparison, the Muslim leaders were in an advantageous position. They could have made full use of this event to demonstrate the brutal and anti-Islamic conduct of the colonial state. Interestingly, by quickly accepting the specific local Muslim demands the colonial state did not provide them any opportunity to transform this event into a major political issue. As a result, as Gail Minault's study of the Khilafat Movement seems to suggest, the Kanpur mosque case gradually lost its political value and the Muslim political discourse was again occupied by larger political issues such as protection of communal rights and separate electorate. Quite similarly in the Shahid Ganj mosque case, the colonial state acted as a neutral arbitrator between two conflicting parties and finally upheld the policy of strict neutrality.

In both the cases, the state did not divert from the established principle of neutrality, which actually marks its own understanding of secularism. Importantly, this kind of secularism drew a very clear line between the secular spheres of state activities and the social and cultural life of Indian communities. It was also established that the secular state would not interfere in the socio-cultural spheres of Indian communities; similarly, the religious communities would not be allowed to intervene in the business of the state. Since this kind of secularism was technically not related to any discourse of rights, the established boundaries between the secular and non-secular activities gradually became the criterion to decide the legitimacy of the claims made by religious communities on their places of worship. In the Kanpur Mosque case, the state favoured the Muslim claim because in principle it recognised the fact that

96 *Muslim Political Discourse in Postcolonial India*

the local authorities were crossing the secular boundaries. In the Shahid Ganj case, the Sikh claims were supported on the basis of secular law of limitation, which was given priority over the wakf status of the mosque. If these two cases are linked to the question of state protected places of worship it could simply be inferred that the protection of monuments was strictly recognised as a secular activity. The state's control over these sites, therefore, could not be considered as an 'adverse possession' of any kind.

So, does it mean that the Muslim politicians accepted the secularism of strict neutrality and decided to ignore the legal ambiguities associated with the notion of secular monuments? Or, alternately does it mean that the colonial state did not allow them to do so? These complex questions cannot be answered merely on the basis of a brief discussion of two relevant cases. In fact, one needs to analyse the relationship between the issues and demands made by the Muslim political groups in colonial India and the secularism of strict neutrality in a detailed manner to find out the responses of the Muslim elite to the colonial administrative-institutional structures and political principles.[49] Yet, on the basis of our discussion, it could be argued that the secularism of strict neutrality, as one of the most important political principles, not only set out rules for the protection of historical monuments but also affected the political discourse in colonial India. Apart from all other ideological and practical political reasons, this aspect also played a very important role in determining the political actions of Muslim elites. To elaborate this point, it is important to compare the colonial archaeological–legal framework of conservation with the postcolonial archaeological agenda. In other words, we have to pay close attention to two competing discourses of secularism: the secularism of strict neutrality and the secularism of participatory neutrality. This is precisely what I am going to discuss in the next chapter.

■

---

[49] Kaviraj's essay (2005) on Gandhi's trial is an excellent example of such possible assessment of political principles on which the colonial state was based.

3

Monumentalisation in Postcolonial India
Conservation, Law and Muslim Politics

This chapter looks at the continuities and discontinuities of the process of monumentalisation in postcolonial India. Concentrating on the postcolonial legal-archaeological framework, a few legal-technical ambiguities and unresolved issues are traced and a link is established between the Muslim political responses and the legal-archaeological changes introduced by the postcolonial state. More precisely, the chapter discusses three aspects of the process of monumentalisation: (*a*) the principles adopted by the Archaeological Survey of India (ASI) for the conservation of protected monuments; (*b*) the nature of archaeological excavation, particularly those excavation projects, which intended to discover ancient Hindu religious places, and (*c*) the conflicting relationship between the right to worship and secular conservation of historical monuments.

Analysing the *secularism of historical monuments*, which as a principle, has been accepted to define the secular character of selected monuments of national importance and the *secularism of minority rights*, which protects the rights and interests of religious minorities, I book at the contested notion of Muslim architectural heritage and its relationship with the national heritage of postcolonial India. I argue that the idea of an Indian Muslim architectural heritage, which had already been shaped by the colonial archaeological efforts, was brought into the public domain by the postcolonial legal framework and archaeological policies and provided a political space to the Muslim groups to articulate political demands in a language of rights.

The chapter is based on a possible reading of existing legal-archaeological framework from the point of view of the changing nature of Muslim political demands. In fact, an attempt has

98   *Muslim Political Discourse in Postcolonial India*

been made to trace a few unclear legal aspects as well. I am not concerned with the policy related implications of this 'political' reading. Nor do I suggest any alternative way to define the existing archaeological policy. Instead, the purpose is to highlight the linkages between the so-called 'neutral policy' of the state and the Muslim political discourse.

I

SEARCH FOR A 'NATIONAL HERITAGE': MONUMENTALISATION AND SECULARISM OF HISTORICAL MONUMENTS

After the Partition of India, the question of 'national heritage' had become a politically sensitive issue. On the one hand, a dominant section of the Congress, led by Nehru, was highly committed to the idea of a composite national heritage. In contrast, there was a strong Hindu rightist lobby, which wanted to adopt Hindu religious-cultural icons as the representative symbols of Indian culture. Despite this clear ideological divide, the notion that the official state symbols should reflect the cultural continuity of ancient Indian civilisation, dominated the proceedings of the Indian Constituent Assembly. The Nehru group supported ancient Indian symbols for underlining the genesis of the tolerant Indian culture and civilisation. The Hindu rightist lobby, on the contrary, appreciated the idea of ancient India for defining the basic Indian culture in strictly Hindu terms. As a result, a synthesis emerged and the Constituent Assembly succeeded in selecting some very 'neutral' national symbols. For instance, the national tricolour flag was selected with a *Chakra* (wheel) symbol, which appears on the abacus of the Sarnath, the capital city built by King Asoka. Similarly, the national emblem was also taken from the Sarnath. These symbols are basically Buddhist in nature and signify ancient Indian civilisation.[1]

---

[1] The debates on national symbols of India, particularly the discussion which took place on 22 July 1947, were very interesting. Nehru, who presented the Resolution on National Flag, repeatedly told the House that the tricolour had no connection with communalism of any kind (Constituent Assembly Debates, Vol. 4. http://parliamentofindia.nic.in/ls/debates/vol4p7.htm, accessed on 8 April 2013).

Monumentalisation in Postcolonial India **99**

It does not mean, however, that the ideological battle between the Hindu rightists lobby and the others, who were later called 'secularists', was over.[2] In fact, the debate on national heritage acquired a wider political significance, particularly for the Hindu rightists in the Congress, who actually started exploiting the state institutions to implement their own political agenda. The campaign to rebuild the Somnath temple, allegedly destroyed by Mehmud of Ghazni in the 12th century, and the forcible conversion of the Babri Masjid — a functional Muslim mosque — into a de-facto temple could be seen as political reflections of this active rightist agenda.[3] In this context, the Nehruvian state articulated its official policy on archaeology.[4]

---

[2] This ideological divide continued to dominate the Indian political discourse in the first decade after independence. In fact, several attempts were made to conceptualise the vexed question of the 'national heritage' from these two ideological perspectives. The Hindu rightists looked at ancient India for tracing the 'unadulterated and authentic' historical sources. Conceptualising 'Muslim rule' as a kind of imperialism, these authors defined medieval India as a 'dark age'. K. M. Munshi, for example, identifies four phases of Indian culture. According to him, the first phase symbolises the 'age of settlement', which began when the Aryan civilisation settled in northern India. The second phase was the 'age of resistance', when Indians 'passively resisted' against the foreign invaders. The third age was the period of 'modern resistance', which began in the 17th century when Shivaji waged a war against the Muslim rule. And finally, the fourth period started in 1947 when India became independent. In this classification the medieval period is described as a 'dark age' (Munshi 1956: 113). On the other hand, the secularists argued for the basic 'accommodative' character of Indian civilisation and composite cultural heritage. Nehru's article 'Epoch of Indian Culture' (1956), S. Abid Hussain's book *The National Culture of India* (1956), and Humayun Kabir's book *The Indian Heritage* (1955) can be cited as examples of this trend.

[3] I do not suggest that the campaign to rebuild Somnath temple and the dispute in Ayodhya on Babri Masjid had any direct linkage. Babri Masjid, at least in the 1950s was a highly localised issue. The Hindu rightist politics realised the political significance of this dispute very late. However, my purpose here is to underline the political context of 1947–49, when religious places of worship turned into the symbols of civilisational conflict.

[4] Two important administrative changes were introduced in the 1950s. First, the archaeological management was decentralised and the

100   *Muslim Political Discourse in Postcolonial India*

Broadly speaking, the policy on archaeology had to deal with three very different kinds of compulsions. First, it had to 'nationalise' the Indian historic sites in a purely legal–administrative terms. This move was not only essential for restructuring the archaeological management in the country but also crucial to publicise the official interpretation of history and culture of India from the point of view of the newly emerged Indian state. Since there was no 'official history' of India at that time, it was fairly obvious for the state to identify historical 'monuments' as the most representative symbols of official postcolonial version of national culture and heritage.

Second, the state had to deal with the question of religion. This was again a very complicated issue. Unlike the colonial state, which followed the principle of strict neutrality in relation to religious affairs, the Indian constitution had already granted a few constitutionally protected fundamental rights to the religious communities, particularly to religious minorities. In addition, the state had also set out long-term social and religious reform agendas. In this sense, the Indian state had been following a kind of secularism, which, to a greater extent, was involved in the religious life of

---

administrative powers were divided between the centre and the states. It changed the legal arrangements made under the Government of India Act 1935 that put archaeology and ancient monuments in the Federal List. Second, the concept of 'national importance' was introduced. It was envisaged that those monuments which had a national importance should be differentiated from the other sites and monuments, which were considered to be less important or which had a local/regional importance. The Constitution of India proposed three administrative categories of monuments and sites: (*a*) the monuments of national importance, which were put in the Union list under the jurisdiction of the centre; (*b*) the monuments other than the declared monuments of national importance, which were put in the state list under the jurisdiction of the state and (*c*) the archaeological sites and remains other than those declared sites of national importance put in the concurrent list under the jurisdiction of both centre and the states. Article 49 of the Constitution, in this regard, says: 'it shall be the obligation of the State to protect every monument or place or object of artistic or historic interest declared by or under law made by the Parliament to be of national importance, from spoliation, disfigurement, destruction, removal, disposal or export as the case may be' (The Constitution of India 2007: 24).

Monumentalisation in Postcolonial India **101**

Indian communities. However, in the political context of the 1950s, when the Hindu rightists were very active, it was not possible for the Nehruvian state to apply this kind of secularism to redefine the religious status of historical monuments, particularly those non-functional Indo-Islamic sites, which had a contested history. As a result, it was a compulsion for the state to stick to the colonial policy of strict neutrality.

Third, the state had to look at the question of 'scientific excavation'. It was also essential because the Partition had already affected the archaeological map of the sub-continent and many ancient sites such as Mohenjo-daro, Harappa and Taxila, which were extremely important for tracing the missing links of Indian history, were under the control of Pakistani authorities. For that reason, the ASI set out two broad objectives for further archaeological excavations in the country: (*a*) excavation for more sites related to Indus Valley civilisation to fulfil the 'loss' of ancient sites such as the Harappa etc., and (*b*) bridging the gap between Harappa and the early historic period (Bhan 1997). These priorities of the ASI also reflect the state's emphasis on ancient India, which had been identified as the most crucial period of Indian history.

Let us now look at the legal framework introduced in postcolonial India to examine how these compulsions were actually managed and a few legal norms were laid down for the archaeological conservation and excavations.

The Official Policy on Archaeology and the Question of 'National Importance'

The Ancient Monuments and Archaeological Sites and Remains [Declaration of National Importance] Act (1951) was the first law on Indian historic sites in postcolonial India. Under this Act, all monuments preserved under the 1904 Act were designated as sites and monuments of national importance. Over 450 monuments and sites of the former princely states were also included in this category. In 1956, the States Reorganisation Act was passed and some more sites and monuments were declared to be of national importance (Chakrabarti 2003: 165).

To deal with these administrative changes, particularly the decentralisation of ASI, a comprehensive law, the Ancient Monuments and Archaeological Sites and Remains Act (1958), was enacted. This new Act was directly related to the management

102   *Muslim Political Discourse in Postcolonial India*

and control of those sites and monuments that had already been declared as the 'monuments of national importance'. These designated national monuments were to be administered by the centre.[5] It was also envisaged that the states would make their own laws to manage other monuments and sites. The 1958 Act replaced the Ancient Monuments and Archaeological Sites and Remains [Declaration of National Importance] Act (1951), the Ancient Monuments and Preservation Act (1904) and Section 126 of the States Reorganisation Act 1956.

The new Act of 1958 was broadly modelled on the 1904 Act. For example, the definition of ancient monument, the process of acquisition, and the policy of preservation were not changed. Yet, this Act elaborated the legal process by which a historic building/ site could be declared as a Protected Monument or in this particular context a 'monument of national importance'. Furthermore, it also deals with the responsibilities and powers of the central government and the status of functional religious sites.

The 1958 Act in principle recognises the central government as the competent authority to define the concept of 'national importance' in four different ways. First, it provides power to the central government to *select* the 'monuments of national importance'. Section 4(1) of the 1958 Act, says:

> [w]here the Central Government is of the opinion that any ancient monuments and the archaeological sites and remains not included in Section 3 of national importance, it may, by notification in the Official Gazette, give two month notice of its intention to declare such ancient monuments or archaeological sites and remains to be of national importance; and a copy of every such notification shall be affixed in a conspicuous place near the monument or site and remain, as the case may be.

Although Section 4(2) provides an opportunity to interested person(s) to make legal objection against such a notification, the

---

[5] This new Act sought to clarify the division of powers between the centre and states in relation to historical sites and monuments. Since the 1904 Act was applicable only to the monuments and sites located in the territory of erstwhile British India, it was extremely important to make a comprehensive law for clearly demarcating the boundaries of the centre and the states to follow the directives given in the Constitution of India.

Monumentalisation in Postcolonial India **103**

Act does not spell out the legal process to deal with such kinds of possible disputes. Thus, technically speaking, the central government enjoys an obvious power in this regard.[6]

Second, the 1958 Act gives powers to the central government to *acquire* historic buildings for preservation. Following the precedent established by the 1904 Act, it outlines four ways to acquire any historic site:

(a) The Director General on behalf of the central government may purchase, take a lease of, or accept a gift or bequest of any building.

(b) In the same way, the building without an owner could also be acquired for protection as the monument of national importance.

(c) Those buildings, which are owned by individuals and/ or concerned religious endowments, could be declared as monuments of national importance.[7]

(d) The compulsory acquisition of those monuments, which are not protected properly. In this case the provisions of the Land Acquisition Act 1894 were to be applied. The protection of this kind of monument is defined as 'public purpose'.

Third, the 1958 Act gives powers to the central government to *'denationalise'* the status of selected historical monuments. Section 35 of the 1958 Act says:

> [i]f the Central Government is of the opinion that any ancient and historical monument or archaeological sites and remain declared to be of national importance, it may, by notification in the Official Gazette, declare that the ancient monuments and or archaeological sites and remain has ceased to be of national importance.

---

[6] According to Section 4(3), the 'Central Government may, after considering the objection, if any, it may receive, declare by notification in the official Gazette, the ancient monument or archaeological site and remains; as the case may be, to be of national importance'.

[7] Section 9 of the 1958 Act empowers the government to ask any owner or owners of a Protected Monument to enter into an agreement with the government. If the owner refuses or fails to enter into an agreement, the government could issue order to him or her in this regard.

104   *Muslim Political Discourse in Postcolonial India*

This section gives power to the central government to terminate the national importance status of any monument at any point of time. Of course, this provision was made to ensure the proper administration of monuments and the division of power between the centre and the states. However, it also indicates that the concept of 'national importance' could easily be appropriated by the ruling political party. If the ruling party feels that it should change its heritage symbols and historic sites of 'national importance', it can simply use this section.[8]

Fourth, the sections related to religious places of worship also empower the central government to *decide the religious identity* of a monument of national importance and the nature of religious observance inside it. Section 16 of the 1958 Act, which has been taken directly from Section 13(2) of the 1904 Act says, 'a place of worship or shrine maintained by the Government under this Act shall not be used for any purpose inconsistent with its character.' Section 16(2) further elaborates this point and notes that the Collector, on behalf of the Government of India, will make necessary arrangements for the protection of such a monument and parts of it from pollution and desecration. This section further suggests two ways by which the Collector could protect the sanctity of such a site: (*a*) 'by prohibiting the entry therein, except in accordance with the conditions prescribed with concurrence of the persons, if any, in religious charge of the said monument or part thereof, of any person not entitled so to enter by religious usages of the community by which the monument of part thereof is used' [Section 16 2a], and (*b*) 'by taking such other actions as he may think necessary in this behalf' [Section 16 2b]. Interestingly, these provisions only talk about the functional protected monuments; the religious status of non-functional religious sites and shrines is left undefined. I shall elaborate this point later. Figure 3.1 illuminates different aspects of the powers of the central government.

---

[8] There is no clear definition of national heritage in the constitution. Article 51 says: 'it shall be the duty of every citizen of India to value and preserve the rich heritage of our composite culture' (The Constitution of India 2007: 24). It is to be noted that this Article was included in the constitution in 1976 when the Congress-led central government brought the controversial 42nd amended bill in the Parliament during the time of National Emergency in 1976!

Monumentalisation in Postcolonial India **105**

Figure 3.1: Powers of the Central Government

```
                    ┌─────────────────────────────────┐
                    │  Powers of the central government │
                    └─────────────────────────────────┘

┌──────────────┐   ┌──────────────┐        ┌──────────────────┐
│ Nationalisation│  │ Acquisition of│        │ Denationalisation │
│ of a monument │   │ buildings/sites│       │ of monuments      │
└──────────────┘   │ as monuments  │        │ (Sec. 35)         │
                    └──────────────┘        └──────────────────┘

┌──────────────────────┐        ┌──────────────────────────┐
│ Identification of a monument│   │ Powers to define the religion│
│ of national importance │       │ of a monument of national  │
│ (intention of the central │    │ importance (Sec. 16)       │
│ government (Sec. 4[i])  │       └──────────────────────────┘
└──────────────────────┘

┌──────────────────────┐
│ Two months' time for │
│ making objection against this│
│ intention (Sec. 4[2]) │
└──────────────────────┘

┌──────────────┐ ┌──────────────┐ ┌──────────────┐ ┌──────────────┐
│ Acquisition of a│ │ Acquisition of│ │ Preservation of│ │ The compulsory│
│ building by the │ │ an abandoned  │ │ a building with│ │ purchase of a │
│ state through  │ │ building      │ │ an agreement  │ │ building      │
│ the collector as│ │ as dead       │ │ with owner or │ │ (Sec. 13)     │
│ a gift (Sec. 5[1])│ │ monuments     │ │ concerned body│ └──────────────┘
└──────────────┘ │ (Sec. 5[2])   │ │ (Sec. 5 & 9)  │
                 └──────────────┘ └──────────────┘
```

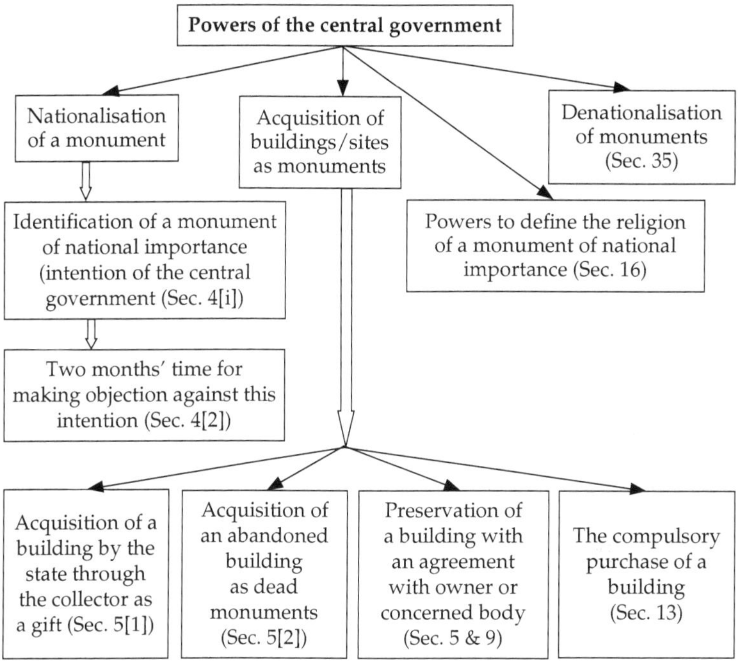

Source: Author.

A broad reading of the 1958 Act suggests that this law follows the principle of strict neutrality that was established as a practical code for the archaeological management by the 1904 Act. Here the 'secular' is juxtaposed with 'religion' and 'traditions'. This form of secularism seeks the separation of religion from official history for the realisation of an ultimate ideal: the objective historical meaning of Indian monuments. The historic sites, as we have seen, were/ are declared as monuments of 'national importance', for commemorating an 'objective', 'rational', 'scientific' and secular idea of national past. The 'secular' in this sense stands for 'objectivity' and 'truthfulness' of official meanings of a particular building. To protect the veracity of this authentic past, 'secularism' is introduced as a kind of administrative category for the effective, proper and efficient management of historic sites.

But, what was the impact of this legal framework on the actual conservation of historic sites? In other words, how did a nationalised

106   *Muslim Political Discourse in Postcolonial India*

version of Indian archaeology come into being? This question is also important to know the placing of Muslim heritage in the broad framework of national heritage. To find out answers to these questions, let us now discuss two very clear manifestations of the archaeological policy: the principles of conservation and the nature of tradition-based archaeological excavation in post-colonial India.

The Postcolonial Neutrality: Principles of Conservation, Tradition-based Archaeology and the Contested Images of Indo-Islamic 'Monuments'

In colonial India, the 'rule of colonial difference' made it possible for the colonial state to stick to the policy of strict neutrality. However, it was a bit difficult for the postcolonial state to follow that kind of neutrality, precisely because of a few political pressures, which I mentioned in the beginning of this discussion. In fact, it was important for the state to identify a secular notion of 'national importance' in such a manner that various types of buildings, including the 'contested' Indo-Islamic monuments, could be conserved and at the same time further archaeological excavation could also be carried out. In this context, three broad principles of neutrality emerged, which actually stemmed from the legal framework established by the 1958 Act. Thus:

1. *The Indian historic sites, particularly the monuments of national importance, are to be conserved in such a manner that the objective national history of India could be displayed.* Following this principle, the existing conservation practice based on *The Conservation Manual* of 1923 was modified and the major Indian historic monuments and sites were developed as tourist spots.[9] Moreover, the international principles of

---

[9] For example, in the 1953 issue of *Ancient India*, the official journal published by the ASI, T. R. Ramachandran identified four main objectives of preservation of a historic building in India: '(a) its preservation without disfigurement or alteration of its character; (b) its maintenance in a proper and attractive condition; (c) the complete examination of its remains and documentary evidence concerning it and (d) the preparation of monograph, guidebooks and reports, so that its historical and artistic interests may be brought home to the scholar and the visitor and may rouse general interest

Monumentalisation in Postcolonial India 107

conservation were also introduced for implementing the national conservation policy and converting a few Indian monuments into the 'World Heritage Sites'.[10]

2. *The monuments would be conserved as 'dead entities' and the state would follow the principle of strict neutrality in relation to religion.* This principle actually intends to demarcate the boundaries between the state and the religious character of a

---

in the past relic of the country' (Ramachandran 1953: 54). These objectives, more broadly, stem from *The Conservation Manual* of 1923. One can also find an additional emphasis on the 'public display' of historic buildings.

[10] The international campaign for the conservation of historic sites and cultural properties has a long history. The Hague Regulation on the Laws and Customs of War (1899 and 1907) established provisions for the protection of the cultural property including the historic sites during the time of war. The Athens Charter of 1931 also endorsed these concerns. The international efforts for the protection of historic sites became truly global after the Second World War. In 1964, the Second International Congress of Architects and Technicians of Historic Monuments introduced the *International Charter for the Conservation and Restoration of Monuments and Sites.* This document is also known as the Venice Charter. In 1965, the International Council on Monuments and Sites (ICOMOS), an international NGO was formed to strengthen the campaign for the protection of historic heritage of the world. The ICOMOS played a significant role in this regard and in 1972, an international treaty, *the Convention concerning the protection of the World Cultural and Natural Heritage,* was adopted by the United Nations Educational Social and Cultural Organisation (UNESCO) in Paris. The Convention more broadly classified the world heritage into two categories: the cultural heritage and the natural heritage. It was decided that the state parties, the countries which have adhered to the Convention, would identify and nominate properties on their national territory to be considered for inscription on the 'World Heritage List'. The state parties would have to provide information about the existing condition of the nominated property/properties and the conservation measures to protect these sites. The selected sites are called the 'world heritage sites'. India ratified the Convention in 1977. In this regard, the National Commission for Co-operation with UNESCO was established. There are 21 cultural heritage sites and four natural heritage sites in India. In fact, all the famous historic sites of India have been already declared as World Heritage Sites. It is important to note that the concept of 'world heritage site' offers a broad framework in which the national principles of conservation operate (Mani 2001).

108   *Muslim Political Discourse in Postcolonial India*

monument, quite similar to the manner in which the colonial state articulated its policy of non-interference. As a result, a 'building-centric' approach to conservation was introduced to protect the non-functional sites as dead monuments and a strong administrative control was established over the functional religious sites.

3. *The state would encourage archaeological excavations by maintaining the principle of neutrality. However, culture is defined in a broader sense to accommodate worldly aspects of religion. Therefore the state could also support the tradition-based archaeological explorations.* Employing this principle of neutrality, the religious literature, mainly the Hindu epics, in conjunction with other historical/archaeological resources, were identified as cultural text for conducting archaeological excavations.

We now look at the impact of these principles of neutrality on the popular images of the Indo-Islamic historic sites. The first principle, which actually transformed Indian monuments into tourist places, brought the contested history of these sites into the public domain. Since no serious discussion took place on the ways by which a nationalist history of Indian monuments could be displayed, the ASI continued to use the old colonial account of most of the Indo-Islamic sites. As a result, the contested notion of Muslim architectural heritage found a new public image. It is true that this process, as I discussed in the previous chapter, actually began in late colonial period, when these sites became tourist attractions for the European 'public'. But, in postcolonial India, the ever-increasing commercialisation of the heritage industry converted these controversial images of Islamic monuments into popular discourse.

Let us take an interesting example to elaborate this point. To provide information to visitors about the famous *Masjid-a-Jami* and the Qutub monument complex, a short inscription inscribed on stone is installed by the ASI at the entrance of the Qutub complex — a monument of national importance and a recognised 'World Heritage Site' (Figure 3.2). The ASI version, which is the most visible and accessible account of the history of this site for tourists and visitors, says that 27 Hindu and Jain temples were demolished by the early Muslim rulers to build this mosque. This inscription very clearly highlights the Islamic iconoclasm as the

Figure 3.2: ASI's Version of Qutub Mosque

Source: HA Collection, 2005.

most important aspect of the history of this site, quite similarly to the ways in which the history of Qutub complex is described in colonial tourists' guidebooks. As a result, the contested history of this mosque, which has been a matter of serious archaeological/historical debates, turns into a subject of popular discourse on the past and present relations between various religious communities.[11]

---

[11] There are several studies which question the colonial account of Qutub complex. For instance, Mohammed Mujeeb highlights the fact that the Islamic principles and local artistic sensibilities are clearly reflected in this mosque and therefore it could also be read as a 'social document'. He argues that the medieval architecture represents a social and cultural assimilation process that produced a remarkably unique culture (Mujeeb 2001). Monica Juneja and Sunil Kumar also support this argument. Juneja

110 *Muslim Political Discourse in Postcolonial India*

The second principle of neutrality, which actually introduced the building-centric approach of conservation, also affected the popular images of Indo-Islamic monuments, particularly after the rapid urbanisation of modern north Indian cities. As I pointed out in the previous chapter, in colonial India, the non-functional sites were almost uninhabited and it was possible for the colonial authorities to focus only the design and features of old buildings. But, the urbanisation in postcolonial India changed the historical profile of major north Indian cities quite significantly. Many protected non-functional monuments, which were situated outside the main city areas, suddenly became an integral part of everyday life. Moreover, commercialised tourism also provided a new life to these non-functional sites. 'Modern tourists' were actually recognised as the legitimised users of these monuments in contrast to irrational communal religious worshippers. Technically speaking, it was now possible for a tourist to use a protected historic mosque for all types of leisure activities, even those acts which are not permitted in Islam. In contrast, it was not possible for a common Muslim to offer Namaz inside these protected mosques. Thus, the relationship between the monument and the community, which had been disconnected by colonial conservation practices, was substantiated by the postcolonial principle of neutrality. For that reason, the question of worship in a protected site turns out to be a serious religious–political demand.[12]

---

focuses on the day-to-day life practices of people in medieval India while Kumar studies the ways in which the Qutub complex is historically interpreted (Juneja 2001; Kumar 2001).

[12] It is useful here to point out that this building centric approach has also been criticised by the Indian National Trust for Art and Cultural Heritage (INTACH), which was established in 1984 to create public awareness for the protection of cultural and historical heritage. The INTACH does not entirely reject the ASI's notion of conservation; rather it interrogates the bureaucratic approach of the ASI and its ineffectiveness in conserving the protected as well as unprotected monuments in India. Therefore the listing and conservation of the 'unprotected' monuments has been the main thrust of the INTACH's activities. Highlighting the relationship between the local communities and the historic sites, the INTACH has introduced the concept of 'heritage zone'. As a concept, it has shifted the focus of archaeological activities from the physical or material conservation of historic buildings to the cultural context in which the particular

Monumentalisation in Postcolonial India **111**

The third principle of neutrality, which paved the way for the tradition-based archaeological excavations, has been one of the most controversial aspects of postcolonial Indian archaeology.[13] Despite the fact that a clear dividing line between the science of archaeology and religious faith was always drawn in such explorations, the virtual rejection of non-Hindu religious/regional/local traditions actually transformed this issue into a politically sensitive question.[14] In fact, a particular version of the tradition-based

---

building(s) is/are located. The INTACH has identified more than 50 heritage zones in India. It has also prepared a *Charter for the Conservation of unprotected Architectural Heritage and Sites in India*. This Charter talks about the participation of local communities in the conservation practices by recognising their traditional methods of building constructions and the cultural values associated with these buildings. Article 3.5.1 of this Charter says 'each community has its own distinctive culture constituted by its traditions, beliefs, rituals and practices — all intrinsic to defining the significance of the unprotected architectural heritage and site. The conservation strategy must respect the fact that local cultures are not static and, therefore, encourage active community involvement in the process of decision-making. This will ensure that the symbiotic relation between the indigenous community and its own heritage is strengthened through conservation' (INTACH 2006: *Charter for the Conservation of unprotected Architectural Heritage and Sites in India*.).

[13] It would be entirely wrong to assume that these types of archaeological efforts in postcolonial India were politically motivated and the ASI was working to establish the Hindutva theories. One must remember that the 'scientific archaeology' was the main thrust of the ASI's work in the 1950s. In fact, one could identify three different positions on this issue. For instance, people like A. Ghosh were in favour of tradition-based archaeology to find out secular 'facts' (Bhan 1997). In contrast, archaeologist B. B. Lal, who actually conducted the Hastinapur excavations of the 1950, wanted to examine Hindu epics as sources. H. S. Sankalia's stand however, was quite different from these two positions. In his opinion, the significance of traditions to trace the past should not be underestimated. Yet, it is the duty of the archaeologists to go beyond the existing understanding of traditions and explore the unknown aspects of cultural past (Sankalia 1977: 893).

[14] Broadly speaking, we can find three phases of the 'tradition-based archaeology' in India. The first phase started in the 1950s, when excavation was carried out in Hastinapur. This excavation produced a number of new discoveries including, the famous Painted Gray Ware (PGW). The PGW

112　　*Muslim Political Discourse in Postcolonial India*

archaeology was used by the right wing Hindutva of the 1980s to justify its position on desecration of Hindu temples in medieval India. In fact, the conservation of these sites and the excavation for unknown sites became two contradictory processes. As a result, those non-controversial Indo-Islamic sites/monuments, which were not targeted by the Hindu rightists, also became symbols of a contested past.[15]

---

were the painted grey colour pottery which was dated by the archaeologist B. B. Lal to between c. 1000 BCE and c. 800 BCE. These discoveries, which were linked to the war of Mahabharata by some archaeologists, paved the way for a long debate on the nature of archaeological findings (Chakrabarti 2003: 12). The second phase of the tradition-based archaeology was started in the 1970s. Noted archaeologist H. D. Sankalia examined the issue of Ramayana. After detailed excavations, Sankalia concluded that some more evidences were required to link the story of Ramayana to present day Ayodhya. In fact, he suggested a multi-dimensional approach to study the archaeology of this religious text (Bhan 1997). In this period, S. P. Gupta and K. S. Ramachandran also attempted to examine different archaeological approaches to the story of Mahabharata (Gupta and Ramachandran 1976). In 1975 a nation-wide project on Ramayana sites led by B. B. Lal was started. This project also endorsed Sankalia's argument on the Ramayana story (Bhan 1997). The third phase of the tradition-based archaeological excavations began in the mid-1980s. By this time the Babri Masjid/Ram Temple site had become the focal point of such kind of excavations. Interestingly, this time the focus shifted from the Ramayana story to medieval India. Even people like B.B. Lal started taking a clear position in favour of the Ram temple (Shrimali 2003).

[15] There are three different Hindutva stands on the 'desecration of Hindu temples issue. P. N. Oak represents the first kind of *polemic soft Hindutva*. He describes almost all the Indo-Islamic historic sites as Hindu temples. Exploring some 'other' blunders of Indian historical research, he concludes that the Hindu contributions had been relegated to the margin in postcolonial India (Oak 1966). R. Nath takes a different *polite soft Hindutva* position. Using all the historical sources and archaeological evidences, he suggests that the Babri Masjid, like many other Hindu temples, was built after demolishing a Hindu temple. He proposes that the Muslims should give up their claims on Babri Mosque to avoid any kind of 'religious politics' (Nath 1991: 78). Sita Ram Goel and Koenraad Elst represent the *radical intellectual Hindutva* position. Goel's two volume book exclusively deals with the issue of temple desecration. Both the volumes revolve around the Babri Masjid–Ram temple site. These volumes focus on three issues: the listing of desecrated temples, Islamic iconoclasm in India and

Monumentalisation in Postcolonial India **113**

The rebuilding of the Somnath temple in the early 1950s can be a good example to elaborate this point. The Somnath Temple was actually situated in the Hindu majority princely state of Junagadh, which was ruled by a Muslim Nawab, Muhammad Mahabat Khanji in the late colonial period. On the eve of independence, the Nawab announced that his state would join Pakistan. However, due to changing political circumstances and local resistance led by the Congress party, the Nawab fled to Pakistan and state of Junagadh became a part of India. It was a significant merger. The Congressmen Sardar Patel and K. M. Munshi, who had been the active campaigners for the Hindu heritage in the Constituent Assembly, visited Junagadh in November 1947. In a public meeting, which was held on 13 November 1947 at the old Ahaliabai temple (which believed to be the old Somnath Temple) Patel announced that the Somnath temple would be rebuilt.[16] Although the Government of India did not extend any direct financial help to the Somnath rebuilding project, an official advisory committee was constituted in 1949 to provide technical support to the project. In fact, the Somnath Temple Trust was formed to collect money for the temple. The first serious objection to the project came from a section of archaeologists who argued that the ruins of old temple should not be demolished. Moreover, the ASI officially proposed that the old structure of the temple should be declared a protected historical monument because the building was more than a hundred years old and by the legal definition of a monument it could not be destroyed (Davis 1997: 214). Sardar Patel, the most powerful man after Nehru at that time, simply rejected this proposal. He argued that such technicalities should not be overemphasised as the construction of temple at this site 'was the question of Hindu faith and sentiments'.[17]

---

the Islamic theology. Koenraad Elst claims to offer an 'intellectual argument' in favour of the Ram Temple. Elst argues that the Muslim rulers destroyed Hindu temples and Buddhist shrines in medieval India purely for religious reasons (Elst 2002: 38).

[16] It is interesting to note that just after the announcement of Patel, the crowd started demolishing the old temple and the Muslim fakirs (beggars) who used to live around the temple were force to leave the site. The officials had to stop the crowd (Davis 1997: 213).

[17] On this question, Patel said: 'Hindu sentiment in regard to this temple is both strong and widespread. In the present condition, it is unlikely that,

114　　*Muslim Political Discourse in Postcolonial India*

K. M. Munshi, who was also a senior minister in the Nehru cabinet, suggested that the excavation could be carried out before demolishing the old structure and subsequently a new temple at Somnath should be rebuilt on the same site. This proposal was accepted and the excavation was conducted by the Archaeological Department of the government under the leadership of B. K. Thapar in November 1950. The excavation report supported the rightist Hindu argument that a temple was actually demolished by Mehmud of Ghazni.[18]

After this excavation the site was cleared and the actual construction of a new Somnath temple began. The temple was opened for the public after the ceremonial *linga* ritual. Dr. Rajendra Prasad, the President of India presided over this public ceremony. In the later years, a museum, which was called the Parbhas Patan Museum, was also established nearby the temple to display all the important archaeological discoveries (ibid.: 215). This example clearly shows that archaeological excavation, particularly those excavations which precisely looked at the Hindu epics/relevant Hindu religious places, directly or indirectly, provided a political space to Hindu rightists. Perhaps for that reason, the excavations at the Somnath site became a point of reference for the Hindu rightists, who demanded that similar kind of excavation should be carried out at the Babri Masjid site.

This discussion shows that the postcolonial legal-archaeological framework based on secularism of historical monuments reproduced the contested notion of an Indian Muslim architectural heritage. In fact, the existence of Indo-Islamic site has been recognised

---

that the sentiment will be satisfied by mere restoration of the temple or by prolonging its life. The restoration of idol would be a point of honor and sentiment with Hindu public' (Munshi 1965: 71).

[18] In the preface of his report of excavation, B. K. Thapar wrote: 'The story of Somnath . . . signifies the faith and reverence of the devout Hindu; it symbolises the racial instinct for survival; it amplifies the theory of creation, destruction and reconstruction and above all it represents the architectural development in Gujarat for over 900 years. A huge literature of fanciful stories developed soon after the victory of Sultan Mehmud whom it intended to glorify by extolling his real or supposed virtues. But, there are many gaps and incongruities. The picture has hitherto been both incomplete and synthetic. Excavation alone could provide material evidence and add precision to our knowledge' (Thapar 1965: 102).

Monumentalisation in Postcolonial India **115**

as the most disruptive phase of Indian history in this archaeological discourse. For that reason, the principles of neutrality adopted by the ASI to conserve Indian buildings as monuments of 'national importance' actually helped the rightist Hindu position.

II

THE SECULARISM OF MINORITY RIGHTS: MONUMENTALISATION AND THE RIGHT TO HERITAGE

I now move on to discuss the second form of secularism: the secularism of minority rights. Here, the state sticks to the principle of 'participatory neutrality' to celebrate the diversity of India without being associated with any particular faith. Theoretically, the state maintains equal distance from all religions; yet some special rights are given to religious and/or cultural minorities so that their cultures and languages could be preserved.[19]

Let us look at how this kind of secularism provides a right to heritage to Muslims of India. Article 26 of the Constitution of India provides freedom to religious minorities to manage their own religious affairs including, their religious places of worship.[20] Article 29(1) further elaborates the scope of this provision by establishing a link between religious affairs and right to culture. According to the Article, 'any section of the citizen residing in the territory of India or any part thereof having a distinct language, script or culture of its own shall have a right to conserve the same'.

Here, the term 'culture' is not specified and it is possible to infer that historically relevant places of worship could also be seen as culturally relevant objects. Thus, a possible reading of these constitutional provisions would suggest that Muslims as a religious minority have a right to preserve their own heritage in accordance with law. In other words, Muslims have a constitutional 'right to heritage'.

---

[19] Article 25(1) says: '[s]ubject to public order, morality and health, all persons are equally entitled to freedom of conscience and right freely to profess, practice and propagate religion'.

[20] Article 26 provides freedom to manage religious affairs, it says: (*a*) to establish and maintain institutions for religious and charitable purposes; (*b*) to manage its own affairs in matters of religion; (*c*) to own and acquire movable and immovable properties; and (*d*) to administer such a property in accordance with law.

116　　*Muslim Political Discourse in Postcolonial India*

There are two very clear legal manifestations of this right to heritage: the wakf laws and the laws related to the protection of religious places of worship. The different wakf laws ensure that Muslims in India could not only dedicate their movable and immovable properties for the pious and chartable acts recognised by Indian law but also underlines the constitutional guarantee that the Muslim community could manage their own religious places of worship on the basis of Islamic norms. In this sense, the 'act of dedication' is legally approved and the Muslim community enjoys a collective right to inherit wakf properties.[21] Since the state

---

[21] The formation of various Wakf boards in India is based on the application of Article 26 of the constitution. The subject relating to Wakf (charitable and religious endowments) are enlisted in the Concurrent List of the Seventh Schedule of the Constitution. The Wakf Act 1954 was the first comprehensive legal document that defined the structure of wakf administration in India. It provided powers to the central government to supervise the administration of wakf. In the states, the state government became responsible to take care of the wakf properties. The Wakf Act 1954 made provision for the establishment of Wakf boards, their functions, power and finances. The Act provides for the survey of Wakf properties, publication of lists of wakfs, registration of wakfs and the superintendence of all Wakfs. However, the issue of historical monuments was not explained by this Act. The Wakf Act 1954 underwent several amendments in 1959, 1964 and 1969 respectively. A comprehensive amendment bill was introduced in the Parliament in 1984 based on the recommendations of the Wakf Inquiry Committee (1976). However, due to some political reasons, the 1984 Act could not be enacted. In 1991, the government announced a package of law and welfare schemes for the development of minorities which led to the implementation of the Wakf Act 1995. The significant aspect of the Act was that it provided more power to the Board to smoothly administer the wakf in the country. However, like the 1954 Act it does not clarify the wakf status of the protected historical monuments. There are two important features of the management of wakfs in India. First, the Wakf is a minority institution where the state has the sole authority to make laws and supervise its functioning. In this sense the Wakf institution has become a government department. At the state level, the state government appoints a minister for handling Wakf issues. At the central level, Wakf comes under the Ministry of Social Justice and Empowerment. Second, the Wakf institution is the largest Islamic philanthropic institution in India. Unlike the other religious boards, the Wakf is not managed and

Monumentalisation in Postcolonial India 117

protected Indo-Islamic historic sites are also religiously identified wakf properties, the Muslim claims on these monuments, as we shall see later, are also linked to the right to heritage.[22]

The laws related to the protection of religious places of worship are the second very clear manifestation of right to heritage. The Indian Penal Code's (IPC) Chapter XV that provides protection to religious places of worship and the Protection of Religious Places of Worship Act 1991 could be cited as examples in this regard. The IPC Chapter XV is on the 'Offences Relating to Religion' (Sections 295 to 298). Section 295 says that *injuring or defiling place of worship with intent to insult the religion of any class is a punishable offence*. In various cases, the Supreme Court has identified this part of the IPC as the most legitimate legal protection given to the religious places of worship in India. Similarly the 1991 Act, which was passed by the Parliament just before the demolition of Babri Masjid in Ayodhya, establishes that the religious character of the religious places of worship existed on the 15th day of August, 1947 shall continue to be the same as it existed on that day [Sections 3, 4(1)]. Despite the fact that the Section 4(3a) of the 1991 Act clearly says that the provisions of this Act would not be applied to any state-protected historical monument, this Act along with the IPC, in principle, ensures that the protection of the Muslim places of worship is the responsibility of the state. In this sense, the Muslim right to heritage is protected.

The Muslim right to heritage based on secularism of minorities' rights is clearly contradictory to the neutral archaeological conservation based on the secularism of historical monuments. In fact, one finds a tension between these two types of secular initiatives, which further generates a number of legal ambiguities. To

---

controlled by the Muslim community. The state either nominates people in these institutions or they are elected by the Muslim elite (Members of Parliament [MPs], Members of Legislative Assemblies [MLAs], Members of the Bar Councils, etc.).

[22] It is to be noted here that Article 26 very clearly points out that the state could interfere in the secular activities associated with the wakf properties and this would not violate the minority rights guaranteed by the Constitution. In this sense the Wakf boards are supposed to manage the religious aspects of wakf properties.

Figure 3.3: Right to Heritage: A Legal Interpretation

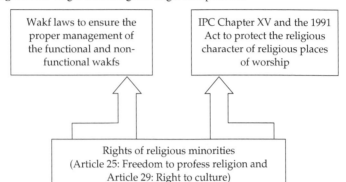

Source: Author.

find out various dimensions of this tension, let us look at the legal status of historical Muslim mosques in India and discuss three most pertinent questions:

(a) Can the state acquire any piece of land including places of worship under the Ancient Monuments and Archaeological Sites and Remains Act (1958)?
(b) What would be the nature of state's acquisition in case of a non-functional historical mosque? Would it lose its basic character as a mosque after being converted into a protected historical monument?
(c) Is it legally possible to worship in a protected historical monument?

Can the State Acquire Any Piece of Land Including Places of Worship under the 1958 Act?

As pointed out earlier, the 1958 Act makes provisions for the state to acquire any historical site/monument under the Land Acquisition Act 1894 for the protection and conservation as a monument of national importance. We have also seen that the concept of 'national importance' is not defined by any of these laws and public purpose and national importance are always to be defined by the ruling party or technically speaking, the central government. It raises another question: Is it legally possible for the state to acquire a

Monumentalisation in Postcolonial India **119**

functional/non-functional religious site? Or more specifically from our point of view: is it possible for the state to acquire a functional or non-functional Muslim mosque for the purpose of protecting it as a monument of national importance? This is a complicated matter because mosques come under the wakf laws and managing and controlling a place of worship comes under the fundamental rights guaranteed to the minorities by the constitution.

Let us first look at the legal status of a historical functional mosque in India, particularly in relation to the wakf laws. According to the Wakf Act 1995 Section 3(r) 'a Wakf means the permanent dedication by a person professing Islam, of any movable or immovable property for any purpose recognised by the Muslim Law as pious, religious or charitable'. There is a long list of charitable and pious purposes for which a valid and legal wakf can be created. However, donating land for mosques and/or Muslim graveyards are two most important religious purposes. Section 3(r) further identifies three kinds of wakf — the wakf by dedication, wakf by user and the family wakf or *wakf-al-ul-aulad*. For our purpose, the 'wakf by user' is an important category because it is directly related to historical mosques. It is recognised that where land has long been used for religious purposes, proof of express dedication is not necessary. In different court cases the wakf status of old mosques and graveyards has been upheld on the ground that wakf by user is a recognisable legal entity.[23] Thus, all the old historical functional mosques are wakf. Could wakf properties be legally acquired for the protection as national monuments? A simple reading of the 1958 Act suggests that the state, for the sake of 'public purpose', could acquire any piece of land including the wakf properties and/or a functional mosque. Furthermore, there could be two possibilities in such a situation:

(*a*) The state can acquire the functional mosque and declare it a protected monument and, as per the provisions of the 1958 Act, allow the religious activities inside it.

(*b*) The state can ask the owners/caretaker, in most of the cases, the wakf board, to enter into an agreement with the state. In this case, the responsibilities would be shared and the

---

[23] In this context two cases can be cited: *Mazhar Hussain v. Adiya Saran* (AIR 1948 P. C. 42) and *Mohd. Shah v. Fasisuddin* (AIR, 1956, SC 713).

120   *Muslim Political Discourse in Postcolonial India*

religious practices would continue inside the monument. The state would protect the architectural and/or historical importance and quite particularly take care of the conservation side. The owner/wakf board/local community will have much more say in the management.

Does this sort of acquisition affect the rights of religious minorities? Let us look at the first case in the context of minority rights. Article 26 has a wide scope and the issue of historical functional mosques also comes under its ambit. For instance the term 'religious affairs' covers a variety of activities including the management of functional religious sites and it simply contradicts the acquisition of any functional religious historical site under the 1958 Act. The Indian judiciary, however, has devised an interesting concept of 'essential practices' of religion to determine the limitations of religious institutions and the secular control of the state. The Supreme Court in various cases has observed that there is an essential part of religion that constitutes the core or the centre of the entire belief system.[24] According to the Supreme Court, this 'essential part of religion' has to be protected and the state can intervene in other 'non-essential religious activities'.[25] In the context of wakf laws, the court verdict in the *Khajamian Waqf Estate etc. v. the State of Madras and Another* (1971[2] SCR 791) is quite significant. In this case, it was held that Article 26(c) and (d) give power to the religious denominations to administer the property as per the laws. However, it does not mean that the property owned by the religious denomination could not be acquired by the state. This judgement very clearly shows that the 'management of the wakf' is not comprehended as an essential religious practice associated with Islam in India and thus any functional (in this case historical) mosque could be acquired by the state.[26] The difference between the

---

[24] In this context the two cases are very important: *Ratilal v. State of Bombay* (1954, SCR 1055), *Commissioner Hindu Religious Endowment v. Lakshmindra* (1954, SCR 1055).

[25] The court verdict in the *Saifuddin v. the State of Bombay* case (AIR 1962, SC 853, 864) could be cited in this regard.

[26] It is also important to clarify the legal status of Muslim Personal Laws in India. Tahir Mehmood's well researched study on Muslim Personal Law shows that the personal laws do not enjoy any special status and the

Monumentalisation in Postcolonial India 121

essential religious practices and the other non-essential religious practices may be understood as a workable legal formula. However, it raises an important question related to the secular nature of Indian judiciary. How could a secular judiciary based on rational principles determine the 'essential practices' and non-essential practices of a religion? (Dhavan 2001). In the next two chapters I shall look at such questions and try to find out how such issues produce burning political controversies. Suffice to say at the moment that legally it is possible for the state to acquire any functional religious place of worship including the functional historical mosques under the 1958 Act and, as the earlier discussion has shown, this acquisition would not be understood as a violation of the minority rights.

The Nature of the State's Acquisition of a Non-Functional Historical Mosque as a Protected Monument

The state's acquisition of a non-functional mosque for converting it into a historical monument could also be linked to the legal positions on the question of 'adverse possession of a mosque'. Technically speaking, in a legal context if a mosque is not used by the Muslims for offering prayers and is under the occupation of a non-Muslim individual/institution, it would be called an adverse possession. The state's possession of non-functional mosques as historical monument is an important question in this regard.

The three important cases related to the status of a mosque are the Shahid Ganj mosque, the Abdul Aziz and the Ismail Faruqui cases, respectively. The first case, which we have already discussed in the previous chapter, was decided by the colonial judiciary on the basis of the principle of strict neutrality and from the perspective of the Limitation Act.[27] This case laid down a legal precedent that if a mosque is adversely possessed by any other group for a period of time, its sacred character would be lost and therefore it cannot

---

legislative powers of the state can scrutinise any set of laws including the personal laws of various communities (Mehmood 1977: 103).

[27] Under the Limitation Acts the title of the true owner would be extinguished if the properties are in adverse possession for twelve or more years. After the partition of India, several wakf properties were adversely possessed by others. It was decided that the provisions of the Limitation Act would not be applicable in the suits filed for the possession of wakf property (Qureshi 1990: 365).

122   *Muslim Political Discourse in Postcolonial India*

be recognised as a mosque. The second case does not approve this precedent. In the *N. R. Abdul Azeez v. E. Sundaresa Chettiar* case (AIR 1993, Madras 169), the Madras High Court held that 'a mosque once so consecrated cannot in any case revert to the founder and every Muslim has a legal right to enter into it and perform Namaz … no Muslim can be denied the right to offer prayers on the ground that the mosque fell into disuse long back. Therefore when the dilapidated structure was proved to be an old mosque, it became a waqf by use' (Ahmad 2000: 262). Obviously, this judgement could have far reaching implications for other historical sites. However, the famous Ayodhya case (*Dr. Ismail Faruqui v. Union of India* [AIR 1994, SC 605]) endorsed the Shahid Ganj mosque case and upheld that if a mosque is adversely possessed by non-Muslims, its sacred character would be lost. This was an important judgement and several pages were devoted to argue that a mosque in India could be acquired by the state. If we come back to the question of non-functional historical mosques, this judgement seems to suggest that the acquisition of non-functional mosque under the 1958 Act does not violate the minority rights given to the Muslims in India. However, the laws and various judgements do not answer a very basic issue in this context: What will be the nature of state's possession of a non-functional mosque? Or in other words, could it be understood as an adverse possession? The 1958 Act does not talk about the status of a non-functional historical place of worship. All the provisions are related to the functional sites and it is assumed that the non-functional religious sites are 'dead' historical monuments. If the 1994 judgement is re-read in the context of 1958 Act, could it be possible to say that the non-functional mosque declared as a protected monument will lose its sacred character and therefore it cannot be recognised as a mosque? Again it is an unanswered question, which requires a more political and sociological explanation because in each case, there was a political context that determined the judicial decisions.

The discussion on the nature of the state's possession cannot be completed without mentioning the Places of Worship (Special Provisions) Act, 1991. As we pointed out earlier this Act is not applicable to the declared historical monuments, and thus, the state's possession of a religious place, particularly of a non-functional religious place, and its status as a dead historical monument cannot be questioned. Legally it is not possible to restart religious worship

Monumentalisation in Postcolonial India **123**

in a non-functional site. And more specifically, the state control cannot be challenged. However, in some particular cases, the state has allowed religious practices in non-functional sites. Yet, it has always been a political issue.

Let us once again place this question in the context of minority rights. Could the state's possession of a non-functional mosque be seen as a violation of minority rights? The Muslim agitation for the protection of Urdu language in the 1950s and 1960s was directly linked to Article 29. But, the connection between Article 29 of the Constitution of India and the Muslim demand to offer prayer in a mosque protected as a national monument is a much more complex issue. It can simply be construed from the discussion so far that the notion of national importance and the right of the state to protect any historical site as national monument for the 'public purpose' can override the commitment shown in this Article.

Right to Worship in a Historical Monument

The right to worship in a functional religious site protected as a monument of national importance and managed exclusively by the state is different from those religious sites where the responsibilities of the management are jointly shared by the state and the religious bodies. In the state-protected religious site, the state has powers to determine which part of the monument would be used for religious observance and decide the timings of these religious practices. In the latter case, the management boards enjoy relatively more powers to decide the nature and timings of the religious practices.[28] The right to worship in both the cases in a protected monument can be seen in the context of the notion of national importance. It is true that the state permits the followers of the concerned religion to perform religious activities inside a monument. But, these activities, in any case, put some sort of legal restriction. The technical requirements of conservation and the national significance of the site determine the limits of religious activities.

The date of notification is considered to be the most important determining factor related to the religious character of a monument. Under the 1958 Act, the state would protect the declared site

---

[28] In this context the Ancient Monuments and Archaeological Sites and Remains Rules 1959 can be cited. Particularly, Rule 3 and 7(2), which talk about access to a protected monument.

124   *Muslim Political Discourse in Postcolonial India*

as well as the religious practices from the very date of notification. If no religious practice was going on the day of notification, the state is bound to protect only the site, not its religious character. This aspect has also raised a number of issues. In some cases, when the monument was not in use on the date of notification, the state simply denied access for any religious observance. In some other incidents, only one particular activity was allowed and people were not given permission to perform other related rituals. Sultan Ghari ka Makbara in New Delhi is a very good example where one can go to the basement of the site and perform rituals but in the adjacent mosque, prayer is not allowed!

This issue is also linked to the right of access to a historical monument. Section 18 of the 1958 Act assures that 'subject to any rule made under this Act, the public shall have a right to access to a historical monument'. It should be noted that this right is granted only for secular activities. Legally, no one can enter or perform religious activities in a declared monument without the permission of the ASI. Thus, the legal control and ambiguities related to the access to a monument gives rise to political mobilisation. Let us look at Figure 3.4 to further illustrate these unsolved legal issues.

This discussion shows that the tension between the secularism of historical monuments and the secularism of minority rights produces a number of legal ambiguities.[29] Unlike colonial India

---

[29] In recent years the policy discourse has changed quite significantly. The secularism of minority rights is seen in a wider sense to find out amicable solution to the question of right to worship in a protected historical monument. More specifically, the problems associated with the conservation of Indo-Islamic historic architecture — functional as well as non-functional are seen in the light of wakf laws. For example, the Joint Parliamentary Committee on the Working of Wakf Boards, 2003 (JPC) in its seventh report, very clearly talks about those mosques, which are under the control of ASI. Section 3.6 of report notes: 'the Sub-Committee was given to understand that some properties which are of the nature of Wakf (such as mosques) are under the control of Archaeological Survey of India. The Committee recommends that Government should consider taking back the protection and maintenance of these properties from the Archaeological Survey of India and pass on the control of these properties to the proposed Wakf Board (JPC: 2003). The Sachar Committee — the Prime Minister's High Level Committee on Social Economic and Educational Status of Muslims in India (PMHLC 2006) — which was set up to collect data/

Figure 3.4: Secularism(s) Compared and a Few Unsolved Issues

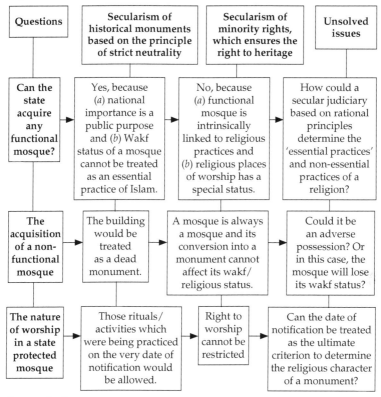

Source: Author.

---

information of the status of social and economic status of India's Muslims, is more specific about the question of those Indo-Islamic buildings — mostly non-functional — which are under the control of ASI. In one of its recommendations the report points out: 'the Ancient Monuments and Archaeological Sites and Remains Act 1958 has often at cross purposes with the Wakf Act. Very often the former has an overriding effect. There are innumerable cases where the wakf properties despite being a place of worship and religious reverence, cannot be touched by the Wakf Board because it is declared as protected monument. Given the present state of large number of wakf properties under the control of ASI, it would be proper if their list are annually reviewed and their condition is assessed in a joint meeting of senior officers of the ASI with representatives of the Central Wakf Council (Prime Minister's High Level Committee 2006: 232).

126 *Muslim Political Discourse in Postcolonial India*

where the principle of strict neutrality did not provide any space to political actors to make use of protected monuments as political sites, the postcolonial legal archaeological framework has offered immense possibilities to the state as well as various political groups, particularly the Muslim groups to articulate their political agendas around these 'monuments'.[30] But, how do Muslim leaders/ groups use these legal ambiguities and the conservation policies for political campaigns? And/or what kinds of political strategies do they use for mobilising Muslims? To answer these questions let us look at the nature of Muslim political demands in postcolonial India and the various ways by which the right to heritage has been asserted.

III

The Secularism of Minority Rights and the Muslim Politics of Protection (1950–70)

The north Indian Muslims as a religiously identifiable community had a strong political presence in colonial India. However the political strength of this 'Muslim community' decreased quite significantly in the aftermath of the Partition, when a sizeable number of educationally dominant and economically powerful Muslim individuals and families migrated to Pakistan.[31] The large scale communal violence in major cities and the aggressive Hindu politics further affected the position of Muslims. In fact, Muslims were blamed for the partition of the country and their 'loyalty' became a serious issue of public discourse (Hasan 1997: Chapter 5).

The Muslim elites of the 1950s had a very little political space to assert the actual grievances and problems of north Indian

---

[30] For an elaborated discussion of this point, see Ahmed (2013).

[31] Interestingly this has been the dominant view about post-Partition Muslims. Azad, for instance, writes: 'The only result of the creation of Pakistan was to weaken the position of the Muslims in the subcontinent of India. The 45 million Muslims who have remained in India have been weakened. On the other hand, there is as yet no indication that a strong and efficient government can be established in Pakistan. If one judges the question only from the point of view of the Muslim community, can anybody deny today that Pakistan has been for them a very unfortunate and unhappy development?' (Azad 1988: 247–48)

Muslims.[32] They had to find out new modes by which such grievances could be transformed into political demands. In this sense, it was crucial for them to understand the nature of the emerging political set up and the possibilities of political alliances with other social groups. In the backdrop of this political context, the Muslim politicians particularly those who were associated with the Congress, decided to mobilise Muslim leaders and intellectuals to assess the emerging political configurations.[33] In order to concretise these efforts, a few major conferences: the All India Azad Muslim Conference (September 1947), the All India Muslim Conference (December 1947, Lucknow) and the All India Muslim Convention (May 1951, Delhi) were organised in a very short span of time. These meetings not only expressed confidence in the policies of Nehru

---

[32] There is an interesting 'Muslim adjustment thesis' which is often evoked to explain the post-Partition Muslim situation. We are informed about various plans of the British government to solve the political stalemate in India in the mid-1940s; then the focus shifted to the Constituent Assembly debates, minority rights and nature of electorates in independent India; finally, in the backdrop of the partition and mass exodus of Muslims to Pakistan, this standard narrative concludes with a few 'touching' and overtly *secular* quotes taken from the famous speeches delivered by Nehru and Azad to show how and why Muslims in India 'adjusted and accommodated' after the Partition! Surprisingly, the Muslim cultural/religious heterogeneity, which constitutes the basic core of this argument, is never expanded, at least analytically, to make sense of the plurality of Muslim political responses in the 1950s. As a result, two obvious concerns: the relationship between Muslim leaders and Muslim communities and the placing of the so-called 'communal Muslim leaders' in the institutional apparatus of the postcolonial state do not get any academic attention. One finds various shades of this thesis in the writings of Mushirul Hasan (1997), A. G. Noorani (2003) and Moin Shakir (1981). My attempt here is to underline the specificity of the postcolonial Muslim politics in north India.

[33] We have to remember that the evolution of the idea of India in actual 'federal' sense — the merger of various princely states in the Indian union and subsequent reorganisation of states in 1956 — contributes significantly to the discursive make-up of a multilayered Muslim politics.
The Muslim League in Kerala and All India Intehadul Muslimeem (AIIM) in Hyderabad are two relevant examples in this regard. The north-Indian Muslim political discourse, therefore, should be seen in relation to this larger picture (see, Wright Jr. 1966; Smith 1950).

128   *Muslim Political Discourse in Postcolonial India*

government but also called upon tall the Muslim organisations to give up political activities of all kinds. It was argued that the Indian Muslims should join secular political parties as legitimate citizens for the protection of their constitutional rights (Noorani 1974). Interestingly, the controversial issues such as rebuilding of the Somnath temple, the tradition-based archaeological excavations, and the Babri Masjid issue were deliberately ignored. In fact, when the Babri Masjid issue was raised in the 1951 convention, Maulana Azad and Syed Mehmud, the most prominent Muslim leaders of that time, advised local Muslims to focus only on the legal aspect of the case and avoid all types of confrontations (Khan K. A. W. 2004, Int.; Sambhali 2005, Int.). In addition, a serious discussion took place on the changing structure of the state and the given legal-constitutional rights. The educational development and the protection of cultural identity were identified as the main concerns of Muslims in India (Khan 2004, Int.). More significantly, these conferences, in a way as it seems, led to a different kind of political discourse, which revolves around three constitutive norms of Muslim politics.[34]

(*a*) The strict adherence to the legal-constitutional discourse of rights/secularism.
(*b*) The propagation of Muslim culture and history as a contribution to Indian civilisation.
(*c*) The emphasis on Muslim unity and collective political action.

These norms were compatible with the legal-constitutional framework of rights and capable of dealing with the emerging political configuration in north India. To elaborate this point let us now look at how these norms were intellectually worked out to articulate Muslim political claims in this period.

(*a*) *The strict adherence to the legal-constitutional discourse of rights/ secularism*: Following this norm, the 'Muslim' political

---

[34] It would be completely wrong to assume that these norms actually govern the forms, ideas and agendas of Muslim political groups. Therefore, it is important to look at these norms as constitutive elements of what could be called *postcolonial Muslim political discourse*.

Monumentalisation in Postcolonial India **129**

demands of this period — protection of Urdu as a language of Muslims and symbol of Muslim heritage, the protection of the minority character of the Aligarh Muslim University, equal employment opportunities for Muslims and the protection of the life and properties of Muslims in communal riots — were defined in purely legal-constitutional terms.[35] Moreover, the protection of wakf properties and the places of worship were also linked to minority rights and it was demanded that the state should introduce a law to protect Muslim Wakf. In this connection, the enactment of the Wakf Act 1954, which paved the way for the formation of various wakf boards in the country and which provided a legal protection to Muslim wakf properties, was a significant outcome of this political norm.

(b) *The propagation of Muslim culture and history as a contribution to Indian civilisation:* Following this norm, the Muslim leaders and intellectuals started focusing on the historical contribution of Muslims as an assertion of Muslim identity.[36]

---

[35] Brass's study on Urdu movement can be cited as a good example here. Brass also shows the wider connection between these demands and the assertion of Muslim identity in UP (Brass 1974). However, it is important to elaborate the Aligarh issue. In 1920 the British government passed the Aligarh Muslim University Act (AMU), which actually transformed the existing MAO College into a university. However, in 1951, the Indian Parliament amended the AMU Act 1920 and made a few new provisions. In fact, the requirement that only a Muslim could be the member of University Court was abolished, the statutory right of the university to always have a Muslim vice chancellor was taken away, the President of India was made the visitor for the university and the Governor of Uttar Pradesh, was appointed as its chief rector. As a result, the supervisory role was taken away from the Muslims and the management of the AMU was converted 'secularised'. For the Muslim elite, who wanted to focus on areas of education and protection of culture, it was a serious blow (Khan 2006).

[36] In November 1947, just after three months of Partition, Maulana Abul Kalam Azad, delivered a very emotional speech at Jama Masjid. He said: It is nothing new for me to address a vast crowd in the historic mosque built by Shah Jahan ... Behold the minarets of this mosque bend down to ask you where you have mislaid the pages of your history! It was yesterday that your caravan alighted on the banks of Jamuna ... how is it that you are afraid of living here today in this Delhi which has been nurtured by

130   *Muslim Political Discourse in Postcolonial India*

Maulana Syed Abul Hasan Ali Nadwi's book *Muslims in India* is the best example to show how historical contribution was defined in purely political terms. In fact, this was one of the very early intellectual attempts to conceptualise the idea of 'Islamic heritage' of Indian Muslim community.[37] The book analysed the Muslim contribution and linked it to the rights of Muslims in postcolonial India. The book offered an interesting response to the Hindu rightist attack on medieval Indian Islam. Nadwi argued that Islam did not come to India to destroy Hinduism. On the contrary, Muslim preachers and saints brought Islam with the message of love. He claimed that Muslims recognised India as their motherland and established great empires.[38] The Muslim contribution was also defined as a kind of cultural development of Indian civilisation.[39] Nadwi suggested that the Muslims

---

your blood' (cf. Gandhi 1990: 248–49). This speech clearly suggests that 'historical contribution' had acquired a political importance to mobilise Muslims.

[37] This book has a very interesting story. Maulana Nadwi was invited by the All India Radio in 1951 for a series of talks in Arabic on the issues and contribution of Indian Muslims. These talks were published as papers in the Arabic journal *Al-Muslimun*. In late 1950s these essays were given a shape of a book and translated into Urdu by Syed Mehmudul Hasan Nadwi in 1976. The impact of this book could be identified by the fact that it was taken very seriously by almost all the commentators and researchers in the 1960s and 1970s. I am using the official English version of the book because of it was recognised as the authoritative translation by the author himself.

[38] In the preface of the book, Nadwi quite openly expresses this view. He writes: 'there is afoot a campaign to present the history of our land in a manner as if the Muslim era was an era of foreign imperialistic domination' (Nadwi 1976: 3). In this sense, he claims to present the 'real' history of Muslim period. Arguing against the forced Islamic conversion debate, Nadwi points out that Muslim saints and preachers came to India basically for spreading the message of Islam. Similarly, in his opinion, the Muslim rulers invaded India for establishing great empires.

[39] Nadwi writes: '[w]hen Muslims had set foot on the Indian soil, there were the ancient sciences and philosophy and an abundance of food and raw materials, but, culturally, India had lapsed from the civilised world for a long time' (1976: 7). This lack of contact with the outside world was responsible for the cultural degradation of India. He further writes:

Monumentalisation in Postcolonial India **131**

rediscovered the ancient sciences and philosophy of India and introduced it to the wider world. In the final part of this book Nadwi tried to link the glorious Muslim past to the present problems of Indian Muslims. Describing the unjust and partial system of education, the decline of Urdu and other socio-economic issues related to Indian Muslims in post-independent India, Nadwi quite implicitly questioned the state policies. He forcefully asserted that *'Muslims are not only citizen of an equal status with anybody in India; they are among its chief builders and architects, and hold position second to none among the people of the world for selfless service to the motherland'* (emphasis added, Nadwi 1976: 5).

(c) *The Muslim unity and collective political action:* The question of Muslim unity has been an important political norm. This norm was used to define the collective political existence of a single Muslim community. In fact, we find two very clear manifestations of this norm. First, the Muslim organisations and leaders decided to organise themselves as a communal vote bank in order to use the combined electoral strength to bargain with the political parties (Ahmad 1974). The second clear manifestation of this norm was to establish the organisational unity among Muslim groups. The formation of the All India Muslim Majlis-e-Mushawarat (AIMMM) — an umbrella organisation that was set up by the Muslim Leaders' Consultative Convention held on 8–9 August 1964 in Lucknow was a good example in this regard. The purpose of the AIMMM was to provide a platform for different Muslim groups and represent the collective Muslim concerns at the national level. Moreover, the notion of peaceful coexistence of different communities was also highlighted by the AIMMM in order to define the Muslim issues as national issues. However, despite this unequivocal stand, the AIMMM was always

---

'[t]hey (Muslims) brought with them to India a new, practical and highly rationalistic religion, mature knowledge, a progressive culture and an evolved civilisation which included within it all that was best in the cultural stock of many nations — it represented a synthesis of the natural wholesomeness of the Arab disposition' (ibid.: 9).

132   *Muslim Political Discourse in Postcolonial India*

seen as a Muslim separatist body, even in the early 1960s.[40] (Sambhali 2005, Int.)

These political norms clearly stem from a creative interpretation of secularism of minority rights and the Nehruvian policy on religious minorities. For example, the adherence to a legal-constitutional discourse of rights provided a legal sanction to Muslim groups to assert their claims in a highly hostile post-Partition environment. This approach also helped to answer the Hindu rightist attack on Muslim 'loyalty'. The Muslim culture and heritage as a contribution thesis simply corresponded to the dominant secular discourse of Indian heritage, which defined India as a melting pot of various civilisations. At the same time, this thesis laid the foundation of the idea of a royal Muslim past, which as a 'constructed memory' was evoked to mobilise Muslims in the later period. Finally, the emphasis on Muslim unity helped the Muslim groups to play an important role in the electoral arithmetic. Since there was no separate electorate system in practice in India, this norm was useful in combining the political strength of Muslims as a pressure group. However, this was not a radical politics of any kind. All the major Muslim organisations in north India, despite severe ideological and political differences, were interested in protecting Muslim identity and consolidating the educational and political power of the community. For that reason, the institutional apparatus of the state was seen as the basic point of reference for all kinds of political actions.

---

[40] The organisations like the Jamaat–e-Islami, Jamiat Ulama-i-Hind and Nadwatul Ulama and individuals like Dr Syed Mehumud, Maulana Madni, Maulana Nadwi and Maulana Manzoor Nomani played a significant role in the formation of AIMMM. The AIMMM also demanded that the Muslim culture and identity should be protected. Interestingly, unlike the 1950, when the Wakf Act 1954 was seen as a kind of legal assurance by the Muslim leaders, the AIMMM in 1965 asserted that the state should give more powers to the Muslims in the management related issues of wakf (Shakir 1972: 57–58). It was a significant change. The wakf properties, particularly in the Punjab region, were occupied by the non-Muslims as well as by the state. Since the government had control over the wakf boards, it was demanded that more Muslim members should be nominated in the boards so that the wakf institutions could work for the welfare of Muslims in the real sense of the term.

Monumentalisation in Postcolonial India **133**

IV

RIGHT TO HERITAGE VERSUS SECULARISM OF HISTORICAL MONUMENTS: THE MUSLIM POLITICS OF AGITATION (1970–92)

The 1971 war with Pakistan and the creation of Bangladesh as an independent country significantly affected the Indian Muslim political discourse. The formation of the All India Muslim Personal Law Board (AIMPLB) on 7 April 1973 at Hyderabad was the first politically organised attempt in the 1970s.[41] The main objective of the AIMBLB was to safeguard the Muslim Personal Law (laws relating to marriage, inheritance, etc., based on the Islamic Shari'ah). Interestingly, unlike the defensive approach of the 1950s and 1960s, the AIMPLB adopted a very strong language against the policies of the state.[42]

The AIMPLB experiment was followed by several radical moves of this kind. For example, in 1975, Imam Abdullah Bukhari openly refuted the authority of the Delhi Wakf Board and the ASI over the Jama Masjid and after a series of riots, established a new management committee. Similarly, a number of local level Muslim organisations were established in the early 1980s to reinstate prayers in the non-functional historic mosques. Even a memorandum was submitted by the AIMMM to the union government to open all protected mosques for prayer in 1984. And finally, a grand Muslim political coalition was formed to restore the religious status of the Babri Masjid! These developments not only underline a very significant change in the overtone of Muslim politics but also show that the secularism of historical monuments has been questioned by the Muslim political groups during this period in a significant way.

Let us concentrate on three crucial events: (*a*) the 'agreement' between the AIMMM and the government to open all the protected mosques for prayers; (*b*) the introduction of a bill in the Parliament to amend the relevant sections of the 1958 Act; and (*c*) the forma-

---

[41] The scope of the AIMPLB's activities is much wider. Apart from the protection of Shari'ah, it also campaigns for the protection of wakf and the illegal acquisition of Islamic mosques (Mujjaddai 1993: 18).

[42] In its very first resolution, the AIMPLB directly opposed Article 44 and clearly stated that the anti-Muslims laws would not be accepted by the Board see The Constitution of AIMPLB, Resolution 1 & 2.

134   *Muslim Political Discourse in Postcolonial India*

tion of a few local Muslim organisations in Delhi to elaborate this interesting political shift.

The Agreement to Restore the Religious Status of Protected Monuments

In 1984, the AIMMM formally submitted a memorandum to the central government for allowing Muslims to offer prayers in those mosques which were being protected by the ASI and other state departments as the protected monuments in India. According to the documents published by the AIMMM, a meeting between the AIMMM delegation led by its President Syed Shahabuddin and the Government of India took place on 1 March 1984. P. V. Narasimha Rao represented the Prime Minister of India along with two other central government ministers. Several Members of Parliament (MPs) also attended this high profile meeting. According to Shahabuddin, the government in principle accepted the Muslim demand to offer prayer in all the protected historical mosques (Shahabuddin 2004, Int.). Syed Shahabuddin, in a letter sent to the Prime Minister in 1987, gives out the details of this agreement. There were five points in the agreement:

(a) In principle there shall be Namaz in all the protected mosques everywhere.

(b) Casual prayers by Muslim tourists and visitors shall be permitted.

(c) Congregational prayers whether Id, Friday or daily shall be permitted if there is local demand and there is no alternative, if mosque is located in a Muslim area, provided it does not call for any amenities or facilities which will require any structural change which would affect the architectural or historical character of the mosque. Such request as and when received shall be considered sympathetically.

(d) As far as possible, the Department of Archaeology shall post Muslim attendants to look after the protected mosques.

(e) The Department shall allocate adequate funds for the maintenance and repairs of protected mosques (Shahabuddin 1987b: 500).

It is interesting to note that following this agreement the Safdarjang Tomb mosque was opened for Friday prayer on 2 March

1984. However, the government did not publish the minutes of this meeting and started ignoring the reminders sent by AIMMM to the Prime Minister and other government departments. Syed Shahabuddin, who happened to be a Member of Parliament in 1988, raised this issue in the Rajya Sabha and demanded an official reply. Finally, in March 1988, almost four years after this so-called agreement, the government of India spelled out its policy on non-functional mosques. In a letter written by L. P. Shahi, on behalf of the Government of India, argued:

> [t]he policy of being followed by the Government has the primary consideration of safeguarding the interests of the ancient and historical monuments which form our prized cultural heritage. . . . Government has not imposed any restriction prohibiting on (sic) offering prayer in protected mosque. The ancient and historical monuments under protection include both living (in religious use) and non-living (not in religious use) mosque, temples, churches, stupas, etc. In protected monuments which are in religious use customary and recognised religious practices already in vogue, are allowed . . . So far as the monuments which are not in religious use are concerned, offering of prayers or worship is not permitted. The policy of the government . . . is not to allow revival of worship at protected monuments which were not in use at the time of protection or where such a use discontinued since long . . . Any concession in regard to revival of religious use at one monument would lead to a movement of revival of worship/prayer at other protected monuments by other communities like Hindus, Buddhists and Jains, etc. . . . As per the Rule 7 of the Ancient Monuments and Archaeological Sites and Remains Rules, 1959 no protected monument can be used for purposes of holding any meeting, reception, party conference, or entertainment except under and in accordance with a permission in writing granted by the central government. Rule 8 (f) of the said Rules further prohibits violation of any practice; usage or custom applicable to or observed in the monument (sic). Any use of a protected monument which is not authorised or is not prevalent is a misuse. The matter regarding revival of worship in a non-living monument came before the High Court of Mysore . . . In the judgement . . . Mr. Justice M. Santosh held that offering of prayers in a long living mosque was a violation of usage under Rule 8 (f) . . . In the interests of conserving our national heritage, the ancient and historical monuments are preserved for the benefit of all, rather allowing worship considering the interests of a particular community (MID 65: 207).

136   *Muslim Political Discourse in Postcolonial India*

This letter simply underlines the fact that the postcolonial state followed the policy of strict neutrality and did not consider the rights to heritage given by the Constitution of India. Even the idea of national heritage is defined in neutral terms by ignoring the religious beliefs of people. Interestingly, the religious practices are described as 'violation of rules'. This aspect shows that the postcolonial legal-archaeological mechanism virtually failed to produce a viable socially sensitive cultural policy on historical monuments. Moreover, this rigid policy stand was justified in a highly unprofessional way by ignoring the 1984 agreement. Consequently, the tension between the right to heritage and secularism of historical monuments was further substantiated.

Amendment in the 1958 Act

Syed Shahabuddin presented a bill (Bill 31 of 1987) in the Parliament in 1987 to amend the Ancient Monuments and Archaeological Sites and Remains Act (1958). In the 'Statement of Objects and Reasons' to this bill, he points out that a number of non-functional religious places of worship, which are being protected by the ASI are not only misused but also desecrated. He notes: '[s]ince the very purpose of the construction of such places of worship was religious observance, in principle, freedom of religion and worship must be guaranteed' (Shahabuddin 1987c: 309). Criticising the policy of the government, Shahabuddin further argues: '[i]t is being obstructed by the Department of Archaeology on the ground that at the time of notification they were not in active service. This is a mistaken view which has caused unnecessary controversy ... many such places of worship because of paucity of resources are not receiving much care. In fact, visitors enter them with their shoes on and sometimes they even become dens for anti-social or frivolous activities which detract from sacred character of the premises' (ibid.: 309).

This proposed bill suggested that two new sub-sections (4A and 6) could be inserted in the 1958 Act. The proposed sub-section (4a) stated:

> [n]othing in this section shall detract the Director General from his duty and responsibility to protect the sanctity of a place of worship declared to be a protected monument and for the time being placed under his guardianship and to regulate accordingly access by the public, or its care and maintenance by the staff (ibid.)

Monumentalisation in Postcolonial India **137**

Furthermore, the new modified Section 6 was added, which pointed out:

> [n]othing in this section shall affect the freedom of worship or bar resumption of religious observance therein at the request of the members of the religious community living within one kilometre radius of the monument; provided that such observance does not entail any construction alteration which could affect the architectural, historical or aesthetical character or the value of the monument (ibid.).

Broadly, these two Subsections stem from the so-called agreement with the central government on protected monuments in 1984. This bill did not become a law. However, it underlined the limitation of the 1958 Act, particularly in relation to the non-functional religious places of worship.

The Masjid Basao Committee

Let us look at a few grassroots examples. In December 1978, a group of young Muslims from old Delhi found one mosque like structure near the Income Tax Office (ITO), New Delhi. They went in this 'mosque' and offered prayer. However, next time when they tried to enter into this 'mosque' they were arrested by the police and later released on bail (Sadar 2004, Int.). However, this incident provoked a section of Muslims of old Delhi to form an organisation, *Masjid Basao Committee* (Mosque Rehabilitation Committee or MBC). The MBC was primarily concerned with those mosques, which were non-functional or had been encroached by non-Muslims (and Muslims as well) in different parts of Delhi. The MBC also tried to contact Delhi Wakf Board but did not get any official support from them.

Initially the MBC focused on two mosques: the ITO mosque which later became the Bhuri Bhatiyari Masjid and the Safdarjang Tomb mosque. Although the Imam of Jama Masjid who became an important political leader in post-1975 period supported this organisation as patron for some time, the established Muslim bodies such as the AIMMM and the AIMPLB, did not offer any kind of institutional help to these grassroots initiatives (Sadar 2004, Int.).

After several court cases of rioting and illegal trespassing against the leader of this agitation Aminuddin Sadar, the prayers were restored in the Bhuri Bhatiyari Masjid with the help of local

138   *Muslim Political Discourse in Postcolonial India*

people. An Imam was appointed for five time prayer. A Madarsa for Muslim children was also established later. This mosque is still in use.

On the other hand, the movement to 'liberate' the Safdarjang tomb mosque took an interesting turn. A close aide of Imam Bukhari, Nawabuddin Naqshbandi, who later became a core member of the All India Babri Masjid Action Committee, established his dominance over this agitation.

It is important to note that the nature of the Safadarjang tomb mosque was case actually quite different from the Bhuri Bhatiyari mosque. It was a protected monument and the ASI had a regional office in the premises of this building. In addition, this mosque was listed in the memorandum submitted by the AIMMM to the government. In this sense, the AIMMM was also a Muslim stakeholder in this case. Interestingly there was no coordination between the AIMMM and MBC. Even the AIMMM was not in favour of the MBC's campaign.[43]

Following the 'agreement' between the AIMMM and the government, the Safdarjang Tomb mosque was opened for the Friday prayer on 2 March 1984. The members of AIMMM and the MBC offered prayer in this mosque. However, their differences became obvious on the same day. After the Friday prayer, when the ASI official decided to close the mosque, Nawabuddin Naqshbandi insisted that he along with his supporters should be allowed to offer regular five times prayers in this mosque (Naqshbandi, 2004, Int.). The ASI did not oblige him and the AIMMM disassociated itself from this demand. However, Nawabuddin Naqshabandi did not stop here. He continued this agitation and after a year declared himself as the Shahi Imam of the Safdarjang mosque! This mosque opens only on Fridays and Naqshbandi still leads the Friday prayer as its Shahi Imam.

These three incidents suggest that the nature of collective Muslim politics changed quite significantly in the 1970s in two ways. First, the notion of 'Muslim heritage', particularly the control over the Indo-Islamic historic sites, emerged as one of the most fundamental Muslim political demand, which actually overshadowed the

---

[43] According to Syed Shahabuddin the MBC actually sabotaged the AIMMM's movement for the restoration of all protected mosques (Shahabuddin 2004, Int.).

Monumentalisation in Postcolonial India 139

other conventional Muslim political issues such as the protection of Urdu and the Muslim personal law. Second, to accommodate this radical approach and to provide justification to radical political moves, the established political norms of the 1950s and 1960s were redefined. For instance, the adherence to the legal-constitutional framework of rights was re-conceptualised to expand the scope of right to worship. Similarly, the Muslim contribution thesis was redefined to assert the idea of a royal Muslim past. In the same way, the bargain with political parties for 'Muslim votes' in the name of 'Muslim unity' paved the way for a new kind of 'Fatwa politics'. I shall discuss these issues in the next two chapters.

■

4

Jama Masjid and the Political Memory of a Royal Muslim Past

The Jama Masjid of Delhi has three huge gates, an architectural feature generally associated with most of the Mughal mosques in India. However, unlike the entrances of other historic mosques, these three gates not only symbolise the historic character of the Jama Masjid as one of the biggest mosques of Asia, but also point towards its controversial status as the 'epicenter' of postcolonial Indian Muslim politics. These three gates bear three different names, introduce us to three different institutions as the caretakers of the mosque and most importantly, disseminate three very different 'histories' of the Jama Masjid![1]

The eastern gate, *Bab-e-Shahjahan*, facing the Red Fort is popularly known as *Shahi Darwaza* (the royal entrance). This popular name is associated with Emperor Shah Jahan, who along with royal caravan, used to enter the mosque from this gate. On the left side of this gate, one can find a makeshift room under the custody of the Archaeological Survey of India (ASI). A small red notice board of the ASI with the national emblem is placed here, which quite astonishingly, does not display any kind of introductory history of the mosque.[2]

---

[1] Except the eastern gate, which was called the *Shahi Darwaza*, other two gates of the Jama Masjid did not have any particular/popular name in the past. However, the Jama Masjid Trust has given three new interesting names to these gates: *Bab-Shah Jahan* (the Shah Jahan Gate), *Bab-e-Abdullah* (the Abdullah Gate) and *Bab-e Abdul Ghafur* (the Abdul Ghafur Gate). These new names quite symbolically commemorate the contributions of three 'personalities': Emperor Shah Jahan, who built the mosque; Imam Abdul Ghafur, who was the first Shahi Imam of the mosque and Imam Abdullah Bukhari, who converted the mosque into a centre of Muslim politics.

[2] The ASI notice board has been removed now and the Jama Masjid Trust has occupied this makeshift room. One of the members of the Jama

Jama Masjid and the Political Memory of a Royal Muslim Past 141

Figure 4.1: Erstwhile Office of the Archaeological Survey of India (ASI) at Jama Masjid

Source: HA Collection, 2005.

The southern entrance (*Bab-e-Abdul Ghafur*) of the mosque is generally used by foreign tourists. Here one can find an old inscription written in English on a white notice board installed by the *Sunni Majlis-e-Auqaf*.[3] This inscription tells us a short history of the mosque and the institution of *Shahi Imam*. The inscription says:

> [t]he history of Jama Masjid and that of its Imam is one and interlinked. ... Muslims have only two inheritances from the emperor Shah Jahan: the highly respected and renowned Jama Masjid and its Royal Imam (JMD1).

Masjid Trust informed me that the ASI used to take care of this building before but they had now withdrawn their support. The concerned ASI official did not comment on this issue but expressed his 'desire' that the entire building complex should be handed over to the ASI for proper up-keeping and management.

[3] In 2007, this old notice board was removed. A new plaque of same size was installed by the Jama Masjid Trust. The Trust did not change the informative history given in the old notice board; however, the name of the Sunni-Majlis-e-Auqaf was replaced by the 'office of the Shahi Imam'.

Figure 4.2: Sunni Majlis-e-Auqaf Board

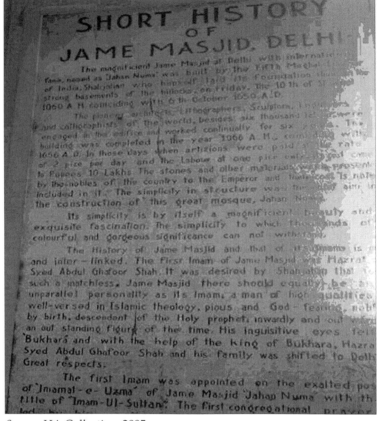

Source: HA Collection, 2005.

The northern gate (*Bab-e-Abdullah*) is the busiest entrance of the mosque. One finds another short inscription written in highly rhetorical Urdu on a white notice board installed by the Jama Masjid Trust.[4] It says:

> *Jama Masjid Delhi aap se hamkalam hai. Wazir-e-Azam Indira Gandhi ke zalim hatho Meri mazlumiyat ki kahani meri zababi. Me Allah tala ki muqadas ibadat gah hun. Ab se 332 sal pehle Mughal tajdar shahjahan badshah ne*

---

[4] After the death of former Imam, Abdullah Bukhari, the Trust has removed this board. One now finds a plaque depicting a chronological table of the Imams of Jama Masjid in its place.

Jama Masjid and the Political Memory of a Royal Muslim Past   **143**

*mujhe tamir karvaya. Is waqt se ab tak mere muqadsat farsh par karor ha
karor afrad bar gahe ilahi me sar justuju ho chuke hai. wazir-e-azam Mrs.
Indira Gandhi ne aur uski government ne watan aur watan walo par
khususan bis karore muslamano aur akhliyato par jo zulm dahaye hai woh
dillo ko larza dene wale hai. Lekin is waqt to me apne upper dahaye gaye
dilo ko tarpa dene wale mazalim hi sunaungi. Suniye aur khun ke aason
bahaiye.*[5] (JMD1a)

(For translation of the full text see Appendix 1)

These notice boards draw our attention to two kinds of issues.
First, one may raise the question of the management of the
mosque: How do three very different institutions — the ASI,
the *Sunni Majlis-e-Auqaf* and the Jama Masjid Trust — function
as the caretaker of the mosque? What is the legal status of these
bodies? Who does what? Second, these notice boards go beyond
such practical issues and point towards a serious politics of representation. For instance, the symbolic presence of the ASI reminds
the visitors that after all the Jama Masjid is a 'monument' and as the
prime custodian of all the ancient monuments, the ASI has a legal
right over it. The Sunni Majlis-e-Auqaf notice board portrays the
Jama Masjid as a 'living' place of worship and Muslim contribution to India. And finally the inscription at the northern entrance
describes the present condition of Muslims in postcolonial India
by narrating the heroic struggles of the Shahi Imam. Thus, these
versions introduce us to the different modes by which Jama Masjid
is represented as a historical monument as well as the centre of
Indian Muslim politics.

The objective of this chapter is to understand this complex
intermingling of official history, conservation laws and the
idea of an Indian Muslim heritage. Focusing on three critical
'events' — the 2 February 1975 riots, the closure of Jama Masjid for

---

[5] I am Jama Masjid Delhi and am speaking to you. I wish to tell you the
story of my persecution at the hands of a despotic Prime Minister Indira
Gandhi in my own words. In the heart of Delhi I am the sacred precinct
for the worship of Allah, the Almighty. Nearly 332 years ago I was built by
the Mughal emperor Shah Jahan. Since then on my sacred floor billions of
worshippers have prostrated before God. The oppressive treatment meted
out by the Prime Minister Mrs. Indira Gandhi and her Government to the
people of this country, specially 20 million Muslims and other minorities,
is heart rending. But here I will stick to narrating the story of my own
persecution. Listen to my woeful story of this barbarity and cry for the
helplessness I have endured during all these times.

144   *Muslim Political Discourse in Postcolonial India*

Figure 4.3: Jama Masjid 'Speaks'

Source: HA Collection, 2005.

regular prayers in 1987 and the construction of the controversial Wazukhana in 1996 — the chapter tries to explore how the memory of a royal Muslim past has been evoked by the Imam to acquire a *political authority* in post-1975 period.[6] The chapter argues that the Imam transformed the Jama Masjid into a centre of Muslim politics and redefined the modes of doing religious politics in India in a significant way.

---

[6] Following Veena Das's conceptualisation of 'critical events' (1995: 1–6), it could be argued that 'critical events' are the most crucial moments of history when different social actors and institutions interact with each other in 'extraordinary, unusual, and often, bizarre situations' and produce new forms of social, cultural and political engagements in a long run. In our case, these three events are 'critical' because the interaction between the state institutions and Muslim political actors redefined the nature of Muslim political discourse in north India.

I

MONUMENTALISATION OF JAMA MASJID: THE 'COMMUNAL' RIOT OF 2 FEBRUARY 1975

The *Masjid-e-Jane-Jahanuma* or Jama Masjid was built by the Mughal Emperor Shah Jahan in the 17th century as the central mosque for the capital city of Shahjahanabad. Shah Jahan invited Hazrat Abdul Ghafur Shah, an established Islamic scholar, to lead the regular prayers at the Jama Masjid. Abdul Ghafur Shah hailed from Bukhara, a central Asian city renowned for Islamic scholarship at that time. Imam Ghafur Shah was designated as the *Imam-ul-Sultan* (the Imam of the Emperor) or the Shahi Imam of the Jama Masjid.

The Shahi Imam had two main functions. First, as the Imam of the mosque he had to perform certain religious activities such as leading regular daily prayers, weekly congregational prayers on Friday and the annual Eid prayers. Second, the Imam had to function as the royal priest. He was bestowed with the responsibility and authority of crowning the Mughal emperor. The Imam of Jama Masjid, thus, over the period of time became some kind of religious-political authority. The *Imamat* of this mosque is still inherited in this very family from generation to generation. The elder son of the Imam succeeds his father as the Shahi Imam of Jama Masjid. The Imam delegates his responsibilities to his son in a public ceremony called *Dastar Bandi.*[7]

Despite having a religious-traditional authority, the Shahi Imam had not been involved in the management-related issues of the mosque in Mughal India. The Emperor dedicated four villages as wakf for Jama Masjid. However, by the end of the 19th century these villages disappeared and the mosque lost its principal source of income. Yet, the royal grants were continued for the maintenance of Jama Masjid. In the last phase of the Mughal Empire, when it became virtually impossible for the emperors to

---

[7] *Dastar Bandi* or Turban Tying ceremony is a highly symbolic act, which signifies the transformation of religious power. The turban of new Imam was ceremonially tied on by the old Imam (father) in a public function. The *Dastar Bandi* of the present Imam Ahmad Bukhari took place on 14 October 2000.

146　*Muslim Political Discourse in Postcolonial India*

provide financial support to the mosque, the local community took up this responsibility.[8]

In the late 19th century a working committee was set up to look after the management of the mosque (Rahman 1987: 37). Besides the monthly collection from the local shops and stalls, the donations given by the rich Muslims were the main source of income of the mosque at that time. The Imam of Jama Masjid used to be an ordinary member of the committee.

After the formation of the Sunni Majils-e-Auqaf on the basis of the Auqaf Act of 1943, all the powers of the working committee of Jama Masjid were delegated to this newly centralised Wakf institution. This administrative system was changed again in 1962 when the Delhi Wakf Board (DWB) was established under the Wakf Act of 1954. Since then, the management of the Jama Masjid became the responsibility of the DWB (Khan 2004, Int.). All the financial matters including the payments of salaries to the Imam, the Naib Imam (the Deputy Imam) and other employees of the mosque were administered by the DWB. This new administrative adjustment was very crucial. Unlike the custodianship of previous caretaker institutions of Jama Masjid, the DWB did not grant any special status to the mosque or the Shahi Imam. The DWB, following the legal principles laid down by the Wakf Act of 1954, simply recognised Jama Masjid as a wakf property. Furthermore,

---

[8] The Jama Masjid, as discussed in the second chapter, was occupied by the British in 1857 and returned to the local community only in 1862 (Gupta 1981; Spear 1951). The mosque continued to play an important role in the social–political life of the city in the post-1857 period. However, I do not focus on this period for two obvious reasons. First, the rise of the Imam as a political personality was somehow contingent upon the postcolonial legal-constitutional discourse and therefore it is important to concentrate on the contextual specificities of 1970s. Second, Abdullah Bukhari never evoked the events of 1857 for establishing any historical legitimacy for his claims as a champion of 'Muslim cause'. This *deliberate* historical deviation — an exercise of selecting/omitting certain events for constructing a politically viable image — in my view, needs to be taken seriously. In other words, to understand the political moves of someone like Abdullah Bukhari, we have to concentrate on his own modes of presenting the past as history. For an excellent discussion on the 19th-century political life of the Jama Masjid, see Kavuri-Bauer (2011).

Jama Masjid and the Political Memory of a Royal Muslim Past **147**

the Act radically transformed the status of the Shahi Imam into a paid employee.

It is important to note that the Jama Masjid has never been declared a protected monument. Following the guidelines given in the Conservation Manual of 1923, the Jama Masjid was put in the special category. Without any formal agreement with concerned religious endowment (in this case, the DWB), the ASI used to take care of the architectural and historic character of the buildings. However, the question of ASI's involvement in the management of the mosque has always been a *politically sensitive* issue.[9]

An Elusive Search for a 'Political' Jama Masjid: The First 'Fatwa' of Abdullah Bukhari

The eleventh Imam of the Jama Masjid, Syed Hamid Bukhari was the Shahi Imam of the mosque in 1970s. He was known for his personal integrity and was respected as a responsible 'elder' by the local Muslim community. In fact, he had never been considered as a political man of any kind. On the other hand, his eldest son and the then *Naib* Imam of the mosque, Syed Abdullah Bukhari, was not an educated man. No one knows about his formal education. He was not a *Hafiz* (a Muslim who knows the Quran by heart), nor an *Alim* or *Mufti* (formal degrees in the Madrasa system). Yet, as the Naib Imam, he used to lead the regular prayers at Jama Masjid in the absence of his father. Unlike Syed Hamid, Abdullah Bukhari was a politically ambitious person. He was fully aware of the religious and historical significance of Jama Masjid, particularly the economic importance of the mosque for the local Muslim population, and very much interested in exploiting this 'emotional attachment' for his own political advancement (Khan 2004, Int.).

It is important to note that the official relationship between the Imam and the DWB was quite paradoxical. The Imam of Jama

---

[9] This has been a highly controversial issue. For instance in 2003 when the BJP was in power, the then Minister for Culture and Tourism, Jagmohan had remarked that the Jama Masjid should be declared a protected monument and handed over to the ASI. Replying to this, the present Shahi Imam, Ahmad Bukhari warned the government that if ASI was involved in the affairs of the Jama Masjid, he would start a mass movement. He also cautioned that Indian Muslims would not hesitate to scarify their lives for the 'protection' of the Jama Masjid (Khan 2003: 32).

148   *Muslim Political Discourse in Postcolonial India*

Masjid was not even a member of the DWB. His religious authority and political reputation did not match with his actual status as a *paid Imam*. In fact, his position was quite vague. He was the Shahi Imam, the symbol of the Mughal era and a religiously recognised person; yet he was financially dependent on the DWB, a semi-government organisation, which derived its legitimacy from a modern law passed by the Indian Parliament to provide legal protection to a variety of Islamic wakf systems in the country.

Abdullah Bukhari was not the Shahi Imam of the mosque at that time. He was simply a Naib Imam of Jama Masjid a position, which had no religious or traditional significance. As a Naib Imam he was not entitled to claim the authority of the Jama Masjid. Thus, Abdullah Bukhari had to inherit the *Imamat* from his father for elevating his position and further establishing his ultimate administrative control over the mosque.

Abdullah Bukhari was also a politically conscious person. He was aware of his limitations and advantages. He must have realised, as it seems, the historic connection between the institution of Shahi Imam and the Jama Masjid. Yet, he was a bit confused, as his first political endeavour clearly shows, about the choice of an applicable political strategy. As a result, he decided not to use his indisputable stature as the true heir of the royal Muslim past in a manner antagonistic to the government and adopted a relatively mild approach.

Instead of waging a war against the Wakf Board, Abdullah Bukhari chose an alternative political move. He issued a statement supporting the family planning programme of the government (Khan 2004, Int.). This statement was widely circulated as a religious decree (fatwa) and presented as the religious sanctioning for family planning among Muslims. He also used the Public Address System (PAS) of the Jama Masjid to encourage the Muslims for family planning.[10]

---

[10] The use of PAS of a mosque was not a new thing at that time. During the national movement the loud speakers of the mosque were used even by Mahatma Gandhi for delivering political speeches. In postcolonial India, this practice took a new form. The state machinery started using the PAS of mosques for spreading its message to the Muslims. It fact, it became a custom in the 1970s when Muslim members of the Union cabinet, Muslim Members of Parliament (MPs) and even the Vice Presidents and

Jama Masjid and the Political Memory of a Royal Muslim Past **149**

Imam's fatwa was compatible with the political trends of the early 1970s when the Congress party wanted to consolidate its position among Muslims.[11] It was desperately looking for a Muslim politician, who could be represented as *the leader* of the entire Muslim community. In this context, Mrs. Gandhi started promoting Abdullah Bukhari. However, Bukhari, on his part followed this pro-Indira politics in a very interesting and innovative manner. He supported the family planning programme by putting aside the local Muslim Congress leaders, and at the same time, introduced himself as a kind of political authority.

This pro-Congress gesture turned out to be a political disaster for Abdullah Bukhari. This 'fatwa' further heightened the anti-government feelings, which were already increasing in the Jama Masjid area because of the forced urbanisation and family planning programme (Tarlo 2003). Many Muslim families decided not to offer Namaz inside this historic mosque to register their protest.[12] The fatwa was also criticised by the local political groups as well as the established Muslim organisations.

This political debacle was a turning point for Abdullah Bukhari. He realised that his political support to Mrs. Gandhi could not help him in mobilising local Muslims. The pro-Congress politics, furthermore, did not give him a stature that he might have been aiming for. On the other hand, the Congress was also not interested in him any longer. The fatwa was unofficially withdrawn and the Congress establishment started ignoring him.[13] These changing cir

---

Presidents of India such as Dr Zakir Husain and Fakhruddin Ali Ahmed, used to deliver speeches in mosques on important occasions like the Eid prayers.

[11] It is very clearly revealed in the speeches of Mrs. Indira Gandhi. For instance, addressing a public meeting in Fatehgarh on 14 February 1974, Mrs. Gandhi said that the Muslim League's tactics could only help the Jan Sangh and not Muslims because the League would not be able to form a government. Thus, only Congress could protect Muslims from the communal politics of the Jan Sangh (JMD2).

[12] Information given by Mr. Latif Beg, who along with his family decided not to offer Namaz in Jama Masjid because of the misuse of the mosque by the Imam (JMD3).

[13] It is important to note that the print version of this 'fatwa' quite strangely disappeared very soon (Khan 2004, Int.).

150   *Muslim Political Discourse in Postcolonial India*

cumstances forced Abdullah Bukhari not only to revolutionise his style of politics but also to rethink creatively about more innovative use of Jama Masjid. In this context, the Socialist Party and the Jan Sangh — ideologically two opposite political groups — discovered Abdullah Bukhari, as a potential ally (Khan 2004, Int.).

THE LAW OF WAKF VERSUS THE TRADITION OF IMAMAT: THE CONTROVERSIAL DASTAR BANDI OF ABDULLAH BUKHARI

The public image of Bukhari was further ruined by allegations made by the DWB. According to the newspaper reports, the Delhi Wakf Board had asked him to give accounts for the money received by him through the sale of tickets to foreign tourists. The Board, as these reports suggest, had already rejected the proposal for levying an entry fee mooted by him. The DWB also alleged that Bukhari wanted to give 50 per cent of the total income of the Jama Masjid to the Board and retain the rest. The Board sent an official letter to Abdullah Bukhari regarding these financial anomalies. However, he did not reply to these letters and ignored the reminders sent to him. At this point of time, the Board decided not to pay salary to the Naib Imam (JMD2a).

In the meantime, in June 1974 the *Dastar Bandi* ceremony of Abdullah Bukhari took place. Syed Hamid, following this age old tradition, appointed Syed Abdullah Bukhari as the new Shahi Imam and Ahmad Bukhari, the elder son of Abdullah Bukhari as the new Naib Imam of Jama Masjid. The DWB, on the other hand, did not endorse the *Dastar Bandi* ceremony and refused to authorise these new appointments. The Board insisted that the selection of the new Shahi Imam of Jama Masjid was a legal prerogative of the Wakf Board (JMD2a).

At this point, Abdullah Bukhari changed his political strategy. He openly repudiated the authority of the Wakf Board by delivering inflammatory speeches before the congregational prayers, particularly on every Friday. He also forced his father, the former Imam, not to apply to the Wakf Board for its formal approval. The Board, on the other hand, followed its routine procedure. Taking no notice of the *Dastar Bandi* ceremony, the Board decided to pay the regular monthly salaries of Syed Hamid, Abdullah Bukhari and other employees of Jama Masjid as per its previous records. This was a good opportunity for Abdullah Bukhari. He did not accept these

Jama Masjid and the Political Memory of a Royal Muslim Past **151**

salaries and persuaded other employees of Jama Masjid to recognise him as the ultimate administrative authority (JMD2a).[14]

Abdullah Bukhari soon figured out other possible implications of this simple administrative conflict between him and the DWB. In his speeches, he attempted to establish a link between the DWB and other government institutions by symbolically representing his battle against the Board as the ultimate struggle of the Muslims in India for justice. In order to further widening his political agenda, the Imam adopted a twofold strategy. First, he started establishing political connections with the opposition parties, particularly with the Socialist and Jan Sangh leaders which helped him to capitalise on the anti-Indira wave created by the Jaiprakash Narayan-led anti-establishment movement. Second, he mobilised the local shopkeepers and kabaris by representing himself as some kind of a politically connected person. This move made him locally popular and also helped him in regaining his lost public credibility (Khan 2004, Int.).

In July 1974, Abdullah Bukhari started his anti-government campaign by using the PAS of the mosque before and after every Friday sermon. On 15 August 1974, when Mrs. Gandhi, the Prime Minister was addressing the nation from the Red Fort, on the eve of the Independence Day, he opened the PAS of the mosque and delivered a very inflammatory speech (JMD3). However, quite surprisingly the authorities did not take any notice of it. Even the national and local media almost ignored him — partly because of the pressure of the ruling Congress and partly because they did not recognise him as an important political leader of any kind.

Finally, Abdullah Bukhari decided to launch a 'direct action' against the Wakf Board. On 31 January 1975, just before the Friday congregational prayer, Abdullah Bukhari delivered a highly provocative speech against the DWB. In this speech, he warned the DWB that he and his supporters would protest against the Board's Area Advisory Committee meeting that was scheduled to be held on 2 February 1975 (JMD3).

---

[14] Abdullah Bukhari had been demanding that the Wakf Board should nominate him as the authorised person for the payment of salaries of other employees. However, the Treasurer of the Board did not accept this demand (Khan 2004, Int.).

Figure 4.4: Clearance of Shops Near the Wall of Jama Masjid by the DDA (1975)

Source: HA Collection, 2005.

The 'Riot' of 2 February 1975

On 2 February 1975, a high profile meeting of the Wakf Board Area Advisory Committee was held at the *Bachchon ka Ghar*, Darya Ganj, the central office of the DWB. The then Union Minister of State for Agriculture, Mr. Shah Nawaz Khan, who was also the Chairman of Delhi Wakf Board, was presiding over the meeting. Around 11 a.m. Abdullah Bukhari, with 50–60 supporters entered the premises of the office and started shouting slogans against the minister. Within a few minutes, the crowd forcibly tried to open the gate of Wakf Board office. They pulled down the *Shamiyana* (tent) and broke the furniture. When the police, as the official news reports claimed, tried to stop this vandalism, the crowd attacked the police. Soon it turned out to be a fight between the police and the violent crowd in which, as newspaper reports allege, some senior

Jama Masjid and the Political Memory of a Royal Muslim Past **153**

police officers got minor injuries. The police, finally, arrested the Imam and his supporters (JMD2b).

This was an 'unusual' demonstration in two ways. First, the agenda of this 'protest' march was quite unclear. There were no placards, no written memorandum, and even no formal picketing. The people who actually participated in the march were not at all informed about the proceeding of this move (JMD3). It was, in a restricted sense, an intentionally 'unorganised' show of strength, which was relying mainly on the negative feelings and apprehensions of the local Muslims. In such a situation, submitting a memorandum to the DWB, or demonstrating in an organised way might give recognition to the institutional supremacy of the Wakf Board. Second, contrary to the newspaper reports of the time, this demonstration was not at all 'spontaneous'. It was a well-planned political act, in which every move was premeditated and the strategic locations and the actions of key players were well set out.

The intervention of the police to 'control' the situation and eventually the arrest of the main leader of an agitating mob, many a time, could be regarded as the end of a public demonstration. However, on the contrary, on 2 February 1975, it was the beginning of a series of violent events, police brutality, curfew and above all a new kind of political manoeuvring. After the arrest of the Imam, his son and the newly appointed Naib Imam, Ahmad Bukhari along with a few supporters decided to proceed back to the Jama Masjid. In a highly dramatic way, Ahmad Bukhari opened the Public Address System (PAS) of the mosque and announced that the Shahi Imam Abdullah Bukhari, who led a peaceful protest march against the DWB, had been assassinated by the police. Ahmad Bukhari also delivered a short emotional speech and pleaded with the Muslims to strike back (JMD3). This news created a stir in the locality. Abdullah Bukhari, in his last speech on Friday had already predicted that in this struggle for 'justice' he might be arrested or even killed by the brutal Indira government. The news of his *assassination* not only proved him blameless and innocent but also quite instantly changed the public opinion in his favour.

The call given by Ahmad Bukhari ignited the anti-government feelings among the local Muslims. The crowd gradually started assembling at the northern stairs of Jama Masjid with Ahmad Bukhari. According to an eye witness of this event, Raisuddin

154   *Muslim Political Discourse in Postcolonial India*

Hashmi, they began shouting slogan '*Nara-e-Takbir Allah-hu-Akabar*' (the call-Allah is great) and the *Imam sahib Zindabad* (long live the Imam). These slogans converted the feelings of anxieties and pain into mass resentment and the crowd began shouting *Delhi police hai hai* (Delhi police down down).

There is a small police post opposite to the northern gate of the mosque, which is locally called the *Jama Masjid Police Chownki*. This police post is an annexe of the main Jama Masjid Police Station, which is situated between the eastern and southern gates of the mosque. This police post suddenly became a target for this irritated crowd. They started throwing stones and soda water bottles at the post. This violent attack on the police almost immediately turned into a riot. The crowd burnt a Delhi Transport Corporation (DTC) bus and a few police vehicles. In retaliation, the police opened indiscriminate fire to disperse the crowd. The firing continued for at least two hours. Many bullets were fired targeting the gates of the Jama Masjid (JMD3).

Around 16 people were supposedly killed and around one hundred people were wounded in this violence. Moreover, according to the official news, 16 shops, two cars, two scooters and one DTC bus were also reported to be burned. The Imam was arrested under the Maintenance of the Internal Security Act (MISA) and an indefinite curfew was imposed on the same day.[15]

The next two days of curfew heightened the communal tension in the Jama Masjid locality. The news of Imam's arrest under the MISA further demoralised the local community since he was the first person who had openly spoken against the government. According to local residents, those two days were the 'blackest days' in the history of the area. In fact, the Jama Masjid locality was 'punished'

---

[15] According to the official police version, 195 people including the Imam were arrested and five cases of rioting, arson, attempted murder and assaults on public servants had been registered. The Imam was arrested under MISA. In a press conference, Shah Nawaz Khan criticised Bukhari for his provocative action. He charged the Imam with spreading baseless and malicious allegations (JMD2b). This incident became national news and Imam Bukhari was recognised as a Muslim leader. However, the Muslim leadership of that time was quite confused on this issue. For instance, a press statement was issued on 3 February 1975 by 14 Muslim leaders who blamed the Imam for the incident and also criticised the role of the police (JMD2c).

Jama Masjid and the Political Memory of a Royal Muslim Past **155**

Figure 4.5: Bullet Marks at Jama Masjid

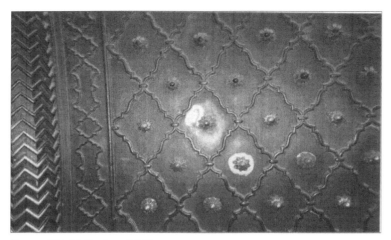

Source: HA Collection, 2005.

for this crime.[16] The electricity and water supplies were stopped and telephone lines were cut off. The situation went from bad to worse when the bodies of those who were killed in police firing were brought back and the police did not allow a public funeral service due to the curfew.[17] Finally, the curfew was relaxed on 5 February 1975 just for two hours between 4.00 p.m. to 6.00 p.m.

At this point of time, when the riot affected area was under curfew and the anti-government feelings were very high, the Friday prayer at Jama Masjid was the perfect opportunity for the Imam's elder son, Ahmad Bukhari, to capitalise upon these advantages. Syed Hamid Bukhari released a press statement requesting the union government to lift the curfew for the Friday congregational

---

[16] The copies of Jamat-e-Islami Hind's newspaper *Dawat*, which published the photographs of those who died in the police firing, were confiscated by the police (JMD2d). In the same way a case against the Urdu daily *Al Jamiyat*, the mouthpiece of Jamiat-Ulema-e-Hind was registered for publishing inflammatory material under Section 153 of the Indian Penal Code (IPC). The paper had alleged that the Jan Sangh was responsible for the deaths on 2 February 1975 (JMD2e).

[17] I am thankful to the family of Mohammed Saif, one of the victims of police firing, for this information (JMD3).

156   *Muslim Political Discourse in Postcolonial India*

prayer. However, it was Ahmad Bukhari who issued a very 'calculated' and 'aggressive' statement. He informed the press that his father had not been treated fairly in jail. *He also told that if the electricity was not restored till Friday prayer, the PAS would be run with the help of dry batteries* (emphasis added, JMD2f).

Friday (7 February 1975), as expected, was an important day for Ahmad Bukhari. He delivered an inflammatory speech before the Friday sermon and informed the congregation that his grandfather had resigned in favour of his father, Abdullah Bukhari. He also pointed out that he had requested his grandfather to lead the Friday prayer as his father, the present Imam, was in jail (JMD2d).[18] Ahmad Bukhari, in an interview with the United News of India (UNI) on the same day alleged that his father's arrest was 'pre-planned by the Government in collusion with a certain Congressman who did not tolerate Abdullah Bukhari for championing the cause of minorities and other weaker sections of the society' (JMD2d).

Ahmad Bukhari's speech on Friday was very significant in two ways. First, the Friday prayer at Jama Masjid was represented as a kind of essential Islamic *religious ritual*. As per the norms laid down by the dominant Islamic Hanafi *Sharia*, which has always been followed in Jama Masjid, leading a prayer in a mosque is not a prerogative of any particular Imam or a family of Imam. Anyone could lead the prayer at any mosque. It is a normal practice at Jama Masjid. Even today the Friday prayers are not always led by the Shahi Imam. However, Ahmad Bukhari's sermon converted the Imam of Jama Masjid into a kind of 'religious-political authority' by evoking the memory of a tradition associated with the Jama Masjid. As a result, the Jama Masjid as a symbol was deliberately connected to the persona of the Shahi Imam.

Second, the interview of Ahmad Bukhari with the UNI evidently provided a national platform to a highly localised administrative tussle between the Imam and the Wakf Board. In a wider sense, Ahmad Bukhari's interview re-conceptualised Muslim politics in India by involving other minorities and weaker sections

---

[18] According to the news reports after the Friday prayer, many Muslims gathered in the Mosque and shouted slogans against the Wakf Board, Minister Shah Nawaz Khan and the police. About 500 people then moved towards the Jama Masjid police post. At this point, the old Imam Syed Hamid requested the crowd to go back home (JMD2d).

Jama Masjid and the Political Memory of a Royal Muslim Past **157**

of the society in the political agenda of the Imam. This was actually the beginning of a new kind of 'aggressive' Muslim politics, which intended to widen its horizon by offering tactical support to other 'weaker' sections.

The arrest of the Imam transformed him into a national leader. He had become a very important 'person' for the Muslim political parties and groups. In fact, the Muslim League and the All India Muslim Majlis started a campaign in favour of Bukhari and decided to observe 14 February 1975, the very next Friday, as anti-repression day. They also demanded that senior Muslim leaders and the family members of the Imam should be allowed to visit him in jail. This demand was accepted and on 11 February 1975, the then Lieutenant Governor of Delhi, Krishan Chand, granted permission to Syed Hamid Bukhari and others Muslim leaders to meet the Imam in jail (JMD2g).

It provided an opportunity for the Muslim leaders to use this event for their own political interests. However, they could not realise that the Imam was well aware of his elevated political status. In fact, Abdullah Bukhari very intelligently used this jail 'meeting' (JMD2h). He requested these Muslim politicians to pursue the famous Kashmiri leader Sheikh Abdullah to mediate between him and the DWB (JMD2i). This attempt had a much wider political implication. It is true that Sheikh Abdullah was a regional political leader, but his anti-government stand, 'secular' approach and his active political involvement in Muslim politics at that time made him a very important political person. The Imam, it seems, was keen to get associated with Sheikh Abdullah simply to enhancing his image as national level Muslim leader.

Abdullah Bukhari also issued a press statement from the Tihar Jail. In this well-drafted written statement, he called upon all the citizens of the country, particularly the residents of Delhi (not old Delhi) to adopt a peaceful and orderly way. This statement was published in all the national newspapers. He wrote:

> The Prophet of Islam has always abhorred violence. Therefore, in order to achieve our fundamental rights and to achieve our purpose, I have issued this appeal to all the citizens of the motherland and particularly of Delhi. I appeal that they should adopt a peaceful and orderly way which will help our national cause. I am praying to God for all of you (JMD2h).

158　*Muslim Political Discourse in Postcolonial India*

Interestingly, this statement does not criticise the wakf board or mention anything related to the events of 2 February 1975. On the contrary, he speaks to all the citizens of India, stresses upon the given 'fundamental rights' and talks about a 'national cause' by citing the ideals of the Prophet Mohammad and praying to God!

The Protest Day organised by the Muslim Majlis in favour of the Imam on 14 February 1975, triggered off a fresh wave of violence in the Jama Masjid area. Black banners were strung across roads to mark the protest. The Muslim Majlis workers distributed black armbands to the congregation. Syed Hamid Bukhari delivered the conventional Arabic Friday sermon and led the congregational prayers. However, after the Friday prayer, the crowds assembled at the stairs of the mosque with black flags. They started shouting slogans against the police and demanded an honourable acquittal of Abdullah Bukhari. Soon this agitation turned violent and the crowd demolished an oven in one of the *dhaba*s in front of the Jama Masjid and started pelting brickbats and coal at the police post. The police then fired tear gas in response to this attack (JMD2j). Two people were killed and several others injured in this violence. According to the official reports, 28 policemen were also injured. This incident further intensified the tension in the locality.

The second wave of rioting in the locality, and the arrest of the Imam simply overshadowed the real administrative conflict. This had become a 'Muslim' issue and a kind of 'intervention in the religious affairs of a minority community'. This was the time for the political parties including the ruling Congress to issue 'customary statements' condemning the police action and expressing their sympathy for the riot affected people.[19]

---

[19] The members of the Congress and the Communist Party of India (CPI) criticised the police and the Lieutenant Governor for their attitude. The Socialist Party decided to move an adjournment motion on the Imamat issue in the Parliament (JMD2l). However, the most interesting statement was issued by Jaiprakash Narayan, the main opposition leader, who was also leading a mass movement for achieving a *'total revolution'* in the country. Narayan was outside Delhi when this incident took place. After coming back to Delhi he issued a press statement saying that the curfew should be lifted from the Jama Masjid area and the Government should not interfere in the *religious matters of the people* (emphasis added, JMD2m).

Jama Masjid and the Political Memory of a Royal Muslim Past **159**

Sheikh Abdullah refused to intervene in this matter. However, the then Minister of State for Railways, Shafi Qureshi, came forward to solve this stalemate. He arbitrated between the Imam, DWB and the government and requested the latter to release the Imam immediately. This request was accepted and the detention order under MISA against the Imam was revoked. Keeping all legal formalities aside, the Imam was finally released on 18 February 1975. He was brought straight to the house of the minister to attend a press conference. The Imam issued the following written statement to the press:

> [t]o serve humanity without taking political advantages would be exactly in keeping with the service of the country and the service of the people. This is the path I am following now and am determined to continue to follow it in future (JMD2k).

Talking to the media, he denied that the speeches he made in the past were political. He asserted that he was a religious man and whatever he did was in accordance with the basic principles of Islam (JMD2k).

In a few months' time, a new committee, the Jama Masjid Trust, was formed by the Imam for the management of the mosque. Interestingly, a white notice board was also installed at the northern entrance of the mosque to describe the events of 2 February 1975 and the 'heroic struggles of the Imam' (Figure 4.3). Meanwhile, in the old records of the DWB, Jama Masjid is still shown as a wakf property.

II

THE CLOSURE OF JAMA MASJID: POLITICAL APPROPRIATION OF THE IDEA OF AN INDO-ISLAMIC HERITAGE

Between 1975 to 1986 Abdullah Bukhari issued several election fatwas. For example, in 1977 he supported the Janta Party, while in the elections of 1980 and 1984, he asked Muslims to vote for the Congress. However, his political status as the leader of the entire Muslim community weakened quite considerably in the post-1984 period. After an impressive electoral success, the Congress government led by Rajiv Gandhi did not show any interest in the 'fatwa politics' of Bukhari. Perhaps for that reason, the Ulema of

160 *Muslim Political Discourse in Postcolonial India*

All India Muslim Personal Law Board (AIMPLB) (particularly Ali Mian Nadwi) were promoted by the government in the Shah Bano case, which eventually became one of the most controversial Muslim issues in the early 1980.[20] In such a political context, he was waiting for a 'right kind' of issue.

The opening of the gates of Babri Masjid in 1986 was a perfect opportunity for the Imam to restore his political status. It is interesting to note that Abdullah Bukhari *was not* introduced to the Babri Masjid issue either by the AIMPLB or any other organisation.[21] In fact, he followed a very different political route. The Imam, as his later moves very clearly showed, was aware that the Babri issue was going to be a nation-wide campaign and therefore it would have many stake holders. In this case, he had to carve out a space for himself. Moreover, the Imam was also conscious about the practical compulsions of UP-based Muslims leaders. The Babri Masjid was situated in UP and it was important for these politicians to search a prominent place in Delhi for disseminating their messages and converting their campaign into a national-level movement. Maulana Zahid Rizvi, who had served as the Convener for the UP Babri Masjid Coordination Committee, told me that the

---

[20] Shah Bano, a 62-year-old Muslim woman and mother of five was divorced by her husband in 1978. She filed a case against her ex-husband for maintenance. In 1985 the Supreme Court ruled in her favour and underlined the need for a common civil law in the country. This judgement created a stir in the country. The AIMPLB and other Muslim organisations launched a nation-wide agitation against the Supreme Court ruling and the protection of Muslim Personal Law and Shariat. Finally, the then Rajiv Gandhi government introduced a bill in the Parliament against this judgement. Importantly, the Imam did not get any media attention in this case and Ali Mian Nadwi and Shahabuddin emerged as the main Muslim leaders. There could be several possible reasons behind the failure of the Imam. He was not a trained *Alim* and had not been involved in the activities of the AIMPLB. In this context, it was not possible for him to hijack this issue. After all, as we have discussed in the previous chapter, the AIMPLB was established primarily for the protection of Islamic Shariat in India and the Supreme Court verdict in the Shah Bano case was a direct challenge against the authority of these Ulema (Bajpai 2002).

[21] I shall discuss in detail the events of 2 February 1986 and the reaction of different Muslim groups in the next chapter. Here I look at the ways by which the Jama Masjid was linked to the Babri Masjid.

Muslim leaders particularly from UP wanted a 'central place' in Delhi so that they could easily approach media and national-level politicians. The Jama Masjid was the perfect place for publicising the political activities in India. Thus, it was inevitable for these leaders to contact the Imam.

The Imam also knew it very well that the leaders associated with the All India Muslim Majlis-e-Mushawarat (AIMMM) were definitely going to approach him for creating extra pressure on the government. Syed Shahabuddin, who is still considered to be the most important leader of the Babri Masjid campaign, told me in a private conversation that the Imam of Jama Masjid had an important political status at that time and it was almost impossible for them to avoid such an important person. Thus, the Jama Masjid as the central place and its Shahi Imam as a powerful Muslim politician were identified by almost all the Muslim political actors in the early 1986.

JAMA MASJID IN THE SHADOW OF BABRI MASJID: THE FORMATION OF 'ADAM SENA'

A photograph depicting the idols of Lord Ram inside the Babri Masjid compound was published by a local Urdu newspaper, the *Faisal Jadeed* on 3 February 1986. These copies were widely distributed by the supporters of the Imam in the Jama Masjid area and it was announced that the Imam would speak on this issue later (JMD3). This was followed by his Friday sermon on 7 February 1986. In a highly provocative speech he warned the government that if the Babri Masjid was not returned to the Muslims, he would start a mass movement.

Following the call given by different Muslim organisations, 14 February 1986 was observed as the Black Day in the Jama Masjid area. The Imam, evoking the feelings of resentments and outrage, delivered a very lucid and eloquent sermon. In fact, this was his first crucial public 'performance' in the Babri Masjid case. The carefully selected contents of this speech were delivered in a very aggressive tone. This speech was so articulated and organised that it was very difficult to directly blame the Imam for spreading any kind of 'communal' feelings. Yet, it was a very decisive speech which outlined his political strategy and determined the course of future political events in the country.

162   *Muslim Political Discourse in Postcolonial India*

His speech ignited the feelings of the worshippers and after the Friday congregational prayer, he stridently called upon all the devotees to say *Nara-e-Takbir Allah ho Akbar* (Allah is supreme). The crowd dispersed chanting slogans related to the Babri Masjid and soon it turned out to be a major communal clash in old Delhi, which is still remembered as the *first Babri Masjid riot*. This riot was followed by a series of communal incidents which took place in the coming months and further elevated the political status of Abdullah Bukhari as a radical Muslim leader.[22]

The formation of *Adam Sena* was his next step.[23] On 15 June 1986, Ahmed Bukhari, the Naib Imam of the mosque, announced that a new Muslim organisation, Adam Sena would be established to fight against the 'communal forces' (MID 43, 331). Two donation boxes were installed at every entrance of the Jama Masjid and Muslims were asked to give moral, religious and above all financial support to this endeavour.[24]

No one knows about the aims, objectives and the formal organisational structure of this outfit.[25] Yet, the Adam Sena as an organised Muslim group for self-defence was praised by the Imam and his son Ahmad Bukhari in almost all their speeches and sermons. In fact, there are only two known incidents in which the 'involvement' of Adam Sena could be found. The first incident took place in September 1986 when the Sena fought a very interesting *war*

---

[22] After the Delhi riots of February 1986 a violent Hindu–Muslim clash took place in Meerut in March 1986. The Imam visited the riot affected areas of Meerut. However, in the outskirts of Meerut, his car was attacked by a Hindu mob. In this confrontation he received some minor injuries. He came back to Jama Masjid and took off his *Kurta* publicly to show his wounds. This incident created a sympathy wave for him in the entire northern India (JMD3).

[23] The term *'sena'* is very significant here. The Imam did not prefer any Urdu/Persian term for his *army*. Instead, he relied on the popular Hindi word so as to make it 'media friendly'.

[24] I am thankful to Mohammad Nadim for providing a detailed account of the events of June–July 1986 (JMD3).

[25] In my discussions with the local residents and particularly with the shopkeepers of Meena Bazaar, this aspect came up very sharply. No one has ever seen any Adam Sena volunteers, except two body guards of Abdullah Bukhari, wearing green uniform. In fact, I also came to know that the idea of Adam Sena was severely criticised by the local people at that time (GD1).

Jama Masjid and the Political Memory of a Royal Muslim Past **163**

with *Trishul* (Trident) clad Bajrang Dal volunteers at the Firoz Shah Kotla.[26] The second more visible involvement of Adam Sena was found in the same month when on the occasion of the *Muharram* the volunteers of the Sena were 'seen' protecting the riot affected areas of old Delhi.[27] In both the cases, the distinction between the local Muslim community and the Adam Sena was almost neglected by the media. The common Muslims were shown as the Adam Sena men and the blind followers of the Imam. The short-lived Adam Sena gave a symbolic legitimacy to Muslim militancy and established the Imam as the champion of radical Muslim politics. Perhaps this was the reason behind the sudden, and astonishingly silent, disappearance of Adam Sena in the late 1980s, which was almost overlooked by the media.

The establishment of Adam Sena on the lines of the Shiv Sena or the Bajrang Dal, was a very interesting move in two ways. First, the Adam Sena had a media value. Unlike the political strategy of the Muslim leaders associated with the AIMMM, the Adam Sena was highlighted as a clear and visibly 'Muslim' answer to Hindu militant organisations. Perhaps for that reason, the Adam Sena was always compared with Bajrang Dal. Second, the Adam Sena

---

[26] It was an interesting case. On 7 September 1986, a group of *Trishul* wielding Bajrang Dal activists entered the historic Kotla Firoz Shah mosque, a protected monument, and stabbed a Muslim boy, who later died in hospital (MID 46: 478). This incident provoked local Muslims and they immediately contacted the Imam. The Naib Imam Ahmed Bukhari along with his Adam Sena visited the Kotla Firoz Shah mosque and delivered a highly inflammatory speech. His speech increased the tension in the old city and finally the police imposed an indefinite curfew (Saxena 1986). However, rumours spread by the supporters of the Imam that a clash between the Adam Sena and Bajrang Dal took place in which an Adam Sena man died!

[27] In September 1986 the Imam announced that the Muslims would not organise the traditional *Tazia* processions in Delhi. It was again a symbolic move. The old Delhi was in the grip of communal tension and the local Muslims were not ready for any kind of public celebration. The Imam simply appropriated this resentment and gave a boycott call. On 15 September 1986, the local Muslims observed a black *Muharram* and no *Tazia* procession was organised. The Imam represented this event as his political victory. It is also claimed that Adam Sena volunteers played an active role in restoring peace in old Delhi (MID 46: 478).

164 *Muslim Political Discourse in Postcolonial India*

was obviously compatible with the radical image of Abdullah Bukhari and his Shahi style politics. It was shown as the Muslim 'army' led by the Shahi Imam to protect the Muslim heritage in India including the Babri Masjid.[28] In this sense, the Adam Sena experiment established an intrinsic link between the Shahi Imam of Jama Masjid and the Babri Masjid.

Non-Observance of the Republic Day and the 30 March Rally

To provide an organised form to Muslim responses on Babri Masjid an All India Conference on Babri Masjid was organised in Delhi on 21–22 December 1986. It was already decided that Maulana Ali Mian Nadwi would inaugurate the conference. However, Ali Mian Nadwi could not make it to the conference on time and it became a practical problem for the organisers to find out someone for the inauguration ceremony.[29] In the final moments, it was decided that Abdullah Bukhari would inaugurate the conference. This was a crucial political gain for the Imam, which actually established his symbolic authority over the Babri Masjid movement. In fact, his informal relationship with the highly institutionalised Babri Masjid movement changed quite significantly after this event.[30] This conference led to the formation of the very first Muslim political coalition, the All India Babri Masjid Movement Coordination Committee (AIBMMCC) on the Babri Masjid issue. This new umbrella organisation introduced two radical proposals: (*a*) the non-observance of the Republic Day call, and (b) a massive Muslim rally for the restoration of the Babri Masjid.

It is very interesting to note that the Imam, who had been known for his radical politics, did not campaign for non-observance of the

---

[28] Abdullah Bukhari, in an interview, pointed out: 'Adam Sena is for the service of the Muslims . . . it is different from the other Hindu senas. It does not believe in violence. When asked about possibility of the arming of the Adam Sena, he gave a very categorical answer. The Imam said: 'Well, it is for self-defense. There is no harm in that' (MID 47: 520).

[29] I am thankful to Syed Shahabuddin for this valuable information (JMD3).

[30] I shall look at the complex institutionalised structure of the Babri Masjid Movement Co-ordination Committee in our next chapter. Here I focus only on the political role played by the Imam.

Jama Masjid and the Political Memory of a Royal Muslim Past   **165**

Republic Day call and decided to keep a low profile.[31] This was an important move. The non-observance of the Republic Day call was an outcome of a collective decision in which several other political players were involved. The success of this call could have benefited the AIBMMCC and above all its convenor and the Imam's main political rival, Syed Shahabuddin. This strategy worked perfectly well for the Imam. The non-observance call was however, withdrawn on 25 January 1987 and the fraction led by Shahabuddin was ultimately held responsible for the failure of this move. On the contrary, the Imam could save his energies for another crucial 'public' event: the massive Muslim rally, which was to be held on 30 March 1987.

The massive rally at the Boat Club, near India Gate, Delhi, on 30 March 1987 is supposed to have been the largest ever Muslim gathering for any political cause in postcolonial India. The Muslim participants, who had come from different parts of the country, mobilised by different Muslim leaders and organisations, assembled at the northern gate of the Jama Masjid and marched towards the Boat Club. This massive rally, which was attended by more than a hundred thousand people, was completely peaceful (JMD2n). Despite the fact that the Imam was not giving his full corporation to the AIBMMCC and had not been participating in its regular meetings, the Jama Masjid as the starting point for the procession was the ultimate choice for the organisers.

This public event was very crucial for the Imam to sideline other Muslim leaders. In fact on this occasion he spoke as an ultimate authority and ignored the actual agenda of the AIBMMCC. His speech was replete with emotions, excitement and frustrations. The Imam called upon the Muslims to reject the 'judicial system of the government which had been unable to protect the religious place of Muslims'. He criticised the Muslim ministers, MPs and MLAs for their unreceptive approach and asked the community *'to burn their houses and break their legs if they were unable to respond to*

---

[31] This rift between the Imam and Shahabuddin became very apparent with a few days. For instance, in an interview, Ahmad Bukhari expressed apprehensions about the effectiveness of the non-observance call and Abdullah Bukhari did not attend the crucial meetings of AIBMMCC which were held on 10 January 1987 (MID 50: 94).

166   *Muslim Political Discourse in Postcolonial India*

the hurt feelings of the Muslims' (JMD2n).[32] During his speech, Syed Shahabuddin, who was sitting just next to him on the podium, tried to pacify him by pulling his *kurta*. Abdullah Bukhari, like a perfect anchor used this minor incident very innovatively. Showing an extreme gesture of anger and irritation, the Imam publicly pushed Shahabuddin over on the dais (JMD2n). This symbolic act marked the beginning of a public rift between the two dominant fractions within the Babri Masjid campaign: one led by Shahabuddin and the other by the Imam.

The Closure of the Jama Masjid

The post-30 March rally scenario was marked by a series of communal riots in the country. The most severe communal clash took place on 23 May 1987 in Maliana, a small Muslim locality in the outskirts of Meerut, where the PAC killed at least 35 Muslims. The Meerut riots were followed by a fresh wave of communal violence in old Delhi, particularly in the last week of *Ramadan* (the Islamic month of fasting) in May 1987.[33]

It was a very disturbing phase for local Muslims, particularly for those families who had lost their relatives in on-going communal violence. In this context, the festival of Eid, which was to be celebrated on 28 May 1987, had to be a very low-key affair in the Jama Masjid locality. The Imam understood this fact correctly and in a statement issued on 26 May 1987, called upon all the Muslims not to offer Eid congregational prayers in big mosques including the Jama Masjid (MID 55: 333). As it was expected, no Eid prayer was held in big mosques. Instead, people performed Eid Namaz on streets and roads.

These riots gave legitimacy to the Imam. He had successfully linked the Jama Masjid with other political events, particularly with

---

[32] Mr Nadeem, who attended this rally as a Khaksar volunteer quoted the Imam as saying: *Meri qaum ke naujawan chahe to tumhari tange tor de aur tumhari kothio me aag laga de* ('If young men of my community want they can break your legs and burn your big houses') (JMD3).

[33] In his *Juma-tul-Vida* sermon on 22 May 1987 the Imam asked the congregation to pray for the Babri Masjid. Despite his emotional speech, a fresh wave of violence erupted in old Delhi and at least four people were killed (Engineer 1988: 80–85).

Jama Masjid and the Political Memory of a Royal Muslim Past **167**

the Babri Masjid issue. Yet, due to on-going communal violence in different cities of north India in which Muslims were the prime target of police brutality, the Imam had not been able to emerge as the key Muslim leader. In fact, the Shahabuddin group was in a relatively good position because several members of this fraction were MPs and MLAs and were in touch with the government agencies in the post-riot relief activities (Khan 2004, Int.). The religious leadership of Nadwa was also with this group. In this context, the Imam needed a breakthrough and Jama Masjid was his ultimate political weapon.

After the Eid prayers on 28 May 1987, Abdullah Bukhari, quite unexpectedly, decided to close down the Jama Masjid from 4 June 1987. Except the staff and the members of the management committee, no one was allowed to enter the mosque for regular prayers. A huge black fabric cover was wrapped around the minarets and domes of the mosque in order to show the resentment of Muslims against the government. A large banner, written in Urdu, Hindi and English, outside the mosque proclaimed:

> Protest against extreme atrocities & barbarism Jama Masjid, Delhi shall remain closed till guilty police officials are severely punished, all innocents arrested are immediately released. Not verbal but practical assurance for the security of life and property for future is made. May 28, 1987 (Engineer 1988: 72).

The black plaques were also installed at southern, northern and eastern gates of Jama Masjid demanding that Vir Bahadur Singh, the then Chief Minister of Uttar Pradesh should immediately be dismissed, and an independent enquiry commission should be set up to investigate the Meerut riots of 1987.

The closure of a functional Muslim mosque for expressing political resentment was a highly controversial decision. A number of Fatwas were issued against this move. The famous Muslim madrasa, *Darul Uloom*, Deoband, which had been known for its pro-Congress stands, also issued a fatwa and declared that the closure of the mosque was an un-Islamic act. The Imam openly refuted this accusation. He criticised these fatwas as *Sarkari Fatwas* and alleged that the government was involved in an anti-Muslim conspiracy. The supporters of the Imam also started a *poster war* against such

Figure 4.6: Black Banner at the Jama Masjid

Source: HA Collection, 2005.

Figure 4.7: Jama Masjid in June 1987

Source: HA Collection, 2005.

Jama Masjid and the Political Memory of a Royal Muslim Past **169**

fatwas. In fact, some pro-Imam fatwas were also obtained and were posted around the walls of Jama Masjid.[34]

The government did not respond immediately. It took nearly two weeks to accept the demands of the Imam. On 13 June 1987, the government assured Bukhari that a departmental enquiry would be initiated against the guilty police officers and those who were arrested would be soon released on bail (Bhushan 1988: 109–10). On the same evening, the Jama Masjid was opened for the common people. The Imam delivered a short speech before the reopening of the mosque and said:

> *A meri qaum tu sun le! Agar choti choti baton me dhoka hua to me kal subha se phir Jama Masjid band karva dunga* (Listen O members of my community, if there is any betrayal on small assurances given, then I shall close down the Jama Masjid tomorrow once again) (ibid.: 110).

Reflecting on these developments later in an interview, the Imam said that he was 'only 75 per cent satisfied . . . therefore the mosque would be opened but the black flags and banners put up in the Jama Masjid and the black cloth covering some of the domes and minarets would not be pulled down'. The Imam further pointed out that the closure of Jama Masjid was an international issue. He claimed that the world media, particularly the Western print and electronic media, had been approaching him in this regard (ibid.: 110).

Let us now discuss these strategic moves of the Imam closely to understand the wide-ranging implications of this event. The entire event had three interlinked elements:

(*a*) The doors of the mosque were closed.
(*b*) The visible parts of the mosque were wrapped with black cloth.
(*c*) A few demands were communicated first through banners and then by permanent plaques.

---

[34] I did not find any copy of any pro-Imam fatwa. However, Mr. Nadim told me that the pro-Imam fatwas were based on the argument that the mosque had been closed only for the general public, particularly for foreign tourists, while the regular prayers were still going on inside it. Thus, this act could not be considered 'a closure of the mosque' (JMD3).

Figure 4.8: Reopening of the Jama Masjid

Source: HA Collection, 2005.

The first element shows that although the gates were closed for public, the staff of Jama Masjid including the Imam and his family continued to offer prayers inside it. So, who was the public in this case? It is important to note that Jama Masjid is surrounded by a large number of mosques, which provide ample space for offering *Namaz* for the local Muslim community. In fact, except Fridays or on the occasion of festivals such Eid, etc., the Jama Masjid remains almost empty. Thus, practically the Jama Masjid is primarily used for congregational prayers by the local community.

However, Jama Masjid also attracts a very different kind of public. We have to note that it is is a part of most of the Delhi based tourist packages. As a result, a large number of tourists, mainly

Jama Masjid and the Political Memory of a Royal Muslim Past **171**

the foreigners, visit the mosque. These tourists are one of the main sources of income for the mosque. Apart from them, Muslims from different parts of the country and the subcontinent also pay customary visit to the mosque. In this scenario, the closure of the mosque was not going to affect the religious or social needs of local Muslims. However, it would have an obvious impact on those who were coming from outside. The Imam, it seems, was well aware of these practical aspects. The closure of a historic mosque could have been shown as a symbol of Muslim resentment and the overseas tourists could be used as messenger to spread this information.

The closure of Jama Masjid also had a media value. The Imam, who had already established an image of a radical Muslim leader, used this opportunity to capture the media space. It is important to note that the nature of media was very different in mid-1980s. National television (Doordarshan) and Radio (Akashvani) were completely under the direct control of the state. People like the Imam were almost non-entity for electronic media. However, print media, especially the English newspapers, was interested in some kind of 'investigative journalism'. The rise of rightist Hindutva politics was already occupying a central stage in these newspaper writings. The media was desperately looking for a Muslim leader who could be juxtaposed with radical Hindutva kind of politics. The Imam's move such as the establishment of Adam Sena, making provocative speeches and finally the closure of the mosque simply contributed to his established media image. So, the Imam, it seems, identified three possible audiences for this act — the tourists, the Muslims from other parts of India and the elite English media.

In order to address these identified audiences, not only to inform them about the Babri Masjid or riots but also to draw their attention, it was important to rethink on the question of language. As we have seen in the previous section, the Imam developed a very different style of Urdu oratory to communicate directly to local Muslims. However, in this case, the identified groups of people were largely non-Urdu speaking. Thus, they had to be communicated in a different language in such a way that the internal nuances of the message were not affected. English was an obvious choice but quite interestingly the messages written in English had a very clear overtone of local Urdu. For instance, the black plaque

172   *Muslim Political Discourse in Postcolonial India*

installed at the entrance of Jama masjid had a caption: *'Quench the fire under our breast'*!

The second important aspect of this act was associated with the public presence of Jama Masjid. It is important to note that the 'public presence' of a mosque situated in an urban environment is constituted by two interlinked domains — the inner domain of religiosity and the outer domain of urbanity. The inner domain of the mosque in this sense is the one where religion and culture interact with each other. While, the outer is a domain where a mosque in its built form responds to the legal-constitutional discourse of secularism and the urban landscape (Ahmed 2012). The closure of the Jama Masjid, in this sense, affected both of these domains in some very interesting ways. The Imam's decision to discontinue the use of PAS to make *Azans* during this period should be seen in relation to the inner public presence of Jama Masjid. The Azan, which reminds the local community that a mosque is situated nearby, was disconnected from the everyday sensibilities. This reconfiguration of the inner domain of the public presence of Jama Masjid actually helped the Imam to create a melancholic atmosphere. The covering of domes and minarets with black fabric were linked to the outer public presence of the Jama Masjid. This act was more significant because it was transforming a mosque into a 'dead entity' of some kind. Jama Masjid, which is known for its eternal architectural features, was given a very different image — that of a mourning site.

Interestingly, the intellectual resources for this act were not drawn from any Islamic religious traditions. It is important to remember that there is a long tradition of mourning in Islam, particularly in Shia Islam and black colour is somehow linked to it. However, in this case, the use of black clothes to wrap the visible parts of the mosque was not at all related to any of the known Islamic traditions, since Jama Masjid is a Sunni mosque and it has not been associated with any Shia rituals. This act, as the Imam's various statements of that time suggest, was a *secular* political act. It was based on a strong assumption that Jama Masjid being the most visible icon of Muslim presence in postcolonial India could also be symbolised to mark the Muslim anger in a strictly modern sense.

Finally, this move was linked to the demands of the Imam. If we closely look at the banners and plaques installed at the various crucial points during this time, we find a few statements in the form of slogans and some short-term demands. For example,

Figure 4.9: Jama Masjid

Source: HA Collection, 2005.

the banner, which was put up outside the northern gate, claims that this move was all about a 'protest against extreme atrocities and barbarism'. However, the plaque situated at the main entrance demanded that the Chief Minister of UP should be dismissed immediately! These were very immediate concerns and had a very clear populist overtone. Precisely for that reason, it was not at all difficult for the government to respond to these demands. This aspect shows an interesting relationship between immediate demands and populist politics.

The closure of Jama Masjid had three political outcomes. First, the Imam successfully portrayed the Jama Masjid as the most important *political symbol* of India's Muslims. He intentionally highlighted the official status of the Jama Masjid as a historical

174   *Muslim Political Discourse in Postcolonial India*

monument by almost ignoring its basic religious position as a mosque. In this sense, it was a radical interpretation of the idea of an Indo-Islamic heritage as a Muslim contribution. The Imam's claim that this event forced the national and international media to give adequate coverage to Muslim issues also demonstrates how he established a direct link between 'Muslim grievances' and 'Muslim contribution'. Second, this move simply destroyed the legal-constitutional type democratic politics of the Shahabuddin groups. This symbolic act not only appealed to the common riot-affected Muslims but also captured the attention of the media. Third, the role of the government is very crucial in this episode. The government did not respond on time and gave a crucial two weeks to the Imam to publicise this event.[35] This provided an official recognition to the Imam as *the Muslim leader*.

The closure of Jama Masjid helped the Imam to consolidate his position on Babri Masjid. It also gave him an opportunity to establish political links with emerging Third Front leaders, including, V. P. Singh. Eventually, these developments led to the collapse of the Muslim coalition on the Babri Masjid in late 1988 and the Imam successfully established a separate Muslim organisation, the All India Babri Masjid Action Committee.

III

Controversial *Wazukhana*: Legal Ambiguities and the Conflict of 'Memories'

The term '*Wazukhana*' refers to a place in a mosque, which is used for making *wadu* (ablutions) before every Namaz. The Jama Masjid has two kinds of wadu facilities. In the centre of the mosque there is a big *Hauz* (tank) which was built originally for this purpose by Emperor Shah Jahan. However, when the number of devotees increased, the water contained in the Hauz became insufficient. Thus, a water tank with running tap-water facility was installed inside the Jama Masjid by the DWB. These two kinds of wadu

---

[35] Asghar Ali Engineer, who conducted a fact-finding survey during that time notes that the government allowed the Imam to use the closure of Jama Masjid for his political purposes (Engineer 1988: 73).

Jama Masjid and the Political Memory of a Royal Muslim Past **175**

facilities are still provided by the Jama Masjid Trust.[36] So, there was no practical need for any new Wazukhana in or around Jama Masjid in the mid-1990s. But in the last week of January 1996, a huge structure as the Wazukhana was constructed near the northern entrance of the Jama Masjid. The Imam defended this structure for the next three months and after much media hype demolished it.[37] So what were the political compulsions, which literally forced Ahmad Bukhari to start the construction of a new Wazukhana?

In 1993, the Bharatiya Janata Party (BJP) secured a comfortable two-third majority in the Delhi Assembly election and emerged as a confident rightist Hindu party. However, in the next two years, the political scenario changed quite considerably. The Ram Temple issue lost its political value and it became essential for the BJP to work out a new political agenda. Thus, in order to widen its mass base as well as to attract other centrist parties for a future coalition, the BJP unofficially adopted a 'pro-Muslim' approach to woo the Muslims.

The Naib Imam was also exploring his options for the next general election. He did not want to rely on the Third Front as well as the ruling Congress. The Congress's position was not very strong and it could not be the 'best bet' for him. Similarly, the Third Front was being dominated by Mulayam Singh-led Samajwadi Party (SP), which had already sidelined Ahmad Bukhari in UP. In fact, Bukhari's open opposition to Mulayam Singh did not stop UP Muslims to vote for the SP. The SP not only won the 1993 UP Assembly election with a significant Muslim support but also formed a coalition government in the state.

---

[36] It is true that a large number of tourists visit this place daily but the number of worshippers (*namazis*) in the mosque is not affected by these daily visitors except on Fridays and/or on the occasion of any Muslim festival. There are more than 20 functional mosques around the Jama Masjid which accommodate many new visitors.

[37] The political rise of Ahmad Bukhari, the Naib Imam of Jama Masjid, compelled Abdullah Bukhari to take retirement from active politics in mid-1990s. Despite the fact that Abdullah Bukhari remained the Shahi Imam of the mosque till October 2000, it was Ahmed Bukhari, who started a new phase of *Shahi* style politics from Jama Masjid in this period. In fact, the construction of the Wazukhana in 1996 as an event is primarily associated with Ahmad Bukhari. Thus, the terms, 'the Imam' and the 'Naib Imam' are used interchangeably here for him.

Thus, Bukhari could not ignore the possibility of an electoral alliance with a new pro-Muslim BJP. In fact, the political significance of the Jama Masjid could benefit both the BJP as well as the Imam. Yet, it was not an easy political shift. The memories of post-Babri Masjid riots were alive and the BJP was still considered to be an anti-Muslim party.[38] To avoid such possible apprehensions, it was important for the BJP to make a symbolic access among Muslims. Perhaps for that reason, they started focusing on the Jama Masjid locality. However, both the Imam and the BJP failed to read the local Muslim reactions and this failure paved the way for the construction of the controversial Wazukhana.

Figure 4.10: The Wazukhana of Jama Masjid

Source: HA Collection, 2005.

---

[38] A number of respondents in old Delhi informed me that in late 1992 the Naib Imam agreed to give the Babri Masjid to the BJP in return of two Rajya Sabha seats in the Parliament (JMD3). This allegation was further justified by Aslam Bhure, the Petitioner in the Babri Masjid case (Bhure 2004, Int.). The relationship between the Imam and the BJP became quite evident when Ahmad Bukhari asked Muslim to vote for the BJP in the 2004 general elections!

Local Muslim Agitation against L. K. Advani's Visit

On 11 January 1996, the DWB started demolition work at the *Kamara Bangash* Maternity Centre which was constructed on a Wakf land and run by the Municipal Corporation of Delhi (MCD). This was a highly surprising move for the local people because it was the only maternity centre of the Jama Masjid locality and the demolition work began without any prior notification.

The activists of the Youth Welfare Society (YWS), a local organisation, which had been campaigning for environment related issues in old Delhi, approached the Wakf officials including its Chairman, who was supervising the demolition work at Kamra Bangash. The Chairman misbehaved with the Secretary of the YWS and asked them to leave the site. These young men started shouting slogans and demanded that the wakf officials should stop the demolition immediately (GD2).

In the meantime, these activists learned that the Delhi Government was going to organise a ceremony at Kamra Bangash site on 16 January 1996 in which the foundation stone for a proposed Sikandar Bakht Girls Memorial School was to be laid down by the then BJP President, L. K. Advani. This was a high profile public meeting in which people like A. B. Vajpayee and other leading BJP politicians were taking part. The YWS activists decided to oppose this function and began mobilising local people and organisations. They also approached Maulana Athar Hussein Dehlavi, the Chairman of a Muslim organisation *Anjuman Minhaj-e-Rasool* (AMR), to lead this protest. Maulana Dehlavi agreed to participate in this agitation and on behalf of the protesters wrote a formal letter to the Home Minister (Dehlavi 2004, Int.).

The protestors made three points in favour of this agitation. First, they argued that the Kamra Bangash centre was situated on a wakf property, which belonged to the Muslim community. Therefore, it was demanded that any change or alteration in this property could only be made in accordance with the principles of Islamic Shariat. Second, it was also claimed that the Delhi government did not have any legal right to acquire this site without the consent of local users of the maternity centre. And finally, it was asserted that if the government wanted to build a girl's school it should be named after any respected Muslim personality. Since Sikander Bakht's Muslim identity had always been a matter of

178 *Muslim Political Discourse in Postcolonial India*

debate, it was suggested that the name of the proposed school should be reconsidered (JMD2o).[39] A pamphlet outlining these claims was issued by these protesters, which was distributed in different mosques (Figure 4.11).[40]

Meanwhile, a section of local Muslims visited the Naib Imam and requested him to intervene in this crisis. Quite unexpectedly, Ahmad Bukhari refused to participate in this agitation and advised these Muslims to ignore this matter. He also told them that this kind of protest would increase communal tension in the locality.[41] The Imam's advice was completely disregarded and an umbrella organieation, the Rabata Islam, was established for this campaign.

The initial plan of the protesters was to organise a peaceful demonstration on 16 January 1996. However, the local police did not grant permission to hold any public activity for next two to three days (JMD3). Moreover, the letters sent to the Home Minister and issued to the press were virtually ignored by administration. In such a situation, the demonstrators decided to take a direct action.[42]

---

[39] Quite intriguingly, Sikander Bakht was alive at that time and in fact he took part in this ceremony which actually intended to establish a school in memory of his services! It was a bizarre event because usually 'memorials' are built to commemorate a dead person. The BJP could not find a Hindutva supporter Muslim personality and finally it had to honour Sikander Bakht.

[40] These activists also sent these pamphlets and press statements to the English, Hindi and Urdu press. However, except the Urdu Daily *Awam*, no one gave importance to this news at this point (GD2).

[41] I am thankful to Hafiz Mohammed Javed and Amin Hayatullah Mir for this information. These two were among those Muslims who approached the Naib Imam on 12 January 1996 (JMD3).

[42] A hand written pamphlet was circulated in the locality (Figure 4.11). It says: Sri Krishna Advani's arrival at the Jama Masjid: Gentlemen, you will be highly distressed to learn that Sri Krishna Advani, who is responsible for (1) the murder of thousands of Muslims and (2) the destruction of the Babri mosque, is now planning to visit the Jama mosque, a wakf property. Mr. Advani, as we know, represents the Fascist and anti-Muslim Bharatiya Janata Party, which, after destroying the Babri Masjid is now intending to seize another endowment with its bloody claws. We leave it to you to decide if such a visit is tantamount to rubbing slat in our wounds, or applying balm to them. Programme: Tuesday, 9:00 AM, 16th January, 1996. Venue: Waqf 'Ali-Ullah', Kamra Bangash, near Khajoor Wali Masjid,

Figure 4.11: Pamphlet Distributed in Different Mosques by the YWS Activists against L. K. Advani's Visit

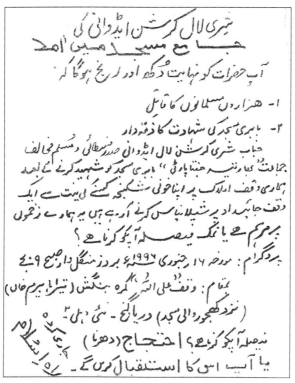

Source: HA Collection, 2005.

On 15 January around 8 p.m. these activists gathered at Kamra Bangash and proceeded towards the Jama Masjid to mobilise Muslims to stop L. K. Advani. As it was expected, the police forcibly stopped the protesters at Jama Masjid and arrested 23 people including Maulana Dehlavi (JMD2o).

These arrests provoked local leaders to make political use of this event. Perhaps for that reason the local Janata Dal MLA Shoib Iqbal and a few local communist leaders came into picture. The MLA joined the protesters and announced that he would stop Advani

---

Darya Ganj, New Delhi 2. Decide whether to welcome him, or protest his visit with a sit-in! Issued by: Rah-i-Islam.

180　*Muslim Political Discourse in Postcolonial India*

and others on 16 January. This action further intensified the local agitation and attracted the national media. In fact, all the national newspapers published this story in their late night edition. The MLA was also arrested later in the morning.

On 16 January 1996, an *unofficial* curfew was imposed in old Delhi to smoothly organise the function at Kamra Bangash. In the presence of senior BJP leaders and a few local supporters, L. K. Advani laid the foundation stone of the Sikander Bakht Memorial School. However, the strong local opposition affected the actual turnout and the BJP virtually failed to attract local Muslims. In fact, it was a highly flop show.

Finally the protesters along with the MLA were released. On the next day, a public meeting was organised by the *Rabata Islam* activists in the Jama Masjid locality. The speakers, including those who were arrested, described their efforts and the apathetic attitude of the authorities. Interestingly, the role of the Shahi Imam was severely criticised. In his speech, Maulana Dehlavi, the main leader of this agitation raised the issue of 'Imamat'. Underlining the religious status of an Imam, Dehlavi criticised Abdullah Bukhari and Ahmad Bukhari for misguiding Muslims (JMD3).

The Wazukhana

This was a very turbulent time for the Naib Imam. He had lost his political credibility. In fact, this was first time when the role of the Imam was directly condemned by the local Muslims. Moreover, the general elections were also fast approaching and this local opposition could have an adverse effect on the long-term political prospects of the Imam. Thus, it was essential for Ahmad Bukhari to work out a clear plan of action to regain his political authority.

In the last week of January 1996, a huge structure adjacent to the main park of the Jama Masjid was constructed as the new Wazukhana. This move created a much needed media hype for the Naib Imam. The Indian National Trust for Art and Cultural Heritage (INTACH) and the Conservation Society of Delhi (CSD) filed two separate Public Interest Litigations (PILs) against the *illegal* Wazukhana in the Delhi High Court (HC) and demanded that the structure should immediately be pulled down (JMD2p).

Following these PILs, the HC issued notices to all the concerned bodies on 12 February 1996 and asked the DDA to demolish this structure. Next day, the DDA demolition squad visited the site.

Interestingly, the Naib Imam and his men did not allow the police and the DDA officials to enter into this controversial structure and as a result of this opposition, these officials had to retreat (JMD2q). The virtual defeat of the police and the DDA to pull down this structure and the statement made by the leading conservationists against the Naib Imam provided a new political stage to Ahmad Bukhari. He started mobilising local Muslims for the protection of the 'sacred Wazukhana'. Several public meetings were organised in the locality and the Wazukhana was described as an integral part of Jama Masjid, which could not be demolished.

When Ahmad Bukhari was totally involved in the Wazukhana episode, something extraordinary happened, which not only strengthened the Wazukhana debate but also opened new political prospects for him. On 29 February 1996, a local court issued a non-bailable warrant against the Naib Imam for delivering a provocative speech in January 1993 after the demolition of the Babri Masjid (JMD2r). The timing of this judgement was crucial. The movement to save the Wazukhana was going on and local Muslims had been fully involved in this issue. In such a scenario, it was impossible for the local Muslims to differentiate between these two cases, which had no direct connection. Eventually, the non-bailable warrant in the 1993 case and the Wazukhana episode provided a great help to the Naib Imam to divert the public attention. He along with local MLAs visited different mosques of the locality and asked people to extend their moral support to save the Wazukhana. Ahmad Bukhari also mentioned that the arrest warrants had been served to him primarily because of his involvement in the construction of Wazukhana for the devotees of Jama Masjid (GD1).

The Naib Imam was aware of the complexities of the legal process and did not want to lose any opportunity in both the cases. In fact, he continued to follow a very subtle course of action. He challenged the arrest warrant issued to him in the HC by raising objection against the contents of this order. He described the order of lower court as anti-Muslim (JMD2s). At the same time on the very next day the Naib Imam submitted an official reply on behalf of the Jama Masjid Trust in the Wazukhana case. His counsel assured the HC that the illegal structure would be demolished within one month. The Naib Imam also requested the court that an alternative place for the Wazukhana should be immediately allotted to the Jama Masjid Trust (JMD2t).

182 *Muslim Political Discourse in Postcolonial India*

The court accepted his petition in the 1993 speech case and granted an interim stay (JMD2s). In the Wazukhana case, the HC also gave him a crucial four weeks' time to demolish the illegal construction (JMD2u). These legal orders encouraged Ahmad Bukhari to take full advantage of the confusion created by the parallel trial of these two court cases. In an interview on 7 April 1996, he said that he would not give up Wazukhana issue and would make a representation in the court (JMD2v). This statement was quite contradictory to his official reply in this case.

By that time, this episode had become a national issue. This was the turn of P.V. Narasimha Rao, the Prime Minister of India, to offer the services of 'his good offices' to solve this vexed question of Wazukhana. Mr. Rao announced that a five-member committee would be constituted for settling the Wazukhana issue (JMD2w). Consequently, the central government filed an application in the HC, seeking four weeks' time to implement the court order in this case (JMD2x). The HC, accepting the centre's plea, gave a further three weeks to demolish this structure on (JMD2y). Finally, on 11 May 1996 the Wazukhana, in which no Muslim had ever performed ablutions, was demolished by the DDA. The Imam announced that three new underground Wazukhanas would be constructed with help of the DDA and other agencies (JMD2z). At present there is no Wazukhana in Jama Masjid, and no one knows when these three Wazukhanas will be constructed for the devotees.

The move to construct a Wazukhana for Jama Masjid was very significant in three respects. First, the 'Wazukhana' was shown as a genuine religious need of devotees. Bukhari asked Muslims that the protection of Wazukhana was a religious issue. Interestingly, he established a direct connection between the 1993 case and the Wazukhana case and mobilised support of the Muslims in the name of religion. Second, the Wazukhana issue provoked the secular conservationists to take legal action against Bukhari. The PILs filed by INTACH actually helped him in highlighting the Wazukhana issue as an infringement of given minority rights. Finally, this move overshadowed his tacit support to the BJP in the Kamra Bangash case. He successfully used the Jama Masjid to sideline the local opposition and regain his political authority. In fact, the Wazukhana episode became a 'Muslim issue'.

Jama Masjid and the Political Memory of a Royal Muslim Past **183**

IV

MONUMENTALISATION OF JAMA MASJID AND THE MEMORY OF A ROYAL MUSLIM PAST

The case of Jama Masjid very clearly shows how history, law and memory were used by the Imam and his son innovatively in three different cases. In fact, these three events demonstrate three different political configurations of law, history and memory. In the first case, the traditional role and religious significance of the institution of Imam was used as the main argument by the Imam. The local memory was juxtaposed with the legal authority of the Wakf Board. Interestingly, the DWB was shown as a kind of coercive institution of the state. Thus, in this case the core of the argument was based on memory. In the second case, the official history and status of Jama Masjid as a historical monument was underlined. The religious status of Jama Masjid was relegated to the margin for purely political purposes. The Imam recognised the legal-constitutional framework of rights for articulating political demands. Finally in the Wazukhana case, the court orders were exploited as political tools to sideline the agendas of secular conservationists as well as the local anti-Imam lobbies and groups. The legal battle over the Wazukhana was justified on the basis of religious needs and at the same time used to challenge the official history and the status of Jama Masjid as a historical monument (Table 4.1).

The significant position of Jama Masjid as a mosque/monument in these three different events gives us an opportunity to explore the symbolic connection between the Shahi Imam and the wider Muslim politics of monuments. In a straightforward sense, this question is linked to the political strategy of the Imam which has been revolving around the memory of a royal Muslim past. I now discuss three significant political techniques of the Imam Abdullah Bukhari and to some extent, Ahmad Bukhari to understand the political construction of this memory.

(*a*) The skillful use of the PAS of the Jama Masjid
(*b*) A clear, simple, and aggressive Urdu language
(*c*) The dress code of a traditional Imam with a *Shahi* touch

Let us begin with the PAS of the Jama Masjid. The Imam recognised the PAS as an instrument to shape the public opinion in a favourable

Table 4.1: Imam's Politics Compared: Memory, Law and History

Imam's politics	1975	1987	1996
What is Jama Masjid?	A religious place of worship which is linked to the *everyday life of Muslim community*.	A religious place of worship which is a historical monument.	A religious place of worship, which has a special legal status.
The problem	Administrative control of the mosque	Occupation of the Babri Masjid by Hindus and anti-Muslim riots.	Muslims have some religious needs therefore some changes are required in the outer structure of the mosque.
Enemy	DWB/The ruling Indira Gandhi-led national government	The state because it does not respond to Muslim demands despite projecting Jama Masjid as Muslim monument.	The secular conservation agencies that do not understand the religious issues related to historic places of worship.
What is to be done?	Liberate Jama Masjid from the DWD	Close down Jama Masjid	A wazukhana needs to be constructed.
Justification given	DWB is a symbol of the state, which is not concerned about the Muslim community.	Closer of a functional monument by a religious authority will affect the image of the government-nationally and internationally	A wazukhana is an inseparable part of mosque therefore it has a religious as well as legal value as per the given minority rights.
What really happened	Jama Masjid is still a wakf property.	Virtually no demand was accepted.	Wazukhana was demolished by the Imam himself.

Source: Author.

Jama Masjid and the Political Memory of a Royal Muslim Past 185

fashion. Bukhari's insistence on the use of PAS, even some times without electric supply, was a conscious decision. In fact, his Friday speeches virtually transformed the PAS of Jama Masjid into a kind of 'mass media', which clearly established a link between the past and the present of Jama Masjid.

Figure 4.12: PAS of the Jama Masjid

Source: HA Collection, 2005.

Most importantly, this 'media' had a specific local significance. The educational backwardness of the majority of local Muslims was a major reason behind the success of this new kind of media. These Muslims did not have access to the conventional media sources. Even the circulation of local Urdu newspapers was very limited. In this context, the PAS of Jama Masjid was easily accessible, more focused on Muslim issues and most importantly capable of communicating with a variety of audiences: the local Muslims, national media and the government, without losing the internal consistency of the immediate political objective of the Imam.[43]

---

[43] This is exactly what I was told in a group discussion. The students of Class IX and X of the Sarvodaya School, Jama Masjid (Urdu Medium), pointed out that there was a significant difference between other mosques

186   *Muslim Political Discourse in Postcolonial India*

The language, the tone and the contents of the speeches of the Imam were equally important political techniques. In fact, the use of straightforward Urdu/Hindustani increased the potential of the PAS of the Jama Masjid. Abdullah Bukhari was the first Muslim political leader who did not follow the traditional style of Urdu oratory. His language was precise, clear, and always to the point. Unlike others, the Imam used an Urdu dialect, which is often denounced as the *Dilli ki bazaru zaban* (the street language of Delhi). In his speech on 15 August 1974, he even used very objectionable language against Mrs. Gandhi, the prime Minister of India. The Imam said *'Yeh Jhuti Hai'* (she is a liar), *'O Indira Gandhi tu sun le'* (Hey Indira Gandhi, listen) (Khan 2004, Int.). This kind of language is often rejected by the modernists and educated Muslim intellectuals and leaders on the ground for its poor literary standard. However, the direct impact of this language on the masses as well as on the national media cannot be ignored.[44] The Imam, in fact, provided a legitimacy to the language of poor and marginalized Muslims of Delhi.

The contents of his speeches are also very significant. His Friday sermons were highly articulate and quite often followed a well-structured pattern. Let us discuss the controversial Friday sermon of 14 February 1986 as an example. This sermon was very crucial because it led to a series of communal clashes in north India.[45]

---

and Jama Masjid. In other mosques of the locality they do not get any kind of 'information'. These mosques are simply treated as religious places of worship. But, the status of Jama Masjid is different. Here they are informed and educated about the important Muslim issues/problems and their possible solutions. It is important to note that these students represent the generation which grew up during the time of Babri Masjid agitation and are not fully aware of the events of 1975. Yet, their memories of Jama Masjid are shaped by the PAS of the mosque (GD 3).

[44] Ahmad Bukhari also tries to imitate Abdullah Bukhari's style of oratory. In a television programme when film actresses Shabana Azmi provoked him to clarify his stand on Talibani regime he said *"Me nachne gane walion ke muh nahi lagta"* (I do not talk to those women who sing and dance) (JMD2aa).

[45] The Imam never used any kind of written text for his sermons and it is impossible to get the full account of this speech. Thus, the PUCL report on Delhi riots, the newspaper reports and the discussions with local residents are employed to find out the basic structure of this speech (PUCL Bulletin:

Jama Masjid and the Political Memory of a Royal Muslim Past **187**

For the purpose of analysis this sermon could be divided into three parts. The first part was intended to provide 'information'. The Imam linked the Babri Masjid case with the secular credentials of the government. The Imam gave a critical appraisal of the 'secular' policies of the government and alleged that the government was trying to disturb the communal harmony by 'inventing' contentious issues like Babri Masjid. He emphatically pointed out that the struggle of Muslims for the mosque was not against the Hindus. On the contrary, the agitation had always been against the *firkhwarana Ta'kate* (communal forces). His version of the Babri Masjid dispute was not based on the fine details of the case. The core 'facts' of the case, were selected, interpreted and delivered as impartial objective information partly to justify his interpretation of secularism and partly to establish credibility of his political acts.

The second part of the sermon contained three elements: the explicit central message that he actually wanted to deliver, a confession to the unity of the Muslims in India to provide a wider acceptability to the central message and a political threat to the government. The Imam used a highly assertive and provocative language. Praising the young men of his *qaum* (community) for their energies, strength, and powers, he claimed that these young Muslim fellows were capable of destroying the entire establishment within an hour! However, he did not want any kind of violence and therefore requested the government to find out an amicable solution. The final part of the sermon focused on local issues such as maintaining peace and communal harmony. The Imam quite dramatically tried to 'pacify' his young men and appealed to all the members of his community to go home peacefully and avoid confrontation with the police.

A simple re-reading of this sermon suggests that the Imam was fully aware of the potential of public oratory. Despite the fact that this was a highly provocative speech no one can deny that he spoke of the unity of all depressed classes and groups, Hindu–Muslim harmony and the need for national integration. But, at the same time, he contrasted the legal power of the secular state with the strength of Muslim community in India. He posed a clear threat

---

1986). Moreover, I am thankful to Nadim and Shafiquddin Khaksar, who were at Jama Masjid on that day, for discussing the content of this speech with me (JMD3).

188   *Muslim Political Discourse in Postcolonial India*

to the existence of the Indian state. These paradoxical statements helped him to communicate with different stakeholders. For local Muslims, it was a courageous act. He openly challenged the authority of the state. For secular media, it was a 'communal' Islamic sermon, which could easily be shown to justify the great communal versus secular divide. And finally for the political parties, it was a clear message that the Imam was the only Muslim leader who could help them in capturing decisive Muslim votes in the elections.

The powerful voice of Imam Bukhari was always complimented by his conventional public appearance, particularly his choice of clothes. The Imam preferred to wear two kinds of clothes for public ceremonies and functions: (*a*) a long white *Kurta*, a green check *Tahmad/Lungi* along with the traditional white or red skull cap. (*b*) Long white *Kurta*, *Pyjama* with a black robe. This kind of dress code is quite unusual for a Muslim politician even today. The Muslim politicians either wear *Sherwani*, an elite dress for the Muslim educated classes or simple white *Kurta Pyjama* with skull cap. Even the Ulema of Deoband or Nadwa prefer to put on *Pyjamas* with *Kurta* for public ceremonies.

The *Tahmad* and the robe were two important changes introduced by the Imam quite symbolically. Wearing a *Tahmad* in public was a symbolic act in two ways. First, *Tahmad* has a religious impact. It is considered a *Sunna* (Imitation) of Prophet Mohammad because he wore *Tahmad* throughout his life. The Imams of the mosques and the other religious minded people, particularly in South Asia, put on *Tahmad* to imitate the pious dress of the Prophet. Second, and perhaps more importantly, poor labourer and lower caste Muslims also wear *Tahmad*. In fact, the *Tahmad* is not recognised as the dress of the *Ashraf* (Upper caste) and usually associated with *Shaboos* (a word used for local uneducated and lower caste Muslims in Delhi) in northern India.

The black robe had a different kind of political significance. The robe simply established a symbolic relationship between the Imam of the holy mosque at Mecca, who wears a big black robe on every important religious occasion, and the Imam of Jama Masjid. On the other hand, it also signifies the eternal bond between the Imam of Jama Masjid and his royal past. As a matter of fact, the robe itself becomes a relic of a bygone era. Abdullah Bukhari identified these two symbolic aspects and re-introduced the traditional Muslim dress code with a touch of royal past. It helped him to get access

Figure 4.13: Imam Abdullah Bukhari in Tahmad and Kurta

Source: HA Collection, 2005.

to the marginalised lower caste Muslims and at the same time provided him a 'media friendly' look. The national media found an ideal 'image' of a pious-poor and aggressive Muslim in Imam Bukhari, who could legitimately be evoked to justify the closed and in-ward looking character of the Indian Muslim community. His provocative language and dress code in the later years established him as a sensational news maker.

The success of the Imam is also related to the changing economic and social profile of old Delhi. The Kabaris were the ardent supporters of the Imam.[46] These Kabaris mostly belong to a lower Muslim Biradari (caste) locally called *Bhihishti/Sakhke*. The Kabaris, who used to work as water suppliers to the local households since

---

[46] The word Urdu/Hindustani 'Kabari' emerges from the word 'Kabara' that literally means 'rubbish'. The Kabari is the person who collects and sells old/second-hand things.

Figure 4.14: Ahmad Bukhari and Abdullah Bukhari Wearing Robes

Source: HA Collection, 2005.

the time of Shah Jahan, became economically powerful in the 1970s. They used to collect old cars and the wreckage of accident cars/vehicle from individuals, companies and quite often from car thieves and sell cheap automobile parts. Despite becoming economically powerful, the lower caste Kabaris did not have a say in mainstream Muslim politics. The local Muslim leadership was in the hands of educated upper caste Muslims from *Syed, Pathan, Mughal* or *Shaikh* backgrounds. There was an obvious feeling of isolation among the *Sakhke Kabari* community of the Jama Masjid area. Despite emphasising the need of 'Muslim brotherhood', the upper caste Muslims, intentionally or unintentionally, did not provide any political space to these *Kabaris*. The Imam, who himself was a Syed by caste, was the first political leader who recognised Kabaris as an emerging political force. In all the institutions and committees established by the Imam, Kabaris were given key positions.

The Imam very creatively placed the Jama Masjid into the dominant Indian political discourse by questioning the ways by which the modern notion of a monument is conceptualised. In this attempt, he highlighted the intrinsic historical connection among the Muslims of India and very silently linked the 'present' of Indian Muslims with a royal Muslim past — reassuring Muslims that they were the past rulers of this country. Interestingly, this memory of the royal Muslim past was placed in the legal-constitutional discourse of secularism and minority rights. In this sense, he not only provided a 'historical foundation' to the idea of a single Muslim community but also redefined the logic of Muslim politics as secular politics.

■

5

Babri Masjid and the Muslim Politics
of Right to Heritage

There are many popular images of the Babri Masjid–Ram Temple
dispute, which have been surviving in public debates for the last
three decades. In the initial phase, the dispute was understood
as a fundamentalist and polemical demand of a few religious
fanatics, which, it was hoped and in fact strongly believed, would
be inevitably rejected by the *secular* people of India.[1] The Meerut
riots of 1987 and rise of the Bharatiya Janata Party (BJP) as an important political force affected these perceptions quite significantly,
though the binaries of base-superstructure/traditional-modern/
communal-secular continued to determine the ways in which this
dispute was analysed. Finally, after the demolition of the Babri
Masjid in 1992, the dispute turned into an ideological struggle
between, what is often called *secularisms* and *Hindu communalism*.
These changing images of the dispute, very intriguingly, hide
the independent and multiple Muslim political responses to this
question. In fact, the relationship between the Babri Masjid case
and the positions of Muslim political groups on wakf properties,
particularly on protected historical mosques was not at all considered. As a result, the Babri Masjid dispute is either conceptualised
as a challenge to Indian secularism or as a symbol of aggressive
Hindu politics. Focusing upon the Muslim political responses

---

[1] I am referring here to the public debates and academic discussions
in the late 1980s which were dominated by a particular kind of 'secular'
interpretation of religious politics. Bipan Chandra, for instance, writes:
'Communalism is not yet the dominant mode of thought of the Indian
people . . . Even where the communalists have come to power, even where
during the last forty years the communal parties have won elections,
they know that even the people who have voted for them have not yet
imbibed communal ideology on a significant scale; the Indian people are
still secular' (1990: 44).

Babri Masjid and the Muslim Politics of Right to Heritage **193**

to Babri Masjid issue, this chapter attempts to explore different political agendas and strategies of various Muslim organisations and political leaders at local, regional and national levels. More precisely, I look at three kinds of issues:

(*a*) What are the Muslim 'histories' of the Babri Masjid dispute? How do such accounts differ from other versions of this case?

(*b*) What has been the role of judiciary in the Babri Masjid case? Why did the Muslim positions on legal proceedings change quite considerably in the post-1986 period?

(*c*) How and why did the Muslim political groups transform the Babri Masjid into a question of secularism and right to heritage? Why did they demand that the mosque should be declared a protected monument? What encouraged them to constitute the grand 'Muslim political coalition' on Babri Masjid? How did this 'fragile' coalition work and why did it collapse within two years?

The chapter concentrates on the relationship between the Babri Masjid issue and changing nature of collective Muslim politics in contemporary India. I try to highlight how the right to heritage is politically interpreted in the post-1970 period and how the Muslim political responses in the Babri Masjid case played a very significant role in the ideological polarisation of Indian politics into secular and communal camps.

I

MONUMENTALISATION OF THE DISPUTE: 'HISTORIES' OF THE BABRI MASJID

To understand the Muslim position(s) on Babri Masjid, particularly in relation to the secular and the Hindutva discourses, let us examine how different narratives present, interpret and explain the selected 'facts' and portray the Babri Masjid either as a 'disputed' site or as an undisputed mosque. For the purpose of analysis, I focus on five narratives: the dominant Hindutva narrative, the local Hindutva narrative, the objective-secular narrative, the dominant Muslim narrative and the local Muslim narrative.

194 *Muslim Political Discourse in Postcolonial India*

The Dominant Hindutva Narrative

The dominant Hindutva narrative is based on the following four claims:

- The Hindus have always believed that there is a very sacred spot at Ayodhya where Lord Ram was born.
- The spot is the very site where the Babri Masjid was built.
- A temple dedicated to Lord Ram stood at this holy site before the Babri Masjid was built.
- The temple was pulled down to construct the Babri Masjid at this spot (Sharma et al. 1991: 2).

A close examination of these assertions suggests that the first two claims concentrate on popular memory and Hindu belief. For example, L. K. Advani during his *rath yatra* campaign pointed out:

> I hold that *there is no mosque there*. There is a structure of a mosque above the temple. And the problem is that the Hindu sentiments are attached to the place . . . I have not heard anyone asking for the birth certificate of [those] great saints. Can you prove archaeologically or historically the birth place of Christ? (emphasis original, MID 103: 309).

This statement shows that Hindutva leaders refute the 'findings' of the secular historians on the basis of Hindu faith in Lord Ram's existence and his birth place while simultaneously using popular memory to mobilise Hindus.[2]

However, it does not mean that the dominant Hindutva politics did not rely on legal and historical facts. Actually, the last two arguments are in many respects more 'historical' and the Hindutva ideologues produce archaeological and legal evidences to prove

---

[2] The 19 Points Questionnaire submitted by the Vishwa Hindu Parishad (VHP) on 3 October 1991 to the AIBMAC is the best example to elaborate these claims. In fact, these 19 questions not only try to substantiate VHP's position but also interrogate the dominant Muslim standpoint that a mosque cannot be altered or shifted (Appendix 2).

Babri Masjid and the Muslim Politics of Right to Heritage **195**

these points. Interestingly, they focus mainly on the writings of British colonial officials and the Muslim scholars of 19th century.[3]

The memory/faith is the focal point of their assertion while official history and law are used to substantiate it. As a result, this version intentionally avoids any detailed discussion on ancient Sanskrit texts and/or the growth of Muslim Sufi traditions in Ayodhya. Above all, this position justifies the destruction of Ram temple at Ayodhya by highlighting other incidents of desecration of Hindu temples by Muslim rulers in medieval India.

The Local Hindutva Narrative

Unlike the dominant and sophisticated Hindutva position of BJP and VHP, the local Hindi literature and guidebooks, which are very popular in Ayodhya, offer us another version of localised Hindutva. In these books, the local myths and folktales are intermingled with the political project of national level Hindutva. The inscriptions and huge paintings depicting the major events of the Ram temple movement at the Kar Sewa Puram, a museum established in Ayodhya during the time of Kar Sewa, is the best example to illustrate this point.[4] According to these inscriptions:

> King Vikramaditya built the grand Ram temple with 84 artistic black pillars. 16 pillars of this kind are still in Ayodhya. When Babar came to Ayodhya, Baba Shayamanada ji was the chief priest of the Ram temple. He was a learned man, who did not believe in social inequality of any kind. Pretending to be the real fakirs, Fazal Abbas and Jalal Shah joined the Baba Shayamanda and became his disciples ... Babar told these fakirs "you people could help me in winning this war, what you want in return". Bearing in mind the status of Ram Janam Bhumi Temple, these fakirs thought that building a mosque on the site of the temple would help in establishing the Islamic supremacy in India. Both of these fakirs compelled Babar to destroy the temple ... Because of the resistance of local Hindus, Babar's army could not enter into the temple. Then, cannons were used to

---

[3] Deoki Nandan's article published on the official website of the VHP is a good example of this position (Nandan 2006, accessed on 13 August 2005).

[4] Such localised version of the dispute is further elaborated in the local guidebooks, which are sold near the disputed site in Ayodhya. See Sharad (n.d.).

196   *Muslim Political Discourse in Postcolonial India*

destroy the temple. Fakir Jalal Shah ordered that the blood of dead Hindus would be used for building the foundation of the mosque (AD1).

The inscription further describes a series of events that show how Hindus and Sikhs had been struggling to liberate the Ram temple. An attempt is also made to highlight the contribution of a few local 'nationalist Muslims', who decided to handover the mosque to Hindus so as to fight against the British colonialism.[5] The inscription says:

> Because of the efforts of Hindu leader Baba Ramcharan Das and the leader of the Muslims Amir Ali, Hindus and Muslims of Ayodhya and Faizabad unanimously decided to give Ram Janam Bhumi to Hindus so that both the communities could wage a war against the British. However, due to the conspiracy of the British, both the leaders were declared as mutineers and were later killed by the British. (AD1)

The Sufis, who are highly praised by local Muslims and even by Hindus, are shown as the main culprit in this story. This version tells us that the destruction of Ram temple was a conspiracy of Muslim Sufis, who helped the royal powers to uproot Hindu religion as well as political control. This *history* simply does not rely on evidence. Instead, local beliefs are exploited to create favourable 'historical' facts.

The Secular Narrative

Let us now move on to the secular version.[6] This explanation was produced by professional historians, who represented their findings as the most authentic 'impartial' historical account of this case. These historians employed a 'scientific' method to systematically

---

[5] There are many conflicting stories about Amir Ali. According to one historical version he was actually killed by the forces of the Nawab. For a detailed discussion on his role, see Srivastva (1989: 22–25).

[6] It is to be clarified that I use the term 'secular/secularists' for those, who prefer to call themselves 'secular' to draw a dividing line between the 'scientific' facts and popular beliefs for producing an 'objective, unbiased and neutral' account of this dispute. Interestingly, this 'neutrality' gradually developed in a well-defined political position. For an excellent discussion on this point see Bhattacharya (2008).

Figure 5.1: Kar Sewa Puram Ayodhya

Source: HA Collection, 2005.

collect historic documents and archaeological evidence. They questioned the Hindutva position and produced well-articulated arguments in favour of the Babri Masjid.

The secular version rests on the following three premises:

- Due to lack of sufficient facts, the historicity of Ram and his birth place cannot be proved.
- There is no evidence which suggests that there was a grand temple dedicated to Lord Ram, which was later destroyed by Babar.
- The recorded history suggests that myth of temple destruction was invented by the disruptive and communal forces: first by the British, then by the communal Muslim authors of 19th century and finally by the Hindutva forces.

I take two examples to illustrate these claims: the *Babari Masjid or Rama's Birth Place: The Historians Report to the Indian Nation* 1991) and Irfan Habib's *Address to the Aligarh Historian Group*.

The *Historians Report* revolves around the historical and archaeological claims made by the VHP and tries to refute these claims on 'historical' grounds. Surprisingly, the report does not talk about

198 *Muslim Political Discourse in Postcolonial India*

the position or claims made by the Babri Masjid Action Committee (BMAC).[7] Instead, we are told that the independent historians of this report requested the government to participate in the negotiations on the Babri Masjid dispute. However, the government did not respond to this demand and maintained a conspicuous silence. Eventually, these independent historians 'thought that national interest required an unbiased and impartial inquiry so that people should be clear about what historical facts are' (Sharma et al. 1991: 1).

The most important part of the report is the section on *'evidence in recorded history'*, which is based on a chronological sequence. The report discuss the translation of the Persian inscription installed at the front gate of the Babri Masjid, the *Ramcharitmanas* of Hindi poet Tulsidas (1575–76), the *Ain-e-Akbari* of Abul Fazal (1598), the travelogue of William Finch (1608), the *Khulastu-Tawarikh* of Sujan Rai Bhandari (1695–96), and the *Chahar Gulshan* of Rai Chaturman (1759–60). The report argues that these authentic documents do not give any indication of the existence of a Ram Temple.

The next section of the report is equally interesting. It further elaborates this sequence and tries to register the *'source of trouble'*. The report points out that the Jesuit priest Joseph Tieffenthaler, who visited Ayodhya in 1788 was the first person who recorded the local Hindu belief that the Babri Masjid was built after destroying a Ram temple. The report quotes Tieffenthaler:

> Emperor Aurangzeb got demolished the fortress of Ramcot, and erected on the same place a Mohomaten temple with three cupolas. Others believe that it was constructed by Babor (Sharma et al. 1991: 9)

Emphasising this account as a major source of trouble, the report suggests that:

> [a] tradition of treating the site of the mosque and its surroundings as sacred was now in its initial phase of creation, marked by the construction of a small rectangular mud platform ... as Rama's crib. No tradition ever remotely existed as yet of there having been a temple

---

[7] The BMAC which had declared that it was ready to abide by the findings of this report, later published the report and circulated it widely. I use the copy published by the BMAC, Lucknow.

here; the entire place was thought to be a part of "Rama's fortress" or "place" (ibid.: 10).

To substantiate this point further, the report uses Francis Buchanan's description of Ayodhya (1810), and concludes that the 'myth' of destroyed Ram Temple gradually strengthened and turned in a local belief in the later period.[8]

If we look at this long sequence, two crucial points emerge. First, the documents which are used to disprove Hindutva claims are completely different from each other. For example, Tulsi Das's *Ramcharitmanas* is a literary-religious text, which does not discuss the major political events of the time when it was written. In contrast, the *Ain-e-Akbari* is a chronicle, which is primarily concerned with the day to day functions of the empire under Akbar. The focus of the other two texts is also very broad. On the basis of a highly mechanical interpretation of these different texts, which were written in various styles and addressed a variety of diverse issues, the report tries to trace the historicity of a politically motivated dispute.

Second, a re-reading of these documents suggests an important shift in the local belief after 1758–59. Tieffenthaler's description of Ayodhya seems to underline a close link between the demolished temples of Benaras and Mathura, which were allegedly destroyed by Aurangzeb and the Babri Masjid. In fact, this account introduces us to the fact that local Hindus started alleging that Aurangzeb was responsible for the destruction of Ram temple or Ram fortress. The Buchanan report further noted that the local Hindus accused Aurangzeb of demolishing the temple. The historians' report does not look at the link between Aurangzeb and Babar, which is crucial in understanding the changing local memory of this dispute. In fact, the political changes that took place in the second half of

---

[8] The Historian Report gives a long quotation of Buchanan: '[t]he people of Ayodhya imagine ... that Vikrama of Ujjain ... erected a fort called Ramgar ... and erected 360 temples ... the destruction (of these temples) is very generally attributed by the Hindus to the furious zeal of Aurangzeb, to whom is imputed the overthrow of the temple in Benaras and Mathura ... the mosque at Ayodhya ... is ascertained by an inscription on its walls to have been built by Babur, five generation before Aurangzeb' (Sharma et al. 1991: 10).

200 *Muslim Political Discourse in Postcolonial India*

18th century in the Awadh region could be traced to look at the growth of this belief.

The secular narrative also questions the books written by Muslim scholars in the 19th century and the reports of the British officials. The Muslim scholars were termed 'communal' and the British reports, which record the popular Hindu belief about the Ram Temple, were rejected for being biased. Let us take Irfan Habib's address to the Aligarh Historians' Group on 12 February 1991 as an example.

In this lecture, Habib tells us about a few Muslim communalists. In his opinion, the works of Muslim scholars of the 19th century, which recorded that the Ram temple was demolished to build the Babri Masjid, represent the Muslim 'communal' position. He points out that Mirza Jaan's *Haqiqa-e-Shohoda* (1855), Azmat Ali Aliv's *Amir Ali Shaheed wa Marka-e-Hanuman Garhi* (1853), Azmat Ali's *Tariq-e-Awadh, Muraqqa-e-Khusarvi* (1854), Mohammad Najmul Ghani Khan's *Tarikh-e-Awadh* (1909, abridged by Zakir Kakorvi), and Maulana Abdul Hai's *HindustanIslami Ahad Mein* are revealing examples, which show that 'the entire evidence which the VHP has created has been put in its lap by Muslim communalists for nearly 150 years' (Habib 1991). He further notes:

> [t]he Babri Masjid is built on a Hindu temple and that too on the Ram Janma Bhumi is the reconstruction of a myth by communalists, Muslims in first place and Hindu in the second ... such communalism has no place in any civilised society ... What is at stake is not a Masjid but the secular content of our heritage (1991).

Now the question arises: is it possible to compare the claims made by the VHP on purely political grounds with the books written by Muslim scholars in the 19th century? This question becomes more complicated when we find that these works are based on popular beliefs, interpretations and memories and do not claim to offer a scientific and factual history of Babri Masjid! Even, if we envisage a link between these 'communal' Muslim 'histories' and the Babri Masjid dispute, a discussion on the ways by which Muslim leaders have accepted, rejected or ignored these accounts would have been more helpful in understanding various Muslim political positions. But, Habib simply overlooks this aspect and seems to justify a grand communal conspiracy theory against 'secular heritage'.

The Dominant Muslim Narrative

The dominant Muslim version rests on the following four arguments:[9]

- Being a mosque as well as a historical monument, Babri Masjid is an inseparable part of India's national heritage.
- The Babri Masjid dispute is a national Muslim issue and therefore it cannot be solved by inviting the local Muslims.
- The claims made by the VHP are not justifiable on historical grounds.
- A mosque is always a mosque, therefore Babri Masjid cannot be shifted anywhere from its original site.

The Declaration of Delhi, which was adopted by the All India Babri Masjid Conference on 22 December 1986, very clearly shows that the dominant Muslim position defined the Babri Masjid as a part of India's national heritage and linked it to the rights of religious minorities. This declaration says:

> The Conference regards the Babri Masjid as a national heritage and as a historical monument but, above all, as a place of Islamic worship whose sanctity must be universally respected by all right minded persons, whatever their religion and whose violation should be regarded as an offence to the religious sentiments of the Muslims but also to the secular order because it contravenes Article 25 of the Constitution (MID 50a: 59–60, 64).

The dominant Muslim version underscores the national significance of the Babri Masjid issue. In 1987, when the government tried to involve local Muslims of Ayodhya for solving the dispute, the AIBMMCC issued a statement and clarified its stand that the Babri Masjid cannot be treated as a local issue. It was asserted that Babri Masjid is a Muslim wakf property and it is symbolically attached to the entire Muslim community (MID 53: 207).

As far as the question of history is concerned, the dominant Muslim position refutes the claims made by the VHP. During the

---

[9] I shall elaborate this position more fully in the second part of this chapter. I simply try to evoke this position to offer a relatively comparative analysis of various conflicting narratives of this dispute.

202   *Muslim Political Discourse in Postcolonial India*

first exchange of documents in 1989, BMMCC issued a long comment on the documents submitted by the VHP. In this statement the emphasis is given to the historical facts presented by the secular historians. Quite interestingly, one does not find any attempt to come out with a well-articulated history of the mosque[10] (MID 79: 305). Quite similarly, the dominant Muslim position gives least importance to the religious or Shariat angle of the case. For instance, defining the status of Babri Masjid during the time of *Shilanyas* in 1990, the All India Muslim Personal Law Board (AIMPLB) issued a statement which says:

> [t]he title [to] and the ownership of a mosque and its site vest in God (*sic*) . . . neither can a mosque be changed nor sold nor purchased nor transferred by way of compromise to any individual or group or govt. nor acquired by a govt . . . That the undeniable historical and legal evidences make it obvious that the Babri Masjid is a mosque. The UP govt. has admitted this fact in its affidavit . . . hence its status in Shariat is that of a mosque. Therefore the (status of a mosque) should be restored . . . as it was till December 22, 1949 (MID 97: 20).

Thus, the dominant Muslim version focuses on the legal side of the case. It does not attempt to produce any 'Muslim history' of the Babri Masjid; instead it sincerely accepts the secular position in this regard.[11]

The Local Muslim Narrative

Tarikh-e-Gumgashta, a popular collection on the Babri Masjid which was first published in 1986 and has been publicised as some kind of 'authentic' history of Muslims of Ayodhya and Faizabad, can

---

[10] All dominant Muslim groups deliberately ignore the books written by the 19th-century Muslim scholars. In fact, Muslim politicians themselves prefer to make their position on history ambiguous and unclear perhaps to avoid any possible discussion on the issue of desecration of Hindu temples.

[11] The questions which were submitted by the AIBMAC to the VHP can be a good example in this regards. The AIBMAC's questionnaire was based on two kinds of questions: the legal questions and the questions related to VHP's campaign. There were only a few historical issues raised in this questionnaire, which shows a serious indifference of Muslim groups towards the formal history of this dispute (Noorani 2003a: 377–80).

Babri Masjid and the Muslim Politics of Right to Heritage **203**

be an example to illustrate the local Muslim version of the dispute. According to the compiler of this history, Ghulam Mohammed, Emperor Babar secretly visited Ayodhya from Kabul during the reign of Sikandar Lodhi. He met two renowned Sufis of that time, Shah Jalaluddin and Musa Ashiqan. These Sufis used to worship in a sacred cottage on a deserted hilltop in Ayodhya. Babar pleaded with the Sufis to make special prayers for his success. The Sufis told him that in order to achieve his objective he would have to build a mosque on that very hilltop. Babar assured the Sufis that a mosque would be constructed there. After defeating Sikander Lodhi in the battle of Panipat in 1526, Babar became the ruler of India. He then ordered his governor of Awadh, Mir Baqi, to construct a mosque on that very spot in Ayodhya. Thus, the Babri Masjid came into existence (Mohammed 1992: 38).

This story simply rules out the demolition of any Ram Temple. Even it does not talk about the religious significance of Ayodhya for Hindus. On the contrary, we are told that the Babri Masjid had a very special status during the Mughal era. The author notes that Emperor Akbar renamed this entire locality as Akbarpur and dedicated land as Wakf for the maintenance of the Babri Masjid and other historic mosques of the city.

The author further informs us that during the reign of Nawab Wajid Ali Shah, the *Bairagi sect* of local Hindus, who belonged to the Hanuman Garhi temple destroyed a mosque supposedly built by Aurangzeb in Ayodhya. They also attacked Babri Masjid and constructed a platform (*Chabutra*) inside the outer compound of the the the mosque. The local Muslims approached the Nawab and asked him to demolish the Chabutra. Instead of taking any action against the Bairagis, the Nawab composed a couplet and sent it back to Muslims (ibid.: 39). The couplet says:

Hum Ishaq ke Bande Hai, Mazahab se nahi waqif,
Gar Kaba kua to kya, Butkhan Hua to kya

(We, the followers of love, are not acquainted with religion, be it a Kaba or be it a pagoda.)

The story further talks about Hindu–Muslim unity in the Awadh region. The author claims that the British played a very dubious role in creating this dispute. According to him, the British fabricated the story of the Ram Temple and provoked the local Hindus to

204 *Muslim Political Discourse in Postcolonial India*

claim the Babri Masjid site (Mohammed 1992: 40). The other part of this story is very similar to the dominant Muslim version. It highlights the subsequent legal battle and the forcible conversion of the mosque into a temple in 1949.

This interesting narrative not only employs the legal facts and historical evidence in support of its claims over Babri Masjid but also links these 'objective' facts with local myths and folktales. In addition, this story very clearly establishes a connection between Sufism and the Muslim rule in medieval India. In fact, the imagination of a royal Muslim past is legitimised by evoking the contribution of local sufi tradition. However, this version pays no attention to the local level conflicts, which are highlighted overwhelmingly by the Hindu story.

This brief review of different narratives of the dispute summarises the details of the case and introduces us to the areas of tensions and conflicts. I find that these descriptions are multi-layered. Every story is based on a conscious selection of a few 'critical' events and interpretations of 'evidence'. Even the local-level versions, which in many respects do not fully deviate from dominant Hindutva and Muslim versions, seem to have 'reinvented' historical facts for sustaining their own explanation of the dispute. So, what do these positions tell us about the dispute? Table 5.1 illustrates the following four important points:

(*a*) The various interpretations of the dispute hold different positions on the existence of a Ram Temple, its alleged destruction and subsequent construction of Babri Masjid. Moreover, these versions also identify the specific areas of struggle, which simply correspond to their own explanation of the dispute. For example, dominant Hindutva seems to over-emphasise politics of faith because its position on law and history is not very strong. Similarly, the dominant Muslim position does not want to get involved in the issues of history; therefore they prefer to call it a 'legal issue'.

(*b*) The dominant Muslim position ignores the works of Muslim scholars of the 19th century, who had claimed that the mosque was built by destroying a Ram temple. Moreover, the Muslim position on desecration of Hindu temples is also not very clear. This deliberate silence on medieval history underscores the point that the dominant Muslim position

Table 5.1: Narratives of the Babri Masjid–Ram Temple Dispute

Version	What is Babri Masjid?	Focus	Main Argument	Preferred Area of Contest/Negotiation	Least Interested in
Dominant Hindutva	It is a structure of a mosque over a site of a temple.	1. Hindu faith 2. History of the desecration of Hindu temples in medieval India by Muslim rulers.	Faith in Ram's birthplace is ultimate and unquestionable. Restoration/construction of a temple is the ultimate goal for the protection of Hindu and dignity.	Actual domain of politics.	1. Sanskrit texts 2. Local Hinduism, which is heavily influenced by regional Sufi tradition.
Local Hindutva	It is a temple, which is converted into a mosque.	Local polemics to construct an imaginary historical narrative.	Ram's birthplace is sacred and therefore the restoration/construction of a temple is religiously desirable.	Actual domain of politics.	Religious significance of Sufis and the shared cultural life of local communities.
Secular	It is a part of India's secular heritage. Its status as a mosque is historically unquestionable. Therefore, its protection as a mosque is a secular act.	Historical sources to construct a legally justifiable narrative.	No evidence of Ram. Construction of a temple on the site a historical monument that is also a mosque is legally and historically unjustifiable.	Professional history.	1. Strong local belief that a temple was actually destroyed. 2. Desecration of Hindu temple debate.

Table 5.1: (*Continued*)

Table 5.1: (*Continued*)

Version	What is Babri Masjid?	Focus	Main Argument	Preferred Area of Contest/Negotiation	Least Interested in
Dominant Muslim	It is a mosque, which is also a part of India's heritage.	It is a legal question which is even supported by secular history.	It is a legal issue and inextricably linked to the constitutional rights given to Muslims.	Law	1. Long history of the dispute and the 19th century texts which talks about desecration of Hindu temples. 2. Islamic notions of a disputed mosque.
Local Muslim	The site of the mosque is recognised very sacred even before the construction of the mosque.	Imaginary History.	It is a mosque, which cannot be shifted.	Law	Muslim participation in local cultural life, especially in those festivals which are associated with local Hindus beliefs.

Source: Author.

Babri Masjid and the Muslim Politics of Right to Heritage **207**

does not directly respond to the issues raised by Hindutva. Rather, it has its own agenda. It supports the secular historians' 'findings/views' to substantiate its claim on the Babri Masjid. However, for the purpose of mobilisation, as we shall see later, this position relies on the memory of a royal Muslim past.

(c) The local Muslim position is also quite different from the dominant Muslim position, which shows the internal diversity of Muslim response on this issue.

(d) The emphasis of Muslim positions on law and minority rights somewhere establishes a link between the Babri Masjid and the legal aspects of the process of monumentalisation, which I have discussed in previous chapters.

Now the question is, if the Babri Masjid has always been recognised purely as a legal issue by the Muslim politicians and if they were committed to solve the dispute through the judicial process, particularly after the re-opening of the mosque in 1986, what was the logic behind their political activities? For analysing this question, we need to look at the complex legal aspects of this case carefully.

II

Understanding the Legal Case(s)

It is important to recognise the specificity of the legal discourse in the Babri Masjid case at least in three crucial ways. First, the legal debates demonstrate the manner in which the 'claims' of the parties in conflict are articulated in a legal language as justifiable assertions. Second, different judicial verdicts illustrate how such contradictory claims have been interpreted by the judiciary with the help of available legal resources at various stages of the case. And finally, the judgements given in various cases reveal how the legal discourse has been playing a significant role in transforming the legal status of the actual disputed site. For these reasons, the specificity of the changing judicial-legal discourse and its precise impact on actual politics turns out to be a crucial aspect of the case. Thus, the changing legal status of disputed site of Babri Masjid needs to be examined for understanding the ways in which its politics is played out.

208 *Muslim Political Discourse in Postcolonial India*

Babri Masjid as a Wakf Property

Let us begin with the wakf status of Babri Masjid. According to official wakf records, after the construction of the mosque, Babar arranged an annual cash grant of INR 60 for the maintenance of the mosque and the family of the *Mutawalli* (caretaker). This grant continued to be paid in cash by subsequent Mughal kings. The arrangement did not change during the regime of the Nawabs. In fact, Nawab Sa'dat Ali Khan increased the annual grant to INR 302. The establishment of British rule after the War of 1857 did not affect this system and the British continued to pay this grant in cash for next seven years. In 1864, the government, instead of paying the grant in cash, donated some revenue-free land in the villages of Burhanpur and Sholeypur for the upkeep of the mosque (Noorani 2003a: 191–95).

This new arrangement was quite complicated because the wakf status of these plots was not clear. After all, British were not Muslims and their dedication of land could not be treated as wakf. In fact, in 1939, the *Mutawalli* of the mosque raised this point and argued that lands given by the British were actually gifted exclusively for the maintenance of his own family. This matter was solved in 1941 when the Faizabad District Waqf Commissioner in his fact-finding report clarified that the Babri Masjid was listed as a Wakf property and the land given by the British inevitably became wakf because it was in continuation of the grant made by the Muslim kings in the past (ibid.: 191–95).

It is to be noted that both Shia and Sunni Muslims had been using the Babri Masjid for religious purposes and the grant for its upkeep had also been given by both Shias and Sunnis rulers. However, it was not clear which Muslim sect was the real owner of the mosque. After the formation of separate Sunni and Shia wakf boards in Uttar Pradesh (UP) in the early 20th century, the ownership of Babri Masjid became questionable. Actually, following the provisions of the UP Muslim Waqf Act 1936, the Babri Masjid was classified as a Sunni Wakf on the grounds that the builder of the mosque, Babar, himself was a Sunni. However, in 1945, the Shia Central Board UP Waqf filed a case against the Sunni Waqf Board in the court of Civil Judge, Faizabad. In this very interesting case, the Shia Board claimed that the mosque was not built by Babar. Instead, Mir Baqi was the real founder of the mosque. Since Mir Baqi

Babri Masjid and the Muslim Politics of Right to Heritage **209**

and all the later *Mutawallis* of the mosque were Shia, it should be handed over to the Shia Board. However, the Civil Judge, Faizabad held that the Babri Masjid was Sunni mosque because it was built by a Sunni ruler. This case was dismissed and the Sunni Board continued to take care of the mosque (Tripathi 1986: 3).

1853 Riots and the Ram Chabutra

According to the official reports, a communal clash took place in Ayodhya over the Babri Masjid between the Bairagis of Hanuman Garhi and the local Muslims in 1853. After the incident, the responsible persons of the two communities decided that the members of both the communities had to be allowed to worship at the same place. It was decided that the main building and the inner compound were to be used as a proper 'mosque' for offering Namaz. On the other hand, Hindus were allowed to worship in front of the inner entrance of the mosque. This arrangement continued even after the British occupied Awadh in 1856 and was extended further up to the 1857–58 (Srivastava 1991: 24).

However, by that time it had become a very sensitive issue. Thus, to avoid the possibility of any future Hindu–Muslim riot, the British officials decided to physically demarcate the places of worship of the two communities. 'The new arrangement was worked out by the administration and it allowed the Hindus to raise a platform in front of the mosque to mark the birthplace of Lord Rama' (Nevill 1928: 77–139). As a result, a grilled fence was put up between the inner compound of the mosque and the raised platform, which was called the *Ram Chabutra* or *Janmsthan Chabutra*. The Hindus were forbidden to enter into the inner part of the mosque and were required to make their offerings before the *Chabutra* in the outer enclosure. The entry from the eastern gate was denied to Muslims (Figure 5.2).

Thus, the entire mosque area was divided into two parts — the inner part occupied by Muslims and a small platform occupied by the Hindus. However, this arrangement further complicated the ownership question in two ways. First, the ownership of land occupied by the Hindus in the outer part of the mosque was highly ambiguous. It was not clear that the raised platform was legally owned by Hindus and Muslims had lost their legal rights over this part of the mosque. Second, there was a much wider issue. Technically, a mosque cannot be divided into the inner or outer parts. The entire land/site of the mosque is considered to be the mosque/wakf. So, it was not clear that the land occupied by Hindus ceased to be a wakf in the religious-legal sense.

Figure 5.2: Babri Masjid Site in 1858

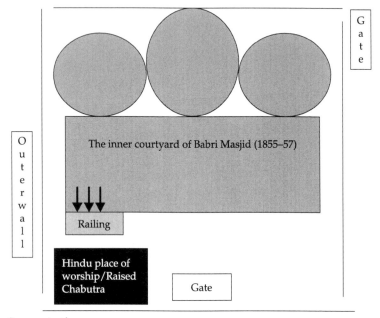

Source: Author.

The 1885 Case and the Question of Ownership of the Chabutra

These ambiguities paved the way for the first legal case between the local Hindus and Muslims. In 1885 a petition was filed by the Mahant of the *Chabutra*, Raghubar Das, in the court of a sub-judge, Faizabad. He requested the court to grant permission to construct a temple on the *Chabutra* (Tripathi 1986: 1). The Mahant also submitted a site plan for the construction of the proposed temple[12] (Figure 5.3). This suit was dismissed and the permission to construct a temple was denied on the ground of the prevailing law and order

---

[12] It was also mentioned in that in May 1883, the Deputy Commissioner of Faizabad had refused permission and prohibited the construction on the basis of objections raised by some Muslims.

Babri Masjid and the Muslim Politics of Right to Heritage **211**

situation. However, the sub-judge accepted the claim of the Mahant that the Janmsthan chabutra was a property of the Hindus.[13]

The Mahant filled another application against this decision in the District Court, Faizabad. After an official enquiry, this appeal was also rejected. In addition, the judge in this case opined that the chabutra did not belong to the Hindus. However, the judge also made a very interesting remark. Underlining the destruction of Ram temple, he wrote:

> It is most unfortunate that a Masjid should have been built on land specially held sacred by the Hindus, but as that event occurred 356 years ago it is too late to remedy the grievances (Noorani 2003a: 183).

Obviously, in this case, the ownership of Chabutra was decided in favour of Muslims. But, the observation made by the judge acquired a legal status for the first time. These remarks, as we shall see, were also used as a legal observation in the later period.

Meanwhile, the Mahant filed another application before the Judicial Commissioner of Awadh, particularly on the question of his ownership right to the chabutra. The Judicial Commission dismissed this application on the ground of public security. But, he also endorsed the views of the District Judge about the destruction of a temple (Noorani 2003a: 183).

Minor Conflicts to Major Dispute (1934–49)

In March–April 1934 communal riots took place in Ayodhya over the slaughtering of cow in a nearby village. In retaliation the local Hindus attacked the Babri Masjid and destroyed the outer part of the building. The mosque was rebuilt and the Muslims continued to use it for regular prayers. This riot was a beginning of Hindu–Muslim conflict over this site. For example, in March–April 1947, the Mutawalli of the mosque lodged a complaint in the court of City Magistrate, Faizabad. He alleged that the local Hindus had been attempting to raise the height of the Chabutra. He also requested

---

[13] Interestingly, in most of the secondary records, the communal situation is shown as the most crucial aspect of this judgement. However, in the original text, the insufficient court fee paid by the Mahant was also emphasised as an important reason for the dismissal of this application. For the original text see Noorani (2003a: 179).

Figure 5.3: Site Plan Submitted by the Mahant in 1885

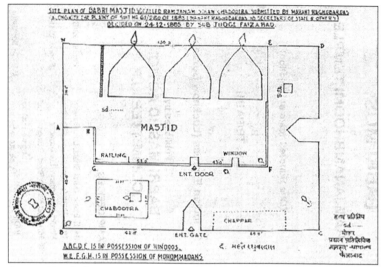

Source: HA Collection, 2005.

that the eastern gates of the mosque, which were opened only for congregational prayers, should be remained open for daily prayers as well. The Magistrate favoured the Muslim claim in this case and ordered that the Chabutra would not be turned into a *Pakka* Chabutra and the eastern doors would not be blocked for Muslims (Noorani 2003a: 207).

The most significant event took place on 22–23 December 1949. A section of Hindus entered the mosque and installed the idols of Lord Ram in the inner part of the mosque and started performing prayers.[14] This incident created a stir in the locality because local Hindus, particularly those who were with the Congress, had been demanding that the entire mosque should be handed over to the them. Interestingly, the installation of idols by the Hindus, as local

---

[14] According to the First Information Report (FIR) of the Station Officer: 'About 9 am in the morning, I came to know that a group of 50–60 people have entered the Babri Masjid by breaking open the locks of the compound ... and placed an idols of Shri Bhagwan in it ... a mob of 5 to 6 thousand people gathered and tried to enter into the mosque ... Committers of crime (*Mujriman-e-waqe*) ... have desecrated (*Napak kiya hai*) the mosque' (Noorani 2003a: 210)

Muslims still claim, was not seen initially as a provocative act; in fact, they were confident that the administration would remove the idols and allow Muslims to make arrangement for the afternoon congressional prayer on that very day. This optimism disappeared very soon. When the local Muslims gathered to offer Friday Namaz at around 1.00 pm, the authorities did not even allow them to enter into the mosque. An eye witness, Hashim Ansari, who went to offer prayer on that day, said:

> We saw a huge collection of senior police officers who assured us that the idols would be removed. We had gathered to offer *Juma* [Friday congregation] prayers but once after the prayer time had elapsed we were told to disperse as that would disturb the peace (Rizvi 2004).

The mosque was later locked without removing the idols.

But, why did the authorities fail to remove the idols on the same day? The two long letters written by the Deputy Commissioner Faizabad to the Chief Secretary of UP explaining his inability to remove the idols from the mosque might help us answer this question.

According to the Deputy Commissioner, within a few days this issue had become a question of *faith*. He cautioned that if the idols were removed forcibly, the local Hindus would not tolerate it and the situation would go out of control. Instead, however, he suggested a 'practical' formula. According to him the administration could take three steps:

(*a*) The mosque would be attached and both Hindu and Muslims should be excluded from it with the exception of a minimum number of *pujari*s who would offer *bhog* to idols.
(*b*) The *Pujari*s would be appointed by the order of a magistrate.
(*c*) The parties will be referred to the Civil Court for adjudication of rights (Noorani 2003a: 215–17).

Following this formula the Additional City Magistrate ordered the attachment of the 'said buildings under Section 145 CrPC and appointed ... the Chairman, Municipal Board Faizabad-cum-Ayodhya as Receiver to arrange for the care of the property in dispute' on 29 December 1949 (ibid.: 218).

214   *Muslim Political Discourse in Postcolonial India*

It is important to point out that the Code of Criminal Procedure 1898 contained an entire chapter on 'dispute as to immovable property', which directly related to Section 145. It explains that after an enquiry of the dispute *'if it appears to the Magistrate that any party has within two months next before the date of such order been forcibly and wrongfully dispossessed, he may treat the party so dispossessed as if he had been in possession on such date'* (emphasis added, ibid.: 219).

It means that the Muslims, who had the actual possession of the building at the time when the idols were put inside it, could have been recognised by the Magistrate as the possessors of the building. In this case, however, the Magistrate simply ignored the technicalities related to the actual possession at the time of the dispute. Furthermore, the placing of the idols was also overlooked and the property was declared 'disputed'.

We must note that the *puja* was going on inside the premises at the time when Section 145 was imposed. In this sense, the status quo of the disputed site would have to recognise *puja* as an ongoing activity. For that reason, the Receiver's scheme which was implemented on 5 January 1950 was all about the proper arrangements of *puja*, etc. At the same time, this arrangement deprived the local Muslims the right to enter the mosque on the ground that they were not using the mosque, when it was taken as a disputed property.

The Title Suits 1950: Unrestricted Puja versus Removal of Idols

On 16 January 1950, Gopal Singh Visharad filed a case in the Court of Civil Judge Faizabad asking permission for *puja* at the site without any restriction (Suit no. 2 of 1950). He also appealed that the defendants (Five Muslims, the State of UP, Deputy Commissioner and Police Superintendent) should be restrained from removing the idols from the site. This was an interesting appeal. The applicant not only wanted a legal sanction for unrestricted permission for the Hindus but also requested that the idols should not be removed. In this sense, the right to perform 'puja' is linked with the existence of idols.

The Civil Judge accepted this application and almost immediately granted interim permission to Visharad. However, the City Magistrate opposed this interim order. In his official reply he pointed out that unrestricted access to Hindus could not be granted as the mosque was a disputed site. He instructed the district counsel

Figure 5.4: Babri Masjid in 1949

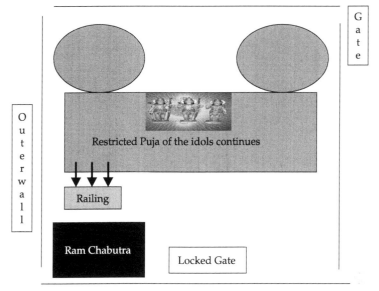

Source: Author.

to move an application for the modification of the interim order (Tripathi 1986: 6–7).

This point was accepted and finally, the order was modified. In a fresh interim order the status quo was maintained and it said: 'Parties are restrained ... to refrain from removing idols in question from the site in dispute and from the interfering with Puja, etc. as at present carried on' (Noorani 2003a: 229). Thus, the restricted entry to Hindu priests was granted for performing the regular religious rites. Meanwhile, on 24 April 1950 the Deputy Commissioner, Faizabad filed an application on behalf of the Government of UP. In this application he admitted that the disputed site is a mosque and it had not been used as a temple of Lord Ram. He also accepted that on the '[n]ight of 22 December 1949 the idols of Shri Ramchanderji were surreptitiously and wrongly put inside it' (ibid.: 229). This was a very crucial statement because the state itself accepted officially that the idols were forcibly kept inside the mosque. However, paying no attention to this application, the civil court confirmed the interim orders on restricted Puja on 3 March 1951.

216   *Muslim Political Discourse in Postcolonial India*

This judgement had two interesting aspects. First, this ruling was based on a few affidavits 'supposedly' filed by the local Muslims. According to the civil judge, a section of local Muslims through their submitted affidavits had actually confirmed that the Muslim community of Ayodhya had not been using the mosque since 1936. Treating these affidavits as 'evidence', the judge gave priority to the restricted 'puja' of idols by the Hindus at the disputed site over the Muslim claims. This line of reasoning gave a new twist to the entire legal debate. After all, placing idols in an 'abandoned' mosque was a less outrageous act in comparison to converting a functional Muslim mosque into a de-facto temple. Thus, this judgement made the ownership question more complicated by interrogating the legal status of Babri Masjid as a functional Muslim mosque.[15]

Second, the judge also made an interesting point. He noted that 'the idols were there inside the property well before the filling of the suit' (Noorani 2003a: 231). In this sense, he gave a legal sanction to idols by not considering the way by which idols were put inside the mosque and the property became a 'disputed' site. In fact, he gave emphasis on the *existence* of the idols. As a result, the Muslim claim to have 'possession of the Babri Masjid' almost disappeared from the legal discourse and in its place 'the removal of idols' and 'unrestricted puja' turned out to be the most focal point of the legal debates.

The Muslim Response 1949–61

From 1949 to 1953 the local Muslim community did not take any legal action. However, an important event took place in 1954, which affected the course of legal proceedings in the case. According to the local Muslims, in 1954 they gave an official notice to the district authorities asking permission for offering Namaz inside the mosque on the last Friday of Ramadan. This application was rejected and Section 144 was imposed in Ayodhya. It was almost predictable that the authorities would not accept such a request. Yet, this absolute dismissal of the Muslim claim somehow provoked the local

---

[15] Interestingly, these affidavits were later used to provide a legal explanation of the case by the Hindutva politicians and lawyers for claiming that the mosque was not in use when the idol incident took place. The case filed by the VHP in 1989 can be taken as the best example in this regard.

Babri Masjid and the Muslim Politics of Right to Heritage **217**

Muslims to take a more radical action. They decided to enter the mosque to register their protest against the decision of the district authority. The local police did not tolerate such protest and used force to disperse the crowd. Moreover, the leaders of this agitation and a few protesters were arrested.[16] After this incident a section of local Muslims decided to take serious legal action. As a result, the first case was filed before the Allahabad High Court in 1954 challenging the 1951 court order.[17]

The petition filed by the Muslims in this case is a good example to understand the evasive and somehow 'self-protective' local Muslim position on Babri Masjid in the mid-1950s. The petition raised a very specific issue. It was asserted that the affidavits, which were supposedly submitted by the local Muslims of Ayodhya and which were treated as evidence by the civil judge, were admitted in the court without the prior knowledge of appellant Muslims. Moreover, they also pointed out that as a defendant they were not given the opportunity to file the counter affidavits in this regard (Noorani 2003a: 231).

On 26 April 1955, the Allahabad High Court (HC) dismissed this appeal and confirmed the Judgement of Civil Court Faizabad on technical grounds. The HC observed that the civil judge applied his discretion and maintained a status quo in a fair manner. However, in this landmark judgement, the court made a very significant remark about the applicability of legal facts. The judges noted:

---

[16] According to Hashim Ansari: 'I gave a notice to the government ... that we would offer Juma-tul-wida [last Friday prayers of Ramadan]. The government had clamped 144 Cr.P.C and had made an assembly of five unlawful. Hence, we made groups of three and proceeded towards the mosque. When we were about 150 yards from the Babri Masjid we were greeted with a brutal lathi [baton] charge which broke my leg. I along with 101 boys were sentenced to six-months imprisonment for breaking the law and INR 500 as fine for saying *Allah-o-Akbar* and in the condition of non-payment, a further jail of 50 days. No Muslim from outside Ayodhya was allowed to enter and we were left helpless from all sides. We did not pay the fine and hence our property was attached. Session judge on our appeal reduced the term to two months and INR 50 as fine. We remained in jail for 1 month and 28 days but did not pay the fine' (Rizvi 2004).

[17] The local Muslims were bit nervous after the incident of 1949 and it was Hashim Ansari who played a significant role in filling a case against the 1951 order in 1955 (Ansari 2004, Int.).

218   *Muslim Political Discourse in Postcolonial India*

[t]he judge [Civil Judge Faizabad] ought not have treated these documents [affidavits submitted by Muslims, which claimed that the mosque had not been in use since 1934] as evidence in the matter then before him without notice to the appellant and affording them an opportunity of filling counter affidavit (Noorani 2003a: 231).

The rejection of this application had two implications. First, the HC, like the civil court, did not consider the 1949 incident and the manner by which the property became disputed on legal–technical grounds. It upheld the status quo on the basis of the verdict given by the civil judge. Second, at the same time, the HC questioned the procedure adopted by the civil judge in this case. The court, in principle, accepted the Muslim claim that they were deprived of the opportunity to represent their stand. Now the question arises: if the High Court found that the lower court had not followed the legal procedure in a proper manner, how could it endorse the 'conclusions', which come out of such an inappropriate process?

By the early 1960s, the Sunni wakf came into the picture. On 6 December 1961, the Sunni Central Waqf Board of UP filed a case in the court of Civil Judge, Faizabad (Regular Suit No. 12 of 1961) on behalf of the Muslim community. In this appeal, the Waqf Board made the following five claims:

(a) 'If the building was not a mosque … the matter ought to have pleaded … in the former suit [1885 suit].
(b) 'No suit challenging the report of the commissioner of Waqf [1936] was filed by the Hindus'.
(c) The Muslims have been in peaceful possession of the mosque till 23 December 1949.
(d) 'Assuming, though not admitting, that there at one time existed a Hindu temple … Muslims, by virtue of their long … possession … perfected their title by adverse possession and the right, title or interest of the temple and or Hindu public, if any, extinguished'.
(e) '[t]he decision of the city magistrate … has the effect of depriving a large section of Muslims from exercising their legal rights' (O.O.S. No. 4 of 1989).

On the basis of these claims, the Waqf Board demanded that, (a) [t]he property is a Muslim wakf (under the possession of the Receiver) and therefore it should be released to the real owner, and (b) '[i]f for any reason, in the opinion of the court, a suit for possession is the proper relief to be claimed, the plaintiffs in the alternative pray for recovery of possession (O. O. S. No. 4 1989).

This petition reveals the actual legal Muslim version of the dispute. From our point of view, the argument that the Muslim claim can legally be justified on the ground of their long possession over the site is very crucial. It imparts priority to the concept of possession. Interestingly, this claim goes against the argument made by the Muslim leaders, particularly the legal constitutionalists, in the later period.

The 1986 Judgement: The Unlocking of the Babri Masjid and Unrestricted Puja

From 1961 to 1984, the Babri Masjid dispute remained a purely legal issue. In 1984, the VHP started its active campaign for the Ram temple. In fact, it launched the first Rath Yatra to 'liberate' Ram Janmbhoomi. However, this 'movement' did not get any mass support until the 1986 court decision, which changed the nature as well as the politics of this dispute completely.

On 25 January 1986, a local lawyer, Umesh Pandey filed an application in the Munsif Court for granting permission to Hindus for unrestricted *puja* at the disputed site. This application was rejected by the court (Tripathi 1986: 7). Nevertheless, Umesh Pandey filed an appeal against the Munsif Court's order before the District Judge Faizabad on 31 January 1986. This time the local Muslims also approached the district court. They filed a counter application in favour of status quo (ibid.: 7). On 1 February 1986, the District Judge rejected the application filed by the local Muslims and after hearing the statements of District Magistrate and the Superintendent of Police allowed the Hindu community to have unrestricted *puja*, etc. inside the Babri Masjid. The judge emphasised the fact that the Hindus had been worshipping at the site, though in a restricted manner for the past 35 years. Thus, he remarked: '[h]eavens are not going to fall if the lock of the gates is removed' (emphasis added, ibid.: 8). Following these orders, on 2 February 1986, the gates of the mosque were opened to Hindus for unrestricted *puja*.

Interestingly, this judgement followed the legal precedents established by previous verdicts in the case. The judgement revolved around one single point that the Hindus had been worshipping inside the mosque, though in a restricted manner, but the Muslims had not even been allowed to enter it. Like previous decisions of

1951 and 1955, this time again, the 1949 events and the title suit was completely ignored and the existence of the idols and the puja of idols were recognised as the most crucial aspects of the case.

Figure 5.5: Babri Masjid (1986)

Source: Author/Impact International, 1987.

In response to the judgement of the District Judge, Hashim Ansari moved an application before the Lucknow Bench of Allahabad High Court on the very next day (Writ Petition 746 of 1986).[18] The High Court did not look at the actual implication of the order of the District Court and followed its routine legal procedure. Thus, without considering the details of the case and/or the nature of the writ petition, the High Court issued a status quo order on the 3 February 1986. The court noted, 'Until further order of the court the nature of property in question *as existing today* shall not be changed' (emphasis added, Noorani 2003a: 270). This order legalised the unrestricted entry of the Hindu community for puja of idols at the disputed site.

---

[18] Sunni Central Waqf Board also filed another petition in this case (Petition No. 3106 of 1986) before the High Court on 12 May 1986.

Disputed Site to Acquired Land: The Expanded Scope of the Case (1986–92)

In the post-1986 period, four important legal developments took place, which affected the subsequent legal proceedings quite considerably and expanded the scope of the dispute.

First, the UP government filed an application before the HC for transferring the title suits to the Lucknow bench and deferring the hearings of the writ petitions filed by Hashim Ansari and the Waqf Board on 10 December 1987. This application, in principal accepted the demand made by the Muslims in the post-1986 period for day-to-day hearing. Although this was just a routine legal move because title suits could not be transferred to the HC immediately, the constitution of a Special Bench of HC and transfer of the title suits gave a wider legal scope to the case.[19] The dispute no long remained an ordinary dispute of property. It became a case of 'national importance'.

The second crucial development was the title suit filed by the VHP on 23 October 1989. This suit, which was actually filed on behalf of the deity, Lord Ram before the HC, was the fifth case in this series (MID 83: 524). The most significant aspect of this petition was that it claimed that: '[t]he entire premises (disputed site and the area around it) . . . belong to the . . . deity therefore defendants should be prohibited from interfering in the . . . construction of new temple building' (Noorani 2003b: 217). By filling this suit the VHP, which did not have any legal standing prior to 1989, became a party in the main case. In fact, the title suit filed on behalf of the deity provided a space to the agenda of Ram temple.

The third important change took place when 2.77 acres of land around the mosque was acquired by the BJP-ruled UP government on 7 October 1991 for 'providing facilities to pilgrims and the development of tourism' in the city (MID 107: 526). This acquisition of land was opposed by the UP Sunni Waqf Board, which filed a writ petition against it before the Special Bench of HC on 17 October 1991 (MID 108: 575). In its interim order, the court permitted the

---

[19] The court cases were transferred to High Court on 10 July 1989 when Allahabad High Court decided to withdraw pending cases on Ayodhya dispute from lower court for expeditious trail by full bench of three judges (MID 80: 384).

222 *Muslim Political Discourse in Postcolonial India*

UP government to take possession of acquired land but at the same time barred the government from transferring the land to anyone or to allow construction of any permanent structure.[20] The acquisition of land by the UP government further widened the scope of the dispute. Henceforth, the acquired area around the Babri Masjid site also became disputed.

The Protection of Places of Worship Act, 1991 was the fourth significant development. The Act was an outcome of a constant struggle led by a section of Muslim leaders, who had been demanding that the state should protect the religious character of all the places of worship including, the disputed site in Ayodhya. More broadly, the provisions of this Act establish that the religious character of the religious places of worship existed on the 15th day of August, 1947 shall continue to be the same as it existed on that day [Sections 3, 4(1)]. Interestingly, the provisions of this Act would not be applied to the Ayodhya site.

The Ownership of the Site versus Right to Worship in the Makeshift Temple

On 6 December 1992, a mob led by the VHP and the BJP demolished the structure of the Babri Masjid. A makeshift temple was constructed and the idol of Lord Ram was installed. This incident forced the union government to launch an 'official Ayodhya policy'. On the very next day of the demolition, four BJP-ruled state governments were dismissed. It was followed by the banning of a few 'communal' organisations. The most significant aspect of this proactive Ayodhya policy was the Ayodhya Ordinance 1993, which was issued on 7 January 1993. This Ordinance empowered the union government to acquire 67 acres of land including the Babri Masjid site and the makeshift temple. The government also made a single point reference to the Supreme Court asking its

---

[20] The acquisition of land was also challenged by a few Muslims of Delhi, who filed two separate petitions as Public Interest Litigation (PIL) before the Supreme Court on 7 November and 10 November 1991, respectively. The petitioners requested that the court should give direction to the authorities to hand over the land to the real owner (Bhure 2004, Int.) On 15 November 1991, the Supreme Court directed the UP government to prevent interference on acquired land and to maintain status quo (MID 108: 576).

Figure 5.6: Babri Masjid (1990)

Source: Impact International, London.

opinion on the prior existence of any Ram temple at the disputed site (MID 137: 207).

However, the VHP, ignoring these grand changes introduced by the union government, decided to concentrate on the question of unrestricted puja at the makeshift temple. A petition was filed before the HC for allowing the Hindus to visit the makeshift temple. The judiciary once again followed a technical approach. This demand was accepted and on 1 January 1993, the puja of the idols inside the makeshift temple and the unrestricted access to general public was allowed.[21]

In the meantime, the legality of the acquisition of land was challenged by Muslims and two PILs were filed before the Supreme Court of India. These petitions raised two legal points: (*a*) the power of the government to acquire the wakf land and, (*b*) the immunity of mosques/religious places of worship from acquisition. Interestingly, the Supreme Court returned the reference unanswered to the government in 1994. It also observed that the acquisition of land by

---

[21] In this judgement the safety of idols was also considered and the authorities were to provide adequate security to the makeshift structure (Noorani 2003a: 247).

224 *Muslim Political Discourse in Postcolonial India*

the government does not contradict with the rights to have wakf. In fact, it opined that the state can acquire any piece of land including the places of worship for public purposes. After this judgement, the title suit again turned out to be the most crucial case. The Special Bench of Allahabad HC at Lucknow gave its verdict in 2010 (Ahmed 2010), which more broadly divided the site into three parts. This judgement has been challenged and the matter is pending before the Supreme Court of India. The functional makeshift temple with the idol of Lord Ram is still protected by the state. As a matter of fact, it has become the de-facto janmbhoomi temple.

Let us now wrap up this discussion on the legal complexities of the Babri Masjid dispute by emphasising following three important observations:

First, the colonial judiciary provided a very 'modern' form to this dispute. The British interpreted this local issue as a symbolic conflict between Hindu and Muslim civilisation. In fact, the judiciary established a link between the Babri Masjid dispute and the colonial theory of desecration of Hindu temples. In this sense, the scope of the conflict expanded and it became a 'communal' question for all Hindus and Muslims of India.

Second, the postcolonial judiciary adopted a rigid and stubborn legal attitude to this issue. Instead of solving the basic problem, the judiciary preferred to sustain the dispute by applying a 'status quo' approach. Table 5.2 shows that this legal attitude complicated the dispute and paved the way for a number of legal ambiguities.

Third, our discussion in this section also points towards various kinds of Muslim responses to legal issues. Broadly, these responses can be divided into four phases. In the first phase (1949–61) of the dispute, the Muslim response was highly evasive. The local Muslims did not show any interest in the case and simply responded to the issues raised by the Hindu parties. In the second phase (1961–86) the Wakf Board became the leading party for the Muslims. In this period, a highly *legal positivistic* position was adopted by the Board. Perhaps for that reason, it did not make any effort to expedite the legal process. In the third phase (1986–92) we find a *radical-political response* to the legal proceedings. The demand to constitute a Special Bench of HC and the filing of PILs before the Supreme Court can be the example of this approach. And finally, in the post-1992 phase, the Muslim position again became very *legalistic*.

Table 5.2: Legal Issues and Political Implications of Babri Masjid Case: 1949–94

Court	Year	Case	Issue Involved	Legal Action Taken	Decision Taken/ Observation Made	Unanswered Issues	Outcome
City Magistrate, Deputy Commissioner, Receiver	1949	Idols of Lord Ram were put inside the mosque	What to do with the idols, which were installed on 22.12.1949?	Section 144 and Section 145	Building is a disputed site and the status quo should be maintained.	As per the Section 145 the claims of the first party (Muslims) were not taken into account.	(a) The Mosque was locked and parties were asked to show their evidences. (b) Restricted permission for *Puja* was granted. (c) The act of placing the idols acquired a legal sanction.
Civil Judge, Faizabad	1950	Suit No. 2 of 1950	(a) Should Hindus be allowed to perform religious rites? (b) Muslims and the government should be restrained to remove the idols.	Interim injunction	In order to maintain the status quo, Hindus will not be allowed to perform unrestricted Puja and Muslims will not be allowed to remove the idols.	The legal right of local Muslim to worship was not considered.	The suit was filed just one day before the date given to the parties to submit their evidence in the case. Thus, the existence of the idols became a legal fact.

Table 5.2: (*Continued*)

Table 5.2: (*Continued*)

Court	Year	Case	Issue Involved	Legal Action Taken	Decision Taken/ Observation Made	Unanswered Issues	Outcome
Civil Judge, Faizabad	1950	Suit No. 2 of 1950		Confirmed the interim injunction	On the basis of some affidavits filled by the local Muslims it is established that the mosque was not in use since 1934. However, 'the existence of idols is a reality'.	The Muslim defendants were not informed about these 'affidavits', which were used as evidence.	This 'fact' was later developed as the popular Hindutva theory that the mosque had not been in use since 1934.
Allahabad High Court	1955	Suit No. 2 of 1950; Case filed by local Muslims	The affidavits were treated as evidence and Muslims were not given an opportunity to file counter affidavit.	Appeal was dismissed and the judgement of the civil judge was confirmed	It was inappropriate to use such affidavit as evidence but temporary injunction was a matter of discretion. The judge on technical ground did not act arbitrarily.	The legal technicalities of the case were over-estimated.	The existence of idols was juxtaposed with the fact that the Muslims did not have possession of the mosque in the later years.
Civil Judge, Faizabad	1986	Application filed by Umesh Chandra Pandey.	Hindus should be allowed to worship the idols without any restriction.	Application was accepted; Application moved by Muslim was rejected.	Since Hindus have been worshipping the idols, 'heaven are not going to fall, if the locks are removed'.	The events of 1949 and the title suit of 1961 were not at all considered.	The mosque was opened for Hindus and it paved the way for a new kind of mass politics, which overshadows the legal position on the title suit.

Allahabad High Court	1986	Writ Petition against the order of the Civil Judge	Quash the order of the Civil Judge and command the authorities to maintain the sanctity of the disputed site.	Writ petition admitted	Until further order of the court the nature of property in question as existing today shall not be changed.	Status quo order did not take into account the changed nature of the disputed property, which after the opening of the gates for Hindus had become a 'functional' temple.	The title suit and the Muslim rights over the site were further ignored because of the technicalities of law.
Allahabad High Court	1993	Petition to have darshans of idols in the make-shift temple	Hindus should be allowed to worship the idols in the makeshift temple.	Petition was accepted	The general public should be allowed to visit the makeshift temple.	The demolition of the mosque as an event and the takeover of the land by force was not considered.	The makeshift structure converted into a de-facto temple and the mosque not only lost its structure but also disappeared from legal discourse.
Supreme Court	1994	Petition against the land acquired by the government	Government cannot acquire a wakf land.	Petition was rejected	The state can acquire any piece of land including the places of worship	Would it be treated as an adverse possession?	The wakf status of the mosque becomes more complicated.

Source: Author.

228   *Muslim Political Discourse in Postcolonial India*

To understand these varied responses, a systematic analysis of the specificity of the Muslim claims is required. We need to know the local as well as national Muslim political discourse on the Babri Masjid. This is precisely what I am going to do in the next section.

III

MUSLIM POLITICS OF BABRI MASJID (1984–86)

From 1949 to 1984, the local as well as the national level Muslim politicians continued to ignore the Babri Masjid case and it was never highlighted as a 'Muslim issue'. Even Abdullah Bukhari, who campaigned for the Janata Party in Faizabad in the 1977 elections, never mentioned the Babri Masjid dispute in his aggressive anti-Congress speeches and sermons (Siddique 2004, Int.). There could be several possible reasons behind this 'evasive' Muslim political response to the Babri Masjid case. The formation of Pakistan and the migration of politically influential Muslims of Ayodhya could be the most important factor that shaped the Muslim response in this period. The Partition not only affected the economic and political strength of the local Muslim community but also had an effect on the religious composition of local administration and judiciary. In such a context, local Muslims adopted a 'self-protective' approach and concentrated on the legal aspects of the case. Quite similarly, the national level Muslim leaders did not want any long term conflict with Hindu rightists and their emphasis was on the legal-constitutional framework of rights to register political grievances. Thus, the Babri Masjid case was nothing more than a local 'property dispute' for Muslim leaders in this period.

In contrast, the local Hindu elite had been very keen to use the political significance of this issue. Even in the 1960s, a Hindu candidate had tried to make use of this dispute for mobilising Hindu voters in the local election (Gould 1966). Yet, the Babri Masjid case remained a highly localised property dispute until 1983 when the VHP established a *Dharmasthan Mukti Yagna Samiti* and launched its nation-wide agitation to 'liberate' sacred Hindu religious places. Within a year the VHP started focusing on the Babri Masjid case and formed the *Sri Ram Janam Bhumi Mukti Yagna Samiti*. To further intensify this campaign, a *Rath Yatra* from Ayodhya to Lucknow was organised, which was followed by a signature campaign (Noorani 2003a: 255). However, despite reasonably good media coverage, the 1984 campaign of VHP did not become a 'national' issue. Perhaps for that reason, the Muslim response to VHP's campaign remained highly scattered.

The Babri Masjid Action Committee, Faizabad (1984)

The most significant event took place in Faizabad. A section of local Muslims of the city decided to form the Babri Masjid Action Committee (BMAC) under the leadership of a Muslim lawyer, Yunus Siddiquie in the last week of October 1984. The Committee was established to reassert the Muslim claims over the Babri Masjid. In fact, there were two objectives of this Committee: (*a*) to solve the dispute through legal action and (*b*) to protect the long term interests, life and property of the Muslim community of Faizabad and Ayodhya (Siddique 2004, Int.). In addition, there were some concrete reasons to set up the BMAC, Faizabad. Yunus Siddiquie, the Chairman of BMAC of 1984 pointed out that the Muslims were a bit anxious about the rising political power of the VHP. The growth of such Hindutva, in his opinion, could affect the communal situation in the district. Furthermore, Muslims were also apprehensive about the role played by the local Congress leaders, including some Congress Muslims, in providing practical support to the VHP. Thus, BMAC had a practical as well as a symbolic importance (Siddiquie 2004, Int.). It had adopted a workable strategy. They submitted a memorandum to the local administration demanding that the legal process should be expedited for solving the title suit. They also tried to persuade the political leaders, including the then Chief Minister of UP N. D. Tiwari, to control the VHP/Rashtriya Swayamsevak Sangh (RSS) activities in the state.

The formation of BMAC in Faizabad had some very interesting implications. This was an organised political attempt, which intended to go beyond the legal proceedings, though in a restricted manner. The Babri Masjid case was not publicised as a national Muslim issue in this period and the activities of the BMAC remained essentially local. In fact, apart from a sizeable number of local Muslims, the Committee was supported by the local left-wing activists and organisations. The national or regional Muslim leaders were not at all involved during this period. Perhaps that was the reason why the local Babri Masjid campaign of 1984 was virtually

230 *Muslim Political Discourse in Postcolonial India*

ignored by the *mainstream* national Muslim politics. Even Ali Mian Nadwi, an *Alim* from Nadwa, who had written a 'public letter' to the then Prime Minister of India, Indira Gandhi on the growing radicalisation of VHP in October 1984, and Syed Shahabuddin, the bureaucrat turned politician, who had published several news items in his journal *Muslim India* on the Babri Masjid case, did not establish any link with the BMAC of Faizabad in this period.[22]

IV

THE MAKING OF A MUSLIM COALITION: BABRI MASJID AS A SYMBOL OF 'COLLECTIVE MUSLIM RESISTANCE' (1986–88)

We have seen that the post-1985 Muslim political discourse was dominated by two very different kinds of issues: the Shah Bano controversy and the demand to offer Namaz inside the protected historical monuments. In both the cases, the Muslim leaders had taken a very radical position. Particularly, the AIMPLB led by Ali Mian had virtually forced the Congress-led government to introduce a bill in the Parliament against the Supreme Court judgement in the Shah Bano case. The 'victory' of Muslim ulema associated with the AIMPLB in this case had a very encouraging impact on other Muslim political organisations. The All India Muslim Majlis-e-Mushawarat (AIMMM) was also in the process of rejuvenation. The memorandum submitted by the AIMMM on historical mosques, which we discussed in Chapter 3, is an example of this newly gained political confidence.

---

[22] Ali Mian Nadwi wrote a letter to Mrs. Gandhi on 24 October 1984. In this letter, Nadwi underlined the degradation of social values in the country and the threat of Hindu communalism. The letter emphasised the importance of 'true secularism' adopted by Nehru and Congress in post-Independence India. Nadwi requested the PM to retrain the activities of VHP in order to save the secular fabric of the nation (Nadwi 2001: 85–87). Due to some postal problems, this letter could not reach to the PM office. In the meantime on 31 October 1984, Indira Gandhi was assassinated. The original text of this letter was published by Nadwi in his autobiography. Similarly, Shahabuddin published a significant news item on VHP's ultimatum on Babri Masjid in the October 1985 issue of *Muslim India*. However, according to the local members of the 1984 BMAC, no Muslim leader tried to establish contact with them. Nor, did they approach them.

Babri Masjid and the Muslim Politics of Right to Heritage **231**

The emergence of radical Muslim politics in mid-1980s should also be seen in the backdrop of wider Indian politics. In post-1984 Indian political discourse, the religious issues occupied a central role in an extraordinary manner. The assassination of Indira Gandhi, who is often alleged to play a 'Hindu card' in the 1980 Lok Sabha election, was followed by Sikh massacres in north India which culminated in a massive electoral success for the Congress in 1984. The Shah Bano case and the Ram temple agitation of VHP further intensified this new politics of religion.[23] In this sense, the old political-ideological division such as Congressism versus anti-Congressism became quite inappropriate to accommodate these new developments. As a result, the ideological equilibrium of Indian politics was disturbed and a search for new forms of political polarisation began. Muslim politics had to play a vital role in this process not only to adjust itself with new political equations but also in a much more significant way, it had to create and sustain the political divide of secularism and communalism. And in this context, on 2 February 1986, the gates of the Babri Masjid were opened.

2 February 1986 and Multiple Muslim Responses

The events of 2 February 1986 were unusual and provocative in many respects. The local judiciary and administration coordinated in a highly exceptional manner in this case. The application was filed on 30 January, the case was discussed and resolved on 1 February and the disputed site was unlocked on 2 February. The legal matter, which had not been decided in past 35 years, was settled within a period of two days! Moreover, the state-controlled national television and radio gave special attention to the unlocking of the site and highlighted it as a historic event of some kind. In addition, the VHP decided to celebrate it as a day of victory.

These developments were enough to provoke Muslims throughout the country, particularly in north India. As expected, the

---

[23] It does not mean the political role of religion was not at all important before 1980s. Religion had always been a major aspect of Indian politics. Yet, in post-1984 period the questions of religion, along with caste, have affected the political discourse in a significant way. For that reason, secularism became a major issue of debate (Nigam 2006).

232 *Muslim Political Discourse in Postcolonial India*

Muslim masses, political leaders, institutions and organisations at various levels overwhelmingly criticised and condemned this act. However, the intensity and magnitude of these responses varied from one place to another. Let us now look at the initial Muslim responses at Ayodhya, Faizabad, Lucknow and Delhi.

Ayodhya and Faizabad

In Ayodhya, VHP's Victory Day celebrations forced the local Muslims to close their shops and take shelter inside the houses of prominent Muslims of the town (Ansari 2004, Int.). Many Muslim families also decided to move to other safe places. In fact, the protection of life and property turned out to be the first priority for local Muslims of Ayodhya. Precisely for this reason, the prominent Muslim of the town decided to establish contact with other Muslims leaders of UP for practical support. In this context, Hashim Ansari visited Faizabad and Lucknow.

The situation was completely different in Faizabad. The administration had already imposed Section 144 of the Indian Penal Code (IPC) and the battalions of the Provincial Armed Constabulary (PAC) were deployed to control the situation. Unlike Ayodhya, the BMAC Faizabad decided to take a clear position on this issue. They planned to organise a public meeting to condemn the judgement of the city court publicly in the afternoon of 2 February 1986 at the Ashfaqullah Colony. However, the District Magistrate refused to grant permission and consequently, this meeting was secretly held at the Masjid-e-Tasha. In this informal meeting it was decided that the prominent Muslim leaders, including the MLAs and MPs of UP should be contacted at Lucknow to work out a practical strategy. The copy of the order was obtained and a small pamphlet was prepared to distribute among local Muslims (Siddiquie 2004, Int.).

Lucknow: The Formation of Babri Masjid Action Committee UP, Lucknow

Lucknow, on the other hand, was quite calm. Although, the Muslim politicians were anxious about the Babri Masjid, they were not fully aware of the complexities of the legal case and the wider political intensity of this issue. Because of this reason, the initial response of Muslim politicians was quite unclear. Zafaryab Jeelani, a lawyer who had been very active in the Shah Bano case, along with other local politicians of Lucknow met Hashim Ansari and other members of the Faizabad Committee and helped them in filing the writ petition against the judgement of the city court. At this point of time, these UP leaders did not want to initiate a mass movement of any kind. They were in favour of legal activism. However, within a few days, Maulana Muzaffar Husain started contacting other UP Muslim leaders to launch a 'political' agitation of some kind. In this regard, an informal meeting was held in Lucknow on 5 February. The prominent Lucknow leaders discussed the Babri Masjid issue and it was decided that a political move should be taken along with the legal proceedings. A formal meeting of Muslim MLAs was also to be arranged (Jilani 2004, Int.). These initiatives were supported by almost all the prominent UP Muslim leaders and finally after the 7 February 1986 meeting, the UP Babri Masjid Action Committee was set up. This newly formed BMAC UP decided to take following four steps:

(a) A memorandum should be given to the Chief Minister urging him to expedite the legal process so that the court case could be settled.
(b) A nation-wide Muslim mass contact campaign for the wider publicity should be initiated.
(c) A call for *Yaum-e-siyah* (Black Day) for 14 February 1986 should be given.
(d) A mass rally should be organised in Lucknow on 26 February 1986 (Jilani 2004, Int.).

Delhi: Mushawarat's Radical Programme and the Imam's Speech at Jama Masjid

The opening of the Babri Masjid for Hindus was highly unexpected news for the AIMPLB. By that time the Congress-led government had literally recognised Nadwi and other Ulema as the most reliable 'representatives' of Muslims in India. In fact, the 'advices' and 'suggestions' given by the Personal Law Board in almost all the matters related to the Shah Bano case were being followed by the Rajiv Gandhi government. In this sense, the Babri Masjid case was an 'astonishing' development. However, unlike the Shah Bano case, the Babri Masjid issue was more complicated because it was directly related to the demands made by Hindu rightists.

234   *Muslim Political Discourse in Postcolonial India*

In this sense, it was imperative for the AIMPLB to give lead to the AIMMM.[24]

The AIMMM announced its initial long-term strategy almost immediately. Their first press statement on this issue can be a useful example to understand their position. In this statement, the AIMMM categorically rejected the claim made by the VHP and requested the government to stop the *Puja* in the premises of the Babri Masjid. Expanding the scope of the agitation, the AIMMM also appealed the Muslim MPs and MLAs to present joint memoranda to the Prime Minister and to the CMs and to raise this issue in their respective legislative bodies.

The AIMMM also proposed a scheme to mobilise Muslims. The statement notes:

> AIMMM calls upon the Muslim community that as a token of their grief ... they should observe Friday the 14 February 1986 as a Black Day ... They should wear Black badges, close their establishment and hoist black flags on their premises; they should offer special prayers ... and then march peacefully in every district and tehsil headquarter to the District Collector or the Sub-Divisional Officer to present a brief memorandum demanding the immediate restoration of the Babri Masjid. In case they are restrained from presenting the memorandum, they should court arrest (MID 39: 118).

The reactions of the Imam of Jama Masjid, as we have seen in Chapter 4, were very different from the resolution passed by the established Muslim organisations. Ignoring the complex local situation of Ayodhya/Faizabad and the resolution passed by the AIMMM and the BMAC UP, the Imam delivered a provocative speech on 7 February 1986 and warned the central government that if the Babri Masjid was not given back to Muslims, he would start a mass campaign. Interestingly, for the first time in his political career, the Imam emphasised that all the Muslim institutions and organisations should work together, and for that reason asked Muslims to support the call given by the AIMMM and the BMAC UP.

---

[24] The AIMMM and the AIMPLB are two independent bodies. However, since its inception the AIMPLB has been working in close association with the AIMMM. In Shah Bano case, AIMPLB was the front organisation and the AIMMM offered background support to the agitation.

These initial reactions at various places suggest two interesting aspects. First, the Babri Masjid was conceived as a national Muslim political issue. Therefore, it was decided that the legal proceedings should be supplemented by a political action of some kind. The Masjid-e-Tasha meeting organised by the BMAC in Faizabad, the formation of the Babri Masjid Action Committee UP, the call given by the AIMMM and the speech of the Imam of Jama Masjid to observe the Black Day, demonstrate very clearly that the Muslim politics at local, regional and even the national level unanimously decided to go for collective action.

Second, in all these attempts, the need for Muslim unity was identified and highlighted to sustain a mass campaign. In fact, all the major political players including Hashim Ansari of Ayodhya, the Muslim leaders of UP, ulema of AIMPLB, the president of the AIMMM, and even the Imam of Jama Masjid showed an eagerness to have a wider Muslim political coalition.

The Necessity of Coalition

To understand the enthusiasm of these Muslim politicians for making a grand coalition, one has to recognise the complex nature of the Babri Masjid issue and the ways by which it was introduced (Table 5.3). In fact, these complexities of the Babri Masjid case were well-suited to the three most dominant Muslim political forces at that time: the Muslim legal-constitutionalists of the AIMMM, the radicals led by Imam Bukhari and the ulema of the AIMPLB.

First, the Babri Masjid dispute was primarily a legal case in which the question of the right to worship was involved. The physical existence of a mosque under the control of the state could have been shown as a form of legal injustice and infringement of minority rights by the legal-constitutionalists. Second, the dispute over the Babri Masjid was also related to the idea of a royal Muslim past or better to say the royal Mughal past. This could be the most attractive aspect of the case for the Shahi Imam of the Jama Masjid. It was possible for him to establish a link between the Jama Masjid and the Babri Masjid. He might have portrayed the Babri Masjid as a symbol of Muslim subjugation in contemporary India. And finally, Babri Masjid was a mosque, which had a specific wakf status under the Islamic Sharia. As a matter of fact, the issue could certainly be

236   *Muslim Political Discourse in Postcolonial India*

approached by the ulema from a Sharia point of view. They could have 'exposed' the crisis of Islam and the virtual dominance of Hindus in secular India through the Babri Masjid!

These issues were closely related to each other and it was not possible, at least at that point of time, for these political forces to focus on any single aspect of the case. The legal constitutionalists were incapable of mobilising common Muslims simply by projecting the Babri Masjid case as a 'constitutional matter'. They had to rely on people like the Shahi Imam for popular politics and ulema for acquiring a 'religious' sanction for their political moves. The Imam, on the other hand, was not in a position to ignore the complex legal issues involved in the case. He needed legal-constitutionalists to establish a link between the Jama Masjid and the crisis of Babri Masjid. Similarly, the politically active ulema were desperately looking for radicals and legal-constitutionalists for establishing a Sharia-based political argument on the Babri Masjid. Thus, the intricacies of the Babri Masjid case forced various ideological forces to come together and form a grand coalition. Moreover, the coalition of Muslim political forces could be the safest option for most of the Muslim leaders. It could give them a secure political start in this case because the responsibility of possible failures was to be shared by all the constituents. At the time, the coalition could also provide them considerable time to refashion their independent agendas.

Table 5.3: Internal Dynamics of Muslim Politics on Babri Masjid in 1986

Group	Strength	Weakness	Immediate Concern
Legal-constitutionalist	Understanding of the limits and scope of minority rights.	No experience of direct mass politics	Making a coalition so that legal proceeding are supported by certain 'pressure politics'.
Ulema	Understanding of Shariat	Unable to lead a mass movement.	Consolidation of already acquired leading role in the post-Shah Bano case period.
Radicals	Understanding of Muslim mass politics.	Unaware of the complexity of the legal case at least initially.	Making a coalition to understand the strength and weaknesses of other players.

Source: Author.

The Formation of the Coalition

The call given by the various Muslim organisations to observe a Black Day on 14 February 1986 triggered off a series of violent clashes at various places. Interestingly, most of these riots were not directly related to the Babri Masjid issue. Yet, in many cases, growing Hindu–Muslim tension, which was a direct repercussion of the Babri Masjid dispute, led to widespread violence and communal clashes. These incidents, particularly the police brutality in many cases, gave a new impetus to Muslim leaders of UP and Delhi to come together. Moreover, these incidents also increased the symbolic status of the Babri Masjid for Muslim politicians. The disputed site was now converted into an emblem of Muslim resistance and Hindu dominance.

In the last two weeks of February 1986, concrete efforts began to constitute a grand coalition for the Babri Masjid 'movement' (Figure 5.7). On 24 February 1986, AIMMM arranged a meeting in Delhi and invited the leaders of the BMAC UP and others Delhi-based Muslim politicians. In this meeting, it was decided that a Central Action Committee for the restoration of the Babri Masjid be set up. Moreover, it was also decided that Action Committees in all states and districts should be formed to widen the scope of the agitation. As a result, finally on 13 March 1986, the Central Action Committee (Rabata Committee) for the restoration of the Babri Masjid was constituted (MID 41: 238).[25]

The symbolic existence of the Rabata Committee played an interesting political role, particularly between March–November 1986. In this period, several communal riots took place in northern and western India, which particularly unsettled the socio-economic

---

[25] The literal meaning of the term 'Rabata' is 'contact'. It originates from word 'Rabt', which means relationship, contact or friendship. In this sense, the Rabata Committee was formed to develop relationship and contact in various isolated and unconnected individual and collective Muslim initiatives. The Rabata Committee was a part of the AIMMM. The main objective of this committee was to coordinate the agitation in order to mobilise wider Muslim opinion. However, the local or state level Babri Masjid Committees were still independent in all respects and free to take their own decisions. The Rabata Committee, however, could provide advice and suggestions to these local initiatives but it could not force the local bodies to follow its instructions.

Figure 5.7: Babri Masjid Agitation: February to November 1986

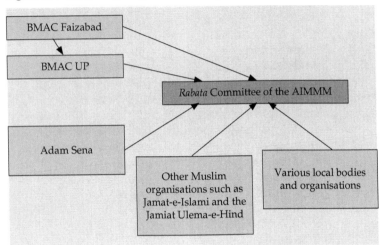

Source: Author.

conditions and the status of Muslims in those riot-affected areas. As a result, the idea of 'Muslim unity' for collective politics, particularly on the Babri Masjid issue was identified as the most viable alternative. This unanimous acceptance of collective Muslim politics provided more space to the Rabata Committee.

This, however, does not mean that the major Muslim ideological forces immediately decided to give up their independent agendas, at least for the time being. In fact, two very clear Muslim political positions on Babri Masjid issue were gradually being articulated. First, there was a legal-constitutionalist position on Babri Masjid which conceptualised the issue in a liberal language of rights. It envisaged the Babri mosque as a legal-religious entity and proposed to solve the dispute through legal-political means by creatively interpreting the existing laws. For example, Syed Shahabuddin, in an interview, proposed a workable formula to solve the dispute. He suggested that: 'The Babri Mosque proper can be declared a protected monument after restoring the status quo obtaining prior to December 22, 1949'. Moreover, he advised that the Ram temple could be built on the 'Rama Chabutra' (MID 43a: 330–31). In this interview, he further opined that: '[t]he status gained by the "mosque" as a national monument will give

Babri Masjid and the Muslim Politics of Right to Heritage **239**

considerable satisfaction to those who now oppose the "Rama Janambhumi" temple move' (MID 43a: 330–31). So, from the legal-constitutionalist point of view, monumentalisation of the Babri Masjid under the legal framework of the 1958 Act was the most possible way out for its 'restoration'.

On the other hand, there was a rather radical position on Babri Masjid.[26] Imam Bukhari of the Jama Masjid and most of the members of the BMAC UP had taken a very extreme yet highly unclear stand. According to them, the mosque was as a symbol of Muslim contribution to Indian heritage. The state control and permission granted to Hindus were seen as a direct 'challenge' to the dignity of India's Muslims. In fact, the dignity of Muslims was the focal point of their political discourse. The legal-constitutional rights of Muslims as a religious minority and the religious status of a disputed mosque in the Islam Shariat were secondary issues in this case. Thus, from this perspective, the restoration of the mosque was a question of Muslim dignity. The formation of Adam Sena by the Imam and the court arrest campaign of the BMAC UP on 7 August 1986 could be two very revealing examples of this radical position (MID 43: 383).

Despite these two very different outlooks, the political zeal to form a coalition was very high. Finally, in November 1986, the Rabata Committee came up with a concrete programme to form a Muslim coalition on the Babri Masjid. In its meeting of 5 November 1986, the Rabata Committee decided to organise an All India Babri Masjid Conference in Delhi on 21–22 December 1986. The Committee also appealed the BMAC UP to withdraw its protest march and suggested that the Central Committee should organise a mass demonstration in the first week of March 1987 in Delhi. It was also suggested that Muslim MPs and political leaders should also be mobilised (MID 48: 542). These proposals were overwhelmingly approved by almost all the major political forces.

---

[26] I use the term 'radical' for the Imam groups primarily to underline their aggressive attitude towards the collective decisions taken by the Muslim coalition on the Babri Masjid. It does not mean that the Imam group wanted to overthrow the democratic system and establish Muslim rule in India. Instead, as we shall see, this group used 'radicalism' as a political tool to strengthen its position. In fact, this group played a very significant role in the formation of the secular camp in the post-1990 Indian politics.

240   *Muslim Political Discourse in Postcolonial India*

The Ideological Composition of the Coalition

On 21–22 December 1986, the All India Conference on the Babri Masjid was organised in Delhi. As we discussed in our previous chapter, the AIMMM had invited Maulana Ali Mian Nadwi to inaugurate the conference. However, he could not come and it was Imam Abdullah Bukhari who inaugurated the conference. The Babri Masjid Conference led to the formation of the All India Babri Masjid Movement Coordination Committee (AIBMMCC) which in many respects was more powerful than the Rabata Committee. As a 'democratic' body, the Conference authorised the BMMCC to take major decisions on behalf of the Babri Masjid movement at the central level. The Conference also issued an overarching document, which was called the *Delhi Declaration*. This document was the very first articulated Muslim statement on Babri Masjid, which also elaborated the wider political strategy of the coalition. Moreover, this document also illustrates the ideological composition of the coalition. In fact, three important aspects of this declaration could easily be identified to understand the internal complexities of this move (Figure 5.8).

First, the Declaration formally recognised the Babri Masjid '[a]s a national heritage and as a historical monument but, above all, as a place of Islamic worship' (MID 50a: 59–60 and 64). In addition, the opening of the mosque was not only described as a setback for Muslims but also as a violation of Article 25 of the Constitution of India. It shows that a compromise between the legal-constitutionalists and radicals like Shahi Imam on the status of Babri Masjid might have been worked out. The carefully written Declaration indicates that the Imam group had to follow the position of legal-constitutionalists on this issue.

Second, in terms of mass politics, legal-constitutionalists had to compromise with radicals. As pointed out earlier, these leaders did not have any experience of mass-based politics; nor did they have any clear political strategy for mobilising common Muslims. It was inevitable for them to rely on the 'expertise' of the radicals like the Imam. That could be a possible reason behind the radical overtone of the Declaration, which suggested a four points plan of action: (*a*) the non-observance of the Republic Day call, (*b*) An all India Bandh on 1 February 1987, (*c*) a rally on 30 March 1987 and if all these fail (*d*) a direct March to Ayodhya (MID 50a: 59–60 and 64).

Babri Masjid and the Muslim Politics of Right to Heritage **241**

Third, the radicals did not have any practical solution for the dispute. Moreover, they did not envisage any long-term strategy for the agitation. Thus, the views of legal-constitutionalists again dominated these aspects. More precisely, the Declaration asserted two long-term objectives: (*a*) it demanded that all the historical mosques, protected by the Archaeological Survey of India (ASI) and the state archaeological departments should be opened for Namaz, and (*b*) it was insisted that: '[i]n the interest of inter-communal harmony, ... a Central Law [should be enacted] to guarantee the status of a place of worship and protecting it as it existed on 15 August 1947, against any claims thereto or any move to alter it' (MID 50a: 59–60 and 64).

Thus, the BMMCC, a coalition of two major Muslim political forces, had a very delicate position. On the one hand, it had adopted a populist political strategy based on radical and to some extent, rhetorical programme of action. This strategy, in any case, could trigger off a fresh wave of communal violence. On the other hand, it wanted to achieve the legal 'restoration' of the Babri Masjid and a constitutional protection to all places of worship. This paradoxical equation between the broader aims of the coalition and its adopted means further created several confusions. Let us now look at three major political initiatives — the non-observation call, the 30 March rally, and the Ayodhya March — to understand how this fragile coalition worked and, finally collapsed.

Figure 5.8: The Ideological Composition of the Coalition

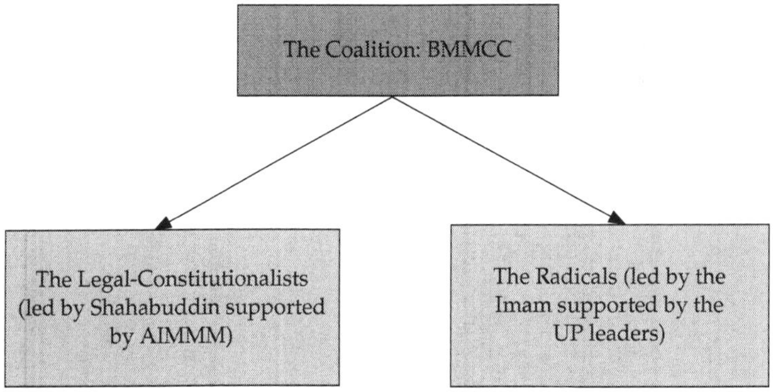

Source: Author.

242   *Muslim Political Discourse in Postcolonial India*

Boycott versus Non-participation: The Babri Masjid and the Question of 'Political Heritage'

It is important to note that the Delhi Declaration very clearly called upon '[t]he Muslim community not to participate in or associate themselves with the observance of the Republic Day on 26 January 1987, except those individuals who are on official duty' (MID 50a).[27] However, there was an inherent confusion. The idea of non-participation in this appeal was not very clear. It could have two possible meanings. First, the non-participation of Muslims could possibly be understood as a kind of 'deliberate action' to register their grievances. Second, the non-participation could also be perceived as an act of boycott or rejection. In this sense, it could challenge the authority of the state.

The mainstream media, particularly the English print media further increased this confusion. In most of the Delhi-based newspapers, the original text of the Delhi Declaration or its broad overview were not published. Instead, the political programme, particularly the radical measures adopted by the BMMCC, was given adequate coverage. Interestingly, the non-participation call was described as the boycott of Republic Day call.

The news of a 'boycott call' provoked all major political forces in the country. The call was criticised, condemned and rejected primarily on the grounds of 'India's unity and integrity'. Moreover, the Babri Masjid agitation was described as a kind of separatist communalism. The sympathisers of the Babri Masjid agitation also disapproved of this move and requested the BMMCC to withdraw it.[28] The most interesting condemnation of this 'boycott call' came from the 'concerned citizens' such as writers, intellectuals, journalists and artists, who prefer to call themselves 'non-political'.[29]

---

[27] Even in the Urdu translation of the Declaration, the phrase '*hissa nahi le*' was used.

[28] The Congress (I), BJP, CPI and VHP officially rejected this call. Janta Party and the CPI (M) asked the BMMCC to review its decisions and requested it to abandon its agitational programme. CPI (ML-Santosh Rana) was the only political front which supported the BMMCC and asked others to join this call. (MID 50, 93–94)

[29] Interestingly, most of these 'non-political' intellectuals were directly associated with the Congress (I), CPI and CPI (M).

Babri Masjid and the Muslim Politics of Right to Heritage **243**

A statement entitled, *Intellectuals' Appeal to Muslims of India* was issued by 25 'eminent persons' on 5 January 1987 (Appendix 3). In this widely circulated statement, these intellectuals supported the demands made by the BMMCC on the Babri Masjid. However, they rejected the 'boycott call' as an unacceptable political means. According to this statement, the Republic Day and Independence Day represent India's common political heritage. Therefore, the statement says:

> [o]n these occasions ... our people should not be drawn into *any controversy of partisan politics, sectarian polemics or conflict with government and administration* ... any attempt to abridge their importance or vitiate their significance is politically unwise, legally impermissible, nationally injurious and morally reprehensible (emphasis added, MID 50b: 63–64).

This lucidly written and well-articulated statement has two very interesting aspects. First, this statement talks about the 'political heritage' of India, which requires some clarification. The notion of political heritage always depends on the ways in which the political identity of a social group is perceived and acknowledged. In case of India, it is impossible to identify any one set of significant historical events and influential individuals which could be remembered as the authentic representatives of the India's 'political heritage'. The anti-colonial struggle is a revealing example to demonstrate the fact that a number of political streams not only rejected British rule on various grounds but also proposed several ideas and imaginations of independent India. Therefore, the official state version, which actually represents the views of most dominant ideological and political forces, could not be designated as ultimate political heritage of India. Second, the statement does not differentiate between 'partisan politics' of any kind and the 'conflict with government and administration'. It implies that any kind of disagreement as well as conflict with the government and administration on these occasions could not be tolerated. In this sense, this statement seems to suggest that any attempt to challenge the given dominant state version of India's heritage and its political legacy are not acceptable.

The legal-constitutionalists, who had dominated the intellectual side of the coalition took up this question of 'political heritage' seriously and came out with an equally well-articulated argument. In a statement entitled, *Call Not against State but against Government*

244　　*Muslim Political Discourse in Postcolonial India*

and Violator of Constitution issued on 11 January 1987, the BMMCC clarified the distinction between the terms 'boycott' and 'non-observance'. The statement notes:

> A boycott call would imply obstruction, resistance and mobilisation, while non-participation or non-association is a voluntary act of sacrifice and self-imposed deprivation . . . The call of non-participation is not against the State but against the government; it is no illegal or un-constitutional in any sense of the term; it is neither unethical nor anti-national; it is not an act of treason or rebellion or revolt; it does not constitute any disrespect to the constitution or to the Republic. The call is against those elements, who violate the Constitution and against a government, which fails to defend and protect the Constitution (MID 50c: 61).

This statement offers a 'democratic' explanation to the radical strategy adopted by the coalition. In addition, it also suggests a creative reading of the constitutional provisions. In fact, this statement emphasised the democratic principles on which the Constitution is based. It derives its strengths from these principles and questions the actual functioning of the government. Nevertheless, as expected, this explanation did not have any impact. The media kept on describing the call as a boycott of Republic Day.

In the meantime, it gradually became a serious political consideration. The sympathisers of the Babri Masjid agitation started pressurising the BMMCC to withdraw the call. Even on 22 January 1987, the then President of India, Giani Zail Singh appealed for the withdrawal of the call for boycott (MID 51: 141). By that time, the BMMCC had achieved its objective, at least symbolically. It had influenced the political system and the 'restoration of the Babri Masjid' had become a national issue. Thus, finally, on 25 January 1987, just one day before the Republic Day, the call was withdrawn.

The radical group of the coalition played a very interesting role in the episode. As we discussed in our previous chapter, the Imam who had been known for his aggressive positions decided to maintain a strange silence. Even he expressed apprehensions about the success of this move. As a result, the legal-constitutionalist camp led by Shahabuddin had to face all sort of criticisms. This crucial 'strategic' difference became more apparent in the next few months.

30 March Rally

The 30 March 1987 rally was the second major initiative of this coalition. Apart from the members, supporters and sympathisers of the BMMCC, almost all the major Muslim organisations and leaders participated in this massive rally at the Boat Club lawn. The participants attended the rally in a peaceful manner. They offered *Zuhur Salat* (afternoon prayer) in the lawns and took part in collective *Dua* (supplication) (JMD2n). Although the rift between the Imam group and the legal-constitutionalists became quite obvious after the withdrawal of the non-participation call, both the groups continued to extend their support to this rally. However, as I have discussed in our previous chapter, the Imam took this opportunity to sideline his competitors. More significantly, he not only neglected Shahabuddin publicly but also challenged the position of the legal-constitutionalists by appealing to the congregation to reject the 'judicial system of the government, which had been unable to protect the religious place of Muslims' (JMD2n). In this sense, the Imam was now in an advantageous position. However, despite these serious differences among the major constituents, the coalition continued to exist. In fact, after the speeches, a resolution on Babri Masjid was passed by the BMMCC and read before a huge gathering.

This resolution, in many respects, was more focussed. First, it emphasised that the Babri Masjid was not a Hindu–Muslim issue, 'but a Constitutional and legal question' (MID 53a: 205–06). However, unlike the previous declaration, it came out with a very clear understanding of the term 'restoration' of Babri Masjid. It pointed out that the '[r]estoration can only be effected by stopping the Puja . . . removing the idols . . . and by guaranteeing the freedom of Namaz (MID 53a: 205–06). Thus, the freedom to perform Namaz inside the Babri Masjid was incorporated in the main programme.

Second, it also proposed an interesting formula to expedite the legal process. The resolution demanded that the '[t]itle suit . . . be heard immediately by a Special Bench of a High Court in South India, consisting of three judges, none of whom may be a Hindu or Muslim and urges . . . the government to take necessary step at the High Court of Allahabad and at the Supreme Court for the purpose' (MID 53a: 205–06). Apart from these two new claims, the BMMCC resolution reiterated its previous demand that 'a central

246   *Muslim Political Discourse in Postcolonial India*

law should be ... enacted to guarantee the status of all places of worship and to protect them as they existed on 15 August 1947, against any claim or any move to alter their status' (MID 53a: 205–06). Moreover, to appease the radicals, the Ayodhya March was also given considerable importance.

Let us now look at the wider political significance of the non-participation call and the 30 March rally, especially from the point of view of the various public debates on religion and politics. First of all, these moves provoked political players to rethink some of the most fundamental issues of Indian political life. For example, in the case of the non-participation call, the difference between the constitutional principles and the actual functioning of the government was thoroughly discussed and the significance of the 'official celebration' was questioned. In fact, the Muslim legal-constitutionalists' position introduced a new kind of politics, which tried to interpret the existence of institutions in a more radical fashion and at the same time searched the possibilities of re-assertion of democratic rights. Second, the ways by which these two moves were denounced are equally significant. Most of the criticisms of these moves stemmed from the assumption that the religion could / should not be taken as a legitimate category for democratic politics. This oversimplified explanation of religious politics further created confusions and somehow provided more legitimacy to those political groups which were actually termed as 'communal'. Finally, the Babri Masjid site acquired a new symbolic political status. It became a point of reference for evoking the 'intrinsic political unity' of India's Muslims and the question of India's political heritage.

V

AYODHYA MARCH AND THE UNMAKING OF THE COALITION

The Congress-led Central and the state governments ignored the Babri Masjid issue almost entirely. For example, the Prime Minister's Office refused to receive the copy of the resolution adopted by the 30 March rally (MID 53b: 207). The then Home Minister, Sardar Buta Singh, who had promised the Muslim MPs in December 1986 that the government would invite Muslim and Hindu leaders for a dialogue on this issue, did not take any initiative (MID 49: 47). Moreover, the state virtually failed to expedite the

Babri Masjid and the Muslim Politics of Right to Heritage **247**

legal process to solve the title suit. In the meantime, a fresh wave of communal riots started in the country. The most severe communal clashes took place in the north Indian towns of Delhi, Meerut and Maliana. In fact, in Maliana, the PAC killed more than 50 Muslims and dumped the bodies in a nearby canal (Pachauri 1987: 120–24). These riots affected the credibility of the central government led by the Congress.

In this context, two very different political forces began to take advantage of the vacuum created by the ambiguous and evasive attitude of the Congress on this issue. The BJP was the first emerging political force. The BJP had a direct organisational and ideological relationship with the RSS and VHP. It had been supporting the VHP on the Ram Temple and had gained considerable popularity in north India. Unlike Congress, which had to take care of the Muslim votes in order to maintain a favourable 'communal equilibrium', the BJP did not have such compulsions, at least in the late 1980s. It was least interested in Muslim support because it had already decided to focus on upper- and middle-caste Hindus. In these circumstances, it was inevitable for the BJP as a political party to work out a full-fledged strategy for mobilising voters in the name of Hinduism.

The Muslim disenchantment with Congress at various levels was also helping the socialists and a few Congress rebels.[30] These leaders were trying to create a new political front on the lines of the old Janata Party model of 1977, which was totally dependent on anti-Congress feelings. However, they were aware that the popular discontent with Congress alone could not help them in setting up a viable alternative front. Since the Congress had been ignoring

---

[30] The impact of JP movement on this front cannot be ruled out. In fact, there were three major constituents of this front which emerged as the Janata Dal in October 1988. One group was led by Chandra Shekhar and other old socialists, who belonged to the defunct Janata Party. The second group was dominated by the Charan Singh fraction of Janata Party. And finally the third major constituent of this front was led by V. P. Singh and other Congress rebels (Fickette 1993). It is important to note that the Congress rebels, particularly V. P. Singh took the lead. He attacked the popular image of Rajiv Gandhi as honest leader by focusing on the issue of corruption and the public accountability of the Congress government. Perhaps for this reason, he emerged as the most powerful contender for the leadership of this front.

248 *Muslim Political Discourse in Postcolonial India*

the Muslims and the BJP had already committed itself to the Ram Temple, the most possible and attractive option for these leaders was to establish effective communication with the Muslim coalition on the Babri Masjid to mobilise Muslim support.

It is important to note that in this period (1986–88) the Muslim coalition on Babri Masjid had not been affected by the compulsions of electoral politics. Nevertheless, election time was fast approaching and it was inevitable for different constituents of this coalition to adjust themselves with emerging electoral alliances. Most importantly, they had to decide the fate of the coalition. In the backdrop of these changing political equations, the Ayodhya March became the focal point of the debate.

Ayodhya March: What, When, Why?

The application filed by the UP government in December 1987 to transfer the title suit and deter the proceedings on the writ petitions filed by the Muslims, further provoked Muslim coalition leaders. In a statement, the BMMCC described this legal attempt as highly unsatisfactory and 'too technical' (MID 63: 109). However, this move by the government initiated a new debate inside the coalition. The group led by the Imam openly criticised the coalition for not adopting a radical approach on the Babri Masjid question. They suggested that the time had come for the Muslim community to march to Ayodhya and 'liberate' the Babri Masjid.

In a broader sense, this radical posture had two very obvious reasons. This apparent radicalism could attract the emerging anti-Congress front leaders. Since the internal complexities of the coalition had already given an opportunity to the radicals to work on mass mobilisation of Muslims, they were in a position to bargain for Muslim votes. At the same time, their radical approach was quite appropriate for translating Muslim grievances into anti-Congress feelings in the riot-affected areas of north India. In this sense, the Ayodhya March issue offered the radicals a possibility to enter into a greater, though informal, electoral alliance with anti-Congress forces. Therefore, it was important for them to either challenge the existing distribution of power within the coalition or alternately, discard it completely.

The legal-constitutionalist group, on the other hand, wanted to pressurise the government to initiate a dialogue. For this group, the Ayodhya March was nothing more than a symbolic threat

Babri Masjid and the Muslim Politics of Right to Heritage **249**

to increase political pressure on the government. Moreover, the structure of the coalition was in their favour. They were leading the intellectual side of the agitation, and therefore, were in a position to deal with the governments and the media. In contrast, they did not have any control over the Muslim mobilisation politics.[31] In such a situation their prime objective was to adhere to the 'organisational framework' of the coalition. For example, a statement issued on 8 October 1987 said:

> [t]he Co-ordination Committee alone is competent to decide whether the stage has been reached to undertake the March and to fix the date thereof. This Committee is expected to meet soon to decide the future course of action. (emphasis in original, MID 59: 497).

In January 1988, finally, the coalition issued a statement that the government's evasive attitude had forced the BMMCC to call upon Muslims for a direct Ayodhya March (MID 63, 109). This declaration gave some kind of satisfaction to the radicals. However, the legal-constitutionalist took this opportunity to approach the government to avoid the Ayodhya March and thus maintain the balance in their favour. Syed Shahabuddin wrote a letter to the Prime Minister on the very next day on 25 January. He writes:

> [r]equest you to . . . to instruct the Group of Ministers . . . to consider the two demands of the Movement — expeditious determination of a title suit by a special bench, [and] . . . the enactment of law to protect the status of all places of worship as on 15 August 1947'. He gave assurance that '. . . Committee would be glad to participate in any endeavour, under the auspices of the govt. for a just and fair settlement of the controversy' (MID 63a: 110).

---

[31] In an editorial published in *Muslim India*, Shahabuddin outlined this aspect of the Babri Masjid agitation. He writes: [t]he Movement has had its quota of extremist and opportunists. The extremists follow a blind strategy: their objective is confrontation. The opportunists blow hot and cold depending on what suits their personal interests. Neither serves the cause, neither are they committed to its success. For the fulfilment is future, as far as they are concerned. Both act as agent's provocateur. Mass psychology loves extremism and admires rhetoric. Moderation is taken as defeatism, reasonableness is taken as surrender' (Shahabuddin 1988b: 195–96).

250   *Muslim Political Discourse in Postcolonial India*

This letter was taken seriously by the radicals. The Imam openly criticised Shahabuddin and described him as a 'Congress agent' (MID 64, 191). However, the radicals continued to maintain a wait and watch policy and did not challenge the authority of the coalition. Instead, internal pressure, particularly from the UP leaders, was used to compel the coalition for the Ayodhya March.

Finally on 22 May 1988, the coalition declared that it would organise an Ayodhya March. According to various press releases, issued during this time, it was decided that the Ayodhya March programme would be scheduled in two phases. In the first phase, the leaders of the Muslim community would take part in March on 12 October 1988. In the second phase, common Muslims would have to March to Ayodhya on 14 October 1988. Moreover, it was also clarified that the 'March shall be peaceful and non-violent and it is not against the Hindu community but against an insensitive and ineffective government and the chauvinist forces' (MID 66: 250).

The modus operandi, at least the official programme of action, was not elaborated in this statement. Furthermore, there were other unresolved issues. For example, the role of local Muslims of Faizabad and Ayodhya was not at all clear. In fact, after the formation of BMAC UP and subsequently the BMMCC, the Faizabad committee literally disappeared from the Muslim political discourse. They were also not consulted about the Ayodhya March (Siddique 2004, Int.). On the other hand, their life and property was at risk; such a March could trigger off massive communal violence that would directly affect them.

The legal-constitutionalists came out with a well-defined 'democratic strategy' for the Ayodhya March. In an editorial published in *Muslim India*, Shahabuddin proposed an interesting blueprint of a *peaceful Ayodhya March*. He points out:

> Unarmed volunteers shall peacefully move on foot from the base camp (at Lucknow or Faizabad) towards Ayodhya in organised and identifiable batches with the intention of performing Friday congregational prayers in the Babri Masjid, violating Section 144 if in force and the existing ban on the access of the Muslim Indian to the mosque. If the march is resisted by the Govt., they shall not disperse but court arrest; if they are attacked, they shall not reiterate; if arrested, they shall not ask for bail; if tried, they shall offer no defence (Shahabuddin 1988b).

More broadly, this programme simply reminds us of the Gandhian strategy of civil disobedience. Even the prayer at Babri Masjid seems to offer a link between Satyagraha and the Ayodhya March. But, this was just an imaginary outline. The radicals had their own plans, which they did not want to share.

The Islamic Relevance of the Ayodhya March

Meanwhile, a very interesting development took place. On 6 July 1988, the *Mufti-e-Azam* (Chief Mufti) of the Darul Uloom (Wakf) Deoband, issued a fatwa against the religious legitimacy of the Ayodhya March. He argued that the March was bound to be resisted by force and the Muslim participants could be attacked by the 'government forces and the Hindu militants. Therefore, the March could amount to suicide, which is not permitted in Islam' (MID 68: 381). This was a massive blow for both the fractions. In spite of everything, they were fighting for the 'Islamic cause', and such a fatwa could challenge their authority to speak on behalf of Islam.

The fatwa received two very different kinds of criticisms. First, the radical group did not question the contents of the fatwa but questioned the ways by which such a fatwa was issued. They argued that the Deoband ulema had been associated with the Congress for a long time and therefore the Congress had used these *Sarkari Mullah*s (Official Mullahs) for issuing favourable religious sanction for its own politics. Several posters were issued in this regard in different cities of north India.[32]

The legal-constitutionalists, however, criticised the fatwa on different counts. Rejecting the fatwa on legal and political grounds, Shahabuddin wrote:

> Republic of India is not *Darul Harab*, neither is it *Darul Islam*. But, it is *Darul Aman* and *Darul Muhada*. This is because the Muslim community enjoys freedom of religion and other fundamental rights and guarantees under the Constitution including the right to agitate democratically and peacefully if any constitutional and legal rights, individual or collective, are infringed' ... The fatwa on Ayodhya march is inappropriate as it is in Indian context, becomes thus a test of

---

[32] I am thankful to Mohammed Nadim, Shafiquddin Khaksar and Mohamed Arif for discussing this aspect of the Babri Masjid agitation (JMD3).

252 *Muslim Political Discourse in Postcolonial India*

the holds of the religious establishment over the Muslim community. If the Muslim community treat such Fatwas with disdain, it can deal a fatal blow to the authority of the Ulema in the matters political ... It is for the Ulema with vision to avoid such a break, they must come forward, bridge the gap and join the political struggle for the defence of the constitutional rights' (Shahabuddin 1988a: 339–40).

These two examples illustrate that the coalition was a purely political outfit, which operated on the basis of practical political compulsions. Moreover, the emphasis given by the legal-constitutionalists on the separate spheres of constitutional framework and the Islamic principles further justify the assertion that the Muslim politics in India should/cannot be understood purely on the basis of Islam.

Postponement of the Ayodhya March and Disintegration of the Coalition

The Ayodhya March became a serious issue for the government. Responding to the demands made by the BMMCC on 31 July 1988, the then Home Minister, Buta Singh proposed that the government was ready to coordinate the negotiation on the Ayodhya controversy. He also gave an assurance that if such negotiations failed, the government would attempt to expedite the judicial process by involving the High Court (MID 68: 383). This assurance was a victory for the legal-constitutionalists. After a long discussion, the BMMCC accepted this offer on 8 August 1988. Although the radicals openly criticised this move, the BMMCC decision for talks with the government was endorsed by the coalition unanimously (MID 69: 432). Consequently, the formal talks with the government began.

Meanwhile, ignoring these developments, the Imam wrote a public letter to the Chief Minister (CM) of UP. In this letter, he pointed out that he was in full agreement with the decision of BMMCC but had not announced his own stand. Thus, he requested that Dr Karan Singh should be involved in the negotiation (MID 69a: 396). This move was quite astonishing because the Congress-led central government was ready for talks and the CM of UP, who was also a Congressman, had a less significant role in these negotiations. But, from a political point of view this letter had a wider importance. The Imam did not want to operate within the BMMCC's institutional framework, which in any case, was restricting his own political status. His purpose was to demonstrate that

Babri Masjid and the Muslim Politics of Right to Heritage **253**

he was 'above' the BMMCC and therefore his individual stand mattered.

The pressures created by the legal-constitutionalists worked well and on 12 October 1988, the government officially announced that that 'steps would be initiated for expediting hearing of the pending title suit in Allahabad High Court' (MID 71: 491). It was also announced that ... the next round of talks with the members of *Ram Janam Bhumi Mukti Yajna Samiti* and other Hindu leaders on the subject will be held' (MID 71: 491). This was another moral victory for the legal-constitutionalists because the government had virtually accepted their demands and in principle the Muslim coalition had been recognised as a party in the dispute. As a result of this assurance, the BMMCC decided to postpone the Ayodhya March programme.

The postponement of the Ayodhya March was taken as an excuse by the radical group to break their relationship with the coalition. They decided to organise another conference in November 1988 to form a separate Muslim body on the Babri Masjid issue. The legal-constitutionalists opposed this move and issued several 'official letters' to the organisers. However, without paying any attention to these letters, finally on 27 November 1988, the break-away group organised the second major conference on Babri Masjid at the Jama Masjid Park, New Delhi and formed the All India Babri Masjid Action Committee (AIBMAC).

In a statement issued by the newly established AIBMAC, these radical leaders highlighted three very technical points justifying this split. First, they argued that the role of the BMMCC was over because after the programme of action adopted by the All India Babri Masjid Conference in 1987, its role had been 'exhausted'. Thus, the BMMCC was no longer a competent authority. Second, it is said that these leaders were not satisfied with the talks going on between the BMMCC and the Home Minister. Third, and perhaps most importantly, the Ayodhya March was shown as a crucial point. The statement says: 'The ways the dates of the Ayodhya March have been extended and finally ... indefinitely postponed has created differences in the leadership and frustration among the masses and gave the communalists an opportunity to indulge in provocation and violence' (MID 73: 14).

However, the most significant part of this statement was the demands made by the AIBMAC. It made three demands: (*a*) the title

254   *Muslim Political Discourse in Postcolonial India*

suit should be transferred to High Court in south India for a neutral trial, (*b*) The 31 January 1986 status of Babri Masjid should be restored and (*c*) A central law should be enacted to protect the religious status of all places of worship including the Babri Masjid.

Table 5.4 shows that the AIBMAC adopted the line initially taken by the BMMCC. But, there was a slight variation. First, the demand to restore the 31 January 1986 status of the Babri Masjid is quite interesting. It is true that the entry for Hindus was restricted before this date. But, it is also true that even on this very day, the Babri Masjid site was almost as disputable as it was in late December 1949. In this sense, the unrestricted entry of Hindus was considered to be the main hurdle not only in solving the title suit but also restoring the 'status of Babri Masjid'. In comparison to the resolution passed by the BMMCC on 30 March 1987, it was a reasonably open position on the nature of the status of Babri Masjid. Second, the issue of the Ayodhya March was also not very clear. The BMMCC was criticised for delaying the Ayodhya March. Yet, no concrete plan or strategy was chalked out for such a move. In fact, the idea of the Ayodhya March was kept highly ambiguous. Third, the talks with the government were criticised and dissatisfactions were expressed about the outcome of these talks. But again no alternative proposal was suggested to solve the dispute. These ambiguities show that the AIBMAC programme was vague and unclear. Even its own strategy was bit 'moderate' because the AIBMAC did not put forward any extreme demand. So, what were the reasons behind the formation of AIBMAC in late 1988 which eventually led to the collapse of the Muslim coalition?

A simple and politically correct line of reasoning would suggest that political opportunism and/or personality clashes were the main factors which forced the radical group to form a new outfit. However, no one can deny the value of such claims. But such oversimplification would not help us in considering wider political processes that contributed to the divide at this crucial point of time. The placing of the Muslim coalition in the wider ideological polarisation of Indian politics, which was taking a concrete shape in the late 1988, is very crucial. We have seen that the Ram Temple movement had established the BJP as an independent political force. In opposition to the BJP, a 'secular' camp was also coming into existence under the leadership of the Janata Dal (JD) with the help of the Left parties. But, interestingly, both the camps

Table 5.4: Positions of BMMCC and AIBMAC on Babri Masjid

Issues	BMMCC	AIBMAC
The talks with the government	We should concentrate on talks because written assurance given by the government has far-reaching legal and political implication	The talks are useful; but there is a politics behind it. If we do not go for the radical steps like Ayodhya March it will affect the morals of activists.
The role of the BMMCC	It was established to guide the movement by a conference in 1986 and it has been playing an effective role.	The role of this body is over because after the programme of action adopted by the All India Babri Masjid Conference has been 'exhausted'.
Ayodhya March	It will be on the last instance; if it happens it would be most saddest aspect for the movement.	It is important because it is our way of protests and it might reflect the strength of the Muslims community.
What is Babri Masjid?	It is a symbol, a vantage point to look at the systematic exclusion of the community. It is a national issue and it needs collective Muslim political action.	Not clarified.
The demands	1. Expeditious determination of a title suit by a special bench of a HC, preferably in south India. 2. The enactment of law to protect the status of all places of worship as on 15 August 1947.	1. 'We are not satisfied with the talks so far held by the BMMCC with Home Minister, we stick to the demand …that the matter should be referred to a special bench of HC of south India with no judge being a Hindu or a Muslim and status quo as on 31.1.1986 being restored in the mean time. … The announcement of expediting the judicial proceeding is nothing more than delaying tactics we do not consider such assurance conductive to the settlement. 2. 'The Home Minister has said nothing so far about our demand for legislature to protect … the status and character of all places of worship' (MID 73: p. 14).

Source: Author.

256   *Muslim Political Discourse in Postcolonial India*

were not very strong and, to some extent, were still depending on anti-Congressism of some kind. For this reason they required each other's help to displace the broken yet powerful Congress.

The position of JD was quite delicate. Despite the fact that they had opposed the Ram Temple issue ideologically, the party was not in a position to reject the possibilities of an electoral alliance with the BJP. Similarly, it also required Muslim backing at any cost. Yet, the radical ways in which the Muslim coalition had framed the Babri Masjid issue as an exclusive 'Muslim issue' was not well-suited for the political requirement of the JD. In this situation, the best option was to eventually re-shape the image of the Babri Masjid issue to accommodate it into the wider ideology of secularism.

From the point of Muslim leaders, the JD had emerged as political *compulsion*. The Congress, which had traditionally been the secure political hub for Muslim politicians, had lost its credibility among the Muslims and it could not be the best bet for any electoral adventure. In this sense, the JD leadership had an advantage to select the favourable partners from the Muslim coalition. This 'selective patronage' of JD was going to be the most determining aspect to influence the Muslim collation. In this context, the V.P. Singh fraction, which was the most dominant group in the JD, started supporting the Imam group by ignoring the activities of the Shahabuddin group.[33] This was a very obvious choice. The JD leadership wanted to use the symbolic importance of the Shahi Imam of the Jama Masjid, which had been playing a very crucial role in almost every election since 1977. Similarly, the Babri Masjid issue had produced a number of Muslim leaders in north India, particularly in UP, which had a considerable mass base. These Muslim leaders could help the JD in capturing the grassroots Muslim support. On the other hand, the Shahabuddin group could

---

[33] The political relationship between V. P. Singh and the Imam became very visible in the later months, particularly during the time of the general elections in late 1989. For example, in July 1989, the AIBMAC decided to support the JD. Even, with some hesitation it eventually accepted the JD–BJP electoral alliance (MID 81: 430). On the other hand, two members of the AIBMAC and the Imam's aides, M. Afzal and Ubbaidullah Azmi, were elected to Rajya Sabha on ruling party's ticket, in return. Furthermore, an unofficial package for repairing of the Jama Masjid was also sanctioned (JMD3).

Babri Masjid and the Muslim Politics of Right to Heritage **257**

not be a challenge for JD. He had been a Janata Party MP and in this situation was not in a position to extend his support to the Congress.[34]

Thus, V. P. Singh's support encouraged the radical group led by the Imam to disassociate itself from the coalition and form the AIBMAC. This new outfit could give him ample space to make full use of the Babri Masjid issue for election purposes. However, in order to balance the relationship with the JD, it was important for the Imam to soften his radicalism. This could be the possible reason behind the flexible stand of AIBMAC on some of the crucial aspects of the Babri Masjid issue.

By that time, the wider demands of the coalition had been accepted by the secularists' camp, including the Congress. The judicial process and negotiations had been initiated and discussions to introduce a bill to protect the status of all places of worship as of 15 August 1947 began. As a matter of fact, the coalition had achieved its main objectives. Yet, Babri Masjid dispute was still alive and there was a need to re-fashion the nature of politics in significant way.

VI

'NEGOTIATIONS' AS A MODE OF POLITICS

In general, negotiations are often understood as processes by which two or more parties try to reduce or remove a conflict. A successful negotiation, in this sense, is one, which allows the opposite parties to reach a compromise. However, in the Babri Masjid case, the nature of negotiations was very different. Both the groups were not participating to reduce or resolve the conflict; rather they were keen to 'use' the platform provided by the state for consolidating their

---

[34] Shahabuddin initially opposed the JD–BJP alliance (MID 79a: 333). However, at the same time, he continued to interact with the 'secular' front. For example, he organised a Muslim political convention on 8 July 1989, in which he invited V. P. Singh and other JD leaders (MID 80: 384). However, instead of supporting any political front, Shahabuddin finally formed a new political party: the *Insaf Party* (Justice Party) (MID 82, 478). In 2001, Shahabuddin clarified the objective of the Insaf Party. He writes, '*Insaf Party* was a protest against the behind the scene deals with the BJP, as soon as V. P. Singh govt. fell, *Insaf Party* was dissolved' (Shahabuddin 2001).

258   *Muslim Political Discourse in Postcolonial India*

respective political positions. In fact, a 'successful failure' of these negotiations was more advantageous than a successful resolution of the dispute.

Moreover, the state played a very substantial role in these negotiations. It introduced itself as a 'neutral arbitrator' and emphasised the process of negotiations as an impartial endeavour to reconcile the conflicting interests of Hindus and Muslims on the Babri Masjid. Table 5.5 very clearly shows that although the process of negotiation started in 1989, it became the most crucial state initiative in the post-1991 period. Thus, negotiations provided political advantages to the state and it emerged as the sole authority to delineate the scope of a 'negotiated settlement' on the Babri Masjid.

From the point of view of Muslim leaders, negotiation was a rhetorical action, which was intended to enhance the symbolic meanings of their other political moves.[35] In fact, in various declarations, they had regretted that the state did not pay attention to this 'sincere' demand. After the collapse of the Muslim coalition, however, negotiations on the Babri Masjid issue became a dominant form of Muslim politics. All the major groups almost suspended the mass mobilisation programme on the Babri Masjid and accepted negotiations with the VHP as the most adequate form of politics to safeguard 'Muslim interests'.

But why did they recognise negotiations with the VHP on Babri Masjid as a viable form of Muslim politics, which could have an effect on their own credibility among the common Muslims? After all, the VHP had been publicly demanding that the mosque should be shifted to some other place otherwise it could possibly be demolished by the devotees of Lord Ram. Let us now look at the different rounds of negotiations to examine the changing Muslim responses in this period.

Round 1: Negotiation and the Question of Muslim Representation

After the 1989 elections, the BMMCC offered to participate in the negotiation with VHP without 'prejudice to the judicial process' (MID 86: 94). It was an interesting move because the negotiation as a political technique suited the legal-constitutionalism of the BMMCC and could again give them a new political opening in this

---

[35] For a detailed analysis of the 'symbolic' aspects of political actions, see Kaviraj (2005).

Babri Masjid and the Muslim Politics of Right to Heritage **259**

case. However, we should not forget that the AIBMAC had helped the JD to come into power and it did not want to lose the political opportunity to find out a negotiated settlement. To outline these objectives, the Imam issued a press statement. He said:

> [t]he government has had a dialogue with the VHP and the BMMCC but not with the BMAC ... They have not talked to us or invited us for any talks ... They have not talked to the people who have been active on Lucknow or Ayodhya ... And you can imagine if the Muslim community will agree to what Shahabuddin says. They will never do so (MID 85: 13).

To put these intentions into action, on 26 December 1989, a delegation of the AIBMAC met the the the then Home Minister and proposed that it would intend to take part in the dialogue with the VHP (MID 85a: 94).

When these two organisations were approaching the state for talks, a very interesting development took place. On 23 January 1990, the Shankaracharaya of Kanchi expressed hope that the Ram Mandir could be constructed without disturbing the Babri Masjid (MID 87: 142). These views were quiet opposite to the extremist Hindutva position of the VHP. However, the direct involvement of Shankaracharaya played an important role and finally on 28 January 1990, the VHP accepted to participate in the negotiations with Muslim parties on the Ram Temple issue (MID 87: 142).

The government responded quite enthusiastically. A three-member committee was set up under the leadership of Madhu Dandvate on 15 February 1990 for facilitating the talks between Hindu and Muslim leaders (MID 88: 191). However, quite intriguingly, the state ignored the BMMCC, AIBMAC and even the VHP and approached the religious leaders of the two communities, the Shankaracharaya of Kanchi and Ali Mian Nadwi, for finding a solution of Babri Masjid case.[36]

At this point of time, quite informally, a meeting between Ali Mian Nadwi and the Shankaracharaya of Kanchi took place in Kanchi near Madras (Chennai) on 19 March 1990. No one knows what actually happened in these talks. In fact, Nadwi's autobiog-

---

[36] Ali Mian Nadwi was contacted by Yunus Salim and Krishan Kant in December 1989 for a proposed talk between him and the Kanchi Shankaracharaya on the Babri Masjid issue (Nadwi 2003: 202).

260 *Muslim Political Discourse in Postcolonial India*

raphy is the best source to know his assessment of these talks. He writes, 'the *Shankaracharaya* was not very clear about the removal of idols from the mosque yet, he was of the view that the Babri mosque should be opened for Namaz' (Nadwi 2003: 202). As it was expected, this first round of talks ended with a happy note. In fact, this informal meeting between the Shankaracharaya and Nadwi encouraged the V. P. Singh government to facilitate the second crucial round of talks between these leaders. Interestingly the National Integration Council was also involved in this issue to provide an official institutional framework to these talks.

In general, this move could be seen as an 'honest attempt' by the state to find an amicable solution by involving 'non-political' religious leaders. However, this was a very significant political move. The JD-led coalition government was depending on the support of the BJP.[37] In this context inviting VHP and any other Muslim group could disturb the political equilibrium at the centre. On the other hand, no one could object the religious significance of the dispute and in this sense the religious leaders could have been the most responsible stakeholders for the two communities. Therefore, the talks between these leaders could defend the position of the coalition government.

Ali Mian Nadwi's name for second crucial round of talks with Hindu religious leaders created a stir in Muslim political circles. He was juxtaposed with other active Muslim religious personalities. In fact, as Nadwi himself pointed out, his name was suggested and supported by the Chandra Shekhar group against Imam Bukhari, whose name was backed by the powerful V. P. Singh camp (Nadwi 2003: 335). This tussle became public when a writ petition was filed in the Lucknow bench of Allahabad High Court challenging the candidature of Nadwi as the representative of the Muslim side for the proposed talks.[38] It was alleged that Nadwi could not represent Muslims primarily because he did not subscribe to the position taken up by the entire Muslim community on the Babri Masjid. It was also said that Nadwi's father, Maulana Abul Hai in

---

[37] V. P. Singh formed a coalition government with help of the BJP and the Left parties in 1989.

[38] This petition was filed by Aas Mohammed Ansari against the central government, state government, UP Sunni Waqf Board and Ali Mian Nadwi (Nadwi 2003: 341).

Babri Masjid and the Muslim Politics of Right to Heritage **261**

his book *Hindustan Islami Ahad Mein* had accepted that the Babri Masjid was built on a desecrated Ram Temple and Nadwi himself believed in this theory. Therefore, he could not be trusted as the Muslim representative (Nadwi 2003: 335).

This case, which was primarily filed to gain media attention, was dismissed by the court. However, to counter this propaganda, Nadwi publicly announced that he did not believe in the Ram Temple story. He also made it clear that his father's book was not based on historical facts and with due respect to his father's intellect, he did not consider his words as 'divine judgment' of any kind. Furthermore, Nadwi also clarified that his name was actually 'chosen' to represent the Muslim community by some people; he never approached anyone in this regard (Nadwi 2003: 334).

The second round of talks was scheduled to begin in October 1990. Nadwi set two preconditions for these talks: (*a*) the government should take some official responsibilities to protect the Babri Masjid and (*b*) these talks should not be considered as the final negotiations. Nadwi insisted that after his meeting with the Shankaracharaya, the AIMPLB and other Muslim parties should also be involved to endorse the final agreement (ibid.: 335).

These two preconditions somehow reflect the conscious approach of Nadwi. He did not want to ignore the political strength of other Muslim groups. Moreover, he knew that after the collapse of the Muslim coalition and subsequent series of riots, the credibility of every Muslim leader was at stake. Nadwi, who had emerged as *the leader* of Ulema in the Shah Bano case, did not want to take any risk. For these reasons, he adopted a very safe and consistent approach to the question of negotiation.

This self-protective attitude at last forced him to almost give up the idea of leading the negotiations. In the final moment, he declined to participate in the second round of talks in person. He insisted that due to his poor health he was unable to take part in the proposed meeting and thus, his friend and close aide Maulana Abdul Karim Parekh should be involved this time.

This demand was accepted by the government and Maulana Parekh as the Muslim representative went to see the Shankaracharaya. Interestingly, this time, the Shankaracharaya also refused to meet the Muslim representative. It was not very clear what forced the Shankaracharaya to disregard this well-publicised state initiative. But according to Nadwi, the Hindu rightists had

262 *Muslim Political Discourse in Postcolonial India*

threatened the Shankaracharaya that if he went against the wishes of the VHP, the *math* of Kanchi would be destroyed (Nadwi 2003: 344).

The ultimate failure of these talks was not very astonishing. However, this first round of talks shows that the question 'who represents Muslims', in fact, overshadowed the actual Babri Masjid issue. In this context the government's invitation for negotiations became a question of *political legitimacy* for Muslim groups/individual. The debate on Nadwi's candidature clearly illustrates the fact that the official invitation turned out to be the ultimate criterion by which the political weight of any fraction/individual had to be determined. For that reason Nadwi, who had always been known for taking a very 'conscious' position against his political rivals, had to openly participate in the internal battle over Muslim representation. He issued a statement and somehow denounced the authority of the Shahi Imam. His final denial is also very crucial. It is possible that he might have identified the expected failure of these negotiations and thus became over-sensitive towards the 'negative' impact of such outcome.

Round 2: Negotiations and the Limits of a Negotiated Settlement

The VHP did not stop its active mobilisation programme, which was directly supported by the BJP.[39] In fact, when the idea of a negotiated settlement was being introduced, the BJP President L. K. Advani started his famous *Rath Yatra* to mobilise Hindus for Ram temple. This Rath Yatra changed the political scenario quite significantly. Advani was arrested by the V.P. Singh government and in retaliation, the BJP decide to withdraw its support. As a result, the JD-led coalition government fell.[40] At this moment, the

---

[39] On 23 June 1990, the VHP announced the *Sant Sammelan*'s decision to fix 30 October 1990 as the date of construction for the proposed temple. On 27 June, however, VHP offered to resume talks with Muslim leaders but insisted that it would not be ready to talk on date, plan and site of the proposed Ram temple (MID 92: 382–83).

[40] Advani started his *Rath Yatra* on 25 September 1990 from Somnath. However, he was arrested on 23 October 1990. Consequently, the BJP decided to withdraw its support. Meanwhile, the VHP sponsored *Kar Sewa* held on 30 October 1990 at Ayodhya. The JD government of UP led by

Chandra Shekhar group formed a minority government with the help of the Congress, which was the largest party in the Lok Sabha. This government also fell within a period of four months. Finally after another national election in 1991 the Congress returned to power. Most significantly, this time the BJP emerged as the main opposition party in the Lok Sabha. It even formed a government in UP, which was going to be an advantage for the VHP. In the backdrop of these political uncertainties, particularly when the talks between the religious leaders were seen as the final solutions of the dispute, in July 1990, the BMMCC approached the government for another round of talks with the VHP. In fact, on 30 July 1990, the then Minister of State for Home Affairs Mufti Mohammad Sayeed arranged an initial meeting with the BMMCC and the VHP and set off a process of negotiation. However, the AIBMAC did not participate in this discussion and even criticised this move.[41] The situation changed almost completely within a few months. After the failure of the talks between Nadwi and the Shankaracharaya in October 1990, the state started promoting the AIBMAC. As a result, when the idea of having a face to face negotiation was proposed, the AIBMAC was recognised as the main Muslim party for talks. Finally, in December 1990, the AIBMAC and the VHP were invited for negotiation.

It is important to note that this was the first occasion when the leading Hindu and Muslim political groups were going to *discuss* the fate of the Babri Masjid. These talks were highly publicised by the media and it was argued that an extensive discussion on the Babri Masjid issue would pave the way for a negotiated settlement. However, it was not going to happen. After initial discussion, the VHP demanded that the historicity of Ram and his birth places could not be discussed in these talks. On the other hand, the AIBMAC adhered to 'once a mosque always a mosque' position.

Mulayam Singh Yadav adopted a very strict approach did not allow the *Kar Sewak*s to enter the disputed site. When *Kar Sewak*s tried to break the barriers, the police started indiscriminate firing. Around 30 people killed in this incident (Noorani 2003b).

[41] On 31 July 1990 AIBMAC convenor Jilani argued that the dialogues with the VHP were futile in view of the rigid stand of the Hindutva forces on Ram Temple (MID 93: 431).

264   *Muslim Political Discourse in Postcolonial India*

Despite these rigid stands of both the parties, this round of talks continued for a period of three months.[42]

From the point of view of the VHP, these talks were simply a rhetorical action by which it could demonstrate its radicalism to its supporters. However, the AIBMAC's position was different. Negotiations were more than a rhetorical move for them. They have to articulate a position which could justify their adherence to a legal solution of the dispute and at the same time defend their participation in talks for finding out a 'negotiated settlement'. In this sense, the *limits of a negotiated settlement* had to be identified.

The Imam formula to solve the dispute could be an example to illustrate this poser. In an interview the Imam said:

> [t]he mosque be locked up and a Ram Temple be constructed around the existing Ram *Chabootra* in the mosque compound ... Idols should be removed from the mosque and a wall can be constructed between the temple and the mosque ... The mosque would be declared as monument of national importance by the ASI (MID 87: 103).

This formula suggests three very interesting points (Figure 5.9). First, the AIBMAC decided to divide the mosque into two parts and in principle accepted that the outer part of the mosque could be given to the VHP. As our previous discussion shows that the Ram *Chabutra* was an inseparable part of the mosque. Moreover, from the point of view of Islamic Shariat, the wakf area occupied

---

[42] The talks started on 1 December 1990 in the presence of the Chief Ministers of UP, Maharashtra, Gujarat and Rajasthan (MID 97a: 46). In this initial meeting preliminary speeches were made. The second round of talks began on 4 December 1990, in which both the parties decided to exchange documentary evidences (MID 97a: 47). These crucial papers were eventually submitted to the government on 26 December 1990 (MID 98: 95). However, in a public statement issued on the same day, the VHP reiterated that the location of *Ramjanmbhumi* site was not negotiable. The AIBMAC also criticised the stubborn attitude of the VHP (MID 98: 95). Despite these essential differences, the third round of negotiation began on 10 January 1991. In this meeting the VHP and the AIBMAC nominated some historians and archaeologist to form expert committees (MID 98: 96). A few meetings of 'these nominated experts' also took place in the first week of February. However, both the parties did not move from their respective public stands and on 13 February 1991, VHP decided to discontinue negotiations with AIBMAC (MID 99: 144).

Figure 5.9: The Imam Formula

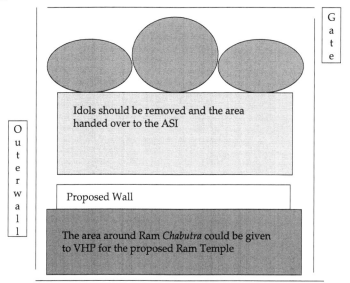

Source: Author.

by a mosque cannot be divided into various parts on the basis of their religious significance. There is no possibility to make a distinction between a purely 'sanctified' space and a 'less-sacred' area. By proposing this formula, the AIBMAC simply transcended the legal and religious boundaries. Interestingly, the VHP refused to accept this partition of the mosque and argued that the entire mosque area was the sacred birth place of Lord Ram, which could not be divided. Second, the ownership of the site was disputed and it was not possible for the ASI to take over the mosque without recognising the owner of the site for a proper agreement under the 1958 Act (MID 87: 103). In such a situation, the ASI could not declare it a protected historical monument. Third, this formula also disregarded the Muslim demand to offer Namaz inside the protected historical monuments. The 1958 Act very clearly points out that if a non-functional mosque is locked up and declared as a protected monument, its religious status would no longer be recognised and it would be protected simply as a dead historical monument. In this sense, the Imam formula would simply mean a division of the Babri Masjid into two parts: the outer part, which

266   *Muslim Political Discourse in Postcolonial India*

could be given to the VHP for the Hindu temple and the inner part, which could be handed over to the state for converting it into a dead historical monument.

The most elaborated explanation of this dilemma, however, can be found in the criticism made by the BMMCC. Shahabuddin, in a long letter to the then PM Chandra Shekhar, not only argued that the BMMCC was the authentic Muslim representative but also questioned the limits of negotiated settlement. He wrote:

> [t]he BMMCC ... fails to understand the objective and the role of the government ... because Executive cannot substitute the Judiciary and government cannot function as court ... the object of negotiation should be confined to define an area of agreement ... which would safeguard the vital ... interests of both the parties and negotiations cannot be stretched to a quasi-judicial process of lining up evidence and assessing their relevance and comparative weight, leading to an award or finding by the Government. Negotiation is neither mediation nor arbitration (MID 99a: 144).

This letter, which was written basically to denounce the position of the AIBMAC, clearly indicates a very crucial problem of the dominant Muslim position. It is true that in many cases, the area of the negotiation could be clearly defined. It is also true that negotiations should not substitute the judicial process. However, it does not mean that the 'area of agreement' cannot go beyond the legal process. In the particular case of Babri Masjid where both the parties were not ready to give up their stand, it was not possible. In fact, the VHP had been showing an eagerness for a negotiated settlement in place of a judicial solution.

However, it was very difficult for the Muslim parties to ignore the judicial process not only because the legal position of the Muslim side was stronger but also because the legal-constitutional framework of rights had been an accepted as a political norm of Muslim politics. In this sense, Shahabuddin was almost correct to suggest that the negotiation should not substitute the legal process.

Round 3: From 'Restoration' to 'Protection' of Babri Masjid

In mid-1991, two very important incidents took place — the publication of the famous *Historians' Report to the Nation* and the enactment of the Protection of Religious Places of Worship Act (1991).

Babri Masjid and the Muslim Politics of Right to Heritage **267**

These two developments almost changed the direction of Muslim politics. The *Historians Report to the Nation* consolidated the position of the Muslim parties on the history of the dispute. As we noted that the Muslim leaders had been avoiding the historical questions and their emphasis was on the 'history' of the legal proceedings. After the publication of this Report, they found a legitimate historical ground.

Quite similarly, the enactment of the 1991 Act, which as a matter of fact, was not applicable to the Babri Masjid dispute, provided a moral victory to Muslim parties. Their fundamental demand had not only been accepted but also quite significantly, assimilated into the wider 'secular' discourse. The Muslim politicians, who had been well-placed in the secular political camp, found an ideological justification for their political loyalties towards 'secular parties' and intelligentsia. In fact, after the publication of the Report and the enactment of the 1991 Act, the 'collapse of the Muslim coalition' became a less-important issue, even for the BMMCC. Perhaps for these reasons, the AIBMAC and BMMCC decided to work together. Just before the 1991 election, Shahabuddin dissolved the Insaaf Party and joined the JD. Even he openly supported the Imam's *prerogative* to choose Muslim candidates for the JD (MID 102: 287). The victory of the Congress in these elections did not affect this unity and both the committees continued to organise joint programmes.

The idea of a negotiation on the Babri Masjid came from the BJP government of UP this time. In June 1991, the UP state government proposed that the dialogue with Muslim leaders should be initiated (MID 104: 383). In the wake of aggressive Hindutva politics, this invitation was very significant for the legitimacy of Muslim groups.[43] They could justify their soft/defensive strategy by emphasising on the process of negotiations as the best way to

---

[43] The BJP–VHP did not stop their radical programmes. In September 1991, the UP government acquired the 2.77 acres of land around the Babri Masjid site. Despite the intervention of the court, the VHP supporters attacked the structure of Babri Masjid on several occasions. In the meantime, the BJP president Murali Manohar Joshi started the *Ekta Yatra* from Kanya Kumari to Kashmir on 10 December 1991 to sensitise people for national issues including the Ram Temple (Noorani 2003b).

268   *Muslim Political Discourse in Postcolonial India*

stop the 'fascism of Hindutva'. Moreover, negotiations as a mode of politics were also compatible with their loyalties for the secular camp.

Finally in September 1992 the Home Minister once again invited VHP, the AIBMAC and associated historians to 'talks under the auspices of government' (MID 119: 526). Interestingly, the short-lived unity of the both Muslim groups also broke down with this invitation. On 30 September, the BMMCC decided not to partici-pate in talks (MID 119: 526). On 3 October 1992, the third round of negotiations between the VHP and the AIBMAC began, which continued till 8 November 1992.[44] The nature of discussion was very different this time. The VHP, which had been less interested in the archaeological and historical debates agreed to nominate a few historians and came out with a series of archaeological and historical facts. The Ayodhya excavations of B. B. Lal were pro-duced as the most reliable finding to establish the fact that a temple was demolished to construct the Babri Masjid. On the other hand, the AIBMAC fully endorsed the position of the secular historians and claimed that as per the Islamic law, the mosque could not be shifted elsewhere.

These talks could not produce any concrete result. However, the VHP proposed a very interesting formula. It suggested that the union government should consider the evidence submitted by both the parties and solve the dispute by a political award (such as a bill in the Parliament). This demand further increased the problems for the Muslim side. Now the AIBMAC had to deal with two very different kinds of pressures. First, it had to mark out the boundary of negotiations in order to emphasise its adherence to the legal process. Second, it had to clarify its stand on the question of a political award.

---

[44] In this initial meeting the VHP submitted 19 points questionnaire to AIBMAC (MID 119: 526). In the second meeting held on 16 October 1992, both the parties agreed to continue negotiation on the basis of historical and archaeological materials. In this meeting the AIBMAC submitted a questionnaire to the VHP (MID 121: 46). On 23 October 1992, VHP and AIBMAC historians inspected the records of excavation by B. B. Lal (MID 121: 46). The talks broke down on 8 November 1992, when the VHP demanded that the central government should enact a law on the basis of evidence before it (MID 121: 46).

Babri Masjid and the Muslim Politics of Right to Heritage **269**

Interestingly, the AIBMAC adopted a highly ambiguous approach and decided not to respond to the controversial issues, particularly the question of a political award. In fact in the last phase of this round of negotiation, they almost gave up their independent position. Instead of demanding the restoration of Babri Masjid, they pleaded for its protection at any cost.[45]

A simple reading of this evasive attitude would suggest that the AIBMAC had virtually failed to reply to the issues raised by the VHP and therefore it had subscribed to a defensive and/or pessimistic position. Even the BMMCC also criticised AIBMAC on these grounds.[46] However, if we look at the wider political nexus between the Muslim politicians and the secular camp, a different explanation of this attitude emerges.

In the post-1991 period, Congress emerged as the leader of the 'secular' camp. It replaced the fractured JD, which was not in a position to retain the Muslim politicians. On the other hand, the BJP was fast emerging as the powerful independent force. In such a situation, the negotiations on Babri Masjid could be used by the Congress in two different ways. First, it could re-establish its hegemony over its traditional Muslim support by inviting the suitable Muslim group for talks. In this sense, the Imam's AIBMAC was the ultimate choice. Second, these talks could provide the Congress an opportunity to utilise the stubborn and radical stand of the VHP to appease Hindu rightists.

---

[45] The AIBMAC's questionnaire in these talks can be taken as example to illustrate its approach. There were three types of questions in this questionnaire. In the first category, there were questions related to the 1949 events and the archaeological evidences. In the second category, there were six questions, which loosely revolved around the political legitimacy of the VHP as the sole Hindu representative. In the third category, again there six questions, which were highly vague, unrealistic and full of rhetoric. In one of these questions, the VHP was asked to suggest the best way to solve the dispute! This questionnaire does make not any attempt to respond to the issues raised by the VHP questionnaire. It seems that the purpose of these questions was not to engage VHP in a dialogue; rather the objective was to refute the political authority of the VHP (Noorani 2003).

[46] In a statement BMMCC alleged that: '[t]he AIBMAC held negotiation with VHP . . . without due preparation, for the sake of publicity and became a party to the VHP line that the fate of the Masjid should be decided by a political award by the Executive' (MID 122: 60).

270   *Muslim Political Discourse in Postcolonial India*

From the point of view of AIBMAC, the Congress support had some crucial long term implications.[47] After all, despite being supported by a group of small parties, it had very good chances to complete a full five year term. As far as Babri Masjid and other Muslim issues are concerned, the Congress government had already announced a package for the development of minorities. It had been instrumental in passing the 1991 Act, which had secured all the Muslim historical places of worship. Furthermore, it had, in principle, already taken the responsibility to protect the Babri Masjid. Thus, in this sense, the independent Muslim position on Babri Masjid, particularly the demand for its restoration gradually became less important.

The AIBMAC used these talks to convert the Babri Masjid issue into a conflict between the Hindutva and secular forces. The evasive approach adopted by the AIBMAC helped it to erase independent Muslim stand. In fact, the responsibility to protect the mosque was successfully assigned to the secular camp. Thus, as a result of the failure of these talks, a new public image of the Babri Masjid dispute emerged. It had now become a symbol of a struggle between secularism and communalism.

The demolition of the Babri Masjid on 6 December 1992 in the presence of top BJP and VHP leaders further consolidated this popular image. The Muslim legal activists, who had filed Public Interest Litigations (PILs) in 1991, were the first to accept the Babri Masjid case as a purely legal-secular issue. In fact, they criticised the dominant Muslim leaders, including the legal-constitutionalists, for politicising this issues and ignoring the constructive role of the secular judiciary.[48] The position of other parties also changed

---

[47] On 3 August 1991, Ahmad Bukhari and Qari Mazhari convened a meeting of Muslim leaders to discuss important Muslim issues. In this meeting, Ahmed Bukhari criticised the JD and other Muslim leaders for adopting a pessimistic approach. They also submitted a memorandum to the President outlining the major Muslim issues including a demand for establishing the Minority Development Corporation (MID 106: 455). The government accepted most of these demands. Interestingly, the National Minorities Development & Finance Corporation was set up and Qari Mazhari was appointed its Chairperson!

[48] These Muslim legal activists had been approaching the Supreme Court for the protection of the mosque by filing PILs. Mohammad Aslam (or Aslam Bhure), a former political supporter of the Imam, filed a PIL

Table 5.5: Negotiation on Babri Masjid Dispute

Year	Parties	Nature of Talks	Hindutva Argument	Argument of Muslim Leaders	Talks Opposed by	Main Argument of the Opposing Party	Outcome
1988–89	BMMCC, VHP	BMMCC reviewed and commented on the documents submitted by the VHP.	A list of documents to support that a Ram temple was destroyed by Babar	Historical records are insufficient to prove that there was a Ram temple.	The Radicals (before the formation of AIBMAC).	Talks are not productive.	Due to the formation of AIBMAC, Shilanyas programme of the VHP, face to face talks could be organised.
March 1990/ September 1990	Ali Mian Nadwi and the Kanch Shankaracharaya	A formal meeting between them in March; no talks in September 1991	No clear statement from Shankaracharaya	Shankaracharaya was opposed to transfer the mosque.	No opposition.		Nadwi did not show any interest and sent his colleague for talks; Shankaracharaya maintained a silence.
July 1990	BMMCC	BMMCC was invited by the Dandvate Committee informally.	–	–	AIBMAC	Dandvate Committee set up by the government cannot produce results therefore it is not acceptable.	No formal Talks with the VHP
December 1990– March 1991	VHP, AIBMAC	Open discussion and exchange of documents.	The identity of Ayodhya and Ram's birth-place are not negotiable.	A mosque cannot be divided.	BMMCC	VHP cannot be considered a party for talks.	In the wake of Rath yatra of L. K. Advani and VHP's demand for Kar Sewa at site, negotiations failed.

Source: Author.

272   *Muslim Political Discourse in Postcolonial India*

quite significantly.[49] The Babri Masjid was finally recognised as a question of secularism and the idea of its legal restoration was almost accepted by all the major Muslim groups. Consequently, in the post-demolition period, Babri Masjid once again became a question of law.[50]

VII

BABRI MASJID AND THE POLITICS OF MEMORY

Let us come back to our main question: What is the significance of Babri Masjid case in relation to wider Muslim politics of monuments and memory in India? This question is directly related to the specificity of Muslim claims and the ways by which the Muslim groups make appropriate configurations of suitable sets of laws, objective history and collective memory. On the basis of our discussion in this chapter, three broader points could be underlined.

---

in December 1992 and demanded that the Supreme Court should direct the government to make appropriate arrangements for the protection of the mosque. This PIL was not supported by any of the established political group, including the legal-constitutionalists of BMMCC (Bhure 2004, Int.).

[49] It is interesting to note that the Imam gave a call to boycott the Republic Day celebration in the aftermath of the demolition. However, the BMMCC not only criticised the Imam but also declared that it would organise a *Defence of Constitution and Democracy Day* on 25 January 1993 (MID 123: 141). Despite the fact that around 4,000 supporters of the AIBMAC court arrested, the boycott call could not work this time. Due to this failure, the AIBMAC publicly announced that it would not organise any agitational programme for next two months (MID 123: 142). This tussle shows how secularism, Constitution and democracy became the political idioms to commemorate the Babri Masjid.

[50] The AIMPLB's High Power Committee, which was unanimously formed by the all the Muslim parties and groups after the demolition, passed a resolution on 20 February 1993. It says: 'The AIMPLB shall accept the responsibility for all cases and judicial proceedings in connection with Babri Masjid' (MID 124: 155). Quite similarly, the AIBMAC passed a resolution on 1 December 1993 to suspend all the agitational programme. It notes: [s]ince the Committee had decided on 26 January 1993 to suspend agitational programme for some time and to cooperate with the AIMPLB . . . In order to maintain the unity of *Millat* [the community], we do not consider it proper to announce a protest programme for the present' (MID 134: 62).

Babri Masjid and the Muslim Politics of Right to Heritage 273

First, the discussion shows that Muslim politics on the Babri Masjid is directly related to the question of monumentalisation of protected historical sites. We find that in the first phase of the Babri Masjid agitation (1986–88), the question of protected monuments was raised quite constantly. The state control over the protected mosques was seen as a direct infringement of right to worship. It was demanded that the Babri Masjid should be given back to Muslims and all the protected mosques should be opened for Namaz. In the later period (1988–92), however, the protection of the Babri mosque became the main objective and the question of other historical sites disappeared. Surprisingly, in order to find out a solution for the dispute, it was suggested that the inner part of the Babri Masjid could be declared as a protected historical monument! This aspect shows that the question of state control over the protected religious places of worship is used in a number of ways by the Muslim groups for justifying their political actions.

Second, we find that all the Muslim groups unanimously accepted the legal-constitutional discourse of rights to articulate their claims. The 1991 Act, which eventually provided a legal cover to all historical places of worship and the ongoing legal proceeding in the Babri Masjid title suit, could be described as positive outcome of this constant legal approach. Even in the Ismail Faruqi case, the Supreme Court judgement simply reversed the dominant Muslim position that 'once a mosque always a mosque', and legalised state's right to acquire wakf land. Despite these legal defeats, Muslim politicians, including, the radicals like the Imam continued to recognise law as the most preferred sphere of politics. This aspect shows that the political discourses of religious minorities, particularly the discourse of Muslim politics in India, adhere to legal constitutionalism for the protection of cultural-religious rights. This legal adherence in Babri Masjid case actually helped Muslim groups in placing their demands in the wider secular discourse. That is why the Muslim agitation of Babri Masjid could also be described as the Muslim politics of right to heritage.

Finally, the Muslim political discourse on the Babri Masjid redefined the collective political existence of a single Indian Muslim community. For example, the legal-constitutionalists looked at the violation of minority rights in the Babri Masjid case as the most visible manifestation of the crisis of Indian Muslim identity. They outlined the contribution of India's Muslims and conceptualised the

274 *Muslim Political Discourse in Postcolonial India*

Babri Masjid as a national Muslim issue. On the contrary, the leaders like the Imam envisaged the Babri Masjid issue as an attack on the dignity of Muslims. He evoked the memory of a royal Muslim past to remind the Muslims that they had actually ruled this country as kings and emperors. Therefore, Muslims as the previous ruling community of India, have a legitimate collective existence.

Moreover, the Muslim collective identity was also be defined by the state as well as the Hindutva. The state for example, converted the Babri Masjid issue into a 'Muslim problem'. In fact, the Babri Masjid issue was 'given' to Muslim politicians as an *exclusive* Muslim subject in the post-1986 period. Similarly, the right-wing Hindutva also provided legitimacy to a 'homogeneous Muslim political identity'. In order to outline the 'intrinsic unity' of the Hindu community in India, the Hindutva forces quite deliberately constructed an image of an aggressive Indian Muslim community as their main enemy. In fact, the universal Islamic community and its radical assertions were seen as 'instructive models' not only for creating a 'fear psyche' among the Hindus but also fashioning the 'Hindutva unity' of similar kind.

■

6

Conclusion

This chapter tries to elaborate the points which have been made in previous chapters and recapitulates the main line of arguments of this study. More specifically, the three research questions — the clash between the modern idea of monument and traditional Indo–Islamic modes of commemoration, the contested nature of an Indian Muslim architectural heritage and the placing of historic sites in the Muslim political discourse — which have already been examined, are reassessed to develop a few specific arguments on contemporary Muslim politics.

This study has attempted to demonstrate that the modern concept of monument, which is based on an assumption that monuments are built to commemorate a historic, dead and lifeless past, is very different from the local and traditional modes by which Muslim communities comprehend the historicity of Indo-Islamic buildings. The specific forms of this contestation in colonial India have been examined in Chapter 2. I have discussed how the process of monumentalisation — the enumeration, listing and categorising of Indian building — produced the idea of an Indian Muslim architectural heritage, which was also linked to the colonial conceptualisation of a single homogeneous Indian Muslim community. This chapter also underlines the contested nature of Muslim heritage on archaeological, historical and legal grounds.

The continuities and discontinuities of these archaeological and legal processes in postcolonial India are examined in Chapter 3. I have discussed two types of secularism(s): *secularism of minority rights,* based on the principle of participatory benign neutrality and the *secularism of historical monuments,* based on the principle of strict neutrality to identify a few crucial, yet unanswered questions. This chapter highlights a broad framework in which Muslim politics of monuments and memory operates. Analysing various trajectories of the postcolonial north Indian Muslim political discourse, this chapter has tried to establish a link between the broad

276   *Muslim Political Discourse in Postcolonial India*

legal-archaeological framework of monumentalisation and the Muslim politics of heritage.

The next two chapters examine the political reincarnation of two historic mosques — the Jama Masjid and the Babri Masjid — as case studies. These chapters show how the monumentalisation of these two mosques in a legal administrative sense produces a number of significant political issues. These case studies also underline the multiplicity of Muslim politics of monuments and memory and its strategic placing in the secular political discourse.

CONTEXTS, LOCATION(S) AND MUSLIM POLITICS

Let us begin with a simple question: Why were the Indo-Islamic historic sites recognised as a political symbol only in the 1970s? This question becomes more complicated when we find that the desecration of religious places of worship including the non-functional religious places has always been an important aspect of communal violence in India. In our brief discussion on colonial Muslim politics in Chapter 2 of this study, I have noted that the Muslim demands in colonial India were more or less centred on the legal-constitutional issues. For instance, the demands for separate representation in legislative bodies, separate set of laws and even the separate state for Muslims were directly related to the political–administrative structures. The *cultural* issues, in this framework, were considered to be the part of an inner domain, which was either used to strengthen the main political agenda or to evoke the Muslim exclusiveness and/or Muslim unity.[1] In addition, Muslim political elites did not show any interest in the 'history' of Indo-Islamic sites; instead, their focus was on the memories of these buildings. That is why, except a few books on historic sites (such as Syed Ahmad Khan's *Asar us Sanadid*), most of the discussion on Indo-Islamic historic sites could be found in poetry and historical novels. Thus, historic sites were actually treated as 'secondary symbols' for popular mobilisation.

---

[1] Partha Chatterjee's argument on the construction of *inner* and *outer* domains by the Indian nationalists could be employed here to explain the strategic placing of 'heritage' in the dominant Muslim political discourse in colonial India (Chatterjee 1993). Yet, as I have pointed out in the second chapter, this aspect needs to be examined in a comprehensive manner.

Conclusion 277

In the period between 1947 and 1970, the Muslim political discourse changed quite considerably, though its 'self-protective' nature was quite mistakenly understood as a kind of defensive politics' by many observers. The Muslim politicians of the 1950s invented a new politics of minority rights and began focusing on cultural–educational issues such as the protection of Urdu, the Muslim Personal law and the minority character of the Aligarh Muslim University. Paul Brass argues that this changed focused of Muslim politics was compatible with an unwritten 'informal rule' of politics, which evolved in 1950s., This informal rule does not permit any political group to evoke religion directly for political mobilisation. In this context, the Muslim elite identified Urdu as an acceptable political symbol to articulate Muslim grievances (Brass 1974: 183–85). However, the most elaborated expression of this shift can be found in the writings of Shahabuddin. In one of his editorials published in *Muslim India*, he writes:

> [b]ecause of the psychic impact of partition in India we tend to consider religious identity as illegitimate or even an act of treason, while linguistic, cultural, regional, racial, geographical and even caste identity is not only legitimised but wholeheartedly embraced (Shahabuddin 1988c: 532).

The nature of collective Muslim politics was transformed once again in the 1970s. We have seen in Chapter 3 that the Muslim Majlis-e-Mushawarat became very active in the post-1967 election period. The formation of the All India Muslim Personal Law Board in 1972 further radicalised the Muslim political discourse in north India in an unprecedented manner. In the backdrop of this increasing radicalisation of Muslim politics, the right to heritage emerged as one of the most powerful political demands.

Two explanations are given to make sense of this significant shift in the nature of collective Muslim politics. First of all it is argued that in the aftermath of Bangladesh crisis in the early 1970s, Muslims of north India realised that the idea of Pakistan could not be accepted as the ultimate source of political inspiration (Ahmad 1974). Thus, they decided to focus on emerging Indian political realities in the 1970s. It is also suggested that after first two decades of Independence, the educational and economic status of Muslims in north India changed quite considerably. As a result, they started articulating their demands in a politically sophisticated and

278 *Muslim Political Discourse in Postcolonial India*

radically matured manner.[2] These arguments cannot be ruled out completely.[3] It is true that the Bangladesh war and the growing educational status of Muslims had an impact on the Muslim politics of 1970s. However, on the basis of our discussion, two important aspects of this shift could also be identified.

First, the radical Muslim politics of the 1970s had a direct connection with the crisis of the Indian state. The post-1967 political developments in India, as various studies suggest, mark a deeper institutional crisis (Kaviraj 1986). In order to deal with this crisis, particularly to re-assert its institutional hegemony, the state started encouraging the controversial and disputed issues of religion and caste in an extraordinary way. Interestingly, the established community institutions were disregarded and a few powerful individuals were recognised as the representatives of various religious and caste communities by the state. Redefining the political system as a contested arena where competing interests of various groups and identities could be reconciled, the state assumed the ultimate responsibility to solve these issues. In this sense, as we have seen in the Babri Masjid case, the state not only played a crucial role in intensifying religious conflicts, but also, at the same time, created the possibilities of *negotiations* among these selected political-religious leaders. In such a political context, the question of Muslim heritage was not only compatible with the state's profound interests in irreconcilable religious conflicts but also in a more significant way it had a potential to accommodate various competing Muslim ideologies and individuals. The rise of the Imam of Jama Masjid as the Muslim leader in post-1970 India, the political decline of

---

[2] The various issues of *Seminar*, the social science journal, published between 1970 and 1974 can be the best example to show how these two explanations were debated in the 1970s.

[3] No one can deny the fact that the creation of Pakistan had a significant impact on Indian Muslim politics. However, it does not mean that Muslims had no understanding of postcolonial Indian realities before 1971. The political norms which we discussed in Chapter 3 clearly show that adherence to constitutional secularism was an important norm of Muslim politics in the 1950s and 1960s. This argument thus, is based on an assumption that Muslim politics could only be understood in the communalism versus secularism framework and therefore when the 'communal' idea of Pakistan shattered in 1971, Muslims changed their loyalties almost immediately!

Muslim organisations such as Jamaat-e-Islami, Jamiat-Ulama-i-Hind and even the Muslim Majlis-e-Mushawarat, the formation of a fragile coalition for the restoration of the Babri Masjid and its subsequent collapse due to the emergence of the secular camp underline the fact that the individual leaders gradually became more powerful and the established community institutions were completely overlooked.

The urbanisation of north Indian cities and the commercialisation of heritage tourism also played an important role in widening the scope of Muslim politics of monument. As I have discussed in Chapters 2 and 3, that in colonial India the Indo-Islamic historic sites were not developed as modern tourist spots and the surrounding areas were almost uninhabited. However, after independence, modern urbanisation redefined the past and present of most of the major cities in India. The historic sites as protected monuments were recognised as secular recreational sites and at the same time the surrounding areas were also redeveloped either as heritage parks or posh residential colonies. For Muslims as a social group, who had lost their economic and political strength quite considerably in the aftermath of the Partition, the new landscape of these cities was quite disturbing.

For example, the Indo-Islamic buildings of Delhi, which had a cultural, religious and psychological relationship with local Muslims, were literally separated from them in postcolonial India. As protected monuments, these sites were now being preserved as dead buildings and all religious rituals including Namaz had been legally banned by the Archaeological Survey of India (ASI). In contrast, modern tourists and residents of neighbouring posh colonies were allowed to use these sites for different leisure activities. This strict demarcation between the 'secular-leisure activities' and 'communal-religious rituals', which is considered to be a part of practical conservation of historical monuments, was often seen by the local Muslims as a kind of on-going desecration of their old mosques and graveyards. Moreover, the growing elite status of nearby residential colonies around these 'tourist spots' also intensified this feeling of isolation among the Muslims of Delhi. The ordinary Muslims had no 'dignified presence' around these buildings. In fact, the uneducated and poor Muslims had a very limited access to these 'civilized' areas because the upper class upper caste Hindu and Muslim elite of postcolonial Delhi did not want them

280　　*Muslim Political Discourse in Postcolonial India*

to make 'their city' dirty. Thus, in this sense, urbanisation and tourist development policies provided a new popular character to the hitherto 'hidden' contested image of Muslim heritage. In our discussion on the Jama Masjid, we have seen how the Imam, who was well aware of these anxieties, introduced the Jama Masjid as a historic symbol of Muslim dignity which attracted the majority of Delhi's Muslims, especially the poor and marginalised sections of Muslim society.

This brings us to my first argument. I argue that the Muslim politics of monuments demonstrates a major shift in Muslim political discourse. This new kind of politics focuses on the contested notion of Muslim architectural heritage and links it to the extended meanings of the constitutional right to worship.

Secularism(s) and Muslim Politics

In his study on the 'crisis of secular–nationalism', Aditya Nigam makes a very interesting argument. Analysing the Muslim response to secularism, Nigam claims:

> Muslims ... could not afford to articulate their critiques as stridently as the Dalits, for the simple reason that they were seen as the 'threatening Other, whose loyalties to the nation were always suspect. In some ways their predicament differed from that of the Dalits for this reason' ... the episode of the Shah Bano judgment and subsequent surrender to fundamentalist Muslim pressure by Rajiv Gandhi, went hand in hand with the Shilanyas' (2006: 316).

This observation is very crucial to understand the relationship between 'secularism' and Muslim politics in India. In fact, Nigam very rightly indicates that the orientation of Muslim elite towards the constitutional secularism has always been significantly different from the Dalits. This aspect shows that Muslim politics, particularly the Muslim politics of monuments, forms a very specific relationship with the concept of secularism. Underlining this specific politics of secularism, I argue that the legal-constitutional discourse of secularism is accepted by the Muslim political groups as a broad framework for articulating their demands in a politically acceptable language. On the basis of our discussion, I find two possible reasons behind this strict adherence to secularism.

The Muslim politics of monument, as we have seen, stems from a tension between the secularism of minority rights and secularism

Conclusion

281

of historical monuments. The Muslim political groups realised the fact that legal ambiguities of this kind could be used politically in a number of different ways. It was possible for them to take a radical stand without even moving out from the permissible boundaries set up by the constitutional structure of the Indian state. The politics of the Shahi Imam is the best example in this regard. He used the language of secularism to ignore the authority of the Wakf Board, ASI and even the court and successfully converted the Jama Masjid into a Muslim political site .

Second, the Muslim politics of monuments could be understood as a reflection of a new kind of radical politics, which emerged in the post-1970s. The environment movements, Dalits movements for dignity and the struggles of Adivasis for conventional community rights offered a new interpretation of politics. Reiterating the liberal values of the Constitution of India, these 'people's' movements attempted to define their political agendas in a language of rights (Chandhoke and Ahmed 1996). In fact, a new kind of political thinking has emerged, which tries to interpret the existence of democratic institutions in a radical manner (Mohanty 2002). The legal-constitutionalist explanation of Muslim politics, particularly the writings of Shahabuddin, could also be seen as a manifestation of this stream of politics. In Babri Masjid case, for instance, he extracted a 'right to heritage' from the constitution to refashion a radical politics of Muslim dissent.

Memories and Politics

Employing the history/memory framework, this study has not only examined the diverse ways in which histories and memories produce multiple notions of the past but has also attempted to observe how these imaginations are transformed in political agendas. Our discussion shows that the contestations between the idea of an Indian Muslim architectural heritage and various local memories have been very creatively used by the Muslim elites to construct the *memory of a royal Muslim past*. This study identifies two interesting political manifestations of this memory.

First, in the case of Jama Masjid, the Public Address System (PAS) of the mosque, the dress code of the Imam, and his aggressive political language in a much broader sense, converted the institution of the Shahi Imam into a historic symbol by which all the Indian Muslim communities could be linked to each other.

282 *Muslim Political Discourse in Postcolonial India*

The Imam evoked the *memory of a royal Muslim past* to underline the collective dignity of India's Muslims. As a result, the caste–class differences and cultural-regional variations among the Muslims became less important and the Imam succeeded in defining the collective political interests of a single Indian Muslim community.

Second, the Ayodhya case shows a very different manifestation of this memory. In the wake of the Babri Masjid dispute, the local Muslim elite recognised the political importance of the 'memory' of a royal Muslim past. Hence, those 'abandoned' Muslim buildings, including, the Babri Masjid, which have a direct connection with various ruling Muslim dynasties and individual Muslim rulers, all of a sudden became symbols of Muslim identity.[4] This changed focus of the local Muslim elite on Ayodhya's Muslim past simply goes against the much glamorised version of custom centric local Islam.[5]

This brings us to the third and final argument of this study. I argue that the political construction of the *memory of a royal Muslim past* transforms local memories into a collective memory of a single Indian Muslim community. This argument simply goes beyond

---

[4] Haji Mehboob, a prominent Muslim of Ayodhya, who has been participating actively in the Babri Masjid agitation, has established the *Anjuman Mohafiz Masjid-Wa-Maqabir* after 1992 to protect the Muslim heritage of Ayodhya, including, the old graveyards and non-functional mosques. Mehboob alleges that the Uttar Pradesh Sunni Wakf Board does not bother to take possession of even undisputed wakf properties of Ayodhya. He also argues that the Archaeological Survey of India as well as the Uttar Pradesh State Archaeological Department has not shown any interest in protecting the Muslim heritage of Ayodhya (Mehboob 2004, Int.).

[5] The literature on the Sufis of Ayodhya, interestingly, focuses mainly on the age old teachings of these Sufis and portrays an idealised picture of the composite Hindu–Muslim culture. Such write-ups and booklets lack a clear understanding of the political roles of such Dargahs and shrines at the grassroots level. We have also seen in Chapter 5 that the local Muslim narrative uses the local Sufi tradition to legitimise Muslim claims on Babri Masjid. Two documentaries produced by Vidya Bhushan Rawat, *Ayodhya se Madhar Tak: Ayodhya ki Sanskritik Virasat* (From Ayodhya till Maghar: Cultural Heritage of Ayodhya) and *Virsasat ki Jung* (Struggle for Heritage) can be the best example of this kind of effort. For an excellent review of these documentaries, see Raj Lakshmi (2003).

Conclusion 283

the 'Muslim homogeneity' versus 'Muslim plurality' debate and attempts to show how the 'collective' existence of India's Muslims as a community is politically defined in a number of ways.

These three arguments, in my view, introduce us to a multifaceted postcolonial Muslim political discourse: a discourse in which Muslim political groups, organisations and political elites participate in various forms, exploit available resources, and produce a number of distinct claims and demands. The structure of this political discourse, as I have tried to show, is inextricably linked to the wider postcolonial socio-political processes, which provides it an external stimulus. At the same time, the internal social and cultural dynamics, which determine the placing of various *Islamic* elements in the discursive formation of Muslim identities also affect the terms of this discourse. It is, therefore, important to contextualise the ideas, action, and statements of political actors before drawing any conclusion about the political behaviour of Muslims in India. The explanatory potentials of the arguments presented in this book, thus, need to be evaluated in relation to the political context of 1970–92 that I have tried to examine.

■

Appendices

Appendix 1: Urdu inscription written on white notice board installed at the northern entrance of Jama Masjid

Jama Masjid Delhi aap se hamkalam hai. Wazir –e-Azam Indira Gandhi ke zalim hatho Meri mazlumiyat ki kahani meri zababi. Me Alllah tala ki muqadas ibadat gah hun. ab se 332 sal pehle Mughal tajdar shahjahan badshah ne mujhe tamir karvaya. Is waqt se ab tak mere muqadsat farsh par karor ha karor afrad bar gahe ilahi me sar justuju ho chuke hai. wazir-e-azam Mrs. Indira Gandhi ne aur uski government ne watan aur watan walo par khususan bis karore muslamano aur akhliyato par jo zulm dahaye hai woh dillo ko larza dene wale hai. Lekin is waqt to me apne upper dahaye gaye dilo ko tarpa dene wale mazalim hi sunaungi. Suniye aur khun ke aason bahaiye.

Mere Shahi Imam Maulana Syed Abdullah Bukhari ko 2 Feb san 1975 ko haq gohi aur bepanah muzalim ke khilaf awaz bulan karne ke jurm me giraftar kar liya gaya. Iske fourn bad Zalim Police ne goliyan chala kar ghar ghar jakar mere pure ilake ko shahaide ke khun se La la zar bana diya. Khawateen ki behurmati ki masum bachchoan ke gallon par khanjar chalaye gaye aur begunah naujawan larko aur larkiyon par goliyan dagi gayin. kamopesh 100 naujawano ne Dekhte hi dekhte zalim wazir-e-azam ki zalim police ke hathon jam –e Shahadat naush kar liya aur abdi neend so kar zinda javed ho gaye. zulm ke daraz hathon ne is par bas nahi kiya. mere muqadas farsh ke zaraart me bhi khun ne shohda jasb kiya gaya. humukut ki darindi yahi khatam nahi hoti mere sine par bhi goliyan dagi gayin aur junbu simt ke mere hahani darwaze ko bhi goliyin se chalini kiya gaya. ab zara janiye aur chashme kasirat se ziyarat kijiye. mere mardan-e-gazi darwazo ke jo ek taraf Indira government ke zulm wa tashadud aur daringi ki nishadehi kar rahi hai to dusri taraf momino ko zalimo ke muqable par dawat e jehad bhi de rahi hai.

22 November 1975 ka suraj police aur fauj ke saye me tulu hua. mere ihtraf aur uske do dhai mile ke raghbe me fauj hi fauj thi. Ke achanak meri charo taraf ki market bagher kisi peshgi itla ya notice ke dev hakel bulldozero se muzum kar diya gaya jisses kamo pesh 100 crore rupeye ka nuksan hua. mere gushte ko jis par meri mazbuti qayam thi shahid kar diya gaya. Aaj me iske bager besahara hun. zamin doz mere tarikhi asason ko bhi mismar kar diya gaya. Aaj crore rupeye bhi sarf kiye jayen to who tamir nahi ho sakte. kamobesh 100 crore maliyat ki meri zamin par bhi government ne DDA ke zariye kabza kar liya. Is tarah Wazir azam, uski government, iska mehkama DDA mere tamam

Appendices   **285**

tarikhi asason ko nuksan pahun cha kar aur tabah karke meri zamin ko bhi shire-madar ki tarah hazam kar gaye.

Ab halat yeh hai ki me ek ek paise se muhataj hun:

1. *Aap ki ibabdat ke liye mere pas na to safe hai*
2. *na dhup se bachawon ke liye pure shamiyane aur*
3. *sahi itezam chalne ke liye pura staff hai. aur na hi tankhwa dene ka pura itezam hai.*
4. *mera shahi imam haq ko haq kehat hai aur naq ko na haq. zalim ke age zulmo ke liye seena subre rehta hai aur mazlum ko seene se lagata hai. bas isi khidmat aur haq gohi ki padahish me Indira sarkar ki taraf se mujhe yeh saza mili rahi hai aur me ise khanda e peshani se bardasht kar rahi hun*
5. *Indira government ke hathon dastone zulmo sitaf tul se tul tarin hai. Khun ne jigar pi pi kar madare watan me zindgi guzari ja rahi haiyeh suluk mere hi sath nahi. rajdhani delhi aur pure watan me hazara ha masiden aur kabrastan shahid kiye jo chuke hai aur un par sarkari imarate sarke pul tamir kiye ja chuken hai. purani dasten nahi aaj ki dastan dekhni ho to Asiad 1982 ke liye jo pul aur sarke tamir hun who Masjido aur hamare buzurgo ki haddiyon par tamir huin. Masjid aur kabristan zamin ke barabar kar diye gaye aur inke namo nishan mita diye gaye.*

286   *Appendices*

Translation of the Urdu Inscription

I am Jama Masjid Delhi and am speaking to you. I wish to tell you the story of my persecution at the hands of a despotic Prime Minister Indira Gandhi in my own words.

In the heart of Delhi I am the sacred precinct for the worship of Allah, the Almighty. Nearly 332 years ago I was built by the Mughal emperor Shah Jahan. Since then on my sacred floor billions of worshippers have prostrated before God. The oppressive treatment meted out by the Prime Minister Mrs Indira Gandhi and her Government to the people of this country, specially 20 million Muslims and other minorities, is heart rending. But here I will stick to narrating the story of my own persecution. Listen to my woeful story of this barbarity and cry for the helplessness I have endured during all these times.

On 2 February 1975, my Shahi Imam Maulana Sayyed Abdullah Bukhari was arrested for opening his mouth and telling the truth to the world of the innumerable cruelties being inflicted upon me. Immediately after this action the police raided each and every house in my neighbourhood and with indiscriminate shooting painted the walls of these houses red with the blood of those martyred. Women were molested, children were bayoneted and innocent girls and boys were riddled with bullets. Within no time more or less 100 youths were gunned down and made to embrace martyrdom at the hands of the barbarous police of the Prime Minister. The long hands of atrocity did not stop at this. My sacred floor was soaked with the blood of these martyrs. The bloodthirstiness of the Government did not stop here. Bullets were sprayed on my chest. My iron gate in the south was riddled with bullets. Visit this gate and see with your own eyes the testimony of the cold-bloodedness and savagery of Indira Gandhi on the one hand and on the other the silent call to the Muslims to stand up against this attack on their sacred place of worship and wage jihad against the tyrants.

The sun of 22 November 1975 rose under the shadow of the police and the army. Around me in an area of about two or two and a half miles was totally taken over by the army. All of a sudden and without any prior information or notice the market around me was raised to the ground by giant bulldozers causing damage worth billions of rupees; my *Gushta* [foundation pillar] upon which the firmness and strength of my structure depended was also martyred. Today I stand without this. My underground relics were also demolished. Now they cannot be rebuilt even by spending billions of rupees. The Government through the DDA has usurped my adjoining land worth millions of rupees. Thus by damaging my historical relics the Prime Minister, her Government, its department DDA have usurped my land worth millions of rupees as if it was a gift like their mother's milk.

Appendices **287**

Today I am now a destitute and have been made to beg for pennies.

1. For your worship neither I have safain [prayer mats]
2. Nor do I have full tents for the protection from the sun;
3. Nor do I have full staff to make all of the arrangements; nor do I have the means to pay their salaries;
4. My Shahi Imam calls a spade a spade and speaks against what is wrong. He stands against the despots and embraces the victims. It was this service, a crime of telling the truth for which Indira Government has been punishing me and I have been enduring all of this.
5. The story of Indira Gandhi's oppressive brutalities is very long. I have been crying blood and enduring all of this in my motherland with perseverance. The story of cruelties at the hands of Indira Gandhi is very long and extensive. I am not the only one to be the brunt of this usurpation and oppression. In the capital Delhi and throughout the country thousands of mosques and graveyards have been raised to the ground and roads and bridges have been built upon them. This is not an old story it belongs to the present times. The bridges and roads that have been constructed for the Asiad 1982 have been constructed on the numerous mosques and the bones of our ancestors. Mosques and graveyards have been levelled to the ground and all the signs of their existence have been decimated.

288 *Appendices*

Appendix 2: VHP's 19 Point Questionnaire to AIBMAC

I.
1. Muslim divines and leaders have all along been offering to part with the disputed structures in case it is established that it displaced a temple. Do you endorse the offer?
2. If not why?
3. Do you uphold the formula, 'once a mosque always a mosque'?
4. But the Quran and prophet do not sanction or envisage it ... it prohibits prayer in the evil (masjidu-d'-didar) ... Does it not cut the ground from under the feet of the 'once a mosque always a mosque thesis?
5. If not, why?

II.
6. Was India under the Lodhi's with Ayodhya under the Shariq's Darul Islam or Darul Harab?
7. If a Darul Islam were its Hindus inhabitants not Dhimmins?
8. If they were, is the disputed structure built by Babar in replacement of the temple, styled RJB temple, a mosque built on piety or a mosque of evil?
9. If the latter, does it merit any better treatment than the mosque of evil referred to in Quran?
10. If so, how?
11. Caliph Umar Bin Abdul Aziz restored Christian a Church of Damascus turned by Banu Nasir into a mosque ... did they all violate the Sharia?
12. If not, why should Indian Muslims not follow suit?

III.
13. According to ... [various works are mentioned] the disputed structure was built by Babar ... by demolishing the temple in question. Are their authors all liars?
14. If so, how?
15. Was the veracity of their statement ever called in question before the last decade?
16. If never, why today?
17. Is there any instance of non-existed temples being reported by Muslims as forcibly converted into mosque and that too, when such reports was likely to prejudice the case of the mosque partly pending before the king of Awadh and even the British Residence had a say in decision making?
18. If not, why take it for granted in the instant case that the Ram temple did not exist, in the face of unequivocal statements of its existence and demolition by Babar?
19. If it cannot be so taken for granted, why not put a stop to imbroglio by restoring the RJB to the Hindus?

Source: *Muslim India*, 119, November 1992, p. 490.

Appendices **289**

Appendix 3: Intellectuals' Appeals to the Muslims of India

(Issued on 5 January 1987)

'The people of India observe two national events as common heritage-Independence Day marking the dawn of national sovereignty and the Republic Day commemorating the adoption of the Constitution on the historic day when more than fifty years ago the leaders of the national Movement belonging to all faiths and region of India, had taken the pledge on the bank of the river Ravi, to establish a democratic republic in India'.

'These are not merely official holidays, but national festivals. They should be observed essentially as occasions when our diverse people should exhibit their capacity to rise above the many stresses and strains, tensions and conflicts, which are bound to occur in the process of building a new national identity. Particularly on these occasions we should strive to foster national solidarity for defending our democratic polity, which is a bold venture in this ancient civilization comprising multi-religious, multi-regional, multi-lingual strands'.

'On these occasions our people should not be drawn into any controversy of partisan politics, sectarian polemics or conflict with government and administration . . . It is improper to mar the solemnity, significance and national relevance of these two symbols of our common political heritage. Any attempt to abridge their importance or vitiate their significance is politically unwise, legally impermissible, nationally injurious and morally reprehensible'.

'We therefore express our grave concern and dismay at the misguided call given to the Muslims by certain persons, to boycott the Republic Day celebrations this year in order to focus attention on the otherwise valid demand for an expeditious and just settlement of the needlessly long drawn Babri Masjid problem. We are not questioning the righteousness of that demand which is anyhow self-evident but deploring the means prescribed'.

Issued by 25 eminent persons comprising academics, scientists, jurists, administrators, educationalists, journalists, industrialists, poet and social workers.

Source: *Muslim India*, 50, February 1987, pp. 63–64.

Select Bibliography

Primary Sources
JMD: Jama Masjid Documentation

JMD1: Inscription in English at Eastern gate, 16 May 2004.
JMD1a: Inscription in Urdu at Northern Gate, 16 May 2004.

JMD2: Jama Masjid Documentation:
Newspaper Clipping

JMD2: 'External Forces working against me: *PM*, PTI', *The Times of India*, 15 February 1974. Delhi, p. 5.

JMD2a: 'Simmering Confrontation, M. Shamin', *The Times of India*, 4 February 1975, Delhi, p. 1.

JMD2aa: 'Muslim Condemn Imam's Remark, Javed M. Ansari', *The Hindu*, Delhi, 24 October 2001, p. 1.

JMD2b: 'Curfew in Jama Masjid Area: 8 Killed in Firing as Imam's Men Clash with Police', *The Times of India*, 3 February 1975, Delhi, pp. 1 and 3.

JMD2c: 'Muslim Leaders Blame Imam, PTI', *The Times of India*, Delhi, 4 February 1975, p. 1.

JMD2d: 'Tension in Jama Masjid Area Again', *The Times of India*, Delhi, 8 February 1975, pp. 1 and 7.

JMD2e: 'Curfew in Delhi Area', *The Times of India*, Delhi, 15 February 1975, p. 5.

JMD2f: 'Imam's Terms for Leading Juma Prayer, P. C. Gandhi', *The Times of India*, Delhi, 6 February 1975, pp. 1 and 9.

JMD2g: 'Shahi Imam Allowed to Meet Son in Jail', *The Times of India*, Delhi, 12 February 1975, p. 1.

JMD2h: 'Naib Imam's Peace Appeal From Jail', *The Times of India*, Delhi, 14 February 1975, p. 7.

JMD2i: 'Jama Masjid Imamat Issue: Meditation Likely by Abdullah, M. Shamin', *The Times of India*, Delhi, 18 February 1975, p. 1.

JMD2j: 'Four-Day Curfew Clamped: 2 Die in Fresh Flare-up in Jama Masjid Area', *The Times of India*, Delhi, 15 February 1975, p. 1.

JMD2k: 'Imam Freed on Bail', *The Times of India*, Delhi, 19 February 1975, p. 1.

Select Bibliography   **291**

JMD2l: 'Adjourn Motion Likely on Imam Issue, UNI', *The Times of India*, Delhi, 16 February 1975, p. 1.

JMD2m: 'JP Demands Probe', *The Times of India*, Delhi, 15 February 1975, p. 7.

JMD2n: 'Biggest-Ever Muslim Rally', *The Times of India*, Delhi, 31 March 1987, p. 3.

JMD2o: 'Controversy Over School Named After Bakht', *The Statesman*, Delhi, 17 January 1996, p. 3.

JMD2p: 'Notices Sent to Civic Bodies, Others on Jama Masjid Structure', *The Indian Express*, Delhi, 13, February 1996, p. 1.

JMD2q: 'Order to Halt Work at Jama Masjid', *The Indian Express*, Delhi, 14 February 1996, p. 4.

JMD2r: 'Naib Imam is not Above the Law says Magistrate: Excerpts from the Lower Court Order', *The Indian Express*, Delhi, 7 March 1996.

JMD2s: 'Delhi HC Stays Arrest of Naib Imam', *The Hindu*, 7 March 1996, p. 3.

JMD2t: 'Illegal Structure in Jama Masjid will be Demolished: Naib Imam, Sayatan Chakravarthy', *The Indian Express*, Delhi, 9 March 1996.

JMD2u: 'Deadline to Pull Down Illegal Construction in Jama Masjid, UNI', *The Pioneer*, 9 March 1996, p. 3.

JMD2v: 'Naib Imam to Move to HC over Mosque Annexe', *The Indian Express*, Delhi, 8 March 1996, p. 2.

JMD2w: 'Rao Forms Committee to Settle Wazukhana Issue', *The Indian Express*, Delhi, 12 April 1996, p. 2.

JMD2x: 'Centre Seeks Time on Masjid Order', *The Asian Age*, Delhi, 23 April 1996, p. 3.

JMD2y: 'Centre Given 3 Weeks on Jama Masjid Structure', *The Asian Age*, Delhi, 24 April 1996, p. 3.

JMD2z: 'Demolition Work on Illegal Wazukhana Begins', *The Indian Express*, Delhi, 12 May 1996, p. 1.

JMD3: Field Notes and Observations on Jama Masjid Case AD: Ayodhya Documentation

Muslim India Documentation (MID)

MID 39: 'Mushawarat Condemn Seizure of Babri Masjid: Calls Upon Muslims to Observe Day of Mourning and Prayers on 14 February 1986', *Muslim India*, 39, March 1986, p. 117.

MID 41: 'Chronology of Events', *Muslim India*, 41, May 1986, p. 238.

MID 43: 'Chronology of the Month', *Muslim India*, 43, July 1986, p. 331.

MID 43a: 'Shahabuddin Formula for Ayodhya', *Muslim India*, 43, July 1986, pp. 330–31.

292 *Select Bibliography*

MID 46: 'Chorology of the Month', *Muslim India*, 46, October 1986, p. 478.

MID 47: 'India is in Danger-Shahi Imam', *Muslim India*, 47, November 1986, p. 520.

MID 48: 'Chronology of the Month', *Muslim India*, 48, December 1986, p. 542.

MID 49: 'Chronology of the Month', *Muslim India*, 49, January 1987, p. 47.

MID 50: 'Chronology of the Month', *Muslim India*, 50, February 1987, p. 94.

MID 50a: 'The Declaration of Delhi: Adopted by the All India Babri Masjid Conference, New Delhi, 22 December 1986, issued by the BMMCCC on 23 January 1987', *Muslim India*, 50, February 1987, pp. 59–60 and 64.

MID 50b: 'Intellectuals' appeals to the Muslims of India: Issued on 5 January 1987', *Muslim India*, 50, February 1987, pp. 63–64.

MID 50c: 'Call Not Against State But Against Government and Violator of Constitution, Statement of the BMMCC', *Muslim India*, 50, February 1987, p. 61.

MID 51: 'Chronology of the Month', *Muslim India*, 51, March 1987, pp. 141–43.

MID 53: 'BMMCC statement on Govt.'s Move for Settlement through Local Negotiations', *Muslim India*, 53, May 1987, p. 207.

MID 53a: 'Memorandum Adopted by the Mass Rally, Boat Club, New Delhi, 30 March 1987 Presented by the Babri Masjid Movement Coordination Committee to Parliament and the Government', *Muslim India*, 53, May 1987, pp. 205–06.

MID 53 b: 'Statement on Prime Minister's Refusal to Receive Memorandum', *Muslim India*, 53, May 1987, p. 207.

MID 55: 'Chronology of the Month', *Muslim India*, 55, July 1987, p. 333.

MID 59: 'Committee to meet in November to Decide Future Course of Action', *Muslim India*, 59, November 1987, p. 497.

MID 63: Muslims Have Been Left With no Option but Ayodhya March', *Muslim India*, 63, March 1988, p. 109.

MID 63a: 'Shahabuddin's Letter to PM Rajeev Gandhi', *Muslim India*, 63, March 1988, p. 110.

MID 64: 'Chronology of the Month', *Muslim India*, 64, April 1988, p. 191.

MID 65: 'L. P. Shahi's Letter to Syed Shahabuddin', *Muslim India*, 65, July 1988, p. 207.

MID 66: 'The Call: Ayodhya March on 14 October, Leaders March on 12 October', *Muslim India*, 66, June 1988, p. 250.

MID 68: 'Chronology of the Month', *Muslim India*, 68, August 1988, pp. 381–83.

Select Bibliography

293

MID 69: 'Chronology of the Month', *Muslim India*, 69, September 1988, p. 432.

MID 69a, 'Abdullah Bukhari's Letter to CM of UP 9 July 1988', *Muslim India*, 69, September 1988, p. 396.

MID 71: 'The Ministry of Home Affair Statement on 12 October 1988', *Muslim India*, 71, November 1988, p. 491.

MID 73: 'All India Babri Masjid Conference, New Delhi Press Release 26–27 November 1988', *Muslim India*, 73, January 1989, p. 14.

MID 79: 'BMMCC's Comments on the Documents Presented by VHP to the Government of India on 6 October 1989', *Muslim India*, 79, July, 1989, p. 305.

MID 79a: 'Chronology of the Month', *Muslim India*, 79, July 1989, p. 334.

MID 80: 'Chronology of the Month', *Muslim India*, 80 August 1989, p. 384.

MID 81: 'Chronology of the Month', *Muslim India*, 68, August 1988, pp. 381–83.

MID 82: 'Chronology of the Month', *Muslim India*, 82, October 1989, p. 478.

MID 83: 'Chronology of the Month', *Muslim India*, 83, November 1989, p. 524.

MID 85: 'Shahi Imam on Dialogue', *Muslim India*, 85, January 1990, p. 13.

MID 85a: 'Chronology of the Month', *Muslim India*, 85, January 1990, p. 94.

MID 86: 'Chronology of the Month', *Muslim India*, 86, February 1990, p. 94.

MID 87: 'Chronology of the Month', *Muslim India*, 87, March 1990, p. 142.

MID 87a: 'The Imam Formula', *Muslim India*, 87, March 1990, p. 103.

MID 88: 'Chronology of the Month', *Muslim India*, 88, April 1990, p. 191.

MID 92: 'Chronology of the Month', *Muslim India*, 92, August 1990, pp. 382–83.

MID 93: 'Chronology of the Month', *Muslim India*, 93, September, 1990, p. 431.

MID 97: 'AIMPLB Resolution on Status of Babri Masjid in Shariat, 3 December 1990', *Muslim India*, 97, January 1991, p. 20.

MID 97a: 'Chronology of the Month', *Muslim India*, 97, January 1991, p. 46.

MID 98: 'Chronology of the Month', *Muslim India*, 98, February 1991, pp. 95–96.

MID 99: 'Chronology of the Month', *Muslim India*, 99, March 1991, p. 144.

MID 99a: 'BMMCC Letter to PM /12 Jan 1991', *Muslim India*, 99, March 1991, p. 141.

294 *Select Bibliography*

MID 102: 'Chronology of the Month', *Muslim India*, 102, June 1991, p. 287.

MID 103: 'Advani on Secularism', *Muslim India*, 103, July 1991, p. 309.

MID 104: 'Chronology of the Month', *Muslim India*, 104, August 1991, p. 383.

MID 106: 'Ahmed Bukhari's Memorandum to President 16 August 1991, Adopted by the Muslim Consultative Committee at Jama Masjid on 3 August 1991', *Muslim India*, 106, October 1991, p. 455.

MID 107: 'Chronology of the Month', *Muslim India*, 107, November 1991, p. 526.

MID 108: 'Chronology of the Month', *Muslim India*, 108, December 1991, p. 575.

MID 119: 'Chronology of the Month', *Muslim India*, 119 November 1992, p. 526.

MID 121: 'Chronology of the Month', *Muslim India*, 121, January 1993, p. 46.

MID 122: 'BMMCC: Statement on Rejection of the Unity Proposal by AIBMAC, 12 January 1993', *Muslim India*, February 1993, p. 60.

MID 123: 'Chronology of the Month', *Muslim India*, 123, March 1993, p. 141.

MID 124: 'AIMPLB High Power Committee (HPC) Decisions/20', *Muslim India*, 124, February 1993, April 1993, p. 155.

MID 134: 'AIBMAC Resolution (translated from Urdu by MI)', *Muslim India*, 134, February 1994, p. 62.

MID 137: 'Chronology of the Month', *Muslim India*, 137, May 1994, p. 207.

AD1: Ayodhya Documentation: Other

AD1: Recorder documentation on *Karya Shala, Kar Sewak Puram* (Ayodhya) 23 May 2004 (Hindi).

AD2: Field Notes and Observations on Ayodhya and Faizabad

Tape Recorded Interviews

Ansari, 2004, Int.: Interview with Mr. Mohammed Hashim Ansari, Appellant Babri Masjid Ayodhya, Ayodhya, UP, 22 May.

Bhure, 2004, Int.: Interview with M. Aslam Bhure, Legal Activist, Delhi, 22 February.

Das, 2004, Int.: Interview with Mahant Gyan Das, President Hanuman Garhi, and Akhil Bhartiya Akhara Parishad, Ayodhya, UP, 23 May.

Dehlavi, 2004, Int.: Interview with Maulana S. A. H. Dehlavi, President Anjuman Minhaj-e-Rasool (S), Delhi, 28 January 2004 and 11 February.

Select Bibliography **295**

Hashmi, 2004, Int.: Interview with Mr. Faizi O. Hashmi, Chief Executive Officer, Delhi Wakf Board, Delhi, 27 February.

Jain, 2004, Int.: Interview with Mr. O. P. Jain, Convenor, INTACH, Delhi Chapter, Delhi, 1 June.

Jilani, 2004, Int.: Interview with Mr. Zafaryab Jilani, Member, AIBMAC, and advocate for Sunni Central Wakf Board, UP, Lucknow, UP, 30 April.

Kashmiri, 2004, Int.: Interview with Maulana Anzar Shah Kashmiri, Mutanzmin and Shekhul Hadith, Darul Uloom Deoband, Deoband, UP, 24 February.

Khan, 2004, Int.: Interview with Khan Abdul Wadud Khan, Ex-Member of Legislative Council, Uttar Pradesh, 1984–1990, Ex-Wakf officer, Delhi Wakf Board, Delhi, 27 January.

Khan, 2004, Int.: Interview with Mr. Kahliq Ahmed Khan, Convenor, Helal Committee, Chairman, Ayodhya and Faizabad Study and Research Centre, Faizabad, UP, 23 May.

Mehboob, 2004, Int.: Interview with Haji Mehboob Ahmad, President, AnjumanMohafiz Masjid-Wa-Maqabir and Muddai Babri Masjid, Ayodhya, Ayodhya, 22 May.

Nakshbandi, 2004, Int.: Interview with Maulana Nawabuddin Nakshabandi, Shahi Imam Safdarjang Masjid, member Jama Masjid Trust and Member All India Babri Masjid Action Committee, Delhi, 17 May.

Nomani, 2004, Int.: Interview with Maulana Abdul Hamid Nomani, Press Secretary, Jamiat Ulema-e- Hind, Delhi, 26 February.

Qayamuddin, 2004, Int.: Interview with Chaudhari Qayamuddin, Leader, Teli Biradari, an active member of Turakman Gate community and a victim of 19 April 1976 riot, Delhi, 16 May.

Sadar, 2004, Int.: Interview with Mr. Aminuddin Sadar, President Masjid Bhuri Bhatiyari and Ex-President Masjid Basao Committee, Delhi, 16 May.

Saleem, 2004, Int.: Interview with M. Saleem, Secretary, National Heritage Protection Council, Delhi, 13 February.

Sambhali 2005, Int.: Interview with Maulana Atiqur Rehman, Founder Member, All India Muslim Majlis-e-Mushawarat, London, 9 January.

Shahabuddin, 2004, Int.: Interview with Syed Shahabuddin, President Muslim Mushawarat and BMMCC, Delhi, 3 March.

Shankarcharya, 2004, Int.: Interview with Shankracharya Adhoykshanand Dev Tirathji Maharaj, Shankarachrya Puri Pith, Delhi, 12 February.

Sharma, 2004, Int.: Interview with Pandit N. K. Sharma, Leader Chetna Jagriti Mission, Delhi, 12 February.

Siddique, 2004, Int.: Interview with Mr. Yunus Siddique, Advocate, President Babri Masjid Action Committee, Faizabad, (along with

296 *Select Bibliography*

Mr. M. A. A. Khan, Convenor, Babri Masjid Action Committee, Faizabad) Faizabad, UP, 23 May.

Singh, 2004, Int.: Interview with Raja Shailendra Mohan Pratap Singh, Ayodhya, UP, 23 May.

Taimur, 2004, Int.: Interview with Mufti Mohammed Taimur, Mufti Kandhla, Kandhla, UP, 23 February.

Interviews (not on tape)

Dr Amarindra Nath, Officer for Monuments, Archaeological Survey of India, New Delhi, 14 February 2004.

Maulana Rabe Nadavi, Chairman All India Muslim Personal Law Board, Lucknow, 23 May 2004.

Maulana Zahid Raza Rizvi, Chairman Haj Committee Uttracnchal, Ex-Convenor BMAC-UP, 29 April 2004.

Maulana Sajjad Nomani Nadvi, Member, All India Muslim Personal Law, Lucknow, London, 9 September 2003.

GD: Tape Recorded Group Discussions

GD1: Group Discussion with local shopkeepers, Jama Masjid areas, 22 February 2004.

GD2 : Group Discussion with social activists, Jama Masjid, 20 February 2004.

GD3: Group Discussion with Muslim students of class IX, X and XI, Sarvodaya School Urdu Medium No. 1 Jama Masjid, Delhi, 21 February 2004.

GD4: Group Discussion with non-Muslim students of class IX and X, Mahavir Jain Senior Secondary School, Delhi, Delhi, 20 February 2004.

SECONDARY SOURCES

Ahmad, Aqil. 2000. *Mohammadan Law*. Allahabad: Central Law Agency.

Ahmad, Aziz. 1964. *Studies in Islamic Culture in the Indian Environment.* Oxford: Oxford University Press.

Ahmad, Imtiaz. 2000. 'Basic Conflicts of "We" and "They" between Religious Traditions, between Hindus, Muslims and Christians in India', in Imitaz Ahmad, S. Partha Ghosh and Helmut Reifeld (eds), *Pluralism and Equality: Values in Indian Society and Politics.* Delhi: Sage.

———. 1983. *Modernization and Social Change among Muslims in India.* Delhi: Manohar.

———. 1981. *Ritual and Religion among Muslims in India.* Delhi: Manohar.

Select Bibliography

Ahmad, Imtiaz. (ed.) 1976a. *Caste and Stratification among Muslims in India*. Delhi: Manohar.

———. 1976b. *Family, Kinship and Marriages among Muslims in India*. Delhi: Manohar.

———. 1974. 'An Essential Prerequisite'. *Seminar*, No. 174.

———. 1972a. 'For a Sociology of India', *Contributions to Indian Sociology* (New Series), VI: 172–78.

———. 1972b. 'Religion in Politics: A Comment', *Economic and Political Weekly*, VII (2).

———. 1969. 'Secularism and Communalism', *Economic and Political Weekly*, Special Number, July: 1142–58.

Ahmad, Imtiaz and Helmut Reifeld (eds). 2004. *Lived Islam in South Asia: Adaptation, Accommodation and Conflict*. Delhi: Social Science Press.

Ahmad, Irfan. 2003. 'A Different Jihad: Dalit Muslims' Challenge to Ashraf Hegemony', *Economic and Political Weekly*, XXXVIII (46): 86–91.

Ahmed, Akbar S. 2001. *Jinnah, Pakistan and Islamic Identity: The Search for Saladin*. London: Routledge.

———. 1999. *Islam Today: Introduction to the Muslim World*. London: I. B. Tauris.

Ahmed, Hilal. 2012. 'Public Presence of Mosques and Muslim Identity in Postcolonial Delhi', *The Book Review*, Vol. XXXVI (January).

———. 2010. 'How to not Read the Ayodhya Judgment'. http://kafila. org/2010/10/02/how-to-not-read-the-ayodhya-judgement-hilal-ahmed/ (accessed on 30 April 2013).

Akhter, Andalip. 2002. 'Muslim Dalits Demand Parity with Other Dalits', *Milli Gazette* (16–31 October).

Alam, Javeed. 2004. *Who Wants Democracy?* Delhi: Orient Blackswan.

Alam, Muzaffar. 2004. *The Languages of Political Islam: India 1200–1800*. London: Hurst & Co.

Ali, Ahmed. 1984. *Al-Qur'an: A Contemporary Translation*. Princeton: Princeton University Press.

Ameer Ali, Syed. 1899. *A Short History of the Saracens: Being a Concise Account of the Rise and Decline of the Saracenic Power and the Economic, Social and Intellectual Development of the Arab Nation*. London: Macmillan & Co.

———. 1891. *The Life and Teachings of Mohammed or the Spirit of Islam*. London: W. H. Allen & Co.

Amin, Shahid, 1995. *Event, Metaphor, Memory: Chauri Chaura, 1922–1992*. Berkeley: University of California Press.

Anderson, Benedict. 1991. *Imagined Communities: Reflections on the Origin and Spread of Nationalism*. London: Verso.

Ansari, Asharf Husain. 2004a. 'Reservation Debate: Which Muslim Group is Under Represented', *Milli Gazette* (16–30 September).

298 *Select Bibliography*

Ansari, Asharf Husain. 2004b. 'Rejoinder to Syed Shahabuddin: Reservation for Muslim Backward', *Milli Gazette* (16–30 November).

———. 2004c. 'Rejoinder: Case for Backward Muslims', *Milli Gazette* (16–31 December).

Appadurai, Arjun. (ed.). 1986. *The Social life of Things: Commodities in Cultural Perspective*. Cambridge: Cambridge University Press.

———. 1981. *Worship and Control under Colonial Rule: A South Indian Case*. Cambridge: Cambridge University Press.

Arnold, David. 1986. *Police, Power and Colonial Rule: Madras, 1859–1947*. Delhi: Oxford University Press.

Asharf, Ali. 1982. *The Muslim Elite*. Delhi: Atlantic Publication and Distributors.

Azaryahu, Maoz. 1993. 'From Remains to Relics: Authentic Monuments in the Israeli Landscape', *History and Memory*, 5 (2): 82–103.

Badhwar, Inderjeet, Tania Midha, Prabhu Chawla, Ramindar Singh and Dilip Awasthi. 1988. 'The Agony of Meerut', in Asghar Ali Engineer, *Delhi Meerut Riots*. Delhi: Ajanta.

Bahl, Vinay. 1997. 'Relevance (Or Irrelevance) of Subaltern Studies', *Economic and Political Weekly*, XXXII (23): 1333–44.

Bajpai, Rochana. 2002. 'The Conceptual Vocabularies of Secularism and Minority Rights in India', *Journal of Political Ideologies*, 7 (2): 179–97.

Batra, N. L. 1996. *Heritage Conservation: Preservation and Restoration of Monuments*. Delhi: Arya Book International.

Bauer, Alexander, A. 2002. 'Is What You See All You Get: Recognising Meanings in Archaeology', *Journal of Social Archaeology*, 2 (1): 37–52.

Baxi, Upendra. 1992. 'Discussion: The State's Emissary: The Place of Law in Subaltern Studies', in Gyanendra Pandey and Partha Chatterjee (eds), *Subaltern Studies VII: Writings on South Asian Society and History*. Delhi: Oxford University Press.

Bhan, Suraj. 1997. 'Recent Trends in Indian Archaeology', *Social Scientist*, 25 (1 & 2), January–February.

Bhattacharya, Neeladri. 2008. 'Predicaments of Secular Histories', *Public Culture*, 20 (1): 57–73.

Bhargava, Rajeev. 1998. 'What is Secularism For?', in Rajeev Bhargava (ed.), *Secularism and Its Critics*. Delhi: Oxford University Press.

Bhusan, Bharat. 1988. 'Imam Climbs Down to Victory', in Asghar Ali Engineer (ed.) *Delhi Meerut Riots*. Delhi: Ajanta.

Bilgrami, Akeel. 1998. 'Secularism, Nationalism and Modernity', in Rajeev Bhargava (ed.), *Secularism and Its Critics*. Delhi: Oxford University Press.

Select Bibliography

Blunt, James T. 1799. 'A description of the Cuttub Minar by Ensign James T. Blunt of the Engineers', *The Asiatic Researche*, vol. IV.

Brass, Paul. 2004. 'Development of an Institutionalised Riot System in Meerut City, 1961 to 1982', *Economic and Political Weekly* (30 October): 4839–48.

———. 2002. 'India, Myron Weiner and the Political Science of Development', *Economic and Political Weekly*, XXXVII (29): 3026–40.

———. 1979. 'Ethnic Groups, Symbol Manipulation and Ethnic Identity among the Muslims of South Asia', in David Taylor and Malcolm Yapp (eds), *Political Identity in South Asia*. London: SOAS.

———. 1974. *Language, Religion and Politics in North India*. London: Cambridge University Press.

Cannadine, David. 2001. *Ornamentalism: How the British Saw Their Empire*. London: Viking/Penguin.

Carroll, L. 1983. 'The Muslim Family in India: Law, Customs and Empirical Research', *Contributions to Indian Sociology*, 17: 205–22.

Chakrabarti, Dilip. 2003. *Archaeology in the Third World: A History of Indian Archaeology Since 1947*. Delhi: D. K. Print World.

———. 1988. *A History of Indian Archaeology: From Beginning to 1947*. Delhi: Munshi Ram Manoharlal.

Chakrabarty, Dipesh. 1992a. 'Postcoloniality and the Artifice of History: Who Speaks for "Indian" Pasts?', *Representations*, 37: 1–26.

———. 1992b. 'The Death of History', *Public Culture*, 4 (2).

Chandhoke, Neera and Hilal Ahmed. 1997. *Politics of People's Rights*, Report submitted to Indian Council of Social Science Research (ICSSR). Delhi: Developing Countries Research Centre.

Chandra, Bipan. 1990. Communalism and the State: Some Issues in India, *Social Scientists*, 18 (8/9): 38–47.

Chatterjee, Partha. 1997a. *A Possible India: Essays in Political Criticism*. Delhi: Oxford University Press.

———. 1997b. *The Present History of West Bengal: Essays in Political Criticism*. Delhi: Oxford University Press.

———. 1994. 'Was There a Hegemonic Project of the Colonial State?', in Dagmar Engels and Shula Marks (eds), *Contesting Colonial Hegemony: State and Society in Africa and India*. London: British Academic Press.

———. 1993. *Nation and its Fragments: Histories in Colonial and Postcolonial India*. Delhi: Oxford University Press.

———. 1984. *Bengal, 1920–1947: The Land Question*. Calcutta: K. P. Bagchi & Co.

Chaudhury, B. B. 1986. Subaltern Autonomy and the National Movement, *Indian Historical Review* 12 (1–2).

300 *Select Bibliography*

Choay, Françoise. 2001. *The Invention of the Historic Monument*, trans. by Lauren M. O. Connell. Cambridge: Cambridge University Press.

Cohn, Barnard S. 1996. *Colonialism and Its Forms of Knowledge*. Princeton: Princeton University Press.

————. 1987. *An Anthropologist among the Historians and Other Essays*. Delhi: Oxford University Press.

————. 1983. 'Representing Authority in Victorian India', in Eric Hobsbawm and Terence Ranger (eds), *The Invention of Tradition*. Cambridge: Cambridge University Press.

Cole, H. H. 1882. *Preservation of National Monuments: First Report of the Curator of the Ancient Monuments in India for the Year 1881–82*. Simla: Government Central Bureau Press.

Crooke William. (ed.). 1925. *Travels in India by Jean-Baptiste Tavernier*, vol. 1. London: Oxford University Press.

Cunningham, John. (ed.) 1939. *Revealing India's Past: A Co-operative Record of Archaeological Conservation and Exploration in India and Beyond*. London: The India Society.

Dalrymple, William. 1994. *City of Djinns: A Year in Delhi*. London: Flamingo.

Das, Veena. 1995. *Critical Events*. Delhi: Oxford University Press.

————. 1984. 'For a Folk-Theology and Theoretical Anthropology of Islam', *Contributions to Indian Sociology*, 18 (3): 293–300.

Davis, Richard. 1997. *Lives of Indian Images*. Princeton: Princeton University Press.

————. 1992. 'Loss and Recovery of Ritual Self among Hindu Images', *Journal of Ritual Studies*, 6 (1): 43–61.

Dhawan, Rajeev. 2002. 'The Kubh', *The Hindu*, 26 January.

————. 1994. 'The Ayodhya Judgement: Encoding Secularism in the Law', *Economic and Political Weekly*, XXIX (48): 3034–40.

Dumont, L. 1970. *Homo Hierarchicus: An Essay on the Caste System*. Chicago: Chicago University Press.

Eaton, Richard M. 2003. 'Introduction', in Richard M. Eaton (ed.), *India's Islamic Traditions: 711–1750*. Delhi: Oxford University Press.

————. 2000. *Essays on Islam and Indian History*. Delhi: Oxford University Press.

Elliot, H. M. and John Dowson. 1867. *The History of India as Told by Its Own Historians: The Muhammadan Period*, vol. Seven. London: Trubner and Co.

Elst, Koenraad. 2002. *Ayodhya: The Case against the Temple*. Delhi: Voice of India.

————. 1993. *Negationism in India: Concealing the Record of Islam*. Delhi: Voice of India.

Select Bibliography **301**

Elst, Koenraad. 1991. *Ayodhya and After: Issues before Hindu Society.* Delhi: Voice of India.

———. 1990. *Ram Janmabhoomi vs. Babri Masjid.* Delhi: Voice of India.

Engineer, Asghar Ali. 1994. *Lifting the Veil: Communal Violence and Communal Harmony in Contemporary India.* London: Sangam Books.

———. 1990. *Islam and Liberation Theology.* Delhi: Sterling Publishers.

———. 1988a. *Delhi Meerut Riots.* Delhi: Ajanta.

———. 1988b. 'Old Delhi too in the Grip of Communal Frenzy', in Asghar Ali Engineer (ed.), *Delhi Meerut Riots.* Delhi: Ajanta.

Ernst, Carl W. 1995. 'India as a Sacred Islamic Land', in Donald S. Lopez (ed.), *Religion of India in Practice.* Princeton: Princeton University Press.

Fergusson, James. 1910. *The History of Indian and Eastern Architecture.* (revised and edited by Burgess, James & Spiers, R. P.), vol. 1. London: John Murray.

Fickette Jr., Lewis P. 1993. The Rise and Fall of Janata Dal', *Asian Survey,* 33 (12): 1157–69.

Foster, William. (ed.). 1926. *The Embassy of Sir Thomas Roe to India 1615–19, as Narrated in his Journal and Correspondence.* London: Oxford University Press.

Francois, Bernier. 1891. *Travels in Mogul Empire* (trans. by Archibald Constable). Westminster: Archibald Constable & Co.

Faruqi, Ziya-ul-Hasan. 1966. 'Indian Muslims and the Ideology of the Secular State', in Donald Eugene Smith (ed.), *South Asian Politics and Religion.* Princeton and New Jersey: Princeton University Press.

Freitag, B. Sandria. 1989. *Collective Action and Community: Public Arenas and the Emergence of Communalism in North India.* Oxford: University of California Press.

Galanter, Marc. 1998. 'Hinduism, Secularism, and the Indian Judiciary', in Rajeev Bhargava (ed.), *Secularism and Its Critics.* Delhi: Oxford University Press.

Gandhi, Rajmohan. 1990. *Understanding the Muslim Mind.* New Delhi: Penguin.

Goel, Sita Ram. 1993. *Islam vis-a-vis Hindu Temples.* Delhi: Voice of India.

———. 1991a. *Hindu Temples: What Happened to Them: A Preliminary Survey,* vol. 1. Delhi: Voice of India.

———. 1991b. *Hindu Temples: What Happened to Them: The Islamic Evidence,* vol. 2. Delhi: Voice of India.

Goodfriend, Douglas. 1989. 'The Tyranny of the Right Angle: Colonial and Postcolonial Urban Development in Delhi (1857–1957)', in Patwant Singh and Ram Dhamija (eds), *Delhi: Deepening Urban Crisis.* Delhi: Sterling.

Gopal, Sarvepalli (ed.). 1990. *Anatomy of Confrontation: The Babri-Masjid-Ramjanmabhumi Issue.* Delhi: Penguin.

302   *Select Bibliography*

Goradia, Prafull. 2002. *Hindu Masjids*. Delhi: Contemporary Targett Prafull Pvt. Limited.

Gough, R. (ed.). 1785. *A Comparative View of the Ancient Monuments of India, Particularly Those in the Island of Salset near Bombay as Described by Different Writers*. London: John Nicholas.

Gould, Harold. A. 1966. 'Religion and Politics in a UP Constituency', in Donald Eugene Smith (ed.), *South Asian Politics and Religion*. Princeton and New Jersey: Princeton University Press.

Gramsci, Antonio. 1971. *Selections from Prison Notebooks* (trans. and edited by Quintin Hoare and G. Smith Nowell). London: Lawrence and Wishart.

Guha, Ranajit. 1997. *Dominance without Hegemony: History and Power in Colonial India*. Cambridge: Harvard University Press.

———. 1989. *Subaltern Studies VI: Writings on South Asian History and Society*. Delhi: Oxford University Press.

———. 1988. *An Indian Historiography of India: A Nineteenth Century Agenda and Its Implications*. Calcutta: K. P. Bagchi and Co.

———. 1987. *Subaltern Studies V: Writings on South Asian History and Society*. Delhi: Oxford University Press.

———. 1985. *Subaltern Studies IV: Writings on South Asian History and Society*. Delhi: Oxford University Press.

———. 1984. *Subaltern Studies III: Writings on South Asian History and Society*. Delhi: Oxford University Press.

———. 1983. *Elementary Aspects of Peasant Insurgency in Colonial India*. Delhi; Oxford University Press.

———. ed. 1982a. *Subaltern Studies I: Writings on South Asian History and Society*. Delhi: Oxford University Press.

———. 1982b. *Subaltern Studies II: Writings on South Asian History and Society*. Delhi: Oxford University Press.

Guha, Ranajit and Gayatri Chakravorty Spivak (eds). 1988. *Selected Subaltern Studies*. New York: Oxford University Press.

Guha Thakurta, Tapati. 1997. 'The Museumised Relic: Archaeology and the First Museum of Colonial India', *The Indian Economic and Social History Review*, XXXIV (1): 21–52.

———. 1992. *The Making of a New "Indian" Art: Artists, Aesthesis, and Nationalism in Bengal, c. 1850–1920*. Cambridge: Cambridge University Press.

Gupta, Narayani. 2000. 'From Architecture to Archaeology: The Monumentalising of Delhi's History in the Nineteenth Century', in Jamal Malik (ed.), *Perspectives on Mutual Encounters in South Asian History, 1760–1860*. Leiden: Brill.

———. 1982. *Delhi between the Two Empires*. Delhi: Oxford University Press.

Select Bibliography   **303**

Gupta, S. P. and K. S. Ramachandran. (eds). 1976. *Mahabharata: Myth and Reality: Differing Views*. Delhi: Agam Prakashan.

Habib, Irfan. 1997. 'Unreason and Archaeology-"Painted Grey Ware" and Beyond', *Social Scientist*, 25: 1–2.

———. 1991. 'Basic Question in Babri Dispute is Blind Faith versus Reason, Secularism Versus Theocracy, Democracy versus Fascism', *People's Democracy*, 14 April 1991 and *Muslim India*, 101 (May 1991).

———. 1963. *Agrarian System of Mughal India, 1556–1707*. Bombay: Asia Publishing House.

Habib, Mohammed. 1967. *Sultan Mahmud of Ghaznin*. Delhi: S. Chand.

Halbwachs, Maurice. 1980. *The Collective Memory* (trans. by Francis J. Ditter, Jr. and Vida Yazdi Ditter). New York: Harper Colophone Books.

Haq, Mushir-ul. 1972. *Islam in Secular India*. Simla: IIAS.

Hartung, Jan-Peter. 2003. 'The Land, The Mosque, The Temple: More Than 145 Years of Dispute Over Ayodhya', in Jan-Peter Hartung, Gillian Hawkes and Anuradha Bhattacharjee, *Ayodhya 1992–2003: The Assertion of Cultural and Religious Hegemony*, South Asian History Academic Paper 9, Institute for the Study of Indo-Pak Relation. Leicester: University of Leicester.

Hasan, Mushirul. 1997. *Legacy of a Divided Nation: India's Muslims since Independence*. London: Hurst & Co.

——— (ed.). 1993. *India's Partition: Process, Strategy and Mobilization*. Delhi: Oxford University Press.

Hearn, G. R. 1997. *The Seven Cities of Delhi*. New Delhi: SBW Publishers.

Heehs, Peter. 2003. 'Shades of Orientalism: Paradoxes and Problems in Indian Historiography', *History and Theory*, 42 (May): 169–95.

Henri, Lefebvre 1991. *The Production of Space* (trans. by Donald Nicholson-Smith). Oxford: Blackwell.

Hilberg, Raul. 2001. *Sources of Holocaust Research: An Analysis*. London: Evan Dee.

Hobsbawm, Eric and Terence Ranger (eds). 1983. *The Invention of Tradition*. Cambridge: Cambridge University Press.

Hodder, Ian. 1992. *Theory and Practice in Archaeology*. London: Routledge.

Hunter, William. 1785. 'An Account of Some Artificial Caverns in the Neighbourhood of Bombay', *Archaeologia*, volume VII.

Hussain, S. Abid. 1956. *The National Culture of India*. Bombay: Jaico Books.

Imam, Abu. 1966. *Sir Alexander Cunningham and the Beginning of Indian Archaeology*. Dacca: Asiatic Society of Pakistan.

Imam, Zafar. 1975. 'Some Aspects of Social Structure of the Muslim Community in India', in Zafar Imam (ed.), *Muslims in India*. New Delhi: Orient Longman.

304 *Select Bibliography*

Iqbal, Mohammad. 2006. *Shikwa.* http://oldpoetry.com/opoem/30200 (accessed on 14 January 2014).

———. 1980. *Reconstruction of Religious Thought in Islam.* Delhi: New Taj Office.

Jagmohan. 1975. *Redevelopment of Shahjahanabad.* Delhi: Vikas.

Jalal, Ayesha. 2001. *Self and Sovereignty: Individual and Community in South Asian Islam Since 1850.* Delhi: Oxford University Press.

———. 1998. Exploding Communalism: The Politics of Muslim Identity in South Asia', in Ayesha Jalal and Sugata Bose (eds), *Nationalism, Democracy and Development: State and Politics in India.* Delhi: Oxford University Press.

———. 1996. 'Secularists, Subalterns and the Stigma of "Communalism": Partition Historiography Revisited', *Modern Asian Studies,* 30 (3): 681–737.

Jayakar, Pupul. 1995. *Indira Gandhi.* Delhi: Penguin.

Jones, William. 1788. 'The Third Anniversary Discourse on the Chronology of Hindus', *Asiatic Researchers,* vol. 2.

Juneja, Monica (ed.). 2001a. *Architecture in Medieval India: Forms, Contexts, Histories.* Delhi: Permanent Black.

———. 2001b. 'Introduction', in Monica Juneja (ed.), *Architecture in Medieval India: Forms, Contexts. Histories.* Delhi: Permanent Black.

Kabir, Humayun. 1955. *The Indian Heritage* (Third revised edition). Bombay & Calcutta: Asia Publishing House.

Katju, Manjari. 2003. *Vishva Hindu Parishad and Indian Politics.* Delhi: Orient Longman.

Kaviraj, Sudipta. 2010. *Imaginary Institution of India: Politics and Ideas.* New York: Columbia University Press.

———. 2005. 'Politics of Performance: Gandhi's Trial Read as Theatre', in Julia C. Strauss and Donal Cruise O'Brien (eds), *Staging Politics: Power and Performance in Asia and Africa.* London: I. B. Tauris.

———. 1995. *The Unhappy Consciousness: Bankim Chandra Chattopadhyay and the Formation of Nationalist Discourse in India.* Delhi: Oxford University Press.

———. 1997a. 'The Imaginary Institution of India', in Gyanendra Pandey and Partha Chatterjee (eds), *Subaltern Studies VII: Writings on South Asian History and Society.* Delhi: Oxford University Press.

———. 1997b. 'Introduction', in Sudipta Kaviraj (ed.), *Politics in India.* Delhi: Oxford University Press.

———. 1997c. 'On the Construction of Colonial Power: Structure, Discourse, Hegemony', in Sudipta Kaviraj (ed.), *Politics in India.* Delhi: Oxford University Press.

———. 1997d. 'Religion and Identity in India', *Ethnic and Racial Studies,* 20 (2).

Select Bibliography **305**

Kaviraj, Sudipta. 1997e. 'Filth and the Public Sphere: Concepts and Practices about Space in Calcutta', *Public Culture,* Vol. 10, No. 1. (Fall).

———. 1997f. 'A Critique of the Passive Revolution', in Partha Chatterjee (ed.), *State and Politics in India.* Delhi: Oxford University Press.

———. 1997g. 'On the Construction of Colonial Power: Structure, Discourse, Hegemony', in Sudipta Kaviraj (ed.), *Politics in India.* Delhi: Oxford University Press.

———. 1986. 'Indira Gandhi and Indian Politics', *Economic and Political Weekly,* XXI (38&39): 1697–1708.

Kavuri-Bauer, Santhi. 2011. *Monumental Matters: The Power, Subjectivity, and Space of India's Mughal Architecture.* Durham: Duke University Press.

Kejariwal, O. P. 1988. *The Asiatic Society of Bengal and the Discovery of India's Past 1784–1838.* Delhi: Oxford University Press.

Khan, Danish A. 2003. 'Muslim Express Doubts, Fears over Jagmohan Plan', *Milli Gazette* (1–15 July).

Khan, M. Ghazali. 2006. 'Muslim University is not a Muslim Institution says Indian Court', *Muslim News.* http://www.muslimnews.co.uk (accessed on 14 January 2014).

Khan, Sayed Ahmad. 1978. *Asar-as-Sanadid,* trans. by R. Nath. Delhi: Ambika Publications.

———. 1854. *Asar-as-Sanadid* (Urdu). Delhi: NP.

Koshar, Rudy. 2000. *From Monument to Traces: Artefacts of German Memory 1870–1990.* London: University of California Press.

Krafft, Thomas. 2003. 'Contemporary Old Delhi: Transformation of an Historical Place', in Eckart Ehlers and Thomas Krafft (eds), *Shahjahanabad/Old Delhi: Tradition and Colonial Change,* second edition. Delhi: Manohar.

Krishna Menon, A. G. 2003. 'The Case of an Indian Charter', *Seminar,* no. 503 (October).

Kumar, Sunil. 2001. 'Qutub and Modern Memory', in Suvir Kaul (ed.), *The Partition of Memory.* Delhi: Permanent Black.

Lahiri, Nayanjyoti. 2003. 'Conservation and Destruction: Some Aspects of the Monument Policy of the British Raj during the Time of Lord Curzon'. http://www.wac.uct.ac.za/croatia/lahiri2.htm (accessed on 14 January 2014).

Lang, John, Madhavi Desai and Miki Desai. 1997. *Architecture and Independence: The Search for Identity — India 1880 to 1980.* Delhi: Oxford University Press.

Lindholm, Charles. 1995. 'Caste in Islam and the Problem of Deviant System: A Critique of Recent Theory', in T. N. Madan (ed.), *Muslim Community in South Asia,* second revised edition. Delhi: Manohar.

306 *Select Bibliography*

Mackenzie, John M. 1995. *Orientalism: History, Theory and the Arts.* Manchester: Manchester University Press.

Madan, T. N. 2003. 'Freedom of Religion', *Economic and Political Weekly*, XXXVIII (11): 1034.

———. 1998. 'Secularism in Its Place', in Rajeev Bhargava (ed.), *Secularism and Its Critics.* Delhi: Oxford University Press.

———. 1995. 'Introduction', in T. N. Madan (ed.), *Muslim Community in South Asia.* Delhi: Manohar.

———. 1972. 'Religious Ideology in Plural Society: The Muslims and Hindus of Kashmir', *Contributions to Indian Sociology*, 15: 223–49.

Mani, V. S. 2001. 'Bamiyan Buddhas & International Law', *The Hindu*, 6 March.

Marshal, John. 1928. 'The Monuments of Muslim India', in Wolseley Haig (ed.), *Cambridge History of India, Turks and Afghans*, vol. 3. Cambridge: Cambridge University Press.

———. 1939. 'The Story of the Archaeological Department in India', in John Cunningham (ed.), *Revealing India's Past: A Co-operative Record of Archaeological Conservation and Exploration in India and Beyond.* London: The India Society.

Maurice, Thomas. 1794. *Indian Antiquities: Or Dissertations relative to the Ancient Geography Divisions, the Pure System of Primeval Theology, the Grand Code of Civil Laws, the Original Form of Government, and the Various and Profound Literature of Hindostan*, 7 volumes. London: C&W Galbin.

Mayaram, Shail. 1997. *Resisting Regimes: Myth, Memory and the Shaping of a Muslim Identity.* Delhi: Oxford University Press.

Mayer, Peter B. 1983. 'Tombs and Dark Houses', in Imtiaz Ahmad (ed.), *Modernization and Social Change among Muslims in India.* Delhi: Manohar.

McCrindale, J. W. 1885 [2008]. *Ancient India as Described by Ptolemy.* Kessinger Publishing.

Mehmood, Tahir. 1977. *The Muslim Personal Law: Role of the State in The Subcontinent.* Delhi: Vikas.

Mehra, Ajay K. 1990. *The Politics of Urban Development: A Study of Old Delhi.* Delhi: Sage.

Metcalf, Thomas, 1989. *An Imperial Vision: Indian Architecture and the British Raj.* London: Faber & Faber.

Minault, Gail. 1982. *Khilafat Movement: Religious Symbolism and Political Mobilization in India.* Delhi: Oxford University Press.

Miri, Ali A. 2004. 'Philosophy and Principles of Preservation in Practice'. http://crm.cr.nps.gov/archive/24-07/24-07-4pdf (accessed on 14 January 2014).

Mitter, Partha. 1994. *Art and Nationalism in Colonial India 1850–1922: Occidental Orientations*. Cambridge: Cambridge University Press.

———. 1977. *Much Maligned Monsters: History of European Reactions to Indian Art*. Oxford: Clarendon.

Mohammed, Ghulam. 1986. *Tarikh-e-Gumgashta* (Urdu) Faizabad: Bazm-e-Adab.

Mohan, I. 1992. *Environmental Issues and Urban Development of the Walled Cities*. Delhi: Mittal.

Mohanty, Manoranjan. 2000. *Contemporary Indian Political Theory*. New Delhi: Samskirti.

Monk, Daniel Bertrand. 2002. *An Aesthetic Occupation: The Immediacy of Architecture and the Palestine Conflict*. Durham and London: Duke University Press.

Morris Jones, W. H. 1964. *The Government and Politics in India*. London: Hutchinson University Library.

Mubarakpuri, Shaikh Safiur Rahman. 2002. *History of Mecca*, trans. by Nasiruddin al-khattab. Riyadh: Darussalam.

Mujeeb, Muhammad. 2001. 'The Qutub Complex as a Social Document', in Monica Juneja (ed.), *Architecture in Medieval India: Forms, Contexts, Histories*. Delhi: Permanent Black.

Mujjaddai, Maulana Fazalur Rehman. 1993. *All India Muslim Personal Law Board Ki Kidmaaat Aur Sargarmiyan* (Urdu/Hindi). Jaipur: AIMPLB.

Munshi, K. M. 1965. 'The Story of Somnath', in K. M. Munshi (ed.), *Somnath: The Shrine Eternal*, third edition. Bombay: Bharatiya Vidya Bhawan.

———. 1956. 'Epoch of Indian Culture', in K. M. Munshi (ed.), *Indian Inheritance: Art, History and Culture*, vol. II. Bombay: Bharatiya Vidya Bhawan.

Nadwi, Syed Hasan Ali. 2003. *Karvan-e-Zindagi* (Urdu), vol. V. Lucknow: Matkaba-e-Islam.

———. 2001. *Karvan-e-Zindagi* (Urdu), vol. I. Lucknow: Matkaba-e-Islam.

———. 1976. *Muslims in India* (trans. by Mohammad Asif Kidwai). Lucknow: Academy of Islamic Research and Publication.

Nanda, Ritish. 1999. 'Introduction', in Ritish Nanda, Narayani Gupta and O. P. Jain, *Delhi the Built Heritage: A Listing*, vol. 1. Delhi: INTACH Publications.

Nandan, Deoki. 2006. 'Shri Ramjanmbhoomi: Historical and Legal Perspective'. http://www.vhp.org/englishsite/e.Special_Movements/dRanjanambhumi%20Muti/historical_legalperspective.htm (accessed on 26 January 2006).

Nandy, Ashis, Shikha Trivedi, Shail Mayaram, and Achyut Yagnic. 1995. *Creating a Nationality: The Ram Janambhuni Movement and the Fear of the Self*. Delhi: Oxford University Press.

308 *Select Bibliography*

Nandy, Ashis. 2003. *The Romance of the State and the Fate of Dissent in the Tropics*. Delhi: Oxford University Press.

———. 1998. 'The Politics of Secularism and the Recovery of Religious Toleration', in Rajeev Bhargava (ed.), *Secularism and Its Critics*. Delhi: Oxford University Press.

Narain, Harsh. 1993. *The Ayodhya Temple Mosque Dispute: Focus on Muslim Sources*. Delhi: Penman Publishers.

Nath, R. 1991. *The Baburi Masjid of Ayodhya*. Jaipur: The Historical Research Documentation Programme.

Nehru, J. L. 2002 [1946]. *The Discovery of India*. Delhi: Oxford University Press.

———. 1956. 'The Continuity of Indian Culture', in K. M. Munshi (ed.), *Indian Inheritance: Art, History and Culture,* vol. II. Bombay: Bharatiya Vidya Bhawan.

Nevill, N. R. 1928. *District Gazetteers of the United Province of Agra and Oudh: Fyzabad.* Allahabad: Government Press.

Nigam, Aditya. 2006. *The Insurrection of Little Selves: The Crisis of Secular-Nationalism in India*. Delhi: Oxford University Press.

Noorani, A. G. 2003a. *The Babri Masjid Question 1528–2003: A Matter of National Honour*, vol 1. Delhi: Tulika.

———. 2003b. *The Babri Masjid Question 1528–2003: A Matter of National Honour*, vol. 2. Delhi: Tulika.

———. 1974. 'Non-Partisan Approach', *Seminar*, No. 174 (February).

Nora, Pierre. 1996a. 'Between Memory and History', in Pierre Nora (ed.), *Rethinking the French Past: Realms of Memory: Conflict and Division* (English edition). New York: Columbia University Press.

———. 1996b. 'From Lieux de Memoir to Realms of Memory', in Pierre Nora (ed.), *Rethinking the French Past: Realms of Memory: Conflict and Division* (English edition). New York. Columbia University Press.

Oak, P. N. 1966. *Some Blunders of Indian Historical Research*. Delhi: Institute of Rewriting Indian History.

O'Hanlon, Rosalind. 1988. 'Recovering the Subject: Subaltern Studies and Histories of Resistance in Colonial South Asia', *Modern Asian Studies*, 22 (1): 189–224.

Pachauri, Pankaj. 1988. '117 Missing in Maliana', in Asghar Ali Engineer (ed.), *Delhi Meerut Riots.* Delhi: Ajanta.

Page, J. A. 2001. 'An Historical Memoir on Qutub: Delhi', in Monica Juneja (ed.), *Architecture in Medieval India: Forms, Contexts, Histories*. Delhi: Permanent Black.

Pandey, Gyanendra. 2002. *Remembering Partition: Violence, Nationalism and History in India.* Cambridge: Cambridge University Press.

———. 1990. *The Construction of Communalism in Colonial North India*. Delhi: Oxford University Press.

Select Bibliography

Pandey, Gyanendra. 1984. '"Encounters and Calamities": The History of a North Indian Qasba in the Nineteenth Century', in Ranajit Guha (ed.), *Subaltern Studies IV: Writings on South Asian History and Society*. Delhi: Oxford University Press.

Panja, Sheena. 2002. 'The Third Space: The Creation of Archaeological Knowledge in Post-Independence India', *Studies in History*, 18 (1): 1–22.

Pease, Donald, E. 1992. 'Author', in Frank Lentricchia and Thomas McLaughlin (eds), *Critical Terms for Literary Study*, second edition. Chicago: University of Chicago Press.

Pelizzari, Maria Antonella. (ed.). 2003. *Traces of India: Photography, Architecture, and the Politics of Representation, 1850–1900*. London: Yale University Press.

Perron, Anquetil du. 1785. 'Description of the Pagodas of Iloura', in R. Gough (ed.), *A Comparative View of the Ancient Monuments of India, Particularly those in the Island of Salset near Bombay as Described by Different Writers*. London: Printed by John Nicholas.

Pirzada, Syed Sharifuddin. 1982. *Foundation of Pakistan: All India Muslim League Documents (1906–1941)*, vol. 1. Delhi: Metropolitan Books.

Prakash, Gyan. 1990. 'Writing Post–Orientalist Histories of the Third World: Perspectives from Indian Historiography', *Comparative Study in Society and History*, 32 (2): 383–408.

Pratt, Mary Louise. 1992. *Imperial Eyes: Travel Writing and Transculturation*. London: Routledge.

Prinsep, James. 1831. *Benares Illustratedin a Series of Drawings*. Calcutta: Baptist Mission Press.

Qureshi, M. A. 1990. *Waqfs in India: A Study of Administrative and Legislative Control*. Delhi: Gian Publishing House.

Rahman, Aziz-ur. 1987 [1936]. *History of Jama Masjid and Interpretation of Muslim Devotions*. Delhi: Publications India.

Rajaram, N. S. 2000. *Profiles in Deception: Ayodhya and the Dead Sea Scrolls*. Delhi: Voice of India.

———. 1995. *Secularism, the New Mask of Fundamentalism: Religious Subversion of Secular Affairs*. Delhi: Voice of India.

Rajalakshmi, T. K. 2003. 'Ayodhya, a Picture of Diversity', *Frontline*, 20 (22), 25 October – 7 November.

Raleigh, Thomas. 1906. *Lord Curzon in India: 1898-1905*. London: Macmillan.

Ramachandran, T. A. 1953. 'Preservation of Monuments', *Ancient India*, no. 9 (Special Jubilee Number).

Rawat, Vidya Bhushan. 2002. 'Sufi Shrines of Ayodhya', *Qalandar* (May). http://www.islaminterfaith.org/may2002/issue.html#article2 (accessed on 14 January 2014).

310   *Select Bibliography*

Raz, Ram. 1832. *Architecture of the Hindus*. Varanasi: Ideological Book House.

RSS on Minorities: http://www.rss.org/New_RSS/Mission_Vision/RSS_on_Minorties.jsp (accessed on 14 January 2014).

Riegl, Alois, 1982. 'The Modern Cult of Monument: Its Character and Its Origin', *Opposition*, no. 25 (Fall).

Rizvi, Syed Haidar Abbas. 2004. 'Political Atmosphere Polluted by Congress: Hashim Ansari', *Milli Gazette* (1–15 February).

Robinson, Francis. 2000. *Islam and Muslim History in South Asia*. Delhi: Oxford University Press.

———. 1983. 'Islam and Muslim Society in South Asia', *Contributions to Indian Sociology*, 17 (2).

———. 1979. 'Nation Formation: The Brass Thesis and Muslim Separatism', in David Taylor and Malcolm Yapp (eds), *Political Identity in South Asia*. London SOAS.

———. 1977. 'Nation Formation: The Brass Thesis and Muslim Separatism', *Journal of Commonwealth and Comparative Politics*, 15 (3): 215–30.

Room, Adrian. 2002. *Cassell's Dictionary of Word Histories*. London: Cassell.

Roy, Sourindranath. 1996 [1961]. *The Story of Indian Archaeology 1784–1947*. Delhi: Archaeological Survey of India.

Sahay, Tara Shankar. 2004. 'Muslims Should Cast Away the Crutches of Other Political Parties', An interview with Ahmed Bukhari, the Shahi Imam of Jama Masjid), 16 April. http://www.rediff.com/election/2004/april/17inter/htm (accessed on 14 January 2014).

Said, Edward W. 1994. *Culture and Imperialism*. London: Vintage.

———. 1978. *Orientalism*. New York: Vintage.

Sarkar, Sumit. 1997. 'The Decline of the Subaltern in Subaltern Studies', in *Writing Social History*. Delhi: Oxford University Press.

———. 1993. 'The Fascism of the Sangha Parivar', *Economic and Political Weekly*, XXVIII (5).

Saxsena, Alka. 1986. 'Dilli me dange bharkane wale trishuldhari the: dar aur sandhe ka vatavaran ka yanhai' (Hindi), *Ravivar* (10–14 September).

Schwarts, Barry. 1982. 'The Social Context of Commemoration: A Study in Collective Memory', *Social Force*, 61 (2).

Sen, Amartya. 1998. 'Secularism and Its Discontents', in Rajeev Bhargava (ed.), *Secularism and Its Critics*. Delhi: Oxford University Press.

Shah, Mohammad. 2005. 'Muslim Unity is the Only Guarantee for Proportionate Share in Administration: A reply to Ashraf Husain Ansari', *Milli Gazette* (1–15 January).

Select Bibliography

Shah, Mohammad. 2004. 'Reservation for Muslims is Constitutional and Socially Necessary in National Context', *Milli Gazette* (1–15 October).

———. 2003. 'Muslim Indians — Yesterday, Today and Tomorrow', *Milli Gazette* (16–30 June)

———. 2001. 'Syed Shahabuddin: A Letter to Editor', *Milli Gazette* (1–15 June).

———. 1989. 'State and Violence: The Struggle for Justice and Dignity', *Muslim India*, 75 (March).

———. 1988a. 'Muslim Indians as a Political Community', *Muslim India*, 64 (April).

———. 1988b. 'Babri Masjid Case: A Tragedy for Secularism, An Epitaph on Democracy' *Muslim India*, 65 (May).

———. 1988c. 'And Finally A Fatwa!', *Muslim India*, 68 (August).

———. 1988d. 'On the False and Anti-National Message of Hindu Chauvinism', *Muslim India*, 72 (December).

———. 1987a. 'Shahabuddin's Bill (31 of 1987) to Amend the Ancient Monuments And Archaeological Sites and Remains Act', *Muslim India*, 55 (July).

———. 1987b. 'On Not Embracing a Suitor in a Hurry', *Muslim India*, 57 (September).

———. 1987c. 'On Secularism and Neo-Secularism in a Multi-Religious Society', *Muslim India*, 58 (October).

———. 1987d. 'Shahabuddin's Letter to the PM on Protected Mosques', *Muslim India*, 59 (November).

———. 1986. 'Editorial', *Muslim India*, 48 (December).

——— (ed.). 1972. *Writings and Speeches of Sir Syed Ahmad Khan*. Delhi: Nachiketa.

Shaikh, Farzana. 2005. 'Millat and Mazhab: Rethinking Iqbal's Political Vision', in Mushirul Hasan and Asim Roy (ed.), *Living Together Separately: Cultural India in History and Politics*. Delhi: Oxford University Press.

———. 1989. *Community and Consensus in Islam: Muslim Representation in Colonial India, 1860–1947*. Cambridge: Cambridge University Press.

Shakir, Moin. 1983. *Islam in Indian Politics*. Delhi: Ajanta Publication.

———. 1972. *Muslims in Free India*. Delhi: Kalamkar Prakashan.

Sharad, Ram Gopal Pandey. n.d. *Shri Ram Janam Bhumi ka Raktranjit Itihas* (Hindi) Ayodhya: Dwarka Prasad Shiv Pustkalya.

Shariff, Abusaleh. 1999. *India: Human Development Report*. Delhi: Oxford University Press.

Sharma, R. S., M. Athar Ali, D. N. Jha, and Suraj Bhan. 1991. *Babari Mosque or Rama's Birth Place? Historians' Report to the Indian Nation*. Lucknow: Babri Masjid Action Committee (UP).

312   *Select Bibliography*

Shaw, Annapurna. 1998. *Eminent Historians: Their Technology, Their Line and Their Fraud.* Delhi: ASA.

———. 1996. 'Urban Policy in Post Independent India: An Appraisal', *Economic and Political Weekly*, XXXI (4) : 224–28.

———. 1993a. *Indian Controversies: Essays on Religion in Politics.* Delhi: ASA.

———. 1993b. *A Secular Agenda: For Saving Our Country and Welding It.* Delhi: ASA.

Shourie, Arun. 1989. 'Hideaway Communalism', *The Indian Express*, 5 February.

Shrimali, K. M. 2003. Ayodhya Archaeology: From Imbroglio to Resolutions. http://www.wac.uct.ac.za/croatia/shrimali.htm (accessed on 14 January 2014).

Sikand, Yoginder. 2004. *Indian Muslims Since 1947: Islamic Perspectives on Inter-Faith Relations.* London and New York: Routledge.

Smith, D. E. 1998. 'India as a Secular State', in Rajeev Bhargava (ed.), *Secularism and Its Critics.* Delhi: Oxford University Press.

Smith, R. V. 2004. 'Grand Old City, Good Old Tales', *The Hindu*, 31 May. http://www.thehindu.com/thehindu/mp/2004/05/31/stories/2004053100630200.htm (accessed on 14 January 2014).

Smith, W. Cantwell. 1961. 'Modern Muslim Historical Writings in English', in C. H. Philips, (ed.), *Historians of India Pakistan and Ceylon.* London: Oxford University Press.

Srivastva, Sushil. 1991. *Disputed Mosque: A Historical Inquiry.* Delhi: Vistar.

Tambiah, Stanley. J. 1998. 'The Crisis of Secularism in India', in Rajeev Bhargava (ed.), *Secularism and Its Critics.* Delhi: Oxford University Press.

Tarlo, Emma. 2003. *Unsettling Memories: The Narratives of the Emergency in Delhi.* London: Hurst & Co.

Thapar, B. K. 1965. The Temple of Somnath: History by Excavation. K. M. Munshi. ed. *Somnath: The Shrine Eternal,* 3rd edition. Bombay: Bharatiya Vidya Bhawan.

Thapar, Romila. 2000. *Cultural Past: Essays in Earlier Indian History.* Delhi: Oxford University Press.

The Encyclopaedia Britannica, vol. 15. 1967. London.

The Oxford English Dictionary. 1999. Oxford: Oxford University Press.

Tillotson, G. H. R. 1998. *The Paradigm of Indian Architecture: Space and Time in Representation and Design.* Surrey: Curzon.

Tripathi, S. K. 1986. *Babri mosque or Ramjanmbhoomi Temple: One Hundred Year of Litigation.* Lucknow: Babri Masjid Action Committee (UP).

Select Bibliography **313**

Upadhyay, Sanjay and Bhavani Raman. 1998. *Land Acquisition and Public Purpose*. Delhi: The Other Media.

Veer, Peter Ven Der. 1988. *Gods on Earth: The Management of Religious Experience and Identity in a North Indian Pilgrimage Centre*. London: Athlone Press.

Wheeler, J. Talboys. 1878. *Early Records of British India: A History of the British Settlements in India, as told in the government records, the works of old travellers, and other contemporary documents, from the earliest period to the down to the rise of British Power in India*. London: Trubner & Co.

Wright, Theodore. 1983. 'Inadvertent Modernization of Indian Muslims by Revivalists', in Imtiaz Ahmad (ed.), *Modernization and Social Change among Muslims in India*. Delhi: Manohar.

———. 1966. 'The Effectiveness of the Muslim Representation in India', in Wright Smith and Donald Eugene, (ed.), *South Asian Politics and Religion*. Princeton and New Jersey: Princeton University Press.

Official Publications

The Conservation Manual. 1923. *A Hand Book for the Use of Archeological Officers and other entrusted with the care of Ancient Monuments by John Marshall*. Calcutta: Superintendent Government Printing.

Constituent Assembly Debates. http://parliamentofindia.nic.in (accessed on 14 January 2014).

Master Plan for Delhi. 1961. Prepared by the DDA and Approved by the Central Government under the DDA Act 1957. Delhi: Delhi Development Authority.

Redevelopment of Shahjahanabad. 1975. Seminar Proceeding. New Delhi: Published by Town and Country Planning Organization. Government of India.

The Constitution of India. 2007. Ministry of Law and Justice, Government of India, Delhi.

Joint Parliamentary Committee on the Working of Wakf Boards, Seventh Report. 2003 (JPC). New Delhi: Government of India.

Prime Minister's High Level Committee on Social Economic and Educational Status of Muslims in India. 2006. (PMHLC). New Delhi: Government of India.

The Indian Archeological Policy 1915: Being a Resolution Issued by the Governor General in Council on the 22nd October 1915. 1916. Calcutta: Superintendent Government Printing.

Government Departments: Official Websites

Archeological Survey of India 2005. http://asi.nic.in/index1.asp?linkid=27 (accessed on 14 January 2014).

314 *Select Bibliography*

Court Cases

O. O. S No. 4 of 1989, Amended Plaint: In the Court of Civil Judge Faizabad: Regular Suit No. 12 of 1961.

Dr. Ramesh Yeshwant Prabhoo v. Brabhakar Kashi Nath Kunte, AIR 1996 SC, 1113.

Dr. Mohammed Ismail Faruqui v. Union of India case, AIR, 1994, SC 605.

Masjid Shahid Ganj and Others v. the Shiromani Gurdwara Prabandhak Committee, Amritsar, AIR, 1938, Lahore, 369.

St. Xavier College v. the State of Gujarat, AIR, 1974, SC 1389.

N. R. Abdul Aziz v. E. Sundaresa Chettiar AIR 1993, Madras, 169.

Legal Documents

The Bengal Code, 1810
The Madras Code, 1817
The Religious Endowments Act, 1863
The Charitable Endowment Act, 1890
The Charitable and Religious Trust Act, 1920
Ancient Monuments Preservation Act, 1904
The Archaeological Sites and Remains [Declaration of National Importance] Act 1951
The Ancient Monuments and Archaeological Sites and Remains Act (1958),
The Wakf Act, 1954
The Wakf Act, 1995
The Indian Penal Code, 1860
The Places of Worship (Special Provision) Act, 1991
The Acquisition of Certain Areas at Ayodhya Act, 1991
The Land Acquisition Act, 1894
The Land Acquisition Act, 1994

Published Reports/Fact-Finding Surveys by Non-governmental Agencies

Bulletin. *Terror in the Walled City: PUCL Report on Delhi Firing 14 February 1986.*

The Ayodhya Reference: Supreme Court Judgments and Commentaries (1995). Delhi: Voice of India.

The Concerned Citizens Tribunal Report. 2002. Crime Against Humanity, vols. I, II, III. Delhi.

The Constitution of All India Muslim Personal Law Board. 2003. Delhi: AIMPLB.

Select Bibliography   **315**

Delhi is Ours: Delhi's Master Plan and Delhi's People. A Report of the Convention held in Delhi on Master Plan and People on 6 June 1999. 1999. Delhi: Sanjha Manch and Hazard Centre.

History versus Casuistry: Evidence of the Ramajanmabhoomi Mandir presented by the Vishwa Hindu Parishad to the Government of India in December–January 1990–91. 1994. Delhi: Voice of India.

Hindu Agenda. Passed by the Vishwa Hindu Parishad. 1997. http://www.vhp.org/englishsite/f.Hindu_Agenda/HinduAgenda_E.htm, (accessed on 14 January 2014).

International Charters and Declarations

The Venice Charter. http://www.international.icomos.org/e_venice.htm (accessed on 14 January 2014).

The World Heritage Convention. http://www.whc.unesco.org (accessed on 14 January 2014).

About the Author

Hilal Ahmed is Assistant Professor, Centre for the Study of Developing Societies (CSDS), New Delhi. His areas of interest are political Islam, Muslim Modernities/representation, and politics of symbols in South Asia. He has published essays, articles and commentaries in national and international journals, newspapers and websites. He also participates in currents affairs programs on popular television channels as a political analyst. Ahmed has produced a short documentary, *Encountering Political Jama Masjid* (18m, colour, 2006). He is currently working on a project entitled *Politics of Muslim Political Representation*, which looks at the issues and debates on Muslim political representation in postcolonial India. This project is a part of Lokniti Program's project on *Democracy and New Publics*. He has also completed a project *Mosques as Monuments: Memory, Islam and National Identity in Bangladesh* (funded by the Asian Scholarship Foundation). Ahmed is also editing *Kaviraj Reader* (in Hindi), for the *Lokchintan Granthmala* series of CSDS.

Index

Abdullah, Sheikh 157, 159

Abid Hussain, S. 99

Act of 1904 80–83, 91, 101–05

Act of 1958 102–06, 118–24, 133, 136–37, 239, 265

Act of 1991 117–18, 267, 270, 273

Adam Sena 161–64, 171, 239

Advani, L. K. 177, 194, 262; arrest of 262; foundation stone laying of Sikander Bakht Memorial School 180; pamphlet on Jama Masjid visit 178; visit to Jama Masjid 179

Agra Fort 58

Ahaliabai temple 113

Ahmad, Imtiaz 9–12, 14

Ain-e-Akbari of Abul Fazal 198

Akbar, Emperor 203

Akbarpur 203

Ali, Ameer 74–75

Ali, Amir 196

Aligarh Muslim University 25, 129, 277

Aligarh Muslim University Act (AMU) 129

Aliv, Azmat Ali: *Amir Ali Shaheed wa Marka-e-Hanuman Garhi* of 200; *Tariq-e-Awadh, Muraqqa-e-Khusarvi* of 200

All India Azad Muslim Conference 127

All India Babri Masjid Action Committee (AIBMAC) 138, 174, 194, 202, 253–54, 256, 259, 263–70

All India Babri Masjid Conference 164, 201, 239, 253, 257

All India Babri Masjid Movement Coordination Committee (AIBMMCC) 164–65, 201–02, 240–45, 248–50, 252–54, 257–59, 263, 266–69, 272

All India Bandh on 1 February 1987 240

All India Intehadul Muslimeem (AIIM) 127n33

All India Muslim Convention 127

All India Muslim Majlis-e-Mushawarat (AIMMM) 4, 131–35, 137–38, 157, 161, 163, 230, 234–35, 237, 240–41; resolution by 234

All India Muslim Personal Law Board (AIMPLB) 133, 137, 160, 202, 230, 233–35, 261, 272n50, 277

ancient monuments 76, 80–81, 85, 100–03, 125, 135–36, 143

Ancient Monuments and Archaeological Sites and Remains Act 1958 4, 101, 125, 136

Ancient Monuments and Archaeological Sites and Remains [Declaration of National Importance] Act (1951) 101–02

Ancient Monuments and Archaeological Sites and Remains Rules, 1959 135

Ancient Monuments Preservation Act 1904 80–81

Anjuman Islamia 94

Anjuman Mohafiz Masjid-Wa-Maqabir 282n4

AnjumanTaraqqi Urdu 22

Ansari, Dr 25

318 *Index*

Ansari, Hashim 213, 220–21, 232–33, 235

anti-government feelings 149, 153, 155; *see also* resentment of Muslims

Antiquarian movement 61

Antiquarianism 60–61

Antiquities 63

archaeological: excavations 77, 101, 106, 108, 114; sites 4, 101–02, 123, 125,

Archaeological Survey of India (ASI) 4, 29, 45–46, 69, 101, 108, 110–11, 124–25, 138, 140–41, 264–65; agreement with 82

architectural heritage 2, 35, 39, 50, 79, 89–91, 97, 108, 114, 275, 280–81

architecture 52–53, 60, 63–64, 70, 73; images of Indian historic 87

Aryan civilisation 99

Asar as-Sanadid 71–73

Asharf, Ali 15

Ashiqan, Musa 203

Asiatic Society of Bengal 52–53, 63, 66

Aurangzeb 61, 64, 66, 198–99, 203

Ayodhya March issue 241, 246, 248–54, 257; BMMCC for 249

Ayodhya Ordinance 222

Ayodhya: disputed site in 222, (Babri Masjid); excavations in 77, 268; Francis Buchanan on 199; Muslim community of 216

Azad, Maulana Abul Kalam 25, 27, 126–29, 130n36

Aziz, Abdul 121

Babar 197, 199, 203, 208; in Ayodhya 195; *see also* Akbar, Emberor; Akbarpur

Bab-e-Shahjahan 140

Babri Masjid 'movement' 237

Babri Masjid 44–45, 99n3, 160–62, 164, 192–94, 197–205, 208–12, 228–46, 248–51, 253–63, 265–70, 272–74; agitation 186, 238, 242, 244, 249, 251, 273, 282; Ahmad Bukhari version of dispute 187; Central Action Committee for restoration of 237; as collective Muslim resistance 230–46; conflicting interests on 258; demolition of 270; as functional Muslim mosque 99; local Muslim position on 217; Muslim claims over 193, 216, 229; Muslim coalition on 248; Muslim politics on 228, 273; as non-functional 45; as Sunni mosque 209; as *Wakf* Property 208; worshipping at disputed site of 219–23, 231, 237, 263

Babri Masjid Action Committee (BMAC), Lucknow 18, 27, 198, 229, 232–35, 237, 239, 250, 259

Babri Masjid case 44–45, 161, 176, 187, 192–93, 205, 228–30, 233, 235–36, 256, 273; as 'constitutional matter' 236; Muslim claims 272

Babri Masjid-Ram Janam Bhoomi 18

Babri masjid-Ram temple site 112n15

Bajrang Dal 18, 163

Bakht, Sikander Muslim identity 177

Bernier, Francois 58–59

Bharatiya Janata Party (BJP) 40, 147, 175–76, 180, 182, 192, 221–22, 247–48, 254–55, 262–63, 269–70; in Delhi Assembly 175

Bhargava, Rajeev 41–42

Bhure, Aslam 176n38

Bhuri Bhatiyari Masjid 137–38

Index **319**

Bihar Momin Conference 22
Black Day 234–35, 237; 14 February 1986 as 161
black robe 188
Blunt, Ensign James T. 65n18
bourgeois democracy 16
Brass, Paul 21–24, 129, 277; on Muslim leaders 22
Buddhist shrines, destruction of 113
buildings, Indian 52–55, 60–61, 67, 73–74, 77, 79–81, 83, 275; *Asar as-Sanadid* on 70; classification of 69, 87; legal-archaeological classification of 85
Bukhari, Abdullah 43–44, 133, 138, 142–43, 145–53, 156–62, 164–67, 175–76, 180, 182–83, 188–90; anti-government campaign of 151; Dastar Bandi of 150; speeches of 186
Bukhari, Ahmad 145, 147, 150, 153, 155–56, 162, 165, 175–76, 178, 180–83, 186; inflammatory speech by 156; Muslim politics of 156; and Qari Mazhari 270n47
Bukhari, Syed Hamid 147, 155, 157–58
Bukhari, voice of Imam 188
Buxar, Battle of 61

Central Action Committee 237
Chakrabarti, Dilip 32
Chand, Krishan 157
Chatterjee, P. 41, 90
Chughtai, A. R. 91–92
civil disobedience 251
civilisation 88–89, 99, 128–29
Cole, H. H. 76
collective: memories 2, 35, 43, 51, 272, 282; Muslim concerns 131;

Muslim identity 274; Muslim politics 8, 11, 138, 193, 238, 277
common Muslims 1, 16, 19, 28, 110, 163, 236, 250, 258; mobilising of 240
communal: harmony 15, 187; networks 21; politics 5, 14, 16, 18–19, 21, 27; riots 129, 166, 211, 237, 247; tension 154, 178; violence 166–67, 241, 276
communalism 2–4, 12–14, 25, 192, 200, 231, 270
communal-religious rituals 279
communities 39, 55, 58, 95, 101
community construction, Kaviraj on 39n32
community of monuments 69–76; archaeological categorisation of 76–77; legal categorisation of 69, 77–80
Congress 22, 98–99, 149, 158–59, 230–31, 242, 247, 251, 255–56, 263, 269; as 'secular' camp 269
conservation 29, 42, 53, 67, 80, 84–85, 87–88, 90, 105–08, 110–12, 123–24; building-centric approach of 110; of historic sites 53, 66, 107; of religious places of worship 87; of selected historical monuments 83; of unprotected Architectural Heritage and Sites 111
Conservation Manual, The (1923), John Marshall 84–85, 106–07, 147
Conservation Society of Delhi (CSD) 180
culture 52, 98–99
Cunningham, Alexander 69, 76
Curzon, Lord 31, 80

Dalits 18, 280; movements by 281
Dandvate, Madhu 259
Dargahs 38, 65
Darul Aman 251

Index

Darul Muhada 251
Darul Uloom (*Wakf*) Deoband 251
Darul Uloom 167
Das, Raghubar 210
Das, Ramcharan 196
Das, Veena 144n6
Dastar Bandi or Turban Tying ceremony 145n7, 150
Davis, Richard 30, 43, 44n36
dead: historical monuments 2, 38, 122, 265–66; monuments 83, 87, 108; sites 3, 83
Defence of Constitution and Democracy Day 272n49
Dehlavi, Maulana Athar Hussein 177
Delhi Declaration 201, 240, 242
Delhi Wakf Board (DWB) 44, 146–48, 150–53, 157, 159, 174, 177, 183
Delhi, buildings of 70, 72
democratic politics 8, 246
Deoband 167, 188, 251
Desai, Madhvi 30
Desai, Miki 30
Dharmasthan Mukti Yagna Samiti 228
disputed site 44, 193, 195, 205, 214–16, 219–23, 231, 237, 263
'double movement' 38–39; Richard Eaton on 38

East India Company 63, 67n22
Eaton, Richard M. 30
Elephanta: Jo`ao do Castro on 56–7n8; as Roman style 57
Elst, Koenraad 112–13
Engineer, Asghar Ali 15, 17–19, 21, 174
English East India Company 61
European: planetary consciousness 53–4n4 ; travellers 52–55, 57–58; visitors 53n3
excavations 77–78, 101, 111–12, 114

Faisal Jadeed 161
Faizabad Committee 233
family planning programme 148–49
Farqui, Ismail cases 121
Fatehpuri Masjid 69n23
fatwa 252; politics 139, 159
Fergusson, James 29, 69, 73; on architecture 74n34; classification of 73–74; on Indo-Islamic historic architecture 75
Finch, William 198
freedom: of worship 137; to religious minorities 115
Friday prayer 134, 138, 155–56, 158
functional: mosque 45, 93, 99, 119, 167, 216; religious sites 67, 102, 108, 119–20, 123; sites 3, 55, 77, 122
fundamentalism 4

Gandhi, Indira 142–43, 149, 151, 186, 230–31
Gandhi, Mahatma 27, 148
Gandhi, Rajiv 159, 233, 247n30, 280
Goa 55–57
Goel, Sita Ram 112n15
Gough, R. 63
Gramsci 20–21; analysis of 20; on social group 20
grievances 12, 126–27, 174, 211, 228, 242, 248, 277
Guha, Ranajit 62n15
Guha-Thakurta, Tapati 30, 32, 66
Gupta, Narayani 65n19
Gurudwara 20, 94

Habib, Irfan 26, 197, 200
Habib, Mohammad 25
Hague Regulation on Laws and Customs of War (1899 and 1907) 107n10

Index

321

Hai, Maulana Abul 260; *Hindustan-Islami Ahad Mein* of 200
Halbwachs, Maurice 35n25
Hamid, Syed 147, 150
Hasan, Mushirul, *Legacy* of 24–27
Hashmi, Raissuddin 153–54
Hearn, G. R. *The Seven Cities of Delhi (1907)* 88–89
heritage 44, 77, 83, 89, 132, 239, 243
heritage: commercialisation of tourism 279; definition of 36n27
Hindu temples 50–51, 57, 66, 84, 88, 90, 112, 195, 200, 202, 204; Aurangzeb destroyed 64; desecration of 50–51, 72n33, 73, 88, 90, 112, 195, 224, (*see also* Buddhist shrines, destruction of); destruction of 72n33, 113; into mosques 50; rightists 1, 13, 98–99, 101, 112, 114, 130, 132, 228, 233, 262
Hindu–Muslim: clash at Meerut 1986 162n22; conflict 211; culture 27; harmony 187; relations 65, 88; riot 209; schism 24; tension 25, 237; unity 203
Hindustan Islami Ahad Mein 261
Hindutva 1, 4, 18, 41, 111, 193, 205, 229, 270, 274; politics 26, 171, 194, 267
Historic architecture 30, 33, 51, 62, 83, 87; and 'monument' 33–34
historic buildings 28–29, 34, 50–51, 55, 60, 62–64, 70–71, 73, 77–78, 81, 102–03; of Delhi 29, 65, 71
historic places of worship 81, 91
historic sites 2, 28–29, 32–33, 42, 53, 63–66, 71, 76–80, 89–90, 100–05, 275–76; meanings of 43; memories of 43
historical 'monuments' 3, 30, 33–35, 43–44, 96–98, 100–01, 121–24, 133, 135–36, 183, 201

historical buildings 33–34, 65, 67, 70, 72
historical functional mosques 119–20
historical monuments: classification of 77; conservation of 42; protection of 96
Hunter, William 63
Husain, Maulana Muzaffar 233;
Husain, Zakir 149

Imam: arrest of 154; formula of 264–65; *see also* Shahi Imam, institution of
Indian Archaeological Policy 84
Indian Muslims: Ahmad on 10; architectural heritage of 2, 35, 50, 69, 79–80, 90, 114, 275, 281; identity of 273; modernisation of 14; Shahabuddin on 8
Indian National Trust for Art and Cultural Heritage (INTACH) 29, 110n12, 180, 182
Indian religious literature, translation of 62
Indian Treasure Trove Act (1878) 78
indigenous Hindu civilisation 50
Indo-Islamic and/or Indian Muslim heritage 52; Bernier on 59; buildings 2–3, 35–38, 51, 55, 58, 60, 69, 74, 77, 79, 88; historic architecture 2, 28, 75; historic buildings 2–3, 35, 38, 56; historic sites 4, 74, 90, 108, 117, 138, 276, 279;
Indo-Islamic: monumentalisation of 36; monuments 110; sites 28, 35–37, 40, 42, 68–69, 83, 87, 90, 108, 114, 276; traditions 39
Insaaf Party 267
intellectuals 20, 127, 129, 242–43
intentional/unintentional monuments 34n23

322 Index

International Council on Monuments and Sites (ICOMOS) 107n10
Iqbal, Mohammed 91n47
Islamic: architectural heritage 2, 35, 39, 46, 48, 50, 69, 79–80, 90–91, 275, 280–81, (*see also* Indo-Islamic heritage) ; buildings 2–3, 35–38, 51–52, 55–56, 58, 60, 69, 71, 73–74, 79, 88, 90; iconoclasm 65, 73; heritage 37–38, 50, 76, 106, 129, 138, 275, 278, 280; religious places of worship 69n23 ; Shariat 37, 177, 235, 264
Islamisation 11–14, 39; process of 11; process of, Ahmad on 12

Jaan, Mirza, *Haqiqa-e-Shohoda* of 200
Jagannath Temple, construction of 64
Jahan, Shah 129, 140–41, 145, 174, 190
Jain Lal Mandir, Syed Ahmad Khan 72n29
Jain temples, destruction of 72n33, 108
Jalal, Ayesha 72n31
Jalaluddin, Shah 203
Jama Masjid 4, 43–45, 58–59, 140–51, 153–56, 158–59, 161–62, 164–67, 169–76, 179–83, 185–86, 234–36; black flags and banners on 169; closure of 44, 143, 167, 169, 171, 173–74; constructing Wazukhana 44; as functional mosque 45; as Muslim political site 281; Naib Imam of 148; as 'notorious centre of Muslim politics' 45; as Sunni mosque 172; using Public Address System (PAS) 148, 185
Jama Masjid case (1858–62) 92n48
Jama Masjid Trust 141

Jamaat-e-Islami 11, 14–15, 19, 25, 132n40, 279
Jamia Milla Islamia 25
Jamiat Ulama-i-Hind 22, 25, 132n40, 279
Janata Dal (JD) 247n30, 254–56, 259–60, 262, 267; selective patronage of 255
Janmsthan Chabutra 209
Jantaa Party 159
Jones, William 62–63
Juneja, Monica 30, 71n27

Kabaris 151, 189–90
Kalika Temple, C. M. Naim on 72n30
Kamara Bangash Maternity Centre, demolition of 177, 179; function at 180; *see also* Advani, L. K.
Kanpur Mosque case (1913) 93, 95; Muslim claim on 95
Kaviraj, Sudipta 3, 39, 52
Kavuri-Bauer, Santhi 32, 93
Khan, Mohammad Najmul Ghani, *Tarikh-e-Awadh* of 200
Khan, Shah Nawaz 152, 154, 156
Khan, Sikander Hayat 94
Khan, Syed Ahmad 65n19, 69–70, 72–73, 75, 276
Khanji, Muhammad Mahabat 113
Khanqahs 38
Khilafat Movement 95
Khulastu-Tawarikh of Sujan Rai Bhandari 198
Kidwai, Rafi Ahmad 26
Koshar, Rudy 43, 43n37
Krishna Menon, A. G. 32
Kumar, Sunil 30, 109

Lahiri, Nayanjyot 30–31
Lal, B. B. 111–12, 268
land acquisition 221–23

Index

Land Acquisition Act 1894 78, 103, 118
Lang, John 30
liberation theology 15, 17, 21
Limitation Acts 94, 121n27
Linschoten, on Indian temples 55n6
living: Muslim heritage 43; sites 2–3, 38
Lok Sabha election (1980) 231
Lord Rama birthplace. *See* Rama Chabutra

Madan, T. N. 9, 40
Madan-Nandy thesis 42
Madni, Maulana 132n40
Mahmud of Ghazni 64
Maintenance of the Internal Security Act (MISA) 154, 159
makeshift temple 222–24; *see also* Babri Masjid
Marshall, John 74n35, 80
Masjid Basao Committee (Mosque Rehabilitation Committee or MBC) 4, 137
Masjid-a-Jami 108
Masjid-e-Jane-Jahanuma or Jama Masjid. *See* Jama Masjid
Masjid-e-Tasha 232, 235
mass politics 6, 8, 240
math 67, 262
Maurice, Thomas 63–64
Mehboob, Haji 282n4
Mehmud, Sultan 114n18
Mehumud, Syed 128, 132n40
Metcalf, Thomas 30–31, 65
Minault, Gail 95
minority rights 5, 22, 43, 97, 115, 120–24, 126–27, 129, 132, 182, 191
minorityism 24–25
Mitter, Partha 32, 57n9
modern tourists 110, 279
modernization 14–15

Mohammed, Ghulam 203
Mohenjo-daro 101
monumentalisation 33, 35–36, 38, 40, 42–43, 45–46, 50–52, 69–70, 82–83, 97–98, 275–76; first phase of 52; process of 33, 35–36, 38, 40, 42–43, 45–46, 50–52, 69–70, 77, 83, 90
monuments of national importance 100–04, 108, 118–19, 123, 264
mosque/masjid 44–45, 66, 93–96, 119–24, 137–38, 140–43, 145–49, 166–67, 169–72, 201–04, 208–19, 264–65; architectural forms of 39; Hanafi Sharia on 38n31 38; as national monument 238; *wakf* status of 119
Mufti-e-Azam 251
Mughal mosques in India 140
Mujeeb, Mohammed 26, 109n11
Munshi, K. M. 99, 113–14
Muslim community 5, 8, 15–16, 22, 27, 37–38, 75, 116–17, 126, 250–52, 259–61; homogeneous 3, 5, 283; oneness of 5;
Muslim–Hindu conflict 66
Muslim League 13, 19, 27, 91n46, 93, 157
Muslim Majlis, Protest Day by 158
Muslim Majlis-e-Mushawarat 12, 19–20, 22, 25, 277, 279
Muslim Personal Laws in India 1, 120n26 133
Muslim politics 1–5, 8, 11–15, 17–28, 36, 44–46, 70, 258, 266–67, 272–73, 275–81; class analysis of 19; Imtiaz Ahmad on 12; of monuments 28, 36, 44–48, 51, 93, 183, 272, 275, 280–81; understanding of 48
Muslim: communalism 14, 24, 200; culture 11, 22, 25, 27, 75, 128–29, 132, 282; exclusiveness 70, 276; identity 3, 18, 129, 282–83; in India 6, 9, 15, 19–20, 27, 116, 122,

324 *Index*

127, 151, 187, 233; intelligentsia 15–17, 19–24, 26–28, 33, 48, 51, 91–93, 96, 117, 126, 280–81; invasion 50, 64, 66, 68, 79, 89; issues 18, 131, 158, 174, 182, 185, 228, 255, 270; leaders 2, 16, 19–20, 22–24, 126–27, 157, 165, 233, 235–37, 255, 267; organizations 1, 9, 19, 26, 128, 131–32, 149, 160–62, 174, 193, 234; plurality 3, 127, 283; political coalition 44, 193; political groups 3–4, 35, 43–44, 91, 96, 133, 192–93, 263, 280–81, 283; politicians 21, 26, 96, 127, 149, 157, 188, 232, 237, 269, 273–74; rule 64–65, 99, 204; separatism 13, 21, 26, 70, 73; Shahabuddin on 7; unity/oneness 5, 9, 49, 128, 131–32, 139, 235, 238, 276; votes 139, 247–48; voting patterns 1, 16
Muslim–Sikh communal relations 94
Mustafa, Seema 26

N. R. Abdul Azeez v. E. Sundaresa Chettiar case 122
Nadwatul Ulama 132n40
Nadwi, Maulana Ali Mian 130, 132n40, 160, 164, 230, 240, 259–60; to Mrs Gandhi 230, 231n22
Nadwi, Maulana Syed Abul Hasan Ali 130n37
Naim, C. M. 70n24, 72
Namaz 3, 9, 45, 110, 122, 134, 149, 166, 170, 174, 245
Nandy, on concept of tolerance 41
Nandy-Madan thesis 42
Naqshabandi, Nawabuddin 138
Narasimha Rao, P.V. 134, 182
Narayan, Jaiprakash 151, 158; anti-establishment movement by 151
Nath, R. 112n15
National: heritage 2, 40, 98–99, 104, 106, 135–36, 201, 240; monument

34, 119, 123, 238; tricolour flag, with *Chakra* (wheel) 98
national importance 45, 97, 100–06, 108, 115, 118–19, 123, 221, 264; concept of 100, 102, 104, 118; secular notion of 106
negotiations 198, 252, 256, 258–59, 261–64, 266–69, 278; settlement by 258–59, 262–64, 266
Nehru, Jawaharlal 27, 98–99
Nigham Bodh Ghat, Syed Ahmad Khan 72n29
Nomani, Maulana Manzoor 132, 133n40
non-controversial Indo-Islamic sites/monuments 112
non-essential religious activities 120
non-functional: buildings 3, 56, 64, 67, 71, 77–78; historic buildings 77; historic mosques 3, 121–22, 133; mosques 45, 83, 122–23, 135, 265, 282; state's acquisition of 121–23; religious places of worship 136–37; sites 3, 55–56, 67, 78, 81, 92, 104, 108, 110, 122–23; tombs 83; *wakf* status of 91
non-Hindu communities 9–10; Ahmad on 9
non-participation, call of 244
Noorani, A G 127
Nora, Pierre 36n26

Oak, P. N. 112n15
organic intellectuals 20
organisations, Muslim 9
organisations, socio-political Muslim 22
Ovington, J.57n10

pagan religions 57n9
Pagode 56–57, 203

Index

325

Pandey, Gyanendra 65–66
Panja, Sheena 32
Parivar, Sangh 1
'participatory neutrality', principle of 85, 88, 95, 108, 110–11, 115
partition 24, 26, 101, 126–27, 228, 265, 277, 279
Patel, Sardar 113
Pathan buildings 71
Pelizzari, Maria Antonella 32
Personal Law Board 233
personal laws 120–21, 139
petitions 182, 210, 217, 219–21, 223; by Muslims 248
Plassey, battles of 61
political community 3, 7–9
political heritage 242–43, 246
politics: of monuments 29; of toleration 41; Chatterjee on 41; radical Muslim 163, 231, 278
Prasad, Rajendra 114
preservation 34, 80, 82, 102–03
Prinsep, James 66; and Muharram procession 66n21
protected: historic mosque 110; historical monuments 4, 30, 33–34, 44–45, 53, 81–84, 96–97, 102–03, 113, 121–23, 124–26, 230, 134–38, 265, 273, 279; mosques 110, 133–35, 273; sites 82–83, 92, 110
protection: of life and properties of Muslims 129; of *wakf* properties 129
Protection of Religious Places of Worship Act 1991 30, 117, 266
Provincial Armed Constabulary (PAC) 166, 232, 247
Public Address System (PAS) 148, 151, 153, 156, 172, 183, 185–86, 281; *see also under* Jama Masjid
public buildings 31, 67
public interest litigations (PILs) 180, 182, 223–24, 270, 272

Qureshi, Shafi 159
Qutub Minar 59, 72n33, 73, 108
Quwaatul Islam mosque 72n33

Rabata Committee 237–40
Rabata Islam 178, 180
Rai Chaturman, *Chahar Gulshan* of 198
Ram Janam Bhumi Mukti Yajna Samiti 253
Ram Janam Bhumi Temple 1, 112–13, 175, 192, 195–96, 198–200, 203–04, 211, 239, 247–48, 254–55, 261–62; Shankaracharaya of Kanchi on 259
Ram temple: destruction of 195, 199; Vikramaditya built 195
Rama Chabutra 203, 209–12, 238, 264
Ramachandran, T. R. 106n9
Ramayana story 112
Ramcot fortress, demolished by Aurangzeb 198
Rashtriya Swayamsevak Sangh (RSS) 40, 229, 247
Rath Yatra 219, 228, 262
Religious Endowments Act 1863 30, 78
religious places of worship 42, 47, 50, 67, 77, 85, 94–95, 104, 115–18, 186, 222; Muslim politics of 93; as non-functional sites 92; observance 38, 104, 123–24, 136–37; as 'protected monument' 83; protection of 30, 116–17
religious: communities 7–8, 11–12, 17, 41, 50, 58, 71–72, 83, 92, 95, 100; endowments 30, 67, 78, 84–85, 87, 92, 103, 147; groups minorities 12, 24, 97, 100, 115, 118, 120, 201, 239, 273; Nehruvian policy on minorities of 1326–27; worship 3, 122

326 *Index*

Republic Day celebration, call to boycott 164–65, 240, 242, 272n49
resentment of Muslims 167, 171
restoration: of all protected mosques 138; of Babri Masjid 164, 234, 237, 241, 244, 269, 279; of monuments 107; of temple 114
Riegl, Alois 34n23
rights of Muslims 23, 130
riots 21, 211, 261; Babri Masjid 162, 171, 176,211, 237; at Banaras 66; in Delhi of February 1986 162n22; of February 1975 44, 145, 152; Gyanendra Pandey on 65n20; at Jama Masjid 133, 143, 154–55; at Lat Bhairava 64–65; Lat Bhairava 65; over Maliana Pak killing 247; at Meerut 162, 166–67, 192; of 1809 66; of 1853 209; old Delhi 163
Robinson Brass's instrumentalism 23
Roe, Thomas (Sir) 58
Roy, Sourndranath 29
royal Muslim past 2, 35, 44, 47, 49, 132, 139, 144, 191, 204–05, 281–82
ruins 3, 33, 55–56, 64, 113
rule of colonial difference, of Partha Chatterjee 89n44

Sadar, Aminuddin 137
Safdarjang mosque 134, 137–38
Said, Edward 58n11
Samajwadi Party (SP) 175
Sangh, Jan 149–51
Sankalia, H. D. 112
Sankalia, H. S. 111n13
Sanskrit, discovery of 61
Sanskritisation 11
Santosh, M. 135
Saracenic nation 75
Sarkari Mullahs 251
Sayeed, Mufti Mohammad 263

secular: historical monuments 50; leisure activities 279; modernists 25; politics 1, 13–14, 16, 26, 191; state 7, 13, 83, 95, 187
secularism 2–3, 13–15, 17–18, 24–27, 29, 40–44, 95–96, 99–101, 105, 115, 191–93, 280–81; Chatterjee on 41; constitutional 27, 40, 278, 280; contextual 42; ethical 41, 41n35; of historical monuments 43, 114, 117, 124, 133, 136, 275; Madan on 40n34, 40–41; of minority rights 43, 115, 124, 132, 275, 280 ; political 41n35; of strict neutrality 96
secularists 48, 99, 256
Shah Bano controversy 18, 160n20, 230–33, 261
Shah, Hazrat Abdul Ghafur 145
Shah, Jalal 195–96
Shah, Nawab Wajid Ali 203
Shahabuddin, Syed 5–8, 134–36, 161, 164–66, 230, 238, 241, 244, 249–51, 259, 266–67: groups of 167, 174, 255; on religious community 8; on secular state 7
Shahi Imam, institution of 141, 148
Shahi, L.P. 135
Shahid Ganj Mosque case (1935–37) 93–95, 121–22
Shakir, Moin 15, 19–20, 127; on common Muslims 16
Shankaracharaya of Kanchi 259–63
Shayamanada, Baba 195
Shekhar, Chandra 260, 263
Shia Central Board UP Waqf 208
Shia Islam 172
Shilanyas 202, 280
Siddiquie, Yunus 229
Sikandar Bakht Girls Memorial School 177; *see also* Advani, L. K.

Index

Sikh Gurudwara Act 94
Sikh Gurudwara Tribunal 94
Sikh massacres 231
Singh, Giani Zail 244
Singh, Karan 252
Singh, V. P. 174, 247n30, 255–56, 260, 262
Singh, Vir Bahadur 167
Society of Antiquaries 61, 63
Somnath temple 64–65, 75, 99, 113–14, 128; desecration of 75n36 64, 75
Sri Ram Janam Bhumi Mukti Yagna Samiti 228
state-protected historical monument 117
States Reorganisation Act 101–02
strict neutrality 80, 89, 95–96, 100–01, 105–7, 121, 126, 136, 275; policy of 83–7; 'Contested Nature' of Muslim Heritage 83, 87–90; principle of 53
Sufis 65, 196, 203, 282; shrines of 67
Sultan Ghari ka Makbara 124
Sunni-Majlis-e-Auqaf 141n3, 143, 146

Tablighi Jamaat 11, 25
Tahmad 188
Taj Mahal 58–9
Tavernier, Jean Baptiste 58
Taxila 101
temple 56–57, 60, 66–67, 72, 113–14, 135, 194–96, 198–99, 204, 210, 215; Aurangzeb demolishing 66; demolished by Mehmud of Ghazni 114; destroyed by Portuguese 56; destruction of 88
Thapar, B. K. 114n18
The History of Indian and Eastern Architecture 29, 73
Tillotson, G.H.R. 30–32
Tiwari, N. D. 229
tourists 108, 110, 170–71

traditional intellectuals 20
tradition-based archaeology 106, 111–12
travellers 52–54, 56–59; *see also* European travellers
Treaty of Surji Arjungaon 64
Tulsidas 198

ulema 22, 46, 233, 235–36, 252, 261; of All India Muslim Personal Law Board. (AIMPLB) 159–60
United Nations Educational Social and Cultural Organisation (UNESCO) 107n10 107
UP Muslim Waqf Act 1936 208
urbanisation 92–93, 279–80, of modern north Indian cities 110; in postcolonial India 110
Urdu and Muslim personal law 1, 139
Urdu language, agitation for protection of 123
Uttar Pradesh Sunni Wakf Board 282n4 282

Vajpayee, A. B. 177
violence. *See* riots
Visharad, Gopal Singh 214
Vishwa Hindu Parishad (VHP) 18, 194–95, 197, 200–02, 219, 221–23, 228–31, 247, 258–60, 262–66, 268–70; (*see also* Rashtriya Swayamsevak Sangh (RSS)); Victory Day celebrations of 232

Wakf Aal-ul-Aulad Act 1913 38n30
Wakf Act 1954/95 30, 38, 116, 119, 125, 129, 132n40, 146
Wakf Board Area Advisory Committee 152
Wakf Inquiry Committee (1976) 116n21

328 *Index*

wakf: aspects of 37n29; concept of 37–38; boards 116n21, 124–25, 133, 148, 150–53, 156, 224, 281; buildings 38, 83n39; Hanafi School conceptualization of 37n28; laws 67, 116, 118–20; meaning of 37; properties 3, 38, 83, 90, 116–17, 119, 121, 125, 129, 132n40, 177–78, 208

Wakf-alal-Aulad 91n46

Wazukhana 180; case of 144, 174–75, 180–83; *see also under* Jama Masjid

world heritage sites 107–08

worship places 4, 29–30, 77–78, 80–81, 83–85, 87, 92–96, 115–18, 136–37, 222–24, 273; *see also* mosque/masjid

Wright, Theodore 14–15

Yadav, Mulayam Singh 263

Youth Welfare Society (YWS) 177

Zakat 9

Zeenatul Masjid 69n23